Elasticsearch in Action

Elasticsearch
in Action

RADU GHEORGHE
MATTHEW LEE HINMAN
ROY RUSSO

MANNING
SHELTER ISLAND

For online information and ordering of this and other Manning books, please visit www.manning.com. The publisher offers discounts on this book when ordered in quantity. For more information, please contact

Special Sales Department
Manning Publications Co.
20 Baldwin Road
PO Box 761
Shelter Island, NY 11964
Email: orders@manning.com

 Manning Publications Co.
20 Baldwin Road
PO Box 761
Shelter Island, NY 11964

Development editor: Susan Conant
Technical development editor: David Pombal
Copyeditor: Linda Recktenwald
Proofreader: Melody Dolab
Technical proofreader: Valentin Crettaz
Typesetter: Dennis Dalinnik
Cover designer: Marija Tudor

ISBN: 9781617291623
Printed in the United States of America
1 2 3 4 5 6 7 8 9 10 – EBM – 20 19 18 17 16 15

brief contents

contents

preface

While writing this book, my objective was to provide you the information I needed when I started using Elasticsearch: what its main features are and how they work under the hood. To give you a better overview of this objective, let me tell you a more detailed story of how this book came to life.

I first met Elasticsearch in 2011 while working on a project for centralizing logs. My colleague Mihai Sandu showed me Graylog, which used Elasticsearch for log search, and setting everything up was extremely easy. Two servers could handle all our logging needs at the time, but we expected the data volume to grow hundreds of times in about one year. And it did. On top of that, we had more and more complex analysis requirements, so we quickly found out that tuning and scaling the setup required a deep understanding of Elasticsearch and its features.

There was no book to teach us that, so we had to learn the hard way: lots of experiments, lots of questions and answers to the mailing list. The upside was that I got to know a lot of nice people that posted there regularly. This is how I came to work at Sematext, where I could concentrate on Elasticsearch full-time, and this is why Manning asked me if I would be interested in writing about Elasticsearch.

Of course I was. They warned me it was hard work, but told me that Lee Hinman was also interested, so we joined forces. With two authors, we thought it was going to be easy, especially as Lee and I really clicked and provided useful feedback to one another. Little did we know that it's much easier to present features in the early chapters than to combine those features into best practices for various use cases in later chapters. Then, with feedback from our reviewers, we found that it's even more work to fit everything together, so our pace became slower and slower. That's when Roy Russo joined us and helped with that final push.

After two and a half years of early mornings, late nights, and weekends, I can finally say we're done. It was a tough experience, but a rich one as well. I would surely have loved to have this book in my hands four years ago, and I hope you'll enjoy it, too.

RADU GHEORGHE

acknowledgments

Many people provided their invaluable support to make this book possible:

- Susan Conant, our development editor at Manning, who supported us in so many ways: by providing valuable feedback on draft chapters, helping to plan book and individual chapter structures, giving encouragement, advising us on upcoming steps, helping us overcome bumps in the road, and so on
- Jettro Coenradie, our technical editor, who helped us review big chunks of the manuscript before it went to production and again helped with the final steps before the book went to press
- Valentin Crettaz, who helped with his thorough technical proofread
- Our Manning Early Access Program (MEAP) readers who posted so many helpful comments in the Author Online forum
- The reviewers from the development process who provided such good feedback that I can't even begin to imagine how the book would look without them: Achim Friedland, Alan McCann, Artur Nowak, Bhaskar Karambelkar, Daniel Beck, Gabriel Katenbaumn, Gianluca Rhigetto, Igor Motov, Jeelani Shaik, Joe Gallo, Konstantin Yakushev, Koray Güclü, Michael Schleichardt, Paul Stadig, Ray Lugo Jr., Sen Xu, and Tanguy Leroux

RADU GHEORGHE

I'd like to express my thanks in chronological order. To my colleagues from Avira: Mihai Sandu, Mihai Efrim, Martin Ahrens, Matthias Ollig and many others, for supporting me in learning about Elasticsearch and tolerating my not-always-successful experiments. To my colleagues from Sematext: Otis Gospodnetić, who supported me in learning and interacting with the community, and Rafał Kuć (aka Master Rafał) for his invaluable tips and tricks. Finally, I'd like to thank my family for supporting me in so many ways that I can barely scratch the surface here: my parents, Nicoleta and Mihai Gheorghe, and my in-laws, Mădălina and Adrian Radu, for providing good food, quiet spaces, and the all-important moral support. My wife Alexandra, for being a real hero: she somehow managed to write her own stuff and still take care of everything in order for me to write. Last but not least, my son Andrei, now 6, for his understanding and his creative solutions on spending time together, like working on his own book next to me.

LEE HINMAN

First and foremost I'd like to give my sincerest thanks to my wife Delilah for encouraging me in this endeavor and for being my adventuring partner. You have given me so much support in this and so many other parts of my life. Thank you for continuing to encourage me throughout the birth of our daughter, Vera Ovelia. I'd also like to thank all of the people who have contributed to Elasticsearch. Without you, open source software would not be possible. I'm honored to contribute to such a wide-reaching and powerful piece of software.

ROY RUSSO

I would like to thank my daughters Olivia and Isabella, my son Jacob, and my wife Roberta, for standing beside me throughout my career and acting as a source of inspiration and motivation. You guys make the impossible possible with your support, love, and understanding.

about this book

Since it came out in 2010, Elasticsearch has become increasingly popular. It's being used in a variety of setups, from product search—which is the traditional use case for a search engine—to real-time analytics of social media, application logs, and other flowing data. The strong points of Elasticsearch have always been its distributed model—which makes it scale out easily and efficiently—as well as its rich analytics functionality. All of this was built on top of the already established Apache Lucene search engine library. Lucene has evolved during this time as well, making it possible to process the same amount of data with less CPU, memory, and disk space.

Elasticsearch in Action covers all the major features of Elasticsearch, from relevancy tuning by using different analyzers and query types to using aggregations for real-time analytics, as well as more "exotic" features, like geo-spatial search and document percolation.

You'll quickly find that Elasticsearch is easy to get started with. You can get your documents in, search them, build statistics, and even distribute and replicate your data onto multiple machines in a matter of hours. Default behavior and settings are very developer-friendly, making proof-of-concepts that much easier to build.

Moving from prototypes to production is often more difficult, as you'll bump into various functionality or performance limitations. That's why we explain how each feature works under the hood, so you can tweak the right knobs in order to get good relevance out of your searches and good performance for both reads and writes to your cluster.

What exactly are the features we'll cover? Let's look at the roadmap of this book for more details.

Roadmap

Elasticsearch in Action is divided into two parts: "Core functionality" and "Advanced functionality." We recommend reading chapters in order, as the functionality discussed in one chapter often depends on the concepts presented in previous chapters. Each chapter contains code listings and snippets you can follow if you prefer a hands-on approach, but it's not necessary to have a laptop with you in order to learn the concepts and how Elasticsearch works.

The first part explains the core features—how to model and index data so you can search and analyze it as your use case requires. By the end of it, you'll understand the building blocks of Elasticsearch functionality:

- Chapter 1 gives an overview of what a search engine does in general and Elasticsearch's features in particular. By the end of it you should know what kind of problems you can solve with Elasticsearch.
- Chapter 2 gets your feet wet regarding the major functionality: indexing documents, searching them, analyzing data via aggregations, and scaling out to multiple nodes.
- Chapter 3 covers the options you have while indexing, updating, and deleting your data. You'll learn what kind of fields you can have in your documents, as well as what happens when you're writing them.
- In chapter 4 you'll dive deeper into the realm of full-text search. You'll discover the important types of queries and filters and learn how they work and when to use which.
- Chapter 5 explains how analysis breaks down the text from both documents and queries into the tokens used for searching. You'll learn how to use different kinds of analyzers—as well as how to build your own—in order to fully utilize Elasticsearch's full text search potential.
- Chapter 6 helps you complete your full text search skills by focusing on relevancy. You'll learn about the factors affecting a document's score and how to manipulate them using different scoring algorithms, boosting a particular query or field, or using values from the document itself—such as the number of likes or retweets—to boost the score.
- Chapter 7 shows how to use aggregations to perform real-time analytics. You'll learn how to couple aggregations with queries and how to nest them in order to find the number of needles in the haystack . . . dropped by someone from Poland . . . two years ago.
- Chapter 8 deals with relational data, like bands and their albums. You'll learn how to use Elasticsearch features—such as nested documents and parent-child relationships—as well as general NoSQL techniques (such as denormalizing or application-side joins) to index and search data that isn't flat.

The second part helps you get the core functionality out to production. In doing so, you'll learn more about how each feature works, as well as its impact on performance and scalability:

- Chapter 9 deals with scaling out to multiple nodes. You'll learn how to shard and replicate your indices—for example, by oversharding or using time-based indices—so that today's design can cope with next year's data.
- In chapter 10 you'll find tricks that will help you squeeze more performance out of your cluster. Along the way, you'll learn how Elasticsearch uses caches and writes data to disk, as well as various trade-offs you can make to tweak Elasticsearch for your use case.
- Chapter 11 shows how to monitor and administer your cluster in production. We'll cover the important metrics you should watch, how to back up and restore your data, and how to use shortcuts such as index templates and aliases.

The book's six appendixes cover features you should know about, but these features may not be relevant to some use cases. We hope that the term "appendix" doesn't mislead you into thinking we cover these features superficially. As with the rest of the book, we'll dive into the details of how each feature works under the hood:

- Appendix A is about geospatial search and aggregations.
- Appendix B shows how to manage Elasticsearch plugins.
- In Appendix C you'll learn about highlighting query terms in your search results.
- Appendix D introduces third-party monitoring tools that you may want to use in production to help you manage Elasticsearch.
- Appendix E explains how to use the Percolator in order to match few documents against many queries.
- Finally, appendix F explains how to use different suggesters in order to implement did-you-mean and autocomplete functionality.

Code conventions and downloads

All source code in listings or in text is in a `fixed-width font like this` to separate it from ordinary text. Code annotations accompany many of the listings, highlighting important concepts.

Source code for all the working examples in the book and instructions to run them are available at https://github.com/dakrone/elasticsearch-in-action. You can also download the code from the publisher's website at www.manning.com/books/elasticsearch-in-action.

The code snippets and the source code will work on Elasticsearch 1.5. They should work on all the versions of the 1.x branch. At the time of this writing, the roadmap for version 2.0 is becoming clearer, and it's taken into account: we skipped features that will go away, such as configuration options on most predefined fields. In other places, such as filter caches, where 1.x and 2.x simply behave differently, we specifically pointed this out in a callout.

Author Online

Purchase of *Elasticsearch in Action* includes free access to a private web forum run by Manning Publications where you can make comments about the book, ask technical questions, and receive help from the authors and other users. To access the Author Online forum and subscribe to it, point your web browser to www.manning.com/books/elasticsearch-in-action. This page provides information on how to get on the forum once you're registered, what kind of help is available, and the rules of conduct on the forum.

Manning's commitment to our readers is to provide a venue where a meaningful dialog among individual readers and between readers and the authors can take place. It's not a commitment to any specific amount of participation on the part of the authors, whose contribution to the forum remains voluntary.

The Author Online forum and the archives of previous discussions will be accessible from the publisher's website as long as the book is in print.

about the cover illustration

The figure on the cover of *Elasticsearch in Action* is captioned "A man from Croatia." The illustration is taken from a reproduction of an album of Croatian traditional costumes from the mid-nineteenth century by Nikola Arsenovic, published by the Ethnographic Museum in Split, Croatia, in 2003. The illustrations were obtained from a helpful librarian at the Ethnographic Museum in Split, itself situated in the Roman core of the medieval center of the town: the ruins of Emperor Diocletian's retirement palace from around AD 304. The book includes finely colored illustrations of figures from different regions of Croatia, accompanied by descriptions of the costumes and of everyday life.

Dress codes and lifestyles have changed over the last 200 years, and the diversity by region, so rich at the time, has faded away. It is now hard to tell apart the inhabitants of different continents, let alone of different hamlets or towns separated by only a few miles. Perhaps we have traded cultural diversity for a more varied personal life—certainly for a more varied and fast-paced technological life.

Manning celebrates the inventiveness and initiative of the computer business with book covers based on the rich diversity of regional life of two centuries ago, brought back to life by illustrations from old books and collections like this one.

Part 1

In this part, we will cover what Elasticsearch can do for you in terms of functionality. We'll start with more general concepts in chapter 1, where we'll explore how Elasticsearch is typically used as a search engine, and then move on to how to model, index, search, and analyze data efficiently. By the end of part 1, you'll have a deep understanding of what Elasticsearch can offer from a functionality standpoint and how you can use it to solve your search and real-time analytics problems.

Introducing Elasticsearch 1

This chapter covers

- Understanding search engines and the issues they address
- How Elasticsearch fits in the context of search engines
- Typical scenarios for Elasticsearch
- Features Elasticsearch provides
- Installing Elasticsearch

We use search everywhere these days. And that's a good thing, because search helps you finish tasks quickly and easily. Whether you're buying something from an online shop or visiting a blog, you expect to have a search box somewhere to help you find what you're looking for without scanning the entire website. Maybe it's me, but when I (Radu) wake up in the morning, I wish I could enter the kitchen and type in "bowl" in a search box somewhere and have my favorite bowl highlighted.

We've also come to expect those search boxes to be smart. I don't want to have to type the entire word "bowl;" I expect the search box to come up with suggestions, and I don't want results and suggestions to come to me in random order. I want the search to be smart and give me the most relevant results first—to guess what I want, if that's possible. For example, if I search for "laptop" from an online shop but have to scroll through laptop accessories before I get to a laptop, I'm likely to go somewhere else after the first page of results. And this need for relevant results and suggestions isn't only because we're in a hurry and spoiled with good search interfaces; it's also because there's increasingly more stuff to choose from. For example, a friend asked me to help her buy a new laptop. Typing "best laptop for my friend" in the search box of an online store that sells thousands of laptops wouldn't be effective. Good keyword searching is often not enough; you need some statistics on the results so you can narrow them down to what the user is interested in. I narrowed down my laptop search by selecting the size of the screen, the price range, and so on, until I only had five or so laptops to choose from.

Finally, there's the matter of performance—because nobody wants to wait. I've seen websites where you search for something and get the results in few minutes. *Minutes!* For a search!

If you want to provide search for your data, you'll have to deal with all these issues: returning relevant search results, returning statistics, and doing all that quickly. This is where search engines like Elasticsearch come into play because they're built to meet exactly those challenges. You can deploy a search engine on top of a relational database to create indices and speed up the SQL queries. Or you can index data from your NoSQL data store to add search capabilities there. You can do that with Elasticsearch, and it works well with document-oriented stores like MongoDB because data is represented in Elasticsearch as documents, too. Modern search engines like Elasticsearch also do a good job of storing your data so you can use it as a NoSQL data store with powerful search capabilities.

Elasticsearch is open-source and distributed, and it's built on top of Apache Lucene,[1] an open-source search engine library, which allows you to implement search functionality in your own Java application. Elasticsearch takes this Lucene function and extends it to make storing, indexing, and searching faster, easier, and, as the name suggests, elastic. Also, your application doesn't need to be written in Java to work with Elasticsearch; you can send data over HTTP in JSON to index, search, and manage your Elasticsearch cluster.

This chapter expounds on these searching and data features, and you'll learn how to use them throughout this book. First, let's take a closer look at the challenges search engines are typically confronted with and Elasticsearch's approach to solving them.

1.1   *Solving search problems with Elasticsearch*

To get a better idea of how Elasticsearch works, let's look at an example. Imagine that you're working on a website that hosts blogs and you want to let users search across the entire site for specific posts. Your first task is to implement keyword search. For

---

[1] More information about Apache Lucene can be found at http://lucene.apache.org/core/.

example, if a user searches for "elections," you'd better return all posts containing that word.

A search engine will do that for you, but for a *robust* search feature, you need more than that: results need to come in quickly, and they need to be relevant. It's also nice to provide features that help users search when they don't know the exact words of what they're looking for. Those features include detecting typos, providing suggestions, and breaking down results into categories.

> **TIP** In this chapter you'll get an overview of Elasticsearch's features. If you want to get practical and jump to installing it, skip to section 1.5. You'll find the installation procedure surprisingly easy. And you can always come back here for the high-level overview.

1.1.1 *Providing quick searches*

If you have a huge number of posts on your site, searching through all of them for the word "elections" can take a long time, and you don't want your users to wait. That's where Elasticsearch helps because it uses Lucene, a high-performance search engine library, to index all your data by default.

An *index* is a data structure which you create along with your data and which is meant to allow faster searches. You can add indices to fields in most databases, and there are several ways to do it. Lucene does it with *inverted indexing*, which means it creates a data structure where it keeps a list of where each word belongs. For example, if you need to search for blog posts by their tags, using inverted indexing might look like table 1.1.

Table 1.1 Inverted index for blog tags

Raw data		Index data	
Blog Post ID	Tags	Tags	Blog Post IDs
1	elections	elections	1,3
2	peace	peace	2,3,4
3	elections, peace		
4	peace		

If you search for blog posts that have an `elections` tag, it's much faster to look at the index rather than looking at each word of each blog post, because you only have to look at the place where the tag is `elections`, and you'll get all the corresponding blog posts. This speed gain makes sense in the context of a search engine. In the real world, you're rarely searching for only one word. For example, if you're searching for "Elasticsearch in Action," three-word lookups imply multiplying your speed gain by three. All this may seem a bit complex at this point, but we'll clear up the details when we discuss indexing in chapter 3 and searching in chapter 4.

An inverted index is appropriate for a search engine when it comes to relevance, too. For example, when you're looking up a word like "peace," not only will you see which document matches, but you'll also get the number of matching documents for free. This is important because if a word occurs in most documents, it's probably less relevant. Let's say you search for "Elasticsearch in Action." and a document contains the word "in"—along with a million other documents. At this point, you know that "in" is a common word, and the fact that this document matched doesn't say much about how relevant it is to your search. In contrast, if it contains "Elasticsearch" along with a hundred others, you know you're getting closer to relevant documents. But it's not "you" who has to know you're getting closer; Elasticsearch does that for you. You'll learn all about tuning data and searches for relevancy in chapter 6.

That said, the tradeoff for improved search performance and relevancy is that the index will take up disk space and adding new blog posts will be slower because you have to update the index after adding the data itself. On the upside, tuning can make Elasticsearch faster, both when it comes to indexing and searching. We'll discuss tuning in great detail in chapter 10.

1.1.2 Ensuring relevant results

Then there's the hard part: how do you make the blog posts that are about elections appear before the ones that merely contain the word election? With Elasticsearch, you have a few algorithms for calculating the *relevancy score*, which is used, by default, to sort the results.

The relevancy score is a number assigned to each document that matches your search criteria and indicates how relevant the given document is to the criteria. For example, if a blog post contains "elections" more times than another, it's more likely to be about elections. Figure 1.1 shows an example from DuckDuckGo.

By default, the algorithm used to calculate a document's relevancy score is *TF-IDF*. We'll discuss scoring and TF-IDF more in chapters 4 and 6, which are about searching

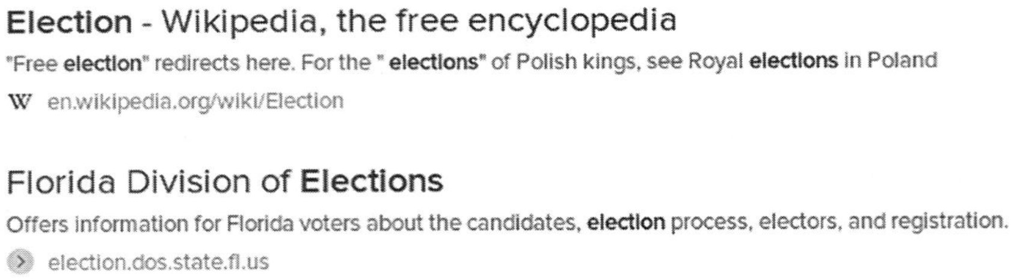

Election - Wikipedia, the free encyclopedia
"Free **election**" redirects here. For the " **elections**" of Polish kings, see Royal **elections** in Poland

W en.wikipedia.org/wiki/Election

Florida Division of **Elections**
Offers information for Florida voters about the candidates, **election** process, electors, and registration.

election.dos.state.fl.us

Figure 1.1   More occurrences of the searched terms usually rank the document higher.

and relevancy, but here's the basic idea: *TF-IDF* stands for *term frequency–inverse document frequency*, which are the two factors that influence relevancy score.

- *Term frequency*—The more times the words you're looking for appear in a document, the higher the score.
- *Inverse document frequency*—The weight of each word is higher if the word is uncommon across other documents.

For example, if you're looking for "bicycle race" on a cyclist's blog, the word "bicycle" counts much less for the score than "race." But the more times both words appear in a document, the higher that document's score.

In addition to choosing an algorithm, Elasticsearch provides many other built-in features to influence the relevancy score to suit your needs. For example, you can "boost" the score of a particular field, such as the title of a post, to be more important than the body. This gives higher scores to documents that match your search criteria in the title, compared to similar documents that match only the body. You can make exact matches count more than partial matches, and you can even use a script to add custom criteria to the way the score is calculated. For example, if you let users like posts, you can boost the score based on the number of likes, or you can make newer posts have higher scores than similar, older posts.

Don't worry about the mechanics of any of these features right now; we discuss relevancy in great detail in chapter 6. For now, let's focus on what you can do with Elasticsearch and when you'd want to use those features.

1.1.3 Searching beyond exact matches

With Elasticsearch you have options to make your searches intuitive and go beyond exactly matching what the user types in. These options are handy when the user enters a typo or uses a synonym or a derived word different than what you've stored. They're also handy when the user doesn't know exactly what to search for in the first place.

HANDLING TYPOS

You can configure Elasticsearch to be tolerant of variations instead of looking for only exact matches. A fuzzy query can be used so a search for "bicycel" will match a blog post about bicycles. We explore fuzzy queries and other features that make your searches relevant in chapter 6.

SUPPORTING DERIVATIVES

You can also use analysis, covered in chapter 5, to make Elasticsearch understand that a blog with "bicycle" in its title should also match queries that mention "bicyclist" or "cycling." You probably noticed that in figure 1.1, where "elections" matched "election" as well. You might have also noticed that matching terms are highlighted in **bold**. Elasticsearch can do that too—we'll cover highlighting in appendix C.

USING STATISTICS

When users don't know what to search for, you can help them in a number of ways. One way is to present statistics through aggregations, which we cover in chapter 7.

Aggregations are a way to get counters from the results of your query, like how many topics fall into each category or the average number of likes and shares for each of those categories. Imagine that upon entering your blog, users see popular topics listed on the right-hand side. One topic may be cycling. Those interested in cycling would click that topic to narrow the results. Then, you might have another aggregation to separate cycling posts into "bicycle reviews," "cycling events," and so on.

PROVIDING SUGGESTIONS

Once users start typing, you can help them discover popular searches and results. You can use suggestions to predict their searches as they type, as most search engines on the web do. You can also show popular results as they type, using special query types that match prefixes, wild cards, or regular expressions. In appendix F, we'll also discuss suggesters, which are faster-than-normal queries for autocomplete and did-you-mean functionality.

Now that we've discussed what high-level features Elasticsearch provides, let's look at how those features are typically used in production.

1.2   *Exploring typical Elasticsearch use cases*

We've already established that storing and indexing your data in Elasticsearch is a good way to provide quick and relevant results to your searches. But in the end, Elasticsearch is just a search engine, and you'll never use it on its own. Like any other data store, you need a way to feed data into it, and you probably need to provide an interface for the users searching that data.

To get an idea of how Elasticsearch might fit into a bigger system, let's consider three typical scenarios:

- *Elasticsearch as the primary back end for your website*—As we discussed, you may have a website that allows people to write blog posts, but you also want the ability to search through the posts. You can use Elasticsearch to store all the data related to these posts and serve queries as well.
- *Adding Elasticsearch to an existing system*—You may be reading this book because you already have a system that's crunching data and you want to add search. We'll look at a couple of overall designs on how that might be done.
- *Elasticsearch as the back end of a ready-made solution built around it*—Because Elasticsearch is open-source and offers a straightforward HTTP interface, a big ecosystem supports it. For example, Elasticsearch is popular for centralizing logs; given the tools already available that can write to and read from Elasticsearch, other than configuring those tools to work the way you want, you don't need to develop anything.

Let's take a closer look at each of these scenarios.

1.2.1 Using Elasticsearch as the primary back end

Traditionally, search engines are deployed on top of well-established data stores to provide fast and relevant search capability. That's because historically search engines haven't offered durable storage or other features that are often needed, such as statistics.

Elasticsearch is one of those modern search engines that provide durable storage, statistics, and many other features you've come to expect from a data store. If you're starting a new project, we recommend that you consider using Elasticsearch as the only data store to help keep your design as simple as possible. This might not work well for all use cases—for instance, when you have lots of updates—so you can also use Elasticsearch on top of another data store.

> **NOTE** Like other NoSQL data stores, Elasticsearch doesn't support transactions. In chapter 3, you'll see how you can use versioning to manage concurrency, but if you need transactions, consider using another database as the "source of truth." Also, regular backups are a good practice when you're using a single data store. We'll discuss backups in chapter 11.

Let's return to the blog example: you can store newly written blog posts in Elasticsearch. Similarly, you can use Elasticsearch to retrieve, search, or do statistics through all that data, as shown in figure 1.2.

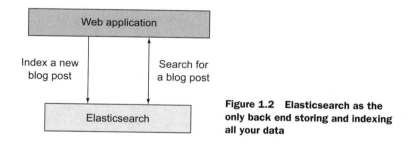

Figure 1.2 Elasticsearch as the only back end storing and indexing all your data

What happens if a server goes down? You can get fault tolerance by replicating your data to different servers. Many other features make Elasticsearch a tempting NoSQL data store. It can't be great for everything, but you should weigh whether including another data store in your overall design is worth the extra complexity.

1.2.2 Adding Elasticsearch to an existing system

By itself, Elasticsearch may not always provide all the functionality you need from a data store. Some situations may require you to use Elasticsearch in addition to another data store.

For example, transaction support and complex relationships are features that Elastic search doesn't currently support, at least in version 1. If you need those features, consider using Elasticsearch along with a different data store.

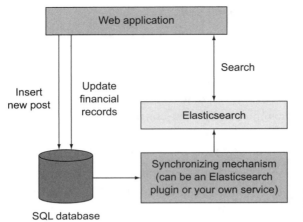

Figure 1.3 Elasticsearch in the same system with another data store

Or you may already have a complex system that works, but you want to add search. It might be risky to redesign the entire system for the sole purpose of using Elasticsearch alone (though you might want to do that over time). The safer approach is to add Elasticsearch to your system and make it work with your existing components.

Either way, if you have two data stores, you'll have to find a way to keep them synchronized. Depending on what your primary data store is and how your data is laid out, you can deploy an Elasticsearch plugin to keep the two entities synchronized, as illustrated in figure 1.3.

For example, suppose you have an online retail store with product information stored in an SQL database. You need fast and relevant searching, so you install Elasticsearch. To index the data, you need to deploy a synchronizing mechanism, which can be an Elasticsearch plugin or a custom service that you build. You'll learn more about plugins in appendix B and about dealing with indexing and updating from your own application in chapter 3. This synchronizing mechanism could pull all the data corresponding to each product and index it in Elasticsearch, where each product is stored as a document.

When a user types in search criteria on the web page, the storefront web application queries Elasticsearch for that criteria. Elasticsearch returns a number of product documents that match the criteria, sorted in the way you prefer. Sorting can be based on a relevance score that indicates how many times the words people searched for appear in each product, or anything stored in the product document, such as how recently the product was added, the average rating, or even a combination of those.

Inserting or updating information can still be done on the "primary" SQL database, so you can use Elasticsearch solely for handling searches. It's up to the synchronizing mechanism to keep Elasticsearch up to date with the latest changes.

When you need to integrate Elasticsearch with other components, you can check for existing tools that may already do what you need. As we'll explore in the next section, there's a strong community building tools for Elasticsearch, and sometimes you don't have to build any custom component.

1.2.3 Using Elasticsearch with existing tools

In some use cases, you don't have to write a single line of code to get a job done with Elasticsearch. Many tools are available that work with Elasticsearch, so you don't have to write yours from scratch.

For example, say you want to deploy a large-scale logging framework to store, search, and analyze a large number of events. As shown in figure 1.4, to process logs and output to Elasticsearch, you can use logging tools such as Rsyslog (www.rsyslog.com), Logstash[2] (www.elastic.co/products/logstash), or Apache Flume (http://flume.apache.org). To search and analyze those logs in a visual interface, you can use Kibana (www.elastic.co/products/kibana).[3]

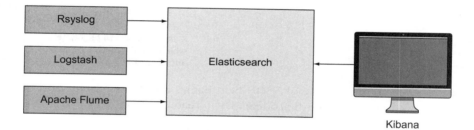

Figure 1.4   Elasticsearch in a system of logging tools that support Elasticsearch out of the box

The fact that Elasticsearch is open-source—under the Apache 2 license, to be precise—isn't the only reason that so many tools support it. Even though Elasticsearch is written in Java, there's more than a Java API that lets you work with it. It also exposes a REST API, which any application can access, no matter the programming language it was written in.

What's more, the REST requests and replies are typically in JSON (JavaScript Object Notation) format. Typically, a REST request has its payload in JSON, and replies are also a JSON document.

---

[2] Ryslog home page: www.rsyslog.com
[3] Kibana home page: www.elastic.co/products/kibana

> **JSON and YAML**
>
> JSON is a format for expressing data structures. A JSON object typically contains keys and values, where values can be strings, numbers, true/false, null, another object, or an array. For more details about the JSON format, visit http://json.org/.
>
> JSON is easy for applications to parse and generate. YAML (YAML Ain't Markup Language) is also supported for the same purpose. To activate YAML, add the `format =yaml` parameter to the HTTP request. For more details on YAML, visit http://yaml.org. Although JSON is typically used for HTTP communication, the configuration files are usually written in YAML. In this book we stick with the popular formats: JSON for LHTT communication and YAML for configuration.

For example, a log event might look like this when you index it in Elasticsearch:

```
{
    "message": "logging to Elasticsearch for the first time",   ◁───┘  A field with a
    "timestamp": "2013-08-05T10:34:00"   ◁───┐                          string value
}                                            │
                                        A string value can be a date,
                                        which Elasticsearch evaluates
                                        automatically.
```

NOTE   Throughout this book, JSON field names are shown in blue and their values are in red to make the code easier to read.

A search request for log events with a value of `first` in the message field would look like this:

```
The value of      {
the query             "query": {
field is                  "match": {                        The match field contains
an object                     "message": "first"    ◁───   another object in which first
containing                }                               is the value of message.
the match             }
field.            }
```

Sending data and running queries by sending JSON objects over HTTP makes it easy for you to extend anything—from a syslog daemon like Rsyslog to a connecting framework like Apache ManifoldCF (http://manifoldcf.apache.org)—to interact with Elasticsearch. If you're building a new application from scratch or want to add search to an existing application, the REST API is one of the features that makes Elasticsearch appealing. In the next section we'll look at other such features.

1.2.4   *Main Elasticsearch features*

Elasticsearch allows you to easily access Lucene's functionality for indexing and searching your data. On the indexing side, you have lots of options for how to process the text in them and how to store that processed text. When searching, you have many queries and filters to choose from. Elasticsearch exposes this functionality through the REST API, allowing you to structure queries in JSON and adjust most of the configuration though the same API.

On top of what Lucene provides, Elasticsearch adds its own, higher-level functionality, from caching to real-time analytics. In chapter 7 you'll learn how to do these analytics through aggregations, which can give you results like the most popular blog tags, the average popularity of a certain group of posts, and endless combinations such as the average popularity of posts for each tag.

Another level of abstraction is the way you can organize documents: multiple indices can be searched separately or together, and you can put different types of documents within each index.

Finally, Elasticsearch is, as the name suggests, elastic. It's clustered by default—you call it a cluster even if you run it on a single server—and you can always add more servers to increase capacity or fault tolerance. Similarly, you can easily remove servers from the cluster to reduce costs if you have lower load.

We'll discuss all these features in great detail in the rest of the book—scaling, in particular, is addressed in chapter 9—but before that, let's have a closer look and see how these features are useful.

1.2.5   *Extending Lucene functionality*

In many use cases, users search based on multiple criteria. For example, you can search for multiple words in multiple fields; some criteria would be mandatory and some would be optional. One of the most appreciated features of Elasticsearch is its well-structured REST API: you can structure your queries in JSON to combine different types of queries in many ways. We'll show you how in chapter 4, and you'll also see how you can use filters to include or exclude results in a cheap and cacheable way. Your JSON search can include both queries and filters, as well as aggregations, which generate statistics from matching documents.

Through the same REST API you can read and change many settings (as you'll see in chapter 11), as well as the way documents are indexed.

What about Apache Solr?

If you've already heard about Lucene, you've probably also heard about Solr, which is an open-source, distributed search engine based on Lucene. In fact, Lucene and Solr merged as a single Apache project in 2010, so you might wonder how Elasticsearch compares with Solr.

Both search engines provide similar functionality, and features evolve quickly with each new version. You can search the web for comparisons, but we recommend taking them with a grain of salt. Besides being tied to particular versions, which makes such comparisons obsolete in a matter of months, many of them are biased for various reasons.

(continued)

That said, a few historical facts help explain the origins of the two products. Solr was created in 2004 and Elasticsearch in 2010. When Elasticsearch came around, its distributed model, which is discussed later in this chapter, made it much easier to scale out than any of its competitors, which suggests the "elastic" part of the name. In the meantime, however, Solr added sharding with version 4.0, which makes the "distributed" argument debatable, like many other aspects.

At the time of this writing, Elasticsearch and Solr each have features that the other one doesn't, and choosing between them may come down to the specific functionality you need at a given point in time. For many use cases, the functionality you need is covered by both, and, as is often the case with competitors, choosing between them becomes a matter of taste. If you want to read more about Solr, we recommend *Solr in Action* by Trey Grainger and Timothy Potter (Manning, 2014).

When it comes to the way documents are indexed, one important aspect is analysis. Through *analysis,* the words from the text you're indexing become terms in Elasticsearch. For example, if you index the text "bicycle race," analysis may produce the terms "bicycle," "race," "cycling," and "racing," and when you search for any of those terms, the corresponding document is included in the results. The same analysis process applies when you search, as illustrated in figure 1.5. If you enter "bicycle race," you probably don't want to search for only the exact match. Maybe a document that contains both those words somewhere will do.

The default analyzer first breaks text into words by looking for common word separators, such as a space or a comma. Then it lowercases those words, so that "Bicycle Race" generates "bicycle" and "race." There are many more analyzers, and you can also build your own. We'll show you how in chapter 5.

At this point you might want to know more about what's in that "indexed data" box shown in figure 1.5 because it sounds quite vague. As we'll discuss next, data is organized in documents. By default, Elasticsearch stores your documents as they are, and it also puts all the terms resulting from analysis into the inverted index to enable the all-important fast and relevant searches. We go into more detail about indexing and

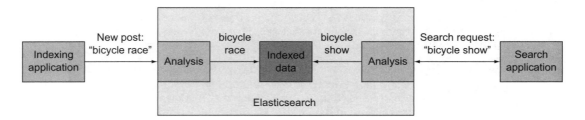

Figure 1.5   Analysis breaks text into words, both when you're indexing and when you're searching.

storing data in chapter 3. For now, let's take a closer look at why Elasticsearch is document-oriented and how it groups documents in types and indices.

1.2.6 Structuring your data in Elasticsearch

Unlike a relational database, which stores data in records or rows, Elasticsearch stores data in documents. Yet, to some extent, the two concepts are similar. With rows in a table, you have columns, and for each column, each row has a value. With a document you have keys and values, in much the same way.

The difference is that a document is more flexible than a row, mainly because—in Elasticsearch, at least—a document can be hierarchical. For example, in the same way you associate a key with a string value, such as `"author":"Joe"`, a document can have an array of strings, such as `"tags":["cycling", "bicycles"]`, or even key-value pairs, such as `"author":{"first_name":"Joe", "last_name":"Smith"}`. This flexibility is important because it encourages you to keep all the data that belongs to a logical entity in the same document, as opposed to keeping it in different rows in different tables. For example, the easiest (and probably fastest) way of storing blog articles is to keep all the data that belongs to a post in the same document. This way, searches are fast because you don't need joins or any other relational work.

If you have an SQL background, you might miss the ability to use joins. Unfortunately, they're not supported, at least in version 1.76 installed. Once that's in place, you're typically only a download away from getting Elasticsearch ready to start.

1.2.7 Installing Java

If you don't have a Java Runtime Environment (JRE) already, you'll have to install it first. Any JRE should work, as long as it's version 1.7 or later. Typically, you install the one from Oracle (www.java.com/en/download/index.jsp) or the open-source implementation, OpenJDK (http://download.java.net/openjdk/).

Troubleshooting "no Java found" errors

With Elasticsearch, as with other Java applications, it might happen that you've downloaded and installed Java, but the application refuses to start, complaining that it can't find Java.

Elasticsearch's script looks for Java in two places: the `JAVA_HOME` environment variable and the system path. To check if it's in `JAVA_HOME`, use the `env` command on UNIX-like systems and the `set` command on Windows. To check if it's in the system path, run the following command: `% java -version`.

If it works, then Java is in your path. If it doesn't, either configure `JAVA_HOME` or add the Java binary to your path. The Java binary is typically found wherever you installed Java (which should be `JAVA_HOME`), in the `bin` directory.

1.2.8   *Downloading and starting Elasticsearch*

With Java set up, you need to get Elasticsearch and start it. Download the package that best fits your environment. The following package options are available from www.elastic.co/downloads/elasticsearch: Tar, ZIP, RPM, and DEB.

ANY UNIX-LIKE OPERATING SYSTEM

If you're running on Linux, Mac, or any other UNIX-like operating system, you can get Elasticsearch from the tar.gz package. Then you can unpack it and start Elasticsearch with the shell script from the archive:

```
% tar zxf elasticsearch-*.tar.gz
% cd elasticsearch-*
% bin/elasticsearch
```

HOMEBREW PACKAGE MANAGER FOR OS X

If you need an easier way to install Elasticsearch on your Mac, you can install Homebrew. Instructions for doing that can be found at http://brew.sh. With Homebrew installed, getting Elasticsearch is a matter of running the following command:

```
% brew install elasticsearch
```

Then you start it in a similar way to the tar.gz archive:

```
% elasticsearch
```

ZIP PACKAGE

If you're running on Windows, download the ZIP archive. Unpack it and then run elasticsearch.bat from the bin/ directory, much as you run Elasticsearch on UNIX:

```
% bin\elasticsearch.bat
```

RPM OR DEB PACKAGES

If you're running on Red Hat Linux, CentOS, SUSE, or anything else that works with RPMs, or Debian, Ubuntu, or anything else that works with DEBs, there are RPM and DEB repositories provided by Elastic. You can see how to use them at www.elastic.co/guide/en/elasticsearch/reference/current/setup-repositories.html.

   Once you get Elasticsearch installed, which basically requires adding the repository to your list and running an install command, you can start it by running:

```
% systemctl start elasticsearch.service
Or, if your operating system doesn't have systemd:
% /etc/init.d/elasticsearch start
```

If you want to see what Elasticsearch is doing, look up the logs in /var/log/elasticsearch/. If you installed it by unpacking the TAR or ZIP archive, you should find them in the logs/ directory within the unpacked archive.

1.2.9   *Verifying that it works*

Now that you have Elasticsearch installed and started, let's take a look at the logs generated during startup and connect to the REST API for the first time.

EXAMINING THE STARTUP LOGS

When you first run Elasticsearch, you see a series of log lines telling you what's going on. Let's take a look at some of those lines and what they mean.

The first line typically provides statistics about the node you started:

```
[node] [Karkas] version[1.4.0], pid[6011], build[bc94bd8/2014-11-05T14:26:12Z]
```

By default, Elasticsearch gives your node a random name, in this case Karkas, which you can modify from the configuration. You can see details on the particular Elasticsearch version you're running, along with the PID of the Java process that started.

Plugins are loaded during initialization, and no plugins are included by default:

```
[plugins] [Karkas] loaded [], sites []
```

For more information about plugins, see appendix B.

Port 9300 is used by default for inter-node communication, called transport:

```
[transport] [Karkas] bound_address {inet[/0.0.0.0:9300]}, publish_address
{inet[/192.168.1.8:9300]}
```

If you use the native Java API instead of the REST API, this is the point where you need to connect.

In the next line, a *master node* was elected and it's the node you started named Karkas:

```
[cluster.service] [Karkas] new_master [Karkas][YPHC_vWiQVuSX-ZIJIlMhg][inet[/
192.168.1.8:9300]], reason: zen-disco-join (elected_as_master)
```

We discuss master election in chapter 9, which covers scaling out. The basic idea is that each cluster has a master node, responsible for knowing which nodes are in the cluster and where all the shards are located. Each time the master is unavailable, a new one is elected. In this case, you started the first node in the cluster, so this is your master.

Port 9200 is used for HTTP communication by default. This is where applications using the REST API connect:

```
[http] [Karkas] bound_address {inet[/0.0.0.0:9200]}, publish_address {inet[/
192.168.1.8:9200]}
```

The next line indicates that your node is now started:

```
[node] [Karkas] started
```

At this point, you can connect to it and start issuing requests.

The gateway is the component of Elasticsearch responsible for persisting your data to disk so you don't lose it if the node goes down:

```
[gateway] [Karkas] recovered [0] indices into cluster_state
```

When you start your node, the gateway looks on the disk to see if any data is saved so it can restore it. In this case, there's no index to restore.

Much of the information we've looked at in these log lines—from the node name to the gateway settings—is configurable. We talk about configuration options, and the concepts around them, as the book progresses. You can expect such configuration options to appear in part 2, which is all about performance and administration. Until then, you won't need to configure much because the default values are developer-friendly.

> **WARNING** Default values are so developer-friendly that if you start another Elasticsearch instance on another computer within the same multicast-enabled network, it will join the same cluster as the first instance, which might lead to unexpected results, such as shards migrating from one to the other. To prevent this, you can change the cluster name in the elasticsearch.yml configuration file, as shown in chapter 2, section 2.5.1

USING THE REST API

The easiest way to connect to the REST API is by pointing your browser to http://localhost:9200. If you didn't install Elasticsearch on your local machine, replace `localhost` with the IP address of the remote machine. By default, Elasticsearch listens for incoming HTTP requests on port 9200 of all interfaces. If the request works, you should get a JSON reply, showing that it works, as shown in figure 1.6.

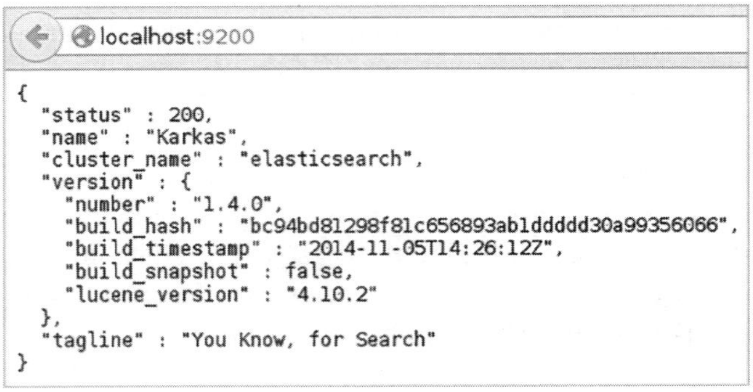

```
localhost:9200

{
  "status" : 200,
  "name" : "Karkas",
  "cluster_name" : "elasticsearch",
  "version" : {
    "number" : "1.4.0",
    "build_hash" : "bc94bd81298f81c656893ab1ddddd30a99356066",
    "build_timestamp" : "2014-11-05T14:26:12Z",
    "build_snapshot" : false,
    "lucene_version" : "4.10.2"
  },
  "tagline" : "You Know, for Search"
}
```

Figure 1.6   Checking out Elasticsearch from your browser

1.3   Summary

Now that you're all set up, let's review what we explored in this chapter:

- Elasticsearch is an open-source, distributed search engine built on top of Apache Lucene.
- The typical use case for Elasticsearch is to index large amounts of data so you can run full-text searches and real-time statistics on it.
- Elasticsearch provides features that go well beyond full-text search; for example, you can tune the relevance of your searches and offer search suggestions.
- To get started, download the package, unpack it if necessary, and run the Elasticsearch start script.

- For indexing and searching data, as well as for managing your cluster's settings, use the JSON over HTTP API and get back a JSON reply.
- You can also look at Elasticsearch as a NoSQL data store with real-time search and analytics capabilities. It's document-oriented and scalable by default.
- Elasticsearch automatically divides data into shards, which get balanced across the available servers in your cluster. This makes it easy to add and remove servers on the fly. Shards are also replicated, making your cluster fault-tolerant.

In chapter 2, you'll get to know Elasticsearch even better by indexing and searching real data.

Diving into the functionality 2

This chapter covers

- Defining documents, types, and indices
- Understanding Elasticsearch nodes and primary and replica shards
- Indexing documents with cURL and a data set
- Searching and retrieving data
- Setting Elasticsearch configuration options
- Working with multiple nodes

Now you know what kind of search engine Elasticsearch is, and you've seen some of its main features in chapter 1. Let's switch to the practical side and see how it does what it's good at. Imagine you're tasked with creating a way to search through millions of documents, like a website that allows people to build common interest groups and get together. In this case, documents could be the get-together groups, individual events. You need to implement this in a fault-tolerant way, and you need your setup to be able to accommodate more data and more concurrent searches, as your get-together site becomes more successful.

In this chapter, we'll show you how to deal with such a scenario by explaining how Elasticsearch data is organized. Then you'll get practical and start indexing and searching some real data for a get-together website using the code samples provided for this chapter. We'll use this get-together example and the code samples throughout the book to allow you to do some "real" searches and indexing.

All operations will be done using *cURL*, a nice little command-line tool for HTTP requests. Later you can translate what cURL does into your preferred programming language if you need to. Toward the end of the chapter, you'll make some configuration changes and start new instances of Elasticsearch, so you can experiment with a cluster of multiple nodes.

We'll get started with data organization. To understand how data is organized in Elasticsearch, we'll look at it from two angles:

- *Logical layout*—What your search application needs to be aware of.

  The unit you'll use for indexing and searching is a document, and you can think of it like a row in a relational database. Documents are grouped into types, which contain documents in a way similar to how tables contain rows. Finally, one or multiple types live in an *index*, the biggest container, similar to a database in the SQL world.

- *Physical layout*—How Elasticsearch handles your data in the background.

  Elasticsearch divides each index into *shards*, which can migrate between servers that make up a cluster. Typically, applications don't care about this because they work with Elasticsearch in much the same way, whether it's one or more servers. But when you're administering the cluster, you care because the way you configure the physical layout determines its performance, scalability, and availability.

Figure 2.1 illustrates the two perspectives.

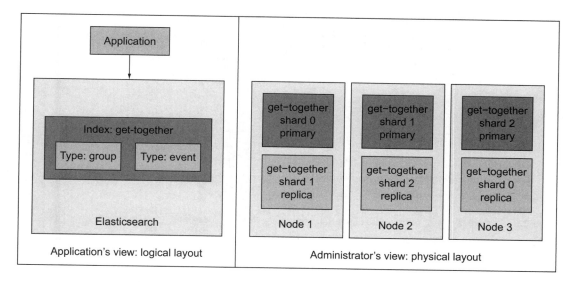

Figure 2.1   An Elasticsearch cluster from the application's and administrator's points of view

Let's start with the logical layout—or what the application sees.

2.1 *Understanding the logical layout: documents, types, and indices*

When you index a document in Elasticsearch, you put it in a type within an index. You can see this idea in figure 2.2, where the get-together index contains two types: event and group. Those types contain documents, such as the one labeled 1. The label 1 is that document's ID.

> **TIP** The ID doesn't have to be an integer. It's actually a string, and there are no constraints—you can put there whatever makes sense for your application.

The index-type-ID combination uniquely identifies a document in your Elasticsearch setup. When you search, you can look for documents in that specific type, of that specific index, or you can search across multiple types or even multiple indices.

At this point you might ask: what exactly are a document, a type, and an index? That's exactly what we're going to discuss next.

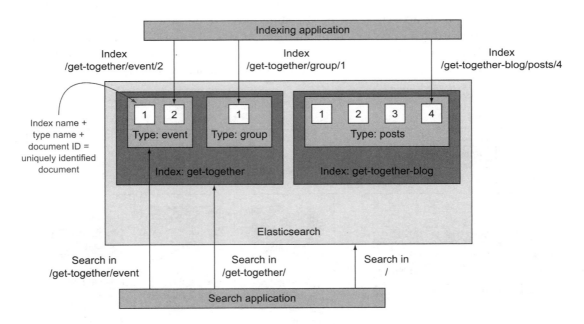

Figure 2.2   Logical layout of data in Elasticsearch: how an application sees data

2.1.1   Documents

We said in chapter 1 that Elasticsearch is *document-oriented*, meaning the smallest unit of data you index or search for is a document. A document has a few important properties in Elasticsearch:

- *It's self-contained.* A document contains both the fields (name) and their values (Elasticsearch Denver).
- *It can be hierarchical.* Think of this as documents within documents. A value of a field can be simple, like the value of the location field can be a string. It can also contain other fields and values. For example, the location field might contain both a city and a street address within it.
- *It has a flexible structure.* Your documents don't depend on a predefined schema. For example, not all events need description values, so that field can be omitted altogether. But it might require new fields, such as the latitude and longitude of the location.

A document is normally a JSON representation of your data. As we discussed in chapter 1, JSON over HTTP is the most widely used way to communicate with Elasticsearch, and it's the method we use throughout the book. For example, an event in your get-together site can be represented in the following document:

```
{
  "name": "Elasticsearch Denver",
  "organizer": "Lee",
  "location": "Denver, Colorado, USA"
}
```

> **NOTE**   Throughout the book, we'll use different colors for the field names and values of the JSON documents to make them easier to read. Field names are darker/blue, and values are in lighter/red.

You can also imagine a table with three columns: name, organizer, and location. The document would be a row containing the values. But there are some differences that make this comparison inexact. One difference is that, unlike rows, documents can be hierarchical. For example, the location can contain a name and a geolocation:

```
{
  "name": "Elasticsearch Denver",
  "organizer": "Lee",
  "location": {
    "name": "Denver, Colorado, USA",
    "geolocation": "39.7392, -104.9847"
  }
}
```

A single document can also contain arrays of values; for example:

```
{
  "name": "Elasticsearch Denver",
  "organizer": "Lee",
  "members": ["Lee", "Mike"]
}
```

Documents in Elasticsearch are said to be *schema-free*, in the sense that not all your documents need to have the same fields, so they're not bound to the same schema. For example, you could omit the location altogether in case the organizer needs to be called before every gathering:

```
{
  "name": "Elasticsearch Denver",
  "organizer": "Lee",
  "members": ["Lee", "Mike"]
}
```

Although you can add or omit fields at will, the type of each field matters: some are strings, some are integers, and so on. Because of that, Elasticsearch keeps a mapping of all your fields and their types and other settings. This mapping is specific to every type of every index. That's why types are sometime called *mapping* types in Elasticsearch terminology

2.1.2 Types

Types are logical containers for documents, similar to how tables are containers for rows. You'd put documents with different structures (schemas) in different types. For example, you could have a type that defines get-together groups and another type for the events when people gather.

The definition of fields in each type is called a *mapping*. For example, name would be mapped as a string, but the geolocation field under location would be mapped as a special geo_point type. (We explore working with geospatial data in appendix A.) Each kind of field is handled differently. For example, you search for a word in the name field and you search for groups by location to find those that are located near where you live.

> **TIP** Whenever you search in a field that isn't at the root of your JSON document, you must specify its path. For example, the geolocation field under location is referred to as location.geolocation.

You may ask yourself: if Elasticsearch is schema-free, why does each document belong to a type, and each type contains a mapping, which is like a schema?

We say *schema-free* because documents are not bound to the schema. They aren't required to contain all the fields defined in your mapping and may come up with new fields. How does it work? First, the mapping contains all the fields of all the documents indexed so far in that type. But not all documents have to have all fields. Also, if a new document gets indexed with a field that's not already in the mapping, Elasticsearch automatically adds that new field to your mapping. To add that field, it has to decide what type it is, so it guesses it. For example, if the value is 7, it assumes it's a long type.

This autodetection of new fields has its downside because Elasticsearch might not guess right. For example, after indexing 7, you might want to index hello world, which will fail because it's a string and not a long. In production, the safe way to go is to define your mapping before indexing data. We talk more about defining mappings in chapter 3.

Mapping types only divide documents logically. Physically, documents from the same index are written to disk regardless of the mapping type they belong to.

2.1.3 *Indices*

Indices are containers for mapping types. An Elasticsearch *index* is an independent chunk of documents, much like a database is in the relational world: each index is stored on the disk in the same set of files; it stores all the fields from all the mapping types in there, and it has its own settings. For example, each index has a setting called refresh_interval, which defines the interval at which newly indexed documents are made available for searches. This *refresh* operation is quite expensive in terms of performance, and this is why it's done occasionally—by default, every second—instead of doing it after each indexed document. If you've read that Elasticsearch is *near-real-time*, this refresh process is what it refers to.

> **TIP** Just as you can search across types, you can search across indices. This gives you flexibility in the way you can organize documents. For example, you can put your get-together events and the blog posts about them in different indices or in different types of the same index. Some ways are more efficient than others, depending on your use case. We talk more about how to organize your data for efficient indexing in chapter 3.

One example of index-specific settings is the number of shards. You saw in chapter 1 that an index can be made up of one or more chunks called shards. This is good for scalability: you can run Elasticsearch on multiple servers and have shards of the same index live on all of them. Next, we'll take a closer look at how sharding works in Elasticsearch.

2.2 *Understanding the physical layout: nodes and shards*

Understanding how data is physically laid out boils down to understanding how Elasticsearch scales. Although chapter 9 is dedicated entirely to scaling, in this section, we'll introduce you to how scaling works by looking at how multiple nodes work together in a cluster, how data is divided in shards and replicated, and how indexing and searching work with multiple shards and replicas.

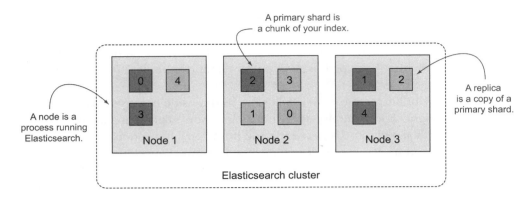

Figure 2.3   A three-node cluster with an index divided into five shards with one replica per shard

To understand the big picture, let's review what happens when an Elasticsearch index is created. By default, each index is made up of five primary shards, each with one replica, for a total of ten shards, as illustrated in figure 2.3.

As you'll see next, replicas are good for reliability and search performance. Technically, a shard is a directory of files where Lucene stores the data for your index. A shard is also the smallest unit that Elasticsearch moves from node to node.

2.2.1   Creating a cluster of one or more nodes

A *node* is an instance of Elasticsearch. When you start Elasticsearch on your server, you have a node. If you start Elasticsearch on another server, it's another node. You can even have more nodes on the same server by starting multiple Elasticsearch processes.

Multiple nodes can join the same *cluster*. As we'll discuss later in this chapter, starting nodes with the same cluster name and otherwise default settings is enough to make a cluster. With a cluster of multiple nodes, the same data can be spread across multiple servers. This helps performance because Elasticsearch has more resources to work with. It also helps reliability: if you have at least one replica per shard, any node can disappear and Elasticsearch will still serve you all the data. For an application that's using Elasticsearch, having one or more nodes in a cluster is transparent. By default, you can connect to any node from the cluster and work with the whole data just as if you had a single node.

Although clustering is good for performance and availability, it has its disadvantages: you have to make sure nodes can communicate with each other quickly enough and that you won't have a split brain (two parts of the cluster that can't communicate and think the other part dropped out). To address such issues, chapter 9 discusses scaling out.

WHAT HAPPENS WHEN YOU INDEX A DOCUMENT?

By default, when you index a document, it's first sent to one of the primary shards, which is chosen based on a hash of the document's ID. That primary shard may be

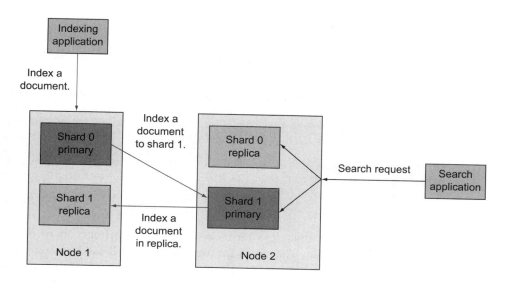

Figure 2.4   Documents are indexed to random primary shards and their replicas. Searches run on complete sets of shards, regardless of their status as primaries or replicas.

located on a different node, like it is on Node 2 in figure 2.4, but this is transparent to the application.

Then the document is sent to be indexed in all of that primary shard's replicas (see the left side of figure 2.4). This keeps replicas in sync with data from the primary shards. Being in sync allows replicas to serve searches and to be automatically promoted to primary shards in case the original primary becomes unavailable.

WHAT HAPPENS WHEN YOU SEARCH AN INDEX?

When you search an index, Elasticsearch has to look in a complete set of shards for that index (see right side of figure 2.4). Those shards can be either primary or replicas because primary and replica shards typically contain the same documents. Elasticsearch distributes the search load between the primary and replica shards of the index you're searching, making replicas useful for both search performance and fault tolerance.

Next we'll look at the details of what primary and replica shards are and how they're allocated in an Elasticsearch cluster.

2.2.2   *Understanding primary and replica shards*

Let's start with the smallest unit Elasticsearch deals with, a shard. A *shard* is a Lucene index: a directory of files containing an inverted index. An *inverted index* is a structure that enables Elasticsearch to tell you which document contains a term (a word) without having to look at all the documents.

Elasticsearch index vs. Lucene index

You'll see the word "index" used frequently as we discuss Elasticsearch; here's how the terminology works.

An Elasticsearch *index* is broken down into chunks: *shards*. A shard is a Lucene index, so an Elasticsearch index is made up of multiple Lucene indices. This makes sense because Elasticsearch uses Apache Lucene as its core library to index your data and search through it.

Throughout this book, whenever you see the word "index" by itself, it refers to an Elasticsearch index. If we're digging into the details of what's in a shard, we'll specifically use the term "Lucene index."

In figure 2.5, you can see what sort of information the first primary shard of your get-together index may contain. The shard get-together0, as we'll call it from now on, is a Lucene index—an inverted index. By default, it stores the original document's content plus additional information, such as *term dictionary* and *term frequencies*, which helps searching.

The *term dictionary* maps each term to identifiers of documents containing that term (see figure 2.5). When searching, Elasticsearch doesn't have to look through all the documents for that term—it uses this dictionary to quickly identify all the documents that match.

Term frequencies give Elasticsearch quick access to the number of appearances of a term in a document. This is important for calculating the relevancy score of results. For example, if you search for "denver", documents that contain "denver" many times are typically more relevant. Elasticsearch gives them a higher score, and they appear higher in the list of results. By default, the ranking algorithm is TF-IDF, as we explained

A shard is a Lucene index.

get-together0 shard		
Inverted index		
Term	Document	Frequency
elasticsearch	id1	1 occurrence: id1->1 time
denver	id1,id3	3 occurrences: id1->1 time, id3->2 times
clojure	id2,id3	5 occurrences: id2->2 times, id3->3 times
data	id2	2 occurrences: id2->2 times

Figure 2.5 Term dictionary and frequencies in a Lucene index

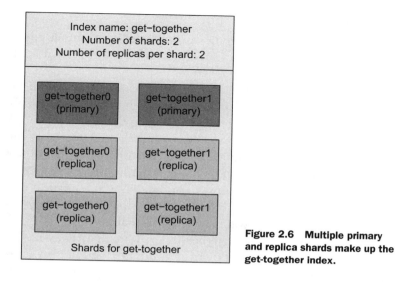

Figure 2.6   Multiple primary and replica shards make up the get-together index.

in chapter 1, section 1.1.2, but you have a lot more options. We'll discuss search relevancy in great detail in chapter 6.

A shard can be either a primary or a replica shard, with *replicas* being exactly that—copies of the primary shard. A replica is used for searching or it becomes a new primary shard if the original primary shard is lost.

An Elasticsearch index is made up of one or more primary shards and zero or more replica shards. In Figure 2.6, you can see that the Elasticsearch get-together index is made up of six total shards: two primary shards (the darker boxes) and two replicas for each shard (the lighter boxes) for a total of four replicas.

Replicas can be added or removed at runtime—primaries can't

You can change the number of replicas per shard at any time because replicas can always be created or removed. This doesn't apply to the number of primary shards an index is divided into; you have to decide on the number of shards before creating the index.

Keep in mind that too few shards limit how much you can scale, but too many shards impact performance. The default setting of five is typically a good start. You'll learn more in chapter 9, which is all about scaling. We'll also explain how to add/remove replica shards dynamically.

All the shards and replicas you've seen so far are distributed to nodes within an Elasticsearch cluster. Next we'll look at some details about how Elasticsearch distributes shards and replicas in a cluster having one or more nodes.

2.2.3   *Distributing shards in a cluster*

The simplest Elasticsearch cluster has one node: one machine running one Elastic-search process. When you installed Elasticsearch in chapter 1 and started it, you created a one-node cluster.

As you add more nodes to the same cluster, existing shards get balanced between all nodes. As a result, both indexing and search requests that work with those shards benefit from the extra power of your added nodes. Scaling this way (by adding nodes to a cluster) is called *horizontal scaling*; you add more nodes, and requests are then distributed so they all share the work. The alternative to horizontal scaling is to scale vertically; you add more resources to your Elasticsearch node, perhaps by dedicating more processors to it if it's a virtual machine, or adding RAM to a physical machine. Although vertical scaling helps performance almost every time, it's not always possible or cost-effective. Using shards enables you to scale horizontally.

Suppose you want to scale your get-together index, which currently has two primary shards and no replicas. As shown in figure 2.7, the first option is to scale vertically by upgrading the node: for example, adding more RAM, more CPUs, faster disks, and so on. The second option is to scale horizontally by adding another node and having your data distributed between the two nodes.

We talk more about performance in chapter 10. For now, let's see how indexing and searching work across multiple shards and replicas.

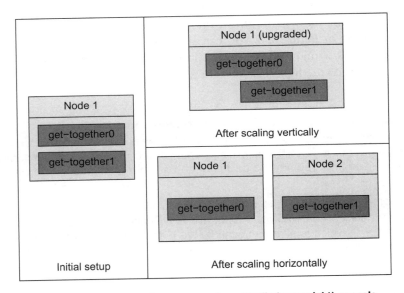

Figure 2.7   To improve performance, scale vertically (upper-right) or scale horizontally (lower-right).

2.2.4 *Distributed indexing and searching*

At this point you might wonder how indexing and searching work with multiple shards spread across multiple nodes.

Let's take indexing, as shown in figure 2.8. The Elasticsearch node that receives your indexing request first selects the shard to index the document to. By default, documents are distributed evenly between shards: for each document, the shard is determined by hashing its ID string. Each shard has an equal hash range, with equal chances of receiving the new document. Once the target shard is determined, the current node forwards the document to the node holding that shard. Subsequently, that indexing operation is replayed by all the replicas of that shard. The indexing command successfully returns after all the available replicas finish indexing the document.

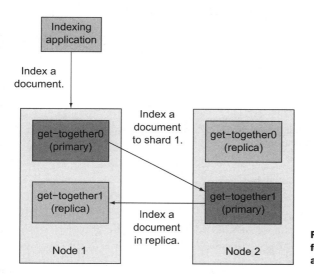

Figure 2.8   Indexing operation is forwarded to the responsible shard and then to its replicas.

With searching, the node that receives the request forwards it to a set of shards containing all your data. Using a round-robin, Elasticsearch selects an available shard (which can be primary or replica) and forwards the search request to it. As shown in figure 2.9, Elasticsearch then gathers results from those shards, aggregates them into a single reply, and forwards the reply back to the client application.

By default, primary and replica shards get hit by searches in round-robin, assuming all nodes in your cluster are equally fast (identical hardware and software configurations). If that's not the case, you can organize your data or configure your shards to prevent the slower nodes from becoming a bottleneck. We explore such options further in chapter 9. For now, let's start indexing documents in the single-node Elasticsearch cluster that you started in chapter 1.

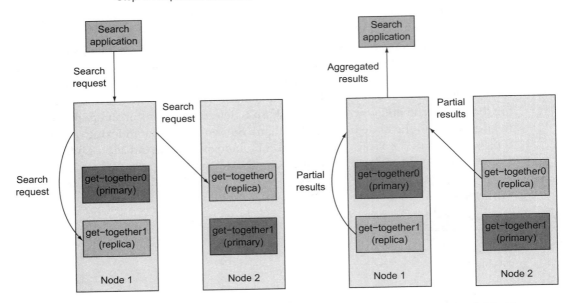

Figure 2.9 **Search request is forwarded to primary/replica shards containing a complete set of data. Then results are aggregated and sent back to the client.**

2.3   *Indexing new data*

Although chapter 3 gets into the details of indexing, here the goal is to give you a feel for what indexing is about. In this section we'll discuss the following processes:

- Using cURL, you'll use the REST API to send a JSON document to be indexed with Elasticsearch. You'll also look at the JSON reply that comes back.
- You'll see how Elasticsearch automatically creates the index and type to which your document belongs if they don't exist already.
- You'll index additional documents from the source code for the book so you have a data set ready to search through.

You'll index your first document by hand, so let's start by looking at how to issue an HTTP PUT request to a URI. A sample URI is shown in figure 2.10 with each part labeled. Let's walk through how you issue the request.

2.3.1   *Indexing a document with cURL*

For most snippets in this book you'll use the cURL binary. *cURL* is a command-line tool for transferring data over HTTP. You'll use the curl command to make HTTP requests, as it has become a convention to use cURL for Elasticsearch code snippets. That's

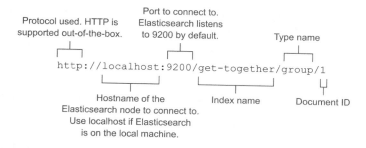

Figure 2.10   URI of a document in Elasticsearch

because it's easy to translate a cURL example into any programming language. In fact, if you ask for help on the official mailing list for Elasticsearch, it's recommended that you provide a *curl recreation* of your problem. A curl recreation is a command or a sequence of curl commands that reproduces the problem you're experiencing, and anyone who has Elasticsearch installed locally can run it.

> **Installing cURL**
>
> If you're running a UNIX-like operating system, such as Linux or Mac OS X, you're likely to have the `curl` command available. If you don't have it already or if you're on Windows, you can download it from http://curl.haxx.se. You can also install Cygwin and then select cURL as part of the Cygwin installation, which is the approach we recommend.
>
> Using Cygwin to run curl commands on Windows is preferred because you can copy-paste the commands that work on UNIX-like systems. If you choose to stick with the Windows shell, take extra care because single quotes behave differently on Windows. In most situations, you must replace single quotes (') with double-quotes (") and escape double quotes with a backslash (\ "). For example, a UNIX command like this
>
> ```
> curl 'http://localhost' -d '{"field": "value"}'
> ```
>
> looks like this on Windows:
>
> ```
> curl "http://localhost" -d "{\"field\": \"value\"}"
> ```

There are many ways to use curl to make HTTP requests; run `man curl` to see all of them. Throughout this book, we use the following curl usage conventions:

- The *method,* which is typically `GET`, `PUT`, or `POST`, is the argument of the `-X` parameter.

  You can add a space between the parameter and its argument, but we don't add one. For example, we use `-XPUT` instead of `-X PUT`. The default method is `GET`, and when we use it, we skip the `-X` parameter altogether.

- In the URI, we skip specifying the protocol; it's always `http`, and curl uses `http` by default when no protocol is specified.
- We put single quotes around the URI because it can contain multiple parameters and you have to separate the parameters with an ampersand (&), which normally sends the process to the background.
- The data that we send through HTTP is typically JSON, and we surround it with single quotes because the JSON itself contains double quotes.

  If single quotes are needed in the JSON itself, we first close the single quotes and then surround the needed single quote with double quotes, as shown in this example:

  ```
  '{"name": "Scarlet O'"'"'Hara"}'
  ```

  For consistency, most URLs will be surrounded by single quotes, too (except when using single quotes prevents escaping a character or including a variable, when double quotes will be used).

The URLs we use for HTTP requests sometimes contain parameters such as `pretty=true` or simply `pretty`. We use the latter, whether the request is done with `curl` or not. The `pretty` parameter in particular makes the JSON reply look more readable than the default, which is to return the reply all in one line.

Using Elasticsearch from your browser via Head, kopf, or Marvel

If you prefer graphical interfaces to the command line, several tools are available.

Elasticsearch Head—You can install this tool as an Elasticsearch plugin, a stand-alone HTTP server, or a web page that you can open from your file system. You can send HTTP requests from there, but Head is most useful as a monitoring tool to show you how shards are distributed in your cluster. You can find Elasticsearch Head at https://github.com/mobz/elasticsearch-head.

Elasticsearch kopf—Similar to Head in that it's good for both monitoring and sending requests, this tool runs as a web page from your file system or as an Elasticsearch plugin. Both Head and kopf evolve quickly, so any comparison might become obsolete quickly as well. You can find Elasticsearch kopf at https://github.com/lmenezes/elasticsearch-kopf.

Marvel—This tool is a monitoring solution for Elasticsearch. We talk more about monitoring in chapter 11, which is all about administering your cluster. Then we'll describe monitoring tools like Marvel in appendix D. For now, the thing to remember is that Marvel also provides a graphical way to send requests to Elasticsearch called Sense, providing an autocomplete feature, which is a useful learning aid. You can download Marvel at www.elastic.co/downloads/marvel. Note that Marvel is a commercial product, though it's free for development.

Assuming you can use the `curl` command and you have Elasticsearch installed with the defaults settings on your local machine, you can index your first get-together group document with the following command:

```
% curl -XPUT 'localhost:9200/get-together/group/1?pretty' -d '{
  "name": "Elasticsearch Denver",
  "organizer": "Lee"
}'
```

You should get the following output:

```
{
  "_index" : "get-together",
  "_type" : "group",
  "_id" : "1",
  "_version" : 1,
  "created" : true
}
```

The reply contains the index, type, and ID of the indexed document. In this case, you get the ones you specified, but it's also possible to rely on Elasticsearch to generate IDs, as you'll learn in chapter 3. You also get the version of the document, which begins at 1 and is incremented with each update. You'll learn about updates in chapter 3.

Now that you have your first document indexed, let's look at what happened with the index and the type containing this document.

2.3.2 Creating an index and mapping type

If you installed Elasticsearch and ran the `curl` command to index a document, you might be wondering why it worked given the following factors:

- The index wasn't there before. You didn't issue any command to create an index named get-together.
- The mapping wasn't previously defined. You didn't define any mapping type called group in which to define the fields from your document.

The `curl` command works because Elasticsearch automatically adds the get-together index for you and also creates a new mapping for the type group. That mapping contains a definition of your field as strings. Elasticsearch handles all this for you by default, which enables you to start indexing without any prior configuration. You can change this default behavior if you need to, as you'll see in chapter 3.

CREATING AN INDEX MANUALLY
You can always create an index with a PUT request similar to the request used to index a document:

```
% curl -XPUT 'localhost:9200/new-index'
{"acknowledged":true}
```

Creating the index itself takes more time than creating a document, so you might want to have the index ready beforehand. Another reason to create indices in advance is if you want to specify different settings than the ones Elasticsearch defaults to—for example, you may want a specific number of shards. We'll show you how to do these things in chapter 9—because you'd typically use many indices as a way of scaling out.

GETTING THE MAPPING

As we mentioned, the mapping is automatically created with your new document, and Elasticsearch automatically detects your name and organizer fields as strings. If you add a new document with yet another new field, Elasticsearch guesses its type, too, and appends the new field to the mapping.

To view the current mapping, issue an HTTP GET to the _mapping endpoint of the index. This would show you mappings for all types within that index, but you can get a specific mapping by specifying the type name under the _mapping endpoint:

```
% curl 'localhost:9200/get-together/_mapping/group?pretty'
{
  "get-together" : {
    "mappings" : {
      "group" : {
        "properties" : {
          "name" : {
            "type" : "string"
          },
          "organizer" : {
            "type" : "string"
          }
        }
      }
    }
  }
}
```

The response contains the following relevant data:

- *Index name*—get-together
- *Type name*—group
- *Property list*—name and organizer
- *Property options*—The type option is string for both properties

We talk more about indices, mappings, and mapping types in chapter 3. For now, let's define a mapping and then index some documents by running a script from the code samples that come with this book.

2.3.3 *Indexing documents from the code samples*

Before we look at searching through the indexed documents, let's do some more indexing by running populate.sh from the code samples. This will give you some more sample data in order to do searches later on.

Downloading the code samples

To download the source code, visit https://github.com/dakrone/elasticsearch-in-action, and then follow the instructions from there. The easiest way to get them is by cloning the repository:

```
git clone https://github.com/dakrone/elasticsearch-in-action.git
```

If you're on Windows, it's best to install Cygwin first from https://cygwin.com. During the installation, add `git` and `curl` to the list of packages to be installed. Then you'll be able to use `git` to download the code samples and bash to run them.

The script first deletes the get-together index you created. Then it recreates it and creates the mapping that's defined in mapping.json. The mapping file specifies options other than those you've seen so far, and we explore them in the rest of the book, mostly in chapter 3. Finally, the script indexes documents in two types: group and event. There is a parent-child relationship between those types (events belonging to groups), which we explore in chapter 8. For now, ignore this relationship.

Running the `populate.sh` script should look similar to the following listing.

Listing 2.1   Indexing documents with `populate.sh`

```
% ./populate.sh
WARNING, this script will delete the 'get-together' index and re-index all data!
Press Control-C to cancel this operation.
Press [Enter] to continue.
```

After running the script, you'll have a handful of groups that meet and the events planned for those groups. Let's look at how you can search through those documents.

2.4   *Searching for and retrieving data*

As you might imagine, there are many options around how to search. After all, searching is what Elasticsearch is for.

NOTE   We look at the most common ways to search in chapter 4; you learn more about getting relevant results in chapter 6 and about search performance in chapter 10.

To take a closer look at the pieces that make up a typical search, search for groups that contain the word "elasticsearch" but ask only for the `name` and `location` fields of the most relevant document. The following listing shows the GET request and response.

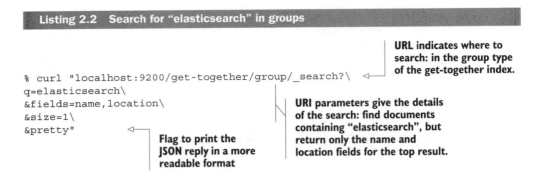

Listing 2.2   Search for "elasticsearch" in groups

```
% curl "localhost:9200/get-together/group/_search?\
q=elasticsearch\
&fields=name,location\
&size=1\
&pretty"
```

URL indicates where to search: in the group type of the get-together index.

URI parameters give the details of the search: find documents containing "elasticsearch", but return only the name and location fields for the top result.

Flag to print the JSON reply in a more readable format

Normally a query runs on a specific field, such as `q=name:elasticsearch`, but in this case we didn't specify any field because we wanted to search in all fields. In fact, Elasticsearch uses, by default, a special field named `_all`, in which all fields' contents are indexed. We'll look more at the `_all` field in chapter 3, but for now it's nice to know that such a query without an explicit field name goes there.

We'll look at many more aspects of searches in chapter 4, but here we'll take a closer look at three important pieces of a search:

- Where to search
- Contents of the reply
- What and how to search

2.4.1   *Where to search*

You can tell Elasticsearch to look in a specific type of a specific index, as in listing 2.2, but you can also search in multiple types in the same index, in multiple indices, or in all indices.

To search in multiple types, use a comma-separated list. For example, to search in both group and event types, run a command like this:

```
% curl "localhost:9200/get-together/group,event/_search\
?q=elasticsearch&pretty"
```

You can also search in all types of an index by sending your request to the `_search` endpoint of the index's URL:

```
% curl 'localhost:9200/get-together/_search?q=sample&pretty'
```

Similar to types, to search in multiple indices, separate them with a comma:

```
% curl "localhost:9200/get-together,other-index/_search\
?q=elasticsearch&pretty"
```

This particular request will fail unless you created `other-index` in advance. To ignore such problems, you can add the `ignore_unavailable` flag in the same way you add the `pretty` flag. To search in all indices, omit the index name altogether:

```
% curl 'localhost:9200/_search?q=elasticsearch&pretty'
```

TIP If you need to search in all indices, you can also use a placeholder called _all as the index name. This comes in handy when you need to search in a single type across all indices as in this example: http://localhost:9200/_all/event/_search.

This flexibility regarding where to search allows you to organize data in multiple indices and types, depending on what makes sense for your use case. For example, log events are often organized in time-based indices, such as "logs-2013-06-03," "logs-2013-06-04," and so on. Such a design implies that today's index is hot: all new events go here, and most of the searches are in recent data. The hot index contains only a fraction of all your data, making it easier to handle and faster. And you can still search in older data or in all data if you need to. You'll find out more about such design patterns in part 2, where you'll learn more about scaling, performance, and administration.

2.4.2 Contents of the reply

In addition to the documents that match your search criteria, the reply of a search contains information that's useful for checking the performance of your search or the relevance of the results.

You might have some questions about listing 2.2 regarding what the reply from Elasticsearch contains. What's the score about? What happens if not all shards are available? Let's look at each part of the reply shown the following listing.

Listing 2.3 Search reply returning two fields of a single resulting document

```
{
  "took" : 2,                          How long your request
  "timed_out" : false,                 took and if it timed out
  "_shards" : {
    "total" : 2,
    "successful" : 2,                   How many shards
    "failed" : 0                        were queried
  },
  "hits" : {
    "total" : 2,
    "max_score" : 0.9066504,           Statistics on all documents
    "hits" : [ {                       that matched
      "_index" : "get-together",
      "_type" : "group",
      "_id" : "3",
      "_score" : 0.9066504,
      "fields" : {                                       The results
        "location" : [ "San Francisco, California, USA" ], array
        "name" : [ "Elasticsearch San Francisco"]
      }
    } ]
  }
}
```

As you can see, the JSON reply from Elasticsearch includes information on time, shards, hits statistics, and the documents you asked for. We'll look at each of these in turn.

TIME

The first items of a reply look something like this:

```
"took" : 2,
"timed_out" : false,
```

The took field tells you how long Elasticsearch needed to process your request. The time is in milliseconds. The timed_out field indicates whether your search timed out. By default, searches never time out, but you can specify a limit via the timeout parameter. For example, the following search times out after three seconds:

```
% curl "localhost:9200/get-together/group/_search\
?q=elasticsearch\
&pretty\
&timeout=3s"
```

If a search times out, the value of timed_out is true, and you get only results that were gathered until the search timed out.

SHARDS

The next bit of the response is information about shards involved in the search:

```
"_shards" : {
    "total" : 2,
    "successful" : 2,
    "failed" : 0
```

This might look natural to you because you searched in one index, which in this case has two shards. All shards replied, so successful is 2, which leaves failed with 0.

You might wonder what happens when a node goes down and a shard can't reply to a search request. Take a look at figure 2.11, which shows a cluster of three nodes,

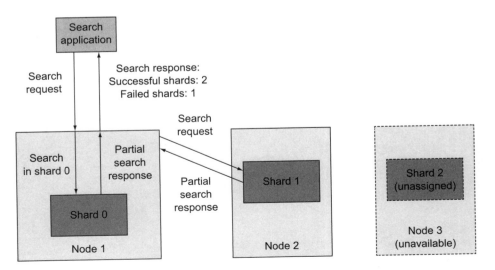

Figure 2.11   Partial results can be returned from shards that are still available.

each with only one shard and no replicas. If one node goes down, some data would be missing. In this case, Elasticsearch gives you the results from shards that are up and reports the number of shards unavailable for search in the `failed` field.

HITS STATISTICS

The last element of the reply is called `hits` and is quite lengthy because it contains an array of the matching documents. But before that array, it contains a couple of statistics:

```
"total" : 2,
"max_score" : 0.9066504
```

In `total`, you see the total number of matching documents, and in `max_score`, you see the maximum score of those matching documents.

> **DEFINITION** The *score* of a document returned by a search is the measure of how relevant that document is for the given search criteria. As mentioned in chapter 1, by default, the score is calculated with the TF-IDF (term frequency-inverse document frequency) algorithm. *Term frequency* means for each term (word) you search, the document's score is increased if it has more occurrences of that term. *Inverse document frequency* means the score is increased more if the term is rare across all documents because it's considered more relevant. If the term occurs often in other documents, it's probably a common term, and is thus less relevant. We'll show you how to make your searches more relevant in chapter 6.

The total number of documents may not match the number of documents you see in the reply. By default, Elasticsearch limits the number of results to 10, so if you can have more than 10 results, look at the value of `total` for the precise number of documents that match your search criteria. As you saw previously, to change the number of results returned, use the `size` parameter.

RESULTING DOCUMENTS

The array of hits is usually the most interesting information in a reply:

```
"hits" : [ {
      "_index" : "get-together",
      "_type" : "group",
      "_id" : "3",
      "_score" : 0.9066504,
      "fields" : {
        "location" : [ "San Francisco, California, USA" ],
        "name" : [ "Elasticsearch San Francisco" ]
      }
   } ]
```

Each matching document is shown with the index and type it belongs to, its ID, and its score. The values of the fields you specified in your search query are also shown. In listing 2.2, you used `fields=name,location`. If you don't specify which fields you want, the `_source` field is shown. Like `_all`, `_source` is a special field, in which, by default, Elasticsearch stores the original JSON document. You can configure what gets stored in the source, and we explore that in chapter 3.

> **TIP**   You can also limit which fields from the original document (_source) are shown, by using source filtering, as explained here: www.elastic.co/guide/ en/elasticsearch/reference/master/search-request-source-filtering.html. You'd put these options in the JSON payload of your search, which is explained in the next section.

2.4.3   *How to search*

So far, you've searched through what's called a *URI request*, so named because all your search options go into the URI. This is good for simple searches you run on the command line, but it's safer to think of URI requests as shortcuts.

Normally, you'd put your query in the data part of your request. Elasticsearch allows you to specify all the search criteria in JSON format. As searches get more complex, JSON is much easier to read and write and offers a lot more functionality.

To send a JSON query for all groups that are about Elasticsearch, you could do this:

```
% curl 'localhost:9200/get-together/group/_search?pretty' -d '{
  "query": {
    "query_string": {
      "query": "elasticsearch"
    }
  }
}'
```

In plain English, this translates to "run a *query* of type *query_string*, where the string is *elasticsearch*." It might seem like too much boilerplate to type in elasticsearch, but this is because JSON provides many more options than a URI request. As you'll see in chapter 4, using a JSON query makes sense when you start to combine different types of queries: squeezing all those options in a URI would be more difficult to handle. Let's explore each field.

SETTING QUERY STRING OPTIONS

At the last level of the JSON request, you have "query": "elasticsearch", and you might think the "query" part is redundant because you already know it's a query. But a query_string provides more options than the string itself.

For example, if you search for "elasticsearch san francisco", Elasticsearch looks in the _all field by default. If you wanted to look in the group's name instead, you'd specify

```
"default_field": "name"
```

Also by default, Elasticsearch returns documents matching any of the specified words (the default operator is OR). If you wanted to match all the words, you'd specify

```
"default_operator": "AND"
```

The revised query looks like this:

```
% curl 'localhost:9200/get-together/group/_search?pretty' -d '{
  "query": {
    "query_string": {
      "query": "elasticsearch san francisco",
      "default_field": "name",
      "default_operator": "AND"
    }
  }
}'
```

Another way to achieve the same results is to specify the field and the operator in the query string itself:

```
"query": "name:elasticsearch AND name:san AND name:francisco"
```

The query string is a powerful tool to specify your search criteria. Elasticsearch parses the string to understand the terms you're looking for and your other options, such as fields and operators, and then runs the query. This functionality is inherited from Lucene[1].

CHOOSING THE RIGHT QUERY TYPE

If the `query_string` query type looks intimidating, the good news is there are many other types of queries, most of which are covered in chapter 4. For example, if you're looking only for the term "elasticsearch" in the `name` field, a `term` query would be faster and more straightforward:

```
% curl 'localhost:9200/get-together/group/_search?pretty' -d '{
  "query": {
    "term": {
      "name": "elasticsearch"
    }
  }
}'
```

USING FILTERS

So far, all the searches you've seen have been queries. Queries give you back results and each result has a score. If you're not interested in the score, you can run a *filtered query* instead. We'll talk more about the filtered query in chapter 4, but the key information is that filters care only whether a result matches the search or not. As a result, they're faster and easier to cache than their query counterparts.

---

[1] If you want to find out more about the query string syntax, visit http://lucene.apache.org/core/4_9_0/queryparser/org/apache/lucene/queryparser/classic/package-summary.html#package_description.

For example, the following query looks for the term "elasticsearch" in the name field of group documents:

```
% curl 'localhost:9200/get-together/group/_search?pretty' -d '{
  "query": {
    "filtered": {
      "filter": {
        "term": {
          "name": "elasticsearch"
        }
      }
    }
  }
}'
```

The results are the same as the ones you get with the equivalent term query, but filter results aren't sorted by score (because the score is 1.0 for all results).

APPLYING AGGREGATIONS

In addition to queries and filters, you can do all sorts of statistics through aggregations. We look at aggregations in chapter 7, but let's look at a simple example here.

Suppose a user is visiting your get-together website and wants to explore the kinds of groups that are available. You might want to show who the group organizers are. For example, if "Lee" comes up in the results as the organizer of seven meetings, a user who knows Lee might click his name to filter only those seven meetings.

To return people who are group organizers, you can use a *terms* aggregation. This shows counters for each term that appears in the field you specify—in this case, organizer. The aggregation might look like this:

```
% curl localhost:9200/get-together/group/_search?pretty -d '{
  "aggregations" : {
    "organizers" : {
      "terms" : { "field" : "organizer" }
    }
  }
}'
```

In plain English, this request translates to "give me an aggregation named organizers, which is of type terms and is looking at the organizer field." The following results display at the bottom of the reply:

```
"aggregations" : {
    "organizers" : {
      "buckets" : [ {
        "key" : "lee",
        "doc_count" : 2
      }, {
        "key" : "andy",
        "doc_count" : 1
```

....

The results show you that out of the six total terms, "lee" appears two times, "andy" one time, and so on. We have two groups organized by Lee. You could then search for the groups for which Lee is the organizer to narrow down your results.

Aggregations are useful when you can't search for what you need because you don't know what that is. What kinds of groups are available? Are there any events hosted near where I live? You can use aggregations to drill down in the available data and see real-time statistics.

At other times you have the opposite scenario. You know exactly what you need and you don't want to run a search at all. That's when it's useful to retrieve a document by ID.

2.4.4 *Getting documents by ID*

To retrieve a specific document, you must know the index and type it belongs to and its ID. You then issue an HTTP GET request to that document's URI:

```
% curl 'localhost:9200/get-together/group/1?pretty'
{
  "_index" : "get-together",
  "_type" : "group",
  "_id" : "1",
  "_version" : 1,
  "found" : true,
  "_source" : {
  "name": "Denver Clojure",
  "organizer": ["Daniel", "Lee"]
....
```

The reply contains the index, type, and ID you specified. If the document exists, you'll see that the found field is true, in addition to its version and its source. If the document doesn't exist, found is false:

```
% curl 'localhost:9200/get-together/group/doesnt-exist?pretty'
{
  "_index" : "get-together",
  "_type" : "group",
  "_id" : "doesnt-exist",
  "found" : false
}
```

As you might expect, getting documents by ID is much faster and less expensive in terms of resources than searching. It's also done in real time: as soon as an indexing operation is finished, the new document can be fetched through this GET API. By contrast, searches are near-real time because they need to wait for a refresh, which by default happens every second.

Now that you've seen how to do all the basic API requests, let's take a look at how to change some basic configuration options.

2.5   Configuring Elasticsearch

One of Elasticsearch's strong points is that it has developer-friendly defaults, making it easy to get started. As you saw in the previous section, you can do indexing and searching on your own test server without making any configuration changes. Elasticsearch automatically creates an index for you and detects the type of new fields in your documents.

Elasticsearch also scales easily and efficiently, which is another important feature when you're dealing with large amounts of data or requests. In the final section of this chapter, you'll start a second Elasticsearch instance, in addition to the one you already started in chapter 1, and let them form a cluster. This way, you'll see how Elasticsearch scales out and distributes your data throughout the cluster.

Although scaling out can be done without any configuration changes, you'll tweak a few knobs in this section to avoid surprises later when you add a second node. You'll make the following changes in three different configuration files:

- *Specify a cluster name in elasticsearch.yml*—This is the main configuration file where Elasticsearch-specific options go.
- *Edit logging options in logging.yml*—The logging configuration file is for logging options of log4j, the library that Elasticsearch uses for logging.
- *Adjust memory settings in environment variables or elasticsearch.in.sh*—This file is for configuring the Java virtual machine (JVM) that powers Elasticsearch.

There are a many other options, and we'll point out a few as they appear, but those listed are the most commonly used. Let's walk through each of these configuration changes.

2.5.1   Specifying a cluster name in elasticsearch.yml

The main configuration file of Elasticsearch can be found in the config/ directory of the unpacked tar.gz or ZIP archive.

> **TIP**   The file is in /etc/elasticsearch/ if you installed it from the RPM or DEB package.

Like the REST API, the configuration can be in JSON or YAML. Unlike the REST API, the most popular format is YAML. It's easier to read and use, and all the configuration samples in this book are based on elasticsearch.yml.

By default, new nodes discover existing clusters via multicast—by sending a ping to all hosts listening on a specific multicast address. If a cluster is discovered, the new node joins it if it has the same cluster name. You'll customize the cluster name to prevent instances of the default configuration from joining your cluster. To change the cluster name, uncomment and change the cluster.name line your elasticsearch.yml:

```
cluster.name: elasticsearch-in-action
```

After you update the file, stop Elasticsearch by pressing Control-C and then start it again with the following command:

```
bin/elasticsearch
```

WARNING If you've indexed some data, you might notice that after restarting Elasticsearch with a new cluster name, there's no more data. That's because the directory in which data is stored contains the cluster name, so you can come back to your indexed data by changing back the cluster name and restarting again. For now, you can rerun populate.sh from the code samples to put the sample data back in.

2.5.2 Specifying verbose logging via logging.yml

When something goes wrong, application logs are the first place to look for clues. They're also useful when you just want to see what's going on. If you need to look in Elasticsearch's logs, the default location is the logs/ directory under the path where you unpacked the zip/tar.gz archive.

> **TIP** If you installed it from the RPM or DEB package, the default path is /var/log/elasticsearch/.

Elasticsearch log entries are organized in three types of files:

- *Main log (cluster-name.log)*—Here you can find general information about what happens when Elasticsearch is running; for example, whether a query failed or a new node joined the cluster.
- *Slow-search log (cluster-name_index_search_slowlog.log)*—This is where Elasticsearch logs when a query runs too slow. By default, if a query takes more than half a second, it logs an entry here.
- *Index-slow log (cluster-name_index_indexing_slowlog.log)*—This is similar to the slow-search log, but by default, it writes an entry if an indexing operation takes more than half a second.

To change logging options, you edit the logging.yml file, which is located in the same place as elasticsearch.yml. Elasticsearch uses log4j (http://logging.apache.org/log4j/), and the configuration options in logging.yml are specific to this logging utility.

As with other settings, the defaults are sensible, but if, for example, you need more verbose logging, a good first step is to change the `rootLogger`, which influences all the logging. We'll leave the defaults for now, but if you wanted to make it log everything, you'd change the first line of logging.yml to this:

```
rootLogger: TRACE, console, file
```

By default, the logging level is `INFO`, which writes all events with a severity level of `INFO` or above.

2.5.3 Adjusting JVM settings

As a Java application, Elasticsearch runs in a JVM, which, like a physical machine, has its own memory. The JVM comes with its own configuration, and the most important one is how much memory you allow it to use. Choosing the correct memory setting is important for Elasticsearch's performance and stability.

Most of the memory used by Elasticsearch is called *heap*. The default setting lets Elasticsearch allocate 256 MB of your RAM for its heap, initially, and expand it up to 1 GB. If your searches or indexing operations need more than 1 GB of RAM, those operations will fail and you'll see out-of-memory errors in your logs. Conversely, if you run Elasticsearch on an appliance that has only 256 MB of RAM, the default settings might allocate too much memory.

To change the default values, you can use ES_HEAP_SIZE environment variable. You can set it on the command line before starting Elasticsearch.

On UNIX-like systems, use the export command:

```
export ES_HEAP_SIZE=500m; bin/elasticsearch
```

On Windows, use the SET command:

```
SET ES_HEAP_SIZE=500m & bin\elasticsearch.bat
```

A more permanent way to set the heap size is by changing bin/elasticsearch.in.sh (and elasticsearch.bat on Windows). Add ES_HEAP_SIZE=500m at the beginning of the file, after #!/bin/sh.

> **TIP**   If you installed Elasticsearch though the DEB package, change these variables in /etc/default/elasticsearch. If you installed from the RPM package, the same settings can be configured in /etc/sysconfig/elasticsearch.

For the scope of this book, the default values should be adequate. If you run more extensive tests, you may need to allocate more memory. If you're on a machine with less than 1 GB of RAM, lowering those values to something like 200m should also work.

> **How much memory to allocate in production**
>
> Start with half of your total RAM as ES_HEAP_SIZE if you run Elasticsearch only on that server. Try with less if other applications need significant memory. The other half is used by the operating system for caches, which make for faster access to your stored data. Beyond that rule of thumb, you'll have to run some tests while monitoring your cluster to see how much memory Elasticsearch needs. We talk more about performance tuning and monitoring in part 2 of the book.

Now that you've gotten your hands dirty with Elasticsearch configuration options and you've indexed and searched through some data, you'll get a taste of the "elastic" part of Elasticsearch: the way it scales. (We cover this topic in depth in chapter 9.) You could work through all chapters with a single node, but to get an overview of how scaling works, you'll add more nodes to the same cluster.

2.6   *Adding nodes to the cluster*

In chapter 1, you unpacked the tar.gz or ZIP archive and started up your first Elasticsearch instance. This created your one-node cluster. Before you add a second node,

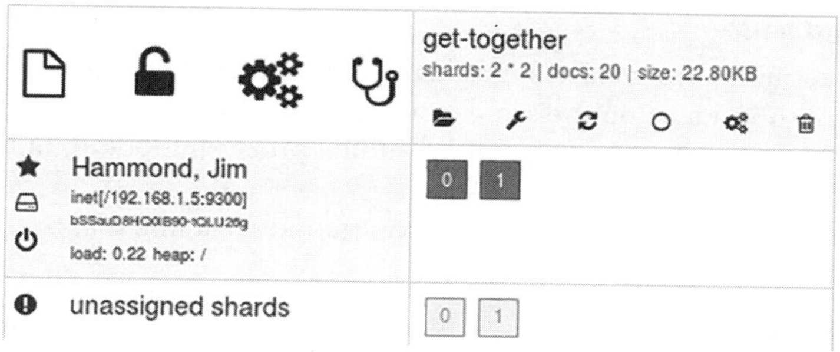

Figure 2.12 One-node cluster shown in Elasticsearch kopf

you'll check the cluster's status to visualize how data is currently allocated. You can do that with a graphical tool such as Elasticsearch kopf or Elasticsearch Head, which we mentioned previously (see section 2.3.1) when you indexed a document. Figure 2.12 shows the cluster in kopf.

If you don't have either of these plugins installed, you can always get most of this information from the Cat Shards API:

```
% curl 'localhost:9200/_cat/shards?v'
index          shard prirep state      docs  store ip            node
get-together 0       p      STARTED      12 15.1kb 192.168.1.4 Hammond, Jim
get-together 0       r      UNASSIGNED
get-together 1       p      STARTED       8 11.4kb 192.168.1.4  Hammond, Jim
get-together 1       r      UNASSIGNED
```

TIP   Most Elasticsearch APIs return JSON, but Cat APIs are an exception to this rule, and the Cat Shards API is one of them. There are many more and they're useful to get information about what the cluster is doing at a point in time in a format that's easy to parse by both humans and shell scripts. We'll talk about Cat APIs more in chapter 11, which is focused on administration.

Either way, you should see the following information:

- Cluster name, as you defined it previously in elasticsearch.yml.
- There's only one node.
- The get-together index has two primary shards, which are active. The unassigned shards represent a set of replicas that were configured for this index. Because there's only one node, those replicas remain unallocated.

The unallocated replica shards cause the status to be yellow. This means all the primaries are there, but not all the replicas. If primaries were missing, the cluster would be red to signal at least one index being incomplete. If all replicas would be allocated, the cluster would be green to signal that everything works as expected.

2.6.1 *Starting a second node*

From a different terminal, run `bin/elasticsearch` or `elasticsearch.bat`. This starts another Elasticsearch instance on the same machine. You'd normally start new nodes on different machines to take advantage of additional processing power, but for now you'll run everything locally.

In the terminal or log file of the new node, you should see a line that begins

```
[INFO ][cluster.service          ] [Raman] detected_master [Hammond, Jim]
```

where `Hammond, Jim` is the name of the first node. What happened was that the second node detected the first one via multicast and joined the cluster. The first node is also the *master* of the cluster, which means it's responsible for keeping information such as which nodes are in the cluster and where shards are located. This information is called *cluster state* and it's replicated to other nodes. If the master goes down, another node can be elected to take its place.

If you look at your cluster's status in figure 2.13, you can see that the set of replicas was allocated to the new node, making the cluster green.

If these two nodes were on separate machines, you'd have a fault-tolerant cluster, which would handle more concurrent searches than before. But what if you need more indexing performance, or need to handle even more concurrent searches? More nodes will certainly help.

> **NOTE** You may have already noticed that the first node starting on a machine listens on port 9200 of all interfaces for HTTP requests. As you add more nodes, it uses port 9201, 9202, and so on. For node-to-node communication, Elasticsearch uses ports 9300, 9301, and so on. These are ports you might need to allow in the firewall. You can change listening addresses in the Network and HTTP section of elasticsearch.yml.

Figure 2.13 Replica shards are allocated to the second node.

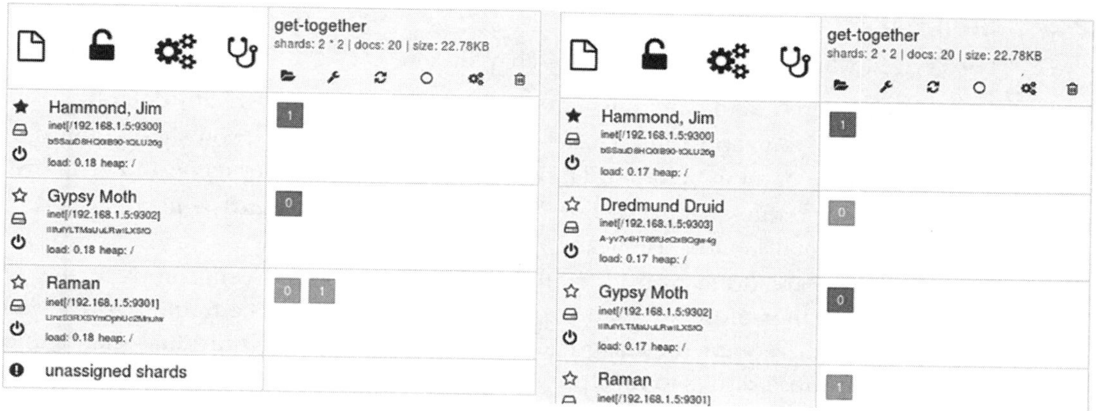

Figure 2.14 Elasticsearch automatically distributes shards across the growing cluster.

2.6.2 Adding additional nodes

If you run bin/elasticsearch or elasticsearch.bat again to add a third node and then a fourth, you'll see that they detect the master via multicast and join the cluster in the same way. Additionally, as shown in figure 2.14, the four shards of the get-together index automatically get balanced across the cluster.

At this point you might wonder what happens if you add more nodes. By default, nothing happens because you have four total shards that can't be distributed to more than four nodes. That said, if you need to scale, you have a few options:

- *Change the number of replicas.* Replicas can be updated on the fly, but scaling this way increases only the number of concurrent searches your cluster can serve because searches are sent to replicas of the same shard in a round-robin fashion. Indexing performance will remain the same, because new data has to be processed by all shards. Also, isolated searches will only run on a single set of shards, so adding replicas won't help.
- *Create an index with more shards.* This implies re-indexing your data because the number of primary shards can't be changed on the fly.
- *Add more indices.* Some data can be easily designed to use more indices. For example, if you index logs, you can put each day's logs in its own index.

We discuss these patterns for scaling out in chapter 9. For now, you can shut down the three extra nodes to keep things simple. You can shut down one node at a time and watch shards get automatically balanced as you go back to the initial state. If you shut them down all at once, the first node will remain with one shard, having no time to get the rest of the data. In that case you can run populate.sh again, which will re-index all the sample data.

2.7   *Summary*

Let's review what you've learned in this chapter:

- Elasticsearch is document-oriented, scalable, and schema-free by default.
- Although you can form a cluster with the default settings, you should adjust at least some of them before you move on; for example, cluster name and heap size.
- Indexing requests are distributed among the primary shards and replicated to those primary shards' replicas.
- Searches are done using a round-robin approach between complete sets of data, whether those are made up of shards or replicas. The node that received the search request then aggregates partial results from individual shards and returns those results to the application.
- Client applications may be unaware of the sharded nature of each index or what the cluster looks like. They care only about indices, types, and document IDs. They use the REST API to index and search for documents.
- You can send new documents and search parameters as the JSON payload of an HTTP request and you'll get back a JSON reply with the results.

In the next chapter you'll get the foundation you need to organize your data effectively in Elasticsearch, learn what types of fields your documents can have, and become familiar with all the relevant options for indexing, updating, and deleting.

Indexing, updating, and deleting data

This chapter covers

- Using mapping types to define multiple types of documents in the same index
- Types of fields you can use in mappings
- Using predefined fields and their options
- All of the above help with indexing, as well as updating and deleting data

This chapter is all about getting data into and out of Elasticsearch and maintaining it: indexing, updating, and deleting documents. In chapter 1, you learned that Elasticsearch is *document-based* and that documents are made up of fields and their values, which makes them self-contained, much like having the column names from a table contained in the rows. In chapter 2, you saw how you can index such a document via Elasticsearch's REST API. Here, we'll dive deeper into the indexing process by looking at the fields in those documents and what they contain. For example, when you index a document like this

```
{"name": "Elasticsearch Denver"}
```

the name field is a string because its value, Elasticsearch Denver, is a string. Other fields could be numbers, booleans, and so on. In this chapter we'll look at three types of fields:

- *Core*—These fields include strings and numbers.
- *Arrays and multi-fields*—These fields help you store multiple values of the same core type in the same field. For example, you can have multiple tag strings in your tags field.
- *Predefined*—Examples of these fields include _ttl (which stands for "time to live") and _timestamp.

Think of these field types as metadata that can be automatically managed by Elasticsearch to give you additional functionality. For example, you can configure Elasticsearch to automatically add new data to documents, such as a timestamp, or you can use the _ttl field to get your documents automatically deleted after a specified amount of time.

Once you know the field types that can be in your documents and how to index them, we'll look at how you can update documents that are already there. Because of the way it stores data, when Elasticsearch updates an existing document, it retrieves it and applies changes according to your specifications. It then indexes the resulting document again and deletes the old one. Such updates can raise concurrency issues, and you'll see how they can be solved automatically with document versions. You'll also see various ways of deleting documents, some faster than others. This is again due to the particular way Apache Lucene, the main library used by Elasticsearch for indexing, stores data on disk.

We'll start with indexing by looking at how you can manage fields from your documents. As you saw in chapter 2, fields are defined in mappings, so before we dive into how you can work with each type of field, we'll look at how you can work with mappings in general.

3.1 Using mappings to define kinds of documents

Each document belongs to a type, which in turn belongs to an index. As a logical division of data, you can think of indices as databases and types as tables. For example, the get-together website that we introduced in chapter 2 uses a different type for groups and events because those documents have different structures. Note that if you also had a blog on that website, you might keep blog entries and comments in a separate index because it's a completely different set of data.

Types contain a definition of each field in the mapping. The *mapping* includes all the fields that might appear in documents from that type and tells Elasticsearch how to index the fields in a document. For example, if a field contains a date, you can define which date format is acceptable.

Types provide only logical separation

With Elasticsearch, there's no physical separation of documents that have different types. All documents within the same Elasticsearch index, regardless of type, end up in the same set of files belonging to the same shards. In a shard, which is a Lucene index, the name of the type is a field, and all fields from all mappings come together as fields in the Lucene index.

The concept of a type is a layer of abstraction specific to Elasticsearch but not Lucene, which makes it easy for you to have different kinds of documents in the same index. Elasticsearch takes care of separating those documents; for example, by filtering documents belonging to a certain type when you search in that type only.

This approach creates a problem when the same field name occurs in multiple types. To avoid unpredictable results, two fields with the same name should have the same settings; otherwise Elasticsearch might have a hard time figuring out which of the two fields you're referring to. In the end, both those fields belong to the same Lucene index. For example, if you have a name field in both group and event documents, both should be strings, not one a string and one an integer. This is rarely a problem in real life, but it's worth remembering to avoid surprises.

In figure 3.1 groups and events are stored in different types. The application can then search in a specific type, such as events. Elasticsearch also allows you to search in multiple types at once or even in all types of an index by specifying only the index name when you search.

Now that you know how mappings are used in Elasticsearch, let's look at how you can read the mapping of a type and how you can write one.

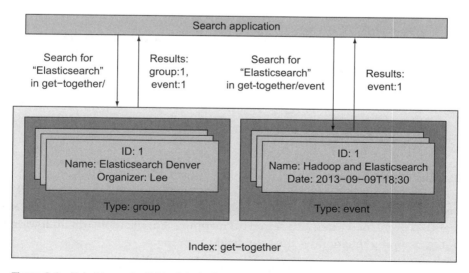

Figure 3.1 Using types to divide data in the same index; searches can run in one, multiple, or all types.

3.1.1 Retrieving and defining mappings

When you're learning Elasticsearch, you often don't need to worry about the mapping because Elasticsearch detects your fields automatically and adjusts your mapping accordingly. You'll look at how that works in listing 3.1. In a production application, you often want to define your mapping up front so you don't have to rely on automatic field detection. We'll explain how to define a mapping later in this chapter.

GETTING THE CURRENT MAPPING

To see the current mapping of a field type, issue an HTTP GET on _mapping under the type's URL:

```
curl 'localhost:9200/get-together/group/_mapping?pretty'
```

In the following listing, you first index a new document from your get-together website, specifying a new type called new-events, and Elasticsearch automatically creates the mapping for you. You then retrieve the created mapping, which shows you the fields from your document and the field types that Elasticsearch detected for each field.

Listing 3.1   Getting an automatically generated mapping

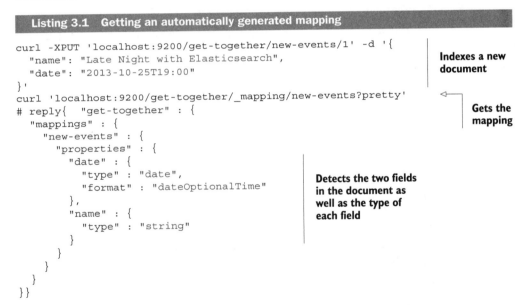

```
curl -XPUT 'localhost:9200/get-together/new-events/1' -d '{      Indexes a new
  "name": "Late Night with Elasticsearch",                        document
  "date": "2013-10-25T19:00"
}'
curl 'localhost:9200/get-together/_mapping/new-events?pretty'     Gets the
# reply{  "get-together" : {                                      mapping
  "mappings" : {
    "new-events" : {
      "properties" : {
        "date" : {
          "type" : "date",              Detects the two fields
          "format" : "dateOptionalTime" in the document as
        },                              well as the type of
        "name" : {                      each field
          "type" : "string"
        }
      }
    }
  }
}}
```

DEFINING A NEW MAPPING

To define a mapping, you use the same URL as previously, but you issue an HTTP PUT instead of GET. You need to specify the JSON mapping in the body using the same format that's returned when you retrieve a mapping. For example, the following request puts a mapping that defines the host field as string:

```
% curl -XPUT 'localhost:9200/get-together/_mapping/new-events' -d '{
  "new-events" : {
    "properties" : {
```

```
        "host": {
          "type" : "string"
        }
      }
    }
  }
}'
```

You can define a new mapping after you create the index but before inserting any document into that type. Why does this PUT work if, as shown in listing 3.1, you already had a mapping in place? We'll explain why next.

3.1.2 Extending an existing mapping

When you put a mapping over an existing one, Elasticsearch merges the two. If you ask Elasticsearch for the mapping now, you should get something like this:

```
{
  "get-together" : {
    "mappings" : {
      "new-events" : {
        "properties" : {
          "date" : {
            "type" : "date",
            "format" : "dateOptionalTime"
          },
          "host" : {
            "type" : "string"
          },
          "name" : {
            "type" : "string"
          }
        }
      }
    }
  }
}
```

As you can see, the mapping now contains the two fields from the initial mapping plus the new field you defined. The initial mapping was extended with the newly added field, which is something you can do at any point. Elasticsearch calls this a merge between the existing mapping and the one you provide.

Unfortunately, not all merges work. For example, you can't change an existing field's data type, and, in general, you can't change the way a field is indexed. Let's take a closer look into why this happens. As shown in the following listing, if you try to change the host field to a long, it fails with a MergeMappingException.

> **Listing 3.2 Trying to change an existing field type from string to long fails**

```
curl -XPUT 'localhost:9200/get-together/_mapping/new-events' -d '{
  "new-events" : {
    "properties" : {
```

```
    "host": {
      "type" : "long"
    }
  }
 }
}'
# reply{"error":"MergeMappingException[Merge failed with failures {[mapper
[host] of different type, current_type [string], merged_type
[long]]}]","status":400}
```

The only way around this error is to re-index all the data in new-events, which involves the following steps:

1 Remove all data from the new-events type; you'll learn later in this chapter how to delete data. Removing data also removes the current mapping.
2 Put in the new mapping.
3 Index all the data again.

To understand why re-indexing might be required, imagine you've already indexed an event with a string in the host field. If you want the host field to be long now, Elasticsearch would have to change the way host is indexed in the existing document. As you'll explore later in this chapter, editing an existing document implies deleting and indexing again. To define correct mappings that hopefully will only need additions, not changes, let's look at the core types you can choose for your fields in Elasticsearch and what you can do with them.

3.2 *Core types for defining your own fields in documents*

With Elasticsearch, a field can be one of the *core types* (see table 3.1), such as a string or a number, or it can be a more complex type derived from core types, such as an array.

There are some additional types not covered in this chapter. For example, there's the *nested* type, which allows you to have documents within documents, or the *geo_point* type, which stores a location on Earth based on its longitude and latitude. We'll discuss those additional types in chapter 8, where we cover relationships among documents, and in appendix A, where we discuss geospatial data.

> **NOTE** In addition to the fields you define in your documents, such as name or date, Elasticsearch uses a set of predefined fields to enrich them. For example, there's a _all field, where all the document's fields are indexed together. This is useful when users search for something without specifying the field— they can search in all fields. These predefined fields have their own configuration options, and we'll discuss them later in this chapter.

Let's look at each of these core types so you can make good mapping choices when you index your own data.

Table 3.1 Elasticsearch core field types

Core type	Example values
String	`"Lee"`, `"Elasticsearch Denver"`
Numeric	`17`, `3.2`
Date	`2013-03-15T10:02:26.231+01:00`
Boolean	Value can be either `true` or `false`

3.2.1 String

Strings are the most straightforward: your field should be `string` if you're indexing characters. They're also the most interesting because you have so many options in your mapping for how to analyze them.

Analysis is the process of parsing the text to transform it and break it down into elements to make searches relevant. If it sounds too abstract, don't worry: chapter 5 explores the concept. But let's look at the basics now, starting with the document you indexed in listing 3.1:

```
% curl -XPUT 'localhost:9200/get-together/new-events/1' -d '{
    "name": "Late Night with Elasticsearch",
    "date": "2013-10-25T19:00"
}'
```

With this document indexed, search for the word `late` in the `name` field, which is a string:

```
% curl 'localhost:9200/get-together/new-events/_search?pretty' -d '{
    "query": {
        "query_string": {
            "query": "late"
        }
    }
}'
```

The search finds the "Late Night with Elasticsearch" document you indexed in listing 3.1. Elasticsearch connects the strings `"late"` and `"Late Night with Elasticsearch"` through analysis. As you can see in figure 3.2, when you index `"Late Night with Elasticsearch"`, the default analyzer lowercases all letters and then breaks the string into words.

Analysis produces four terms: `late`, `night`, `with`, and `elasticsearch`. The same process is then applied to the query string, but this time, "late" produces the same string: `"late"`. The document (doc1) matches the search because the `late` term that resulted from the query matches the `late` term that resulted from the document.

> **DEFINITION** A *term* is a word from the text and is the basic unit for searching. In different contexts, this word can mean different things: it could be a name, for example, or it could be an IP address. If you want only exact matches on a field, the entire field should be treated as a word.

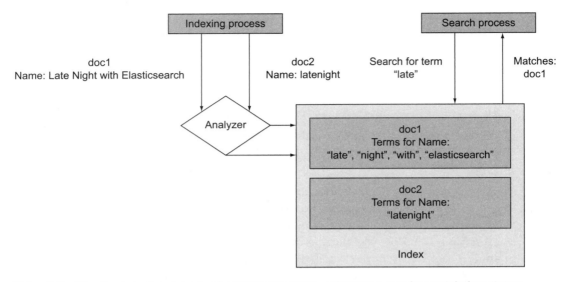

Figure 3.2   After the default analyzer breaks strings into terms, subsequent searches match those terms.

On the other hand, if you index "latenight," the default analyzer creates only one term: latenight. Searching for "late" won't hit doc2 because it doesn't include the term late.

This analysis process is where the mapping comes into play. You can specify many options for analyzing in your mapping. For example, you can configure analysis to produce terms that are synonyms of your original terms, so queries for synonyms match as well. We'll dive into the details of analysis in chapter 5, as promised, but for now, let's look at the index option, which can be set to analyzed (the default), not_analyzed, or no. For example, to set the name field to not_analyzed, your mapping might look like this:

```
% curl -XPUT 'localhost:9200/get-together/_mapping/new-events' -d '{
  "new-events" : {
    "properties" : {
      "name": {
        "type" : "string",
        "index" : "not_analyzed"
      }
    }
  }
}'
```

By default, index is set to analyzed and produces the behavior you saw previously: the analyzer lowercases all letters and breaks your string into words. Use this option when you expect a single matching word to produce a match. For example, if users search for "elasticsearch," they expect to see "Late Night with Elasticsearch" in the list of results.

Setting index to not_analyzed does the opposite: the analysis process is skipped, and the entire string is indexed as one term. Use this option when you want exact matches, such as when you search for tags. You probably want only "big data" to show up as a result when you search for "big data," not "data." Also, you'll need this for most aggregations, which count terms. If you want to get the most frequent tags, you probably want "big data" to be counted as a single term, not "big" and "data" separately. We'll explore aggregations in chapter 7.

If you set index to no, indexing is skipped and no terms are produced, so you won't be able to search on that particular field. When you don't need to search on a field, this option saves space and decreases the time it takes to index and search. For example, you might store reviews for events. Although storing and showing those reviews is valuable, searching through them might not be. In this case, disable indexing for that field, making the indexing process faster and saving space.

Check if your query is analyzed when searching in fields that aren't

For some queries, such as the query_string you used previously, the analysis process is applied to your search criteria. It's important to be aware if this is happening; otherwise results might not be as expected.

For example, if you index "Elasticsearch" and it's not analyzed, it produces the term Elasticsearch. When you query for "Elasticsearch" like this

```
curl 'localhost:9200/get-together/new-events/_search?q=Elasticsearch'
```

the URI request is analyzed, and the term elasticsearch (lowercased) is produced. But you don't have the term elasticsearch in your index; you only have Elasticsearch (with a capital *E*), so you get no hits. In chapter 4, where we'll discuss searches, you'll learn which query types analyze the input text and which don't.

Next, let's look at how you can index numbers. Elasticsearch provides many core types that can help you deal with numbers, so we'll refer to them collectively as numeric.

3.2.2 Numeric

Numeric types can be numbers with or without a floating point. If you don't need decimals, you can choose among byte, short, integer, and long; if you do need them, your choices are float and double. These types correspond to Java's primitive data types, and choosing among them influences the size of your index and the range of values you can index. For example, whereas a long takes up 64 bits, a short takes up only 16 bits, but a long can store ranges up to several trillion times larger than the −32,768 to 32,767 that a short can store.

If you don't know the range you need for your integer values or the precision you need for your floating-point values, it's safe to do what Elasticsearch does when it detects your mapping automatically: use long for integer values and double for floating-point values. Your index might become larger and slower because these two types take up the most space, but at least you're unlikely to get an out-of-range error from Elasticsearch when indexing.

Now that we've covered strings and numbers, let's look at a type that's more purpose-built: `date`.

3.2.3   *Date*

The `date` type is used for storing dates and times. It works like this: you normally provide a string with a date, as in `2013-12-25T09:00:00`. Then, Elasticsearch parses the string and stores it as a number of type `long` in the Lucene index. That `long` is the number of milliseconds that have elapsed since 00:00:00 UTC time on January 1, 1970 (UNIX epoch) and the time you provided.

When you search for documents, you still provide `date` strings and Elasticsearch parses those strings and works with numbers in background. It does that because numbers are faster to store and work with than strings.

You, on the other hand, only have to consider whether Elasticsearch understands the `date` string you're providing. The date format of your `date` string is defined by the `format` option, and Elasticsearch parses ISO 8601 timestamps by default.

> **ISO 8601**
>
> An international standard for exchanging date- and time-related data, ISO 8601 is widely used in timestamps due to RFC 3339 (www.ietf.org/rfc/rfc3339.txt). An ISO 8601 date looks like this:
>
> ```
> 2013-10-11T10:32:45.453-03:00
> ```
>
> It has all the right ingredients of a good timestamp: information is read from left to right, from the most important to the least important; the year has four digits; and the time includes subseconds and the time zone. Much of the information in this timestamp is optional; for example, you don't need to specify milliseconds and you can skip the time altogether.

When you use the `format` option to specify a date format, you have two options:

- *Use a predefined date format.* For example, the `date` format parses dates as `2013-02-25`. Many predefined formats are available, and you can see them all here: www.elastic.co/guide/reference/mapping/date-format/
- *Specify your own custom format.* You can specify a pattern for timestamps to follow. For example, specifying MMM YYYY parses dates as `Jul 2001`.

To put all this date information to use, let's add a new mapping type called `weekly-events`, as shown in the next listing. Then, as is also shown in the listing, add a name and date of the first event and specify an ISO 8601 timestamp for that date. Also add a field with the date of the next event and specify a custom date format for that date.

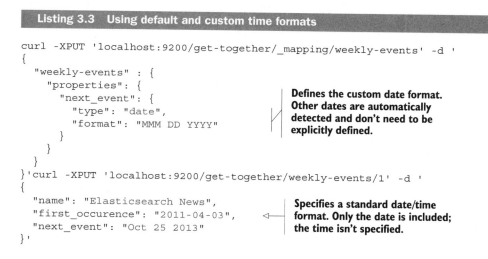

Listing 3.3   Using default and custom time formats

```
curl -XPUT 'localhost:9200/get-together/_mapping/weekly-events' -d '
{
  "weekly-events" : {
    "properties": {
      "next_event": {              Defines the custom date format.
        "type": "date",            Other dates are automatically
        "format": "MMM DD YYYY"    detected and don't need to be
      }                            explicitly defined.
    }
  }
}'curl -XPUT 'localhost:9200/get-together/weekly-events/1' -d '
{
  "name": "Elasticsearch News",
  "first_occurence": "2011-04-03",    Specifies a standard date/time
  "next_event": "Oct 25 2013"         format. Only the date is included;
}'                                    the time isn't specified.
```

We've talked about strings, numbers, and dates; let's move on to the last core type: boolean. Like date, boolean is a type that's more purpose-built.

3.2.4   Boolean

The boolean type is used for storing true/false values from your documents. For example, you might want a field that indicates whether the event's video is available for download. A sample document could be indexed like this:

```
%  curl -XPUT 'localhost:9200/get-together/new-events/1' -d '{
  "name": "Broadcasted Elasticsearch News",
  "downloadable": true
}'
```

The downloadable field is automatically mapped as boolean and is stored in the Lucene index as T for true or F for false. As with date fields, Elasticsearch parses the value you supply in the source document and transforms true and false to T and F, respectively.

We've looked at the core types: string, numeric, date, and boolean, which you can use in your own fields; let's move on to arrays and multi-fields, which enable you to use the same core type multiple times.

3.3   *Arrays and multi-fields*

Sometimes having simple field-value pairs in your documents isn't enough. You might need to have multiple values in the same field. Let's step away from the get-together example and look at another use case: you're indexing blog posts and you want to have a tag field with one or more tags in it. In this case, you need an array.

3.3.1 Arrays

To index a field with multiple values, put those values in square brackets; for example:

```
% curl -XPUT 'localhost:9200/blog/posts/1' -d '{
  "tags": ["first", "initial"]
}'
```

At this point you might wonder, "How do you define an array field in your mapping?" The answer is you don't. In this case the mapping defines the tags field as string, as it does when you have a single value:

```
% curl 'localhost:9200/blog/_mapping/posts?pretty'
{
  "blog" : {
    "mappings" : {
      "posts" : {
        "properties" : {
          "tags" : {
            "type" : "string"
          }
        }
      }
    }
  }
}
```

All core types support arrays, and you can use both single values and arrays without changing your mapping. For example, if the next blog post has only one tag, you can index it like this:

```
% curl -XPUT 'localhost:9200/blog/posts/2' -d '{"tags": "second"}'
```

Internally, it's pretty much the same thing for Lucene, which has to index more or fewer terms in that same field, depending on how many values you provide.

3.3.2 Multi-fields

If arrays let you index more data with the same settings, multi-fields are about indexing the same data multiple times using different settings. For example, in listing 3.4 you configure the tags field from your posts' type with two different settings: analyzed, for matches on every word, and not_analyzed, for exact matches on the full tag name.

> **TIP** You can upgrade a single field to a multi-field configuration without needing to re-index your data. This is what happens if you've already created a tags string field before you run the following listing. The opposite isn't possible, though: you can't remove a sub-field from the mapping once it's there.

> **Listing 3.4 Multi-field for a `string`: once `analyzed`, once `not_analyzed`**

```
% curl -XPUT 'localhost:9200/blog/_mapping/posts' -d '{
  "posts" : {
    "properties" : {
      "tags" : {                          The default tags field is
        "type": "string",                 analyzed, which lowercases
        "index": "analyzed",              and breaks the provided
        "fields": {                       text into words.
          "verbatim": {
            "type": "string",
            "index": "not_analyzed"       The second field, tags.verbatim,
          }                               is not_analyzed, which makes
        }                                 the original tag a single term.
      }
    }
  }
}'
```

You search in the `analyzed` version of the tags field as you do with any other string. To search in the `not_analyzed` version (and get back only exact matches on the original tag), specify the full path: `tags.verbatim`.

Both multi-field and array field types let you have multiple core type values in a single field. Next, we'll look at predefined fields (which are normally handled by Elasticsearch on its own) to add new functionality to your documents, such as automatically expiring them.

3.4 Using predefined fields

Elasticsearch provides a number of predefined fields you can use and configure to add new functionality. These predefined fields are different from the fields you've seen so far in three ways:

- *Typically, you don't populate a predefined field; Elasticsearch does it.* For example, you can use the `_timestamp` field to record the date when a document was indexed.
- *They uncover field-specific functionality.* For example, the `_ttl` (time to live) field enables Elasticsearch to remove documents after a specified amount of time.
- *Predefined field names always begin with an underscore (_).* These fields add new metadata to your documents, and Elasticsearch uses this metadata for various features, from storing the original document to storing timestamp information for automatic expiry.

We'll divide the important predefined fields in the following categories:

- *Control how to store and search your documents.* `_source` lets you store the original JSON document as you index it. `_all` indexes all your fields together.
- *Identify your documents.* These are special fields containing data about where your document was indexed: `_uid`, `_id`, `_type`, `_index`.

- *Add new properties to your documents.* You can index the size of the original JSON with _size[1]. Similarly, you can index the time it was indexed with _timestamp[2] and make Elasticsearch delete it after a specified amount of time with _ttl.[3] We won't cover them here because there are often better ways to achieve the same goals (for example, it's cheaper to expire entire indices, as we'll see in section 3.6.2) and they might get deprecated in future releases.[4]

- *Control the shard where your documents are routed to.* These are _routing and parent. We'll look at _routing in chapter 9, section 9.8, as it's related to scaling, and at _parent in chapter 8, where we talk about relationships among documents.

3.4.1 Controlling how to store and search your documents

Let's start by looking at _source, which lets you store the documents you index, and _all, which lets you index all their content in a single field.

_SOURCE FOR STORING THE ORIGINAL CONTENTS

The _source field is for storing the original document in the original format. This lets you see the documents that matched a search, not only their IDs.

_source can have enabled set to true or false to specify whether or not you want to store the original document. By default it's true, and in most cases that's good because the existence of _source allows you to use other important features of Elasticsearch. For example, as you'll learn later in this chapter, updating document contents using the update API requires _source. Also, the default highlighting implementation requires _source (see appendix C for more details on highlighting).

> **WARNING** Because a lot of functionality depends on the _source field, and storing it is relatively cheap in terms of both space and performance, the ability to disable it might be removed in version 2.0. See the discussion on GitHub: https://github.com/elastic/elasticsearch/issues/8142. For the same reasons, we don't recommend disabling _source.

To see how this field works, let's look at what Elasticsearch typically returns when you retrieve a previously indexed document:

```
% curl 'localhost:9200/get-together/new-events/1?pretty'
[...]
  "_source" : {
  "name": "Broadcasted Elasticsearch News",
  "downloadable": true
```

You also get the _source JSON back when you search because it's returned there by default as well.

---

[1] www.elastic.co/guide/en/elasticsearch/reference/master/mapping-size-field.html
[2] www.elastic.co/guide/en/elasticsearch/reference/master/mapping-timestamp-field.html
[3] www.elastic.co/guide/en/elasticsearch/reference/master/mapping-ttl-field.html
[4] See the discussion here: https://github.com/elastic/elasticsearch/issues/9679.

RETURNING ONLY SOME FIELDS OF THE SOURCE DOCUMENT

When you retrieve or search for a document, you can ask Elasticsearch to return only specific fields and not the entire _source. One way to do this is to give a comma-separated list of fields in the `fields` parameter; for example:

```
% curl -XGET 'localhost:9200/get-together/group/1?pretty&fields=name'
{
  "_index" : "get-together",
  "_type" : "group",
  "_id" : "1",
  "_version" : 1,
  "found" : true,
  "fields" : {
    "name" : [ "Denver Clojure" ]
  }
}
```

When _source is stored, Elasticsearch gets the required fields from there. You can also store individual fields by settings the `store` option to yes. For example, to store only the name field, your mapping might look like this:

```
% curl -XPUT 'localhost:9200/get-together/_mapping/events_stored' -d '{
  "events_stored": {
    "properties": {
      "name": {
        "type": "string",
        "store": "yes"
      }
    }
  }
}'
```

This might be useful when you ask Elasticsearch for a particular field because retrieving a single stored field will be faster than retrieving the entire _source and extracting that field from it, especially when you have large documents.

> **NOTE** When you store individual fields as well, you should take into account that the more you store, the bigger your index gets. Usually bigger indices imply slower indexing and slower searching.

Under the hood, _source is just another stored field in Lucene. Elasticsearch stores the original JSON in it and extracts fields from it as needed.

_ALL FOR INDEXING EVERYTHING

Just as _source is storing everything, _all is indexing everything. When you search in _all, Elasticsearch returns a hit regardless of which field matches. This is useful when users are looking for something without knowing where to look; for example, searching for "elasticsearch" may match the group name "Elasticsearch Denver" as well as the tag `elasticsearch` on other groups.

Running a search from the URI without a field name will search on _all by default:

```
curl 'localhost:9200/get-together/group/_search?q=elasticsearch'
```

If you always search on specific fields, you can disable _all by setting enabled to false:

```
"events": {
    "_all": { "enabled": false}
```

Doing so will reduce the total size of your index and make indexing operations faster.

By default, each field is included in _all by having include_in_all implicitly set to true. You can use this option to control what is and isn't included in _all:

```
% curl -XPUT 'localhost:9200/get-together/_mapping/custom-all' -d '{
  "custom-all": {
    "properties": {
      "organizer": {
        "type": "string",
        "include_in_all": false
      }
    }
  }
}'
```

Using include_in_all gives you flexibility not only in terms of saving space but also regarding how your queries behave. If a search is run without specifying a field, Elasticsearch will only match contents of fields that were also indexed in _all.

The next set of predefined fields includes those used to identify documents: _index, _type, _id, and _uid.

3.4.2 *Identifying your documents*

To identify a document within the same index, Elasticsearch uses a combination of the document's type and ID in the _uid field. The _uid field is made up from the _id and _type fields that you always get when searching or retrieving documents:

```
% curl 'localhost:9200/get-together/group/1?fields&pretty'
{
  "_index" : "get-together",
  "_type" : "group",
  "_id" : "1",
  "_version" : 1,
  "found" : true
}
```

At this point you might wonder, "Why does Elasticsearch store the same data in two places—you have _id, then _type, and then _uid?"

Elasticsearch uses _uid internally for identification because all documents land in the same Lucene indices. The type and ID separation is an abstraction that makes it easy to work with different structures by dividing them into types. _id is normally extracted from _uid because of that, but _type has to be indexed separately so it can easily filter documents by type when you search in a specific type. Table 3.2 shows the default settings for _uid, _id, and _type.

Table 3.2 Default settings for `_id` and `_type` fields

Field name	Store value	Index value	Observations
`_uid`	yes	yes	Used for identifying a document within the whole index.
`_id`	no	no	It's not indexed and not stored. If you search in it, `_uid` is used instead. When you get results, contents are extracted from `_uid` as well.
`_type`	no	`not_analyzed`	It's indexed and it produces a single term. It's used by Elasticsearch to filter documents of specific types. You can search on it, too.

PROVIDING IDs FOR YOUR DOCUMENTS

So far, you've mostly provided IDs manually as part of the URI. For example, to index a document with ID 1st, you run something like this:

```
% curl -XPUT 'localhost:9200/get-together/manual_id/1st?pretty' -d '{
    "name": "Elasticsearch Denver"
}'
```

You could see the ID in the reply:

```
{
  "_index" : "get-together",
  "_type" : "manual_id",
  "_id" : "1st",
  "_version" : 1,
  "created" : true
}
```

Alternatively, you can rely on Elasticsearch to generate unique IDs for you. This is useful if you don't already have a unique ID or you don't need to identify documents by a certain property. Typically, this is what you do when you index application logs: they don't have a unique property to identify them and they're never updated.

To have Elasticsearch generate the ID, use HTTP POST and omit the ID:

```
% curl -XPOST 'localhost:9200/logs/auto_id/?pretty' -d '{
  "message": "I have an automatic id"
}'
```

You can see the autogenerated ID in the reply:

```
{
  "_index" : "logs",
  "_type" : "auto_id",
  "_id" : "RWdYVcU8Rjyy8sJPobVqDQ",
  "_version" : 1,
  "created" : true
}
```

STORING THE INDEX NAME INSIDE THE DOCUMENT
To have Elasticsearch store the index name in the document, along with the ID and the type, use the _index field. As with _id and _type, you can see _index in the results of a search or a GET request, but as with _id and _type, what you see there doesn't come from the field contents. _index is disabled by default.

Elasticsearch knows which index each result came from, so it can show an _index value there, but by default you can't search for _index yourself. The following command shouldn't find anything:

```
% curl 'localhost:9200/_search?q=_index:get-together'
```

To enable _index, set enabled to true. The mapping might look like this:

```
% curl -XPUT 'localhost:9200/get-together/_mapping/with_index' -d '{
  "with_index": {
    "_index": { "enabled": true }
  }
}'
```

If you add documents to this type and rerun the previous search, you should find your new documents.

> **NOTE** Searching for documents belonging to a particular index can be easily done by using the index URL, as you've done so far. But the _index field may turn out to be useful in more complex use cases. For example, in a multi-tenant environment, you might have an index for each user. When you search in multiple indices, you could use the terms aggregation on the _index field to show the number of documents belonging to each user. We'll look at aggregations in chapter 7.

We've looked at how your documents are mapped in Elasticsearch so you can index them in a way that suits your use case. Next, we'll look at how you can modify documents that are already indexed.

3.5   *Updating existing documents*

You may need to change an existing document for various reasons. Suppose you need to change the organizer for a get-together group. You could index a different document to the same address (index, type, and ID), but, as you might expect, you can update documents by sending the changes you want Elasticsearch to apply. The update API in Elasticsearch allows you to send the changes you want to apply to a document and the API returns a reply indicating whether the operation succeeded or not. The update process is shown in figure 3.3.

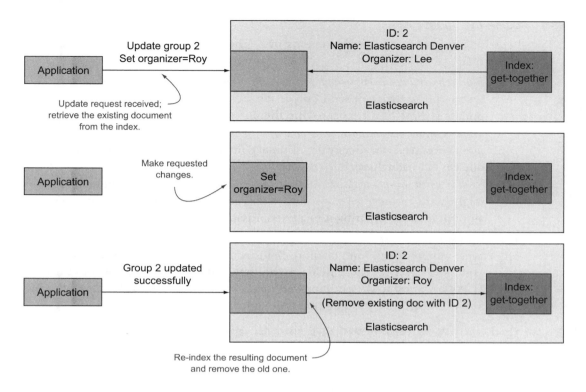

Figure 3.3 Updating a document involves retrieving it, processing it, and re-indexing it while overwriting the previous document.

As figure 3.3 illustrates, Elasticsearch does the following (from the top down):

- *Retrieves the existing document*—For that to work, you must enable the _source field; otherwise Elasticsearch doesn't know what the original document looked like.
- *Applies the changes you specified*—For example, if your document was

  ```
  {"name": "Elasticsearch Denver", "organizer": "Lee"}
  ```

  and you wanted to change the organizer, the resulting document would be

  ```
  {"name": "Elasticsearch Denver", "organizer": "Roy"}
  ```

- *Removes the old document and indexes the new document (with the update applied) in its place*

In this section, we'll look at a few ways to use the update API and explore how to manage concurrency via Elasticsearch's versioning feature.

3.5.1   *Using the update API*

Let's look at how to update documents first. The update API exposes a few ways of doing that:

- *Send a partial document to add or replace the same part from the existing document.* This is straightforward: you send one or more fields with their values, and after the update is done, you expect to find them in the document.
- *When sending partial documents or scripts, make sure that the document is created if it doesn't exist.* You can specify the original contents of a document to be indexed if one isn't already there.
- *Send a script to update the document for you.* For example, in an online shop, you might want to increase the number of T-shirts you have in stock by a certain amount instead of setting it to a fixed number.

SENDING A PARTIAL DOCUMENT

The easiest way to update one or more fields is to send a partial document with the values you need to set for those fields. To do that, you need to send this info through an HTTP POST request to the _update endpoint of the document's URL. The following command will work after running populate.sh from the code samples:

```
% curl -XPOST 'localhost:9200/get-together/group/2/_update' -d '{
  "doc": {
    "organizer": "Roy"
  }
}'
```

This sets the fields you specify under doc to the values you provide, regardless of the previous values or whether these fields existed or not. If the entire document is missing, the update operation will fail, complaining that the document is missing.

> **NOTE**   When updating, you need to keep in mind that there might be conflicts. For example, if you're changing the group's organizer to "Roy" and a colleague changes it to "Radu," one of those updates will be overridden by the other one. To control this, you can use versioning, which we'll cover later in this chapter.

CREATING DOCUMENTS THAT DON'T EXIST WITH UPSERT

To handle the situation when the updating document doesn't exist, you can use *upsert*. You might be familiar with this term from relational databases; the term is a portmanteau of *up*date and in*sert*.

If the document is missing, you can add an initial document to be indexed in the upsert section of the JSON. The previous command looks like this:

```
% curl -XPOST 'localhost:9200/get-together/group/2/_update' -d '
{
  "doc": {
    "organizer": "Roy"
  },
```

```
    "upsert": {
      "name" : "Elasticsearch Denver",
      "organizer": "Roy"
    }
  }'
```

UPDATING DOCUMENTS WITH A SCRIPT

Finally, let's look at how to update a document using the values from the existing one. Suppose you have an online shop, you're indexing products, and you want to increment the price of a product by 10. To do that, you use the same API, but instead of providing a document, you provide a *script*. A *script* is typically a piece of code in the JSON that you send to Elasticsearch, but it can also be an external script.

We'll talk more about scripting in chapter 6 because you'll most likely use scripts to make your searches more relevant. We'll also show you how to use scripts in aggregations in chapter 7 and how to make such scripts run faster in chapter 10. For now, let's look at three important elements of an update script:

- The default scripting language is Groovy. Its syntax is similar to Java, but it's easier to use for scripting.
- Because updating gets the _source of an existing document, changes it, and then re-indexes the resulting document, your scripts alter fields within _source. To refer to _source, use ctx._source, and to refer to a specific field, use ctx._source['field-name'].
- If you need variables, we recommend you define them separately from the script itself under params. That's because scripts need to be compiled, and once they're compiled, they get cached. Running the same script multiple times with different parameters requires the script to be compiled only once. Subsequent runs take the existing script from cache. This is faster than having different scripts because they all need compilation.

In listing 3.5, you'll use a Groovy script to increment the price of an Elasticsearch shirt by 10.

> **NOTE** Depending on the version of Elasticsearch that you're on, running scripts through the API like in listing 3.5 might be forbidden by default for security reasons. This is called *dynamic scripting*, and it can be enabled by setting script.disable_dynamic to false in elasticsearch.yml. Alternatively, you can store scripts on each node's file system or in the .scripts index. For more details, take a look at the scripting module documentation: www.elastic.co/guide/en/elasticsearch/reference/current/modules-scripting.html.

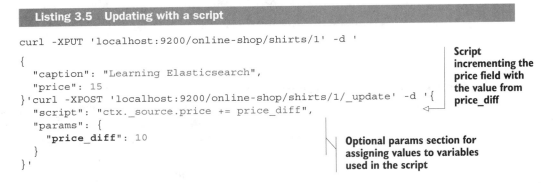

Listing 3.5   Updating with a script

```
curl -XPUT 'localhost:9200/online-shop/shirts/1' -d '
{
  "caption": "Learning Elasticsearch",
  "price": 15
}'curl -XPOST 'localhost:9200/online-shop/shirts/1/_update' -d '{
  "script": "ctx._source.price += price_diff",
  "params": {
    "price_diff": 10
  }
}'
```

Script incrementing the price field with the value from price_diff

Optional params section for assigning values to variables used in the script

You can see that `ctx._source.price` is used instead of the expected `ctx._source['price']`. This is an alternative way to refer to the `price` field. It's easier to use with `curl` because escaping single quotes in shell scripts can be confusing.

Now that you've seen how you can update a document, let's look at how you can manage concurrency if multiple updates happen at the same time.

3.5.2   *Implementing concurrency control through versioning*

If multiple updates are running at the same time, you could encounter concurrency issues. As illustrated in figure 3.4, it's possible that one update re-indexes the document between the time when the other update got the original document and applied its own changes. With no concurrency control, the second re-index will cancel the changes of the first update.

Fortunately, Elasticsearch supports concurrency control by using a version number for each document. The initially indexed document is version 1. When you re-index it through an update, the version number is set to 2. If the version number was set to 2 by another update in the meantime, it's a conflict and the current update fails (otherwise it would override the other update like in figure 3.4). You can retry the update and—if there's no conflict—version will be set to 3.

To see how it works, you'll replicate a process similar to the one shown in figure 3.5 using the code in listing 3.6:

1   Index a document and then update it (update1).
2   Update1 starts in background and includes a waiting time (sleep).
3   During that sleep, issue another `update` command (update2) that modifies the document. This change occurs between update1's fetch of the original document and its re-indexing operation.
4   Instead of canceling the changes of update2, update1 fails because the document is already at version 2. At this point you have the chance to retry update1 and apply the changes in version 3. (See listing 3.6.)

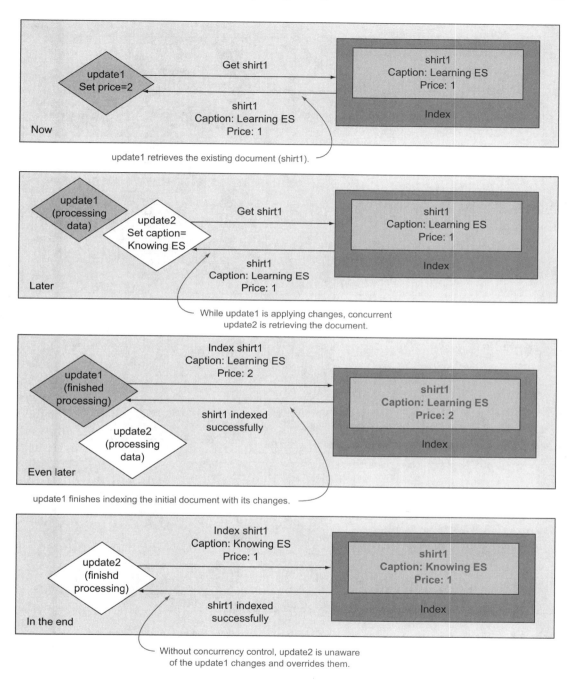

Index shirt1
Caption: Learning ES
Price: 2

update1 retrieves the existing document (shirt1).

While update1 is applying changes, concurrent update2 is retrieving the document.

update1 finishes indexing the initial document with its changes.

Without concurrency control, update2 is unaware of the update1 changes and overrides them.

Figure 3.4   Without concurrency control, changes can get lost.

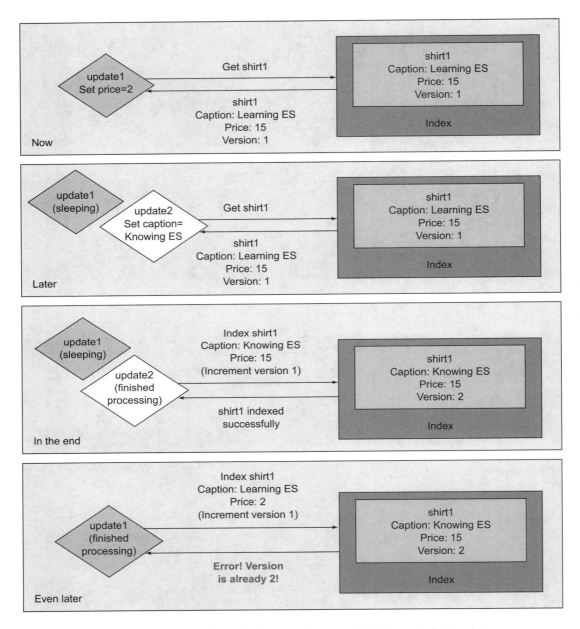

Figure 3.5   Concurrency control through versioning prevents one update from overriding another.

Listing 3.6 Two concurrent updates managed with versioning: one fails

```
% curl -XPOST 'localhost:9200/online-shop/shirts/1/_update' -d '{
  "script": "Thread.sleep(10000); ctx._source.price = 2"
}' &
% curl -XPOST 'localhost:9200/online-shop/shirts/1/_update' -d '{
  "script": "ctx._source.caption = \"Knowing Elasticsearch\""
}'
```

Update1 waits
10 seconds
and goes to
background (&).

If update2 runs within 10 seconds,
it forces update1 to fail because it
increments the version number.

Figure 3.5 is a graphical representation of what happens in this listing.

This kind of concurrency control is called *optimistic* because it allows parallel operations and assumes that conflicts appear rarely, throwing errors when they do appear. This is opposed to *pessimistic* locking, in which conflicts are prevented in the first place by blocking operations that might cause conflicts.

AUTOMATICALLY RETRYING AN UPDATE WHEN THERE'S A CONFLICT

When a version conflict appears, you can deal with it in your own application. If it's an update, you can try applying it again. But you can also make Elasticsearch reapply it for you automatically by setting the retry_on_conflict parameter:

```
% SHIRTS="localhost:9200/online-shop/shirts"
% curl -XPOST "$SHIRTS/1/_update?retry_on_conflict=3" -d '{
    "script": "ctx._source.price = 2"
}'
```

USING VERSIONS WHEN YOU INDEX DOCUMENTS

Another way to update a document without using the update API is to index a new one to the same index, type, and ID. This overwrites the existing document and you can still use the version field for concurrency control. To do that, set the version parameter in the HTTP request. The value should be the version you expect the document to have. For example, if you expect version 3 to be already there, a re-index can look like this:

```
% curl -XPUT 'localhost:9200/online-shop/shirts/1?version=3' -d '{
  "caption": "I Know about Elasticsearch Versioning",
  "price": 5
}'
```

The operation will fail with the version conflict exception you saw in listing 3.6 if the current version is different than 3.

With versions, you can index or update your documents safely. Next, let's look at how you can remove documents.

> ### Using external versioning
>
> So far you've used Elasticsearch's internal versioning, which makes Elasticsearch automatically increment the version number with each operation, whether that's an index or an update. If the source of your data is another data store, maybe you have a versioning system there; for example, one based on timestamps. In that case you might want to keep versions in sync as well as the documents.
>
> To rely on external versioning, you need to add `version_type=external` to every request in addition to the version number:
>
> ```
> DOC_URL="localhost:9200/online-shop/shirts/1"
> curl -XPUT "$DOC_URL?version=101&version_type=external" -d '{
>   "caption": "This time we use external versioning",
>   "price": 100
> }'
> ```
>
> This will make Elasticsearch accept any version number, as long as it's higher than the current version, and it doesn't increment the version number on its own.

3.6   Deleting data

Now that you know how to send data to Elasticsearch, let's look at what options you have for removing some of what was indexed. If you've worked through the listings throughout this chapter, you now have unnecessary data that's waiting to be removed. We'll look at a few ways to remove data—or at least get it out of the way of slowing down your searches or further indexing:

- *Delete individual documents or groups of documents.* When you do that, Elasticsearch only marks them to be deleted, so they don't show up in searches, and gets them out of the index later in an asynchronous manner.
- *Delete complete indices.* This is a particular case of deleting groups of documents. But it differs in the sense that it's easy to do performance-wise. The main job is to remove all the files associated with that index, which happens almost instantly.
- *Close indices.* Although this isn't about removing, it's worth mentioning here. A closed index doesn't allow read or write operations and its data isn't loaded in memory. It's similar to removing data from Elasticsearch, but it remains on disk, and it's easy to restore: you open the closed index.

3.6.1   Deleting documents

There are a few ways to remove individual documents, and we'll discuss most of them here:

- *Remove a single document by its ID.* This is good if you have only one document to delete, provided that you know its ID.
- *Remove multiple documents in a single request.* If you have multiple individual documents that you want to delete, you can remove them all at once in a bulk

request, which is faster than removing one document at a time. We'll cover bulk deletes in chapter 10, along with bulk indexing and bulk updating.

- *Remove a mapping type, with all the documents in it.* This effectively searches and removes all the documents you've indexed in that type, plus the mapping itself.
- *Remove all the documents matching a query.* This is similar to removing a mapping type, in the sense that internally a search is run to identify the documents that need to be deleted, only here you can specify any query you want and the matching documents will be deleted.

REMOVING A SINGLE DOCUMENT

To remove a single document, you need to send an HTTP DELETE request to its URL; for example:

```
% curl -XDELETE 'localhost:9200/online-shop/shirts/1'
```

You can also use versioning to manage concurrency with deletes, just as you did while indexing and updating. For example, let's assume you sold all shirts of a certain type, and you want to remove that document so it doesn't appear in searches at all. But you might not know at that time if a new shipment arrived and the stock data has been updated. To accomplish this, add a version parameter to your DELETE request, as you did with index and update requests before.

There's one particularity to deletes when it comes to versioning, though. Once you delete the document, it's no longer there, so it's easy for an update to come and recreate it, even if shouldn't (for example, because that update's version is lower than the delete version). This is especially a problem if you're using external versioning because any external version will work on a document that doesn't exist.

To prevent this problem, Elasticsearch keeps the version of that document around for a while so it can reject updates with a lower version than that of the delete. That time is 60s by default, which should be enough for most use cases, but you can change it by setting index.gc_deletes in elasticsearch.yml or in each index's settings. We'll talk more about managing index settings in chapter 11, which is about administration.

REMOVING A MAPPING TYPE AND DOCUMENTS MATCHING A QUERY

You can also remove an entire mapping type, which removes the mapping itself plus all the documents indexed in that type. To do that, you provide the type's URL to the DELETE request:

```
% curl -XDELETE 'localhost:9200/online-shop/shirts'
```

The tricky part about removing types is that the type name is just another field in the documents. All documents of an index end up in the same shards regardless of the mapping type they belong to. When you issue the previous command, Elasticsearch has to query for documents of that type and then remove them. This is an important detail when it comes to performance for removing types versus removing complete indices because removing types typically takes longer and uses more resources.

In the same way that you can query for all documents within a type and delete them, Elasticsearch allows you to specify your own query for documents you want to delete through an API called *delete by query*. Using the API is similar to running a query, except that the HTTP request is DELETE and the _search endpoint is now _query. For example, to remove all documents that match "Elasticsearch" from the index get-together, you can run this command:

```
% curl -XDELETE 'localhost:9200/get-together/_query?q=elasticsearch'
```

Similar to regular queries, which we cover in more detail in chapter 4, you can run a delete by query on a specific type, on multiple types, everywhere in an index, in multiple indices, or in all indices. When you search in all indices, be careful when you run a delete by query.

> **TIP** Besides being careful, you can use backups. We talk about backups in chapter 11, which is all about administration.

3.6.2   *Deleting indices*

As you might expect, to delete an index, you issue a DELETE request to the URL of that index:

```
% curl -XDELETE 'localhost:9200/get-together/'
```

You can also delete multiple indices by providing a comma-separated list or even delete all indices by providing _all as the index name.

> **TIP** Does deleting all documents via curl -DELETE localhost:9200/_all sound dangerous to you? You can prevent that by setting action.destructive _requires_name: true in elasticsearch.yml. That will make Elasticsearch reject _all, as well as wildcards in index names, when it comes to deletes.

Deleting an index is fast because it's mostly about removing the files associated with all shards of that index. Deleting files on the file system happens quickly compared to when you delete individual documents. When you do that, they're only marked as deleted. They get removed when segments are merged. *Merging* is the process of combining multiple small Lucene segments into a bigger segment.

On segments and merging

A *segment* is a chunk of the Lucene index (or a shard, in Elasticsearch terminology) that is created when you're indexing. Segments are never appended—only new ones are created as you index new documents. Data is never removed from them because deleting only marks documents as deleted. Finally, data never changes because updating documents implies re-indexing.

When Elasticsearch is performing a query on a shard, Lucene has to query all its segments, merge the results, and send them back—much like the process of querying multiple shards within an index. As with shards, the more segments you have to go though, the slower the search.

As you may imagine, normal indexing operations create many such small segments. To avoid having an extremely large number of segments in an index, Lucene merges them from time to time.

Merging some documents implies reading their contents, excluding the deleted documents, and creating new and bigger segments with their combined content. This process requires resources—specifically, CPU and disk I/O. Fortunately, merges run asynchronously, and Elasticsearch lets you configure numerous options around them. We'll talk more about those options in chapter 12, where you'll learn how to improve the performance of index, update, and delete operations.

3.6.3 Closing indices

Instead of deleting indices, you also have the option of closing them. If you close an index, you won't be able to read or write data from it with Elasticsearch until you open it again. This is useful when you have flowing data, such as application logs. You'll learn in chapter 9 that it's a good idea to store such flowing data in time-based indices—for example, creating one index per day.

In an ideal world, you'd hold application logs forever in case you needed to look back a long time previously. On the other hand, having a large amount of data in Elasticsearch demands increased resources. For this use case, it makes sense to close old indices. You're unlikely to need that data, but you don't want to remove it, either.

To close the online-shop index, send an HTTP POST request to its URL at the _close endpoint:

```
% curl -XPOST 'localhost:9200/online-shop/_close'
```

To open it again, you run a similar command, only the endpoint becomes _open:

```
% curl -XPOST 'localhost:9200/online-shop/_open'
```

Once you close an index, the only trace of it in Elasticsearch's memory is its metadata, such as name and where shards are located. If you have enough disk space and you're not sure whether you'll need to search in that data again, closing indices is better than removing them. Closing them gives you the peace of mind that you can always reopen a closed index and search in it again.

3.6.4 Re-indexing sample documents

In chapter 2, you used the book's code samples to index documents. Running populate.sh from these code samples removes the get-together index you created in this chapter and re-indexes the sample documents. If you look at both the populate.sh script and the mapping definition from mapping.json, you'll recognize various types of fields we discussed in this chapter.

Some of the mapping and indexing options, such as the analysis settings, are dealt with in upcoming chapters. For now, run populate.sh to prepare the get-together index for chapter 4, where we'll explore searches. The code samples provide you with sample data to search on.

3.7 Summary

Before moving on, let's have another look at what we've discussed in this chapter:

- Mappings let you define fields in your documents and how those fields are indexed. We say Elasticsearch is schema-free because mappings are extended automatically, but in production you often need to take control over what's indexed, what's stored, and how it's stored.

- Most fields in your documents are core types, such as strings and numbers. The way you index those fields has a big impact on how Elasticsearch performs and how relevant your search results are—for example, the analysis settings, which we cover in chapter 5.

- A single field can also be a container for multiple fields or values. We looked at arrays and multi-fields, which let you have multiple occurrences of the same core type in the same field.

- Besides the fields that are specific to your documents, Elasticsearch provides predefined fields, such as _source and _all. Configuring these fields changes some data that you don't explicitly provide in your documents but has a big impact on both performance and functionality. For example, you can decide which fields need to be indexed in _all as well.

- Because Elasticsearch stores data in Lucene segments that don't change once they're created, updating a document implies retrieving the existing one, putting the changes in a new document that gets indexed, and marking the old one as deleted.

- The removal of documents happens when the Lucene segments are asynchronously merged. This is also why deleting an entire index is faster than removing one or more individual documents from it—it only implies removing files on disk with no merging.

- Throughout indexing, updating, and deleting, you can use document versions to manage concurrency issues. With updates, you can tell Elasticsearch to retry automatically if an update fails because of a concurrency issue.

Searching your data

This chapter covers

- The structure of an Elasticsearch search request and response
- Elasticsearch filters and how they differ from queries
- Filter bitsets and caching
- Using queries and filters that Elasticsearch supports

Now that we've explored how you get data into Elasticsearch, let's cover how you get data out of Elasticsearch: by searching. After all, what good is indexing your data into a search engine if you can't search through it? Fortunately, Elasticsearch provides a rich API for searching through data, running the gamut of Lucene's search capability. Because of the format Elasticsearch allows for constructing search requests, there are limitless possibilities for how they can be built. The best way to tell which query in combination with filter(s) to use for your data is to experiment, so don't be afraid to try out these combinations on your project's data to figure out which one best suits your needs.

> **Searchable data**
>
> In this chapter, you'll again use the dataset formed around the get-together website we've touched on in previous examples. This dataset contains two different types of documents: groups and events. To follow along and perform the queries yourself, download and run the populate.sh script to populate an Elasticsearch index. The samples are created with a fresh run of the script; if you want to tag along, please run the script again.
>
> To download the script, see the source code for the book at https://github.com/dakrone/elasticsearch-in-action.

To start off, we discuss the components common to all search requests and results so you'll have an understanding of what a search request and the result of that search request look like in general. We then move on to discussing the query and filter DSL as one of the main elements of the search API. Next, we discuss the differences between queries and filters, followed by a look at some of the most commonly used filters and queries. If you're wondering about the details of how Elasticsearch calculates the score for documents, don't worry; we discuss that in chapter 6, where we talk about searching with relevancy. Finally, we provide a quick-and-dirty guide to help you choose which type of query and filter combination to use for a particular application. Make sure to check it out if there seem to be too many types of queries and filters to keep straight!

Before we start, let's revisit what happens when you perform a search in Elasticsearch (see figure 4.1). The REST API search request is first sent to the node you choose to connect to, which in turn sends the search request to all shards (either primary or replica) for the index or indices being queried. When enough information has been collected from all shards to sort and rank the results, only the shards containing the document content that will be returned are asked to return the relevant content.

This search routing behavior is configurable; the default behavior is shown in figure 4.1 and is called "query_then_fetch." We'll look at how to change it later on in chapter 10. For now, let's look at the basic structure that all Elasticsearch search requests share.

4.1 *Structure of a search request*

Elasticsearch search requests are JSON document-based requests or URL-based requests. The requests are sent to the server, and because all search requests follow the same format, it's helpful to understand the components that you can change for each search request. Before we discuss the different components, we have to talk about the scope of your search request.

Step 1: Request is forwarded.   Step 2: Results are aggregated.

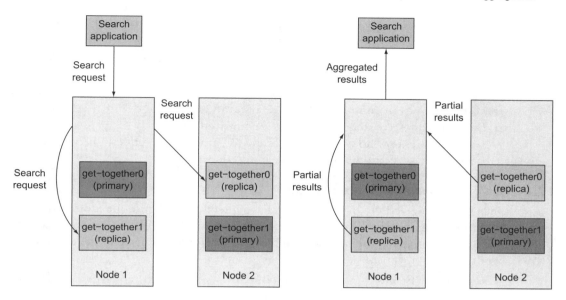

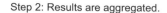

Figure 4.1 How a search request is routed; the index consists of two shards and one replica per shard. After locating and scoring the documents, only the top 10 documents are fetched.

4.1.1 Specifying a search scope

All REST search requests use the _search REST endpoint and can be either a GET request or a POST request. You can search an entire cluster or you can limit the scope by specifying the names of indices or types in the request URL. The following listing provides example search URLs that limit the scope of searches.

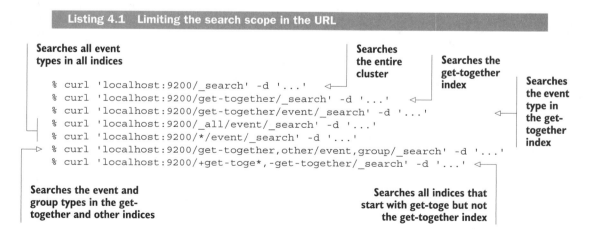

Listing 4.1 Limiting the search scope in the URL

Searches all event types in all indices

Searches the entire cluster

Searches the get-together index

Searches the event type in the get-together index

```
% curl 'localhost:9200/_search' -d '...'
% curl 'localhost:9200/get-together/_search' -d '...'
% curl 'localhost:9200/get-together/event/_search' -d '...'
% curl 'localhost:9200/_all/event/_search' -d '...'
% curl 'localhost:9200/*/event/_search' -d '...'
% curl 'localhost:9200/get-together,other/event,group/_search' -d '...'
% curl 'localhost:9200/+get-toge*,-get-together/_search' -d '...'
```

Searches the event and group types in the get-together and other indices

Searches all indices that start with get-toge but not the get-together index

Next to indexes you can also use aliases to search through multiple indexes. This method is used often to search through all available time-stamped indices. Think about indices in the format logstash-yyyymmdd, with one alias called logstash that points to all indices. You can also do a basic search and limit it to all logstash-based indices: `curl 'localhost:9200/logstash/_search'`. For the best performance, limit your queries to the smallest number of indices and types possible because anything Elasticsearch doesn't have to search means faster responses. Remember that each search request has to be sent to all shards of an index; the more indices you have to send search requests to, the more shards are involved.

Now that you know how to limit the scope for your search request, the next step is to discuss the basic components of the search request.

4.1.2   *Basic components of a search request*

Once you've selected the indices to search, you need to configure the most important components of the search request. These components deal with the amount of documents to return, select the best documents to return, and configure which documents you don't want in your results:

- `query`—The most important component for your search request, this part configures the best documents to return based on a score, as well as the documents you don't want to return. This component is configured using the query DSL and the filter DSL. An example is to search for all events with the word "elasticsearch" in the title limited to events in this year.
- `size`—Represents the amount of documents to return.
- `from`—Together with `size`, `from` is used to do pagination. Be careful, though; in order to determine the second page of 10 items, Elasticsearch has to calculate the top 20 items. If your result set grows, getting a page somewhere in the middle would be expensive.
- `_source`—Specifies how the `_source` field is returned. The default is to return the complete `_source` field. By configuring `_source`, you filter the fields that are returned. Use this if your indexed documents are big and you don't need the full content in your result. Be aware that you shouldn't disable the `_source` field in your index mappings if you want to use this. See the note for the difference between using fields and `_source`.
- `sort`–The default sorting is based on the score for a document. If you don't care about the score or you expect a lot of documents with the same score, adding a `sort` helps you to control which documents get returned.

NOTE Before version 1 of Elasticsearch, field was the component to use for filtering the fields to return. This is still possible; the behavior is to return stored fields if available. If no stored field is available, the field is obtained from the source. If you don't explicitly store fields in the index, it's better to use the `_source` component. Using `_source` filtering, Elasticsearch doesn't have to check for a stored field first before obtaining the field from the `_source`.

RESULTS START AND PAGE SIZE

The aptly named from and size fields are sent to specify the offset to start results from and the size of each "page" of results. For example, if you send a from value of 7 and a size of 5, Elasticsearch will send the 8th, 9th, 10th, 11th, and 12th results back (because the from parameter starts at 0, specifying 7 starts at the 8th result). If these two parameters aren't sent, Elasticsearch defaults to starting at the first result (the "0th"), and sends 10 results with the response. There are two distinct ways of sending a search request to Elasticsearch.

In the next section we discuss sending a URL-based search request; after that we discuss the request body–based search requests. The discussed basic components of the search request will be used in both mechanisms.

URL-BASED SEARCH REQUEST

In this section you'll create a URL-based search request using the four basic components discussed in the previous section. The URL-based search is meant to be useful for quick curl-based requests. Not all search features are exposed using the URL-based search. In the following listing, the search request will search for all events, but you want the second page of 10 items.

Listing 4.2 Paginating results using from and size

```
% curl 'localhost:9200/get-together/_search?from=10&size=10'
```
> Request matching all documents with from and size sent as parameters in the URL

In listing 4.3, you create the search request to return the default first 10 events of all events, but ordered by their date in ascending order. If you want to, you can combine both search request configurations as well. Also try the same search request in descending (desc) order and check if the order of the events is changed, as shown in the next listing.

Listing 4.3 Changing the order of the results

```
% curl 'localhost:9200/get-together/_search?sort=date:asc'
```
> Request matching all documents but returning the default first 10 of all results ordered by date in ascending order

In listing 4.4 you limit the fields from sources that you want in the response. Imagine you only want to have the title of the event together with the date of the event. Again, you want the events ordered by date. You configure the _source component to ask for the title and date only. More options for the _source are explained in the next section when we discuss the request body–based search. The response in the listing shows one of the hits.

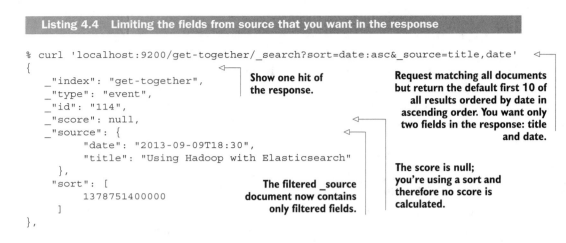

Listing 4.4   Limiting the fields from source that you want in the response

```
% curl 'localhost:9200/get-together/_search?sort=date:asc&_source=title,date'   ◄──┐
{
    "_index": "get-together",       ◄──   Show one hit of
    "_type": "event",                     the response.
    "_id": "114",
    "_score": null,                                                      ◄──
    "_source": {                                                    ◄──
        "date": "2013-09-09T18:30",
        "title": "Using Hadoop with Elasticsearch"
    },
    "sort": [
        1378751400000
    ]
},
```

Request matching all documents but return the default first 10 of all results ordered by date in ascending order. You want only two fields in the response: title and date.

The score is null; you're using a sort and therefore no score is calculated.

The filtered _source document now contains only filtered fields.

So far you've only created search requests using the `match_all` query. The query and filter DSL is discussed in section 4.2, but we do think it's important to show how you can create a URL-based search request where you want to return only documents containing the word "elasticsearch" in the title, as in the next listing. Again you sort by date. Notice the `q=title:elasticsearch` part. This is where you specify that you want to query on the field title for the word "elasticsearch."

Listing 4.5   Changing the order of the results

```
% curl 'localhost:9200/get-together/
_search?sort=date:asc&q=title:elasticsearch'   ◄──
```

Request matching all events with the word "elasticsearch" in their title

With `q=` you indicate you want to provide a query in the search request. With `title:elasticsearch` you specify that you're looking for the word "elasticsearch" in the `title` field.

We leave it up to you to try out the query and check that the response contains only events with the word "elasticsearch" in the title. Feel free to play around with other words and fields. Again, you can combine the mentioned components of the search API in one query.

Now that you're comfortable with search requests using the URL, you're ready to move on to the request body–based search requests.

4.1.3   *Request body–based search request*

In the previous section we demonstrated how to use the basic search request components in URL-based queries. This is a nice way of interacting with Elasticsearch if you're on the command line, for instance. When executing more advanced searches, using request body–based searches gives you more flexibility and more options. Even when using request body–based searches, some of the components can be provided in the URL as well. We focus in this section on the request body because we already discussed all URL-based configurations in the previous section. The example in the following listing searches for the second page of the get-together index when all documents are matched.

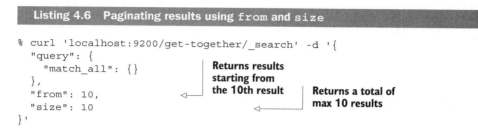

```
% curl 'localhost:9200/get-together/_search' -d '{
  "query": {
    "match_all": {}                    Returns results
  },                                    starting from
  "from": 10,                           the 10th result    Returns a total of
  "size": 10                                               max 10 results
}'
```

Other than noticing the `"query"` section, which is an object in every query, don't worry about the `"match_all"` section yet. We talk about it in section 4.2 when discussing the query and filter DSL.

FIELDS RETURNED WITH RESULTS

The next element that all search requests share is the list of fields Elasticsearch should return for each matching document. This is specified by sending the _source component with the search request. If no _source is specified with the request, Elasticsearch returns either the entire _source of the document by default, or, if the _source isn't stored, only the metadata about the matching document: _id, _type, _index, and _score.

The previous query is used in the following listing, returning the name and date fields of each matching group.

Listing 4.7   Filtering the returned _source

```
% curl 'localhost:9200/get-together/_search' -d '{
  "query": {
    "match_all": {}                    Returns the name and
  },                                    date fields with the
  "_source": ["name", "date"]          search response
}'
```

WILDCARDS IN RETURNED FIELDS WITH _SOURCE

Not only can you return a list of fields, you can also specify wildcards. For example, if you wanted to return both a `"name"` and `"nation"` field, you could specify _source: `"na*"`. You can also specify multiple wildcards using an array of wildcard strings, like _source: `["name.*", "address.*"]`.

Not only can you specify which fields to include, you can also specify which fields you don't want to return. The next listing gives an example.

Listing 4.8 Filtering the returned `_source` showing `include` and `exclude`

```
% curl 'localhost:9200/get-together/_search' -d '{
  "query": {
    "match_all": {}
  },
  "_source": {
    "include": ["location.*", "date"],        ◄── Return fields starting with
    "exclude": ["location.geolocation"]            location and date fields
  }                                                  with the search response.
}'
                                          ◄── Don't return the field
                                              location.geolocation.
```

SORT ORDER FOR RESULTS

The last element most searches include is the sort order for the results. If no sort order is specified, Elasticsearch returns matching documents sorted by the _score value in descending order, with the most relevant (highest scoring) documents first. To sort fields in either ascending or descending order, specify an array of maps instead of an array of fields. You can sort on any number of fields by specifying a list of fields or field maps in the sort value. For example, using the previous organizer search, you can return results sorted first by creation date, starting with the oldest; then by the name of the get-together group, in reverse alphabetical order; and finally by the _score of the result, as shown in the following listing.

Listing 4.9 Results sorted by date (ascending), name (descending), and `_score`

```
% curl 'localhost:9200/get-together/_search' -d '{
  "query": {
    "match_all": {}
  },
  "sort": [
    {"created_on": "asc"},      ◄── Sorts first by the creation date, starting from the oldest to newest
    {"name": "desc"},           ◄── Then sorts by name of the group, in reverse alphabetical order
    "_score"                    ◄── Finally, sorts by the relevancy of the result (its _score)
  ]
}'
```

SORTING ON MULTIVALUED AND ANALYZED FIELDS When sorting on multivalued fields (tags, for instance), you don't know how the sorting uses the values. It will pick one to sort on, but you can't know which one. The same is true for analyzed fields. An analyzed field will regularly result in multiple terms as well. Therefore it's best to sort on not-analyzed or numeric fields.

THE BASIC COMPONENTS IN ACTION

Now that we've covered the basic search components, the next listing shows an example of a search request that uses them all.

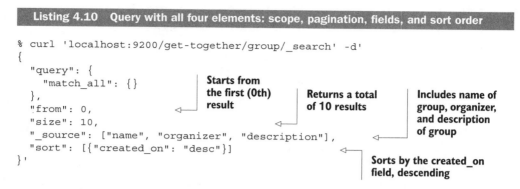

Listing 4.10 Query with all four elements: scope, pagination, fields, and sort order

```
% curl 'localhost:9200/get-together/group/_search' -d'
{
  "query": {
    "match_all": {}
  },
  "from": 0,
  "size": 10,
  "_source": ["name", "organizer", "description"],
  "sort": [{"created_on": "desc"}]
}'
```

- Starts from the first (0th) result
- Returns a total of 10 results
- Includes name of group, organizer, and description of group
- Sorts by the created_on field, descending

Before we go into more details on the query and filter API, we have to cover one other item: the structure of the search response.

4.1.4 Understanding the structure of a response

Let's look at an example search and see what the response looks like. The next listing searches for groups about "elasticsearch." For brevity we used the URL-based search.

Listing 4.11 Example search request and response

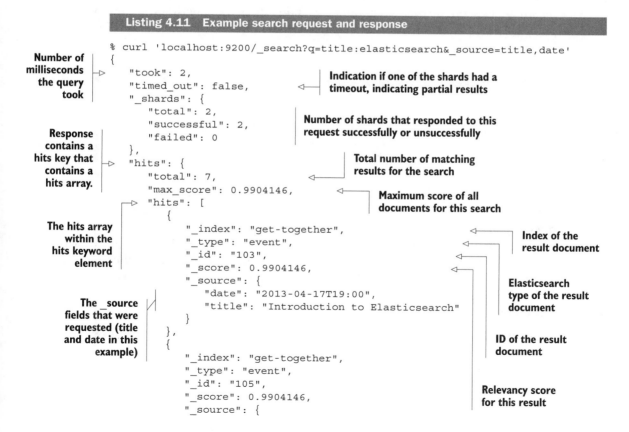

```
% curl 'localhost:9200/_search?q=title:elasticsearch&_source=title,date'
{
  "took": 2,
  "timed_out": false,
  "_shards": {
    "total": 2,
    "successful": 2,
    "failed": 0
  },
  "hits": {
    "total": 7,
    "max_score": 0.9904146,
    "hits": [
      {
        "_index": "get-together",
        "_type": "event",
        "_id": "103",
        "_score": 0.9904146,
        "_source": {
          "date": "2013-04-17T19:00",
          "title": "Introduction to Elasticsearch"
        }
      },
      {
        "_index": "get-together",
        "_type": "event",
        "_id": "105",
        "_score": 0.9904146,
        "_source": {
```

- Number of milliseconds the query took
- Indication if one of the shards had a timeout, indicating partial results
- Number of shards that responded to this request successfully or unsuccessfully
- Response contains a hits key that contains a hits array.
- Total number of matching results for the search
- Maximum score of all documents for this search
- The hits array within the hits keyword element
- Index of the result document
- Elasticsearch type of the result document
- The _source fields that were requested (title and date in this example)
- ID of the result document
- Relevancy score for this result

```
            "date": "2013-07-17T18:30",
            "title": "Elasticsearch and Logstash"
        }
    },
    ...                     ◁─┐  Placeholder for other
    ]                          │  hits left out for brevity
  }
}
```

Remember that if you don't store either the _source of the document or the fields, you won't be able to retrieve the value from Elasticsearch!

Now that you're familiar with the basic components of a search request, there's one component that we haven't really discussed yet: the query and filter DSL. This was done on purpose, because the topic is so big it deserves its own section.

4.2 Introducing the query and filter DSL

In the previous section we discussed the basic components of a search request. We talked about the amount of items to return and support pagination using from and size. We also discussed sorting and filtering the fields of the source to return. In this section we explain the basic component we didn't discuss at length yet, the query component. So far you've used a basic query component, the match_all query. Check the following listing to see it in action.

Listing 4.12 Basic search request using request body

```
% curl 'localhost:9200/get-together/_search' -d '{
  "query": {                          ◁─── The query component
    "match_all": {}   ◁─┐                  in the search API
  }                     │  Basic example of
}'                      │  the query API
```

In this section you're replacing the match_all query with a match query, and you're going to add a term filter from the filter DSL to the search request using the filtered query of the query DSL. After that we dive into what makes filters different from queries. Next, we take a look at some other basic queries and filters. We wrap up the section with compound queries and other more advanced queries and filters. Then, before moving to analyzers, we help you choose the right query for the job.

4.2.1 Match query and term filter

So far almost every search request that you did returned all documents. In this section we show two ways to limit the number of documents to return. We start with a match query to find groups containing the word "Hadoop" in the title. The following code listing shows this search request.

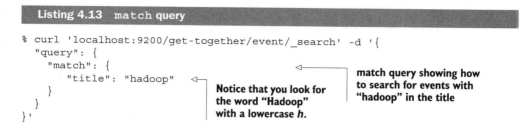

The query returns three events in total. The structure of the response was explained previously in section 4.1.4. If you're following along, look at the score for the first match. The first match is the document with the title "Using Hadoop with Elasticsearch." The score for this document is 1.3958796. You can change the search by searching for the word "Hadoop" with the capital *H*. The result will be the same. Try it if you don't believe us.

Now imagine you have a website that groups events by host, so you get this nice list of aggregates and a count of the number of events per host. After clicking on the events hosted by Andy, you want to find all events hosted by Andy. You can create a search request with a match query looking for Andy in the host field. If you create this search request and execute it, you'll see there are three events hosted by Andy, all having the same score. We hear you ask, "Why?" Read in chapter 6 about how scoring works. This is the right moment to introduce filters.

Filters are similar to the queries we discuss in this chapter, but they differ in how they affect the scoring and performance of many search actions. Rather than computing the score for a particular term as queries do, a filter on a search returns a simple binary "does this document match this query" yes-or-no answer. Figure 4.2 shows the main difference between queries and filters.

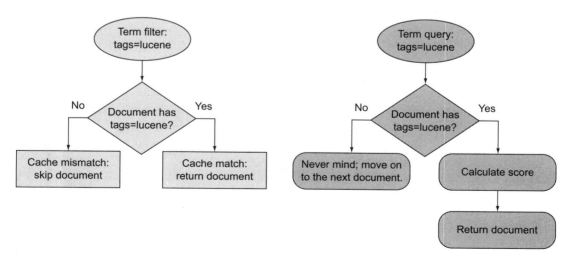

Figure 4.2 Filters require less processing and are cacheable because they don't calculate the score.

Because of this difference, filters can be faster than using a regular query, and they can also be cacheable. A search using a filter looks similar to a regular search using a query, but the query is replaced with a `"filtered"` map that contains the original query and a filter to be applied, as shown in the next listing. This query is called the filtered query in the query DSL. A filtered query contains two components: the query and the filter.

Listing 4.14   Query using a filter

```
% curl 'localhost:9200/get-together/_search' -d '
{
  "query": {
    "filtered": {          <--  Query type, here specifying a
      "query": {                query with a filter attached
        "match": {
          "title": "hadoop"     The query searches for events
        }                       with "hadoop" in the title.
      },
      "filter": {               The additional filter limits the
        "term": {               query to events that are hosted
          "host": "andy"        by andy. Notice the lowercase a
        }                       in andy. This is explained in the
      }                         next chapter about analysis.
    }
  }
}'
```

Here a regular query for events matching "hadoop" is used as the query, but in addition to the query for the word "Hadoop," a filter is used to limit the events. Inside this particular `filter` section, a `term` filter is applied for all documents that have the host `"andy"`. Behind the scenes, Elasticsearch constructs a *bitset*, which is a binary set of bits denoting whether the document matches this filter. Figure 4.3 shows what this bitset looks like.

After constructing the bitset, Elasticsearch can now use it to filter (hence the name!) out the documents that it shouldn't be searching based on the query part of the search. The filter limits the amount of documents for which a score needs to be calculated. The score for the limited set of documents is calculated based on the query. Because of this, adding a filter can be much faster than combining the entire query into a single search. Depending on what kind of filter is used, Elasticsearch can cache the results in a bitset. If the filter is used for another search, the bitset doesn't have to be calculated again!

Other types of filters aren't automatically cached if Elasticsearch can tell they'll never be used again or if the bitsets are trivial to recreate. An example of a query that's hard to cache is a filter that limits the results to all documents of the last hour. This query changes every second when you execute it and therefore there's no reason to cache it. Check listing 4.17 to see an example. Additionally, Elasticsearch gives you the ability to manually specify whether a filter should be cached, as well as

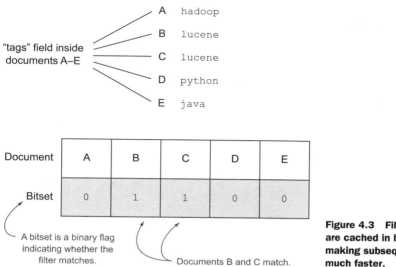

Figure 4.3   **Filter results are cached in bitsets, making subsequent runs much faster.**

the ability to manually specify whether a filter should be cached. All of this translates into faster searches with filters. Therefore, you should make parts of your query into filters if you can.

We'll revisit bitsets to explain the details of how they work and how they affect performance in chapter 10, which discusses ways to speed up searches. Now that you understand what filters are, we'll cover several different types of filters and queries, and you'll run some searches against data.

4.2.2 *Most used basic queries and filters*

Although there are a number of ways to query for things in Elasticsearch, some may be better than others depending on how the data is stored in your index. In this section, you learn the different types of queries Elasticsearch supports and try out an example of how to use each query. We assess the pros and cons of using each query and provide performance notes about each one so you can determine which query best fits your data.

In the previous sections of this chapter, a number of queries and filters were already introduced. You started with the match_all query to return all documents, moved on to the match query to limit results of an occurring word in a field, and used the term filter to limit the results using a term in a field. One query that we didn't discuss but that you did use is the query_string query. This query was used in the URL-based search. More on this later in this section.

In this section we recap these queries but now introduce some more advanced options. We also look at more advanced queries and filters like the `range` filter, the `prefix` query, and the `simple_query_string` query. Let's start with the easiest queries, beginning with the `match_all` query.

MATCH_ALL QUERY

We'll give you a guess as to what this query does. That's correct! It matches all documents. The `match_all` query is useful when you want to use a filter instead of a query (perhaps if you don't care about the score of documents at all) or you want to return all documents among the indices and types you're searching. The query looks like this:

```
% curl 'localhost:9200/_search' -d '
{
  "query" : {
    "match_all" : {}
  }
}'
```

To use a filter for a search instead of any regular query parts, the query looks something like this (with the filters omitted):

```
% curl 'localhost:9200/get-together/_search' -d '
{
  "query": {
    "filtered": {
      "query": {
        "match_all": {}
      },
      "filter": {
        ... filter details ...
      }
    }
  }
}'
```

Simple, huh? Not too useful, though, for a search engine, because users rarely search for everything. You can even make this search request easier; using the `match_all` query is the default. Therefore the query elements can be left out completely in this case. Next, let's look at a query that's a bit more useful.

QUERY_STRING QUERY

In chapter 2, you used the `query_string` query to see how easy it is to get an Elasticsearch server up and running, but we'll cover it again in more detail so you can see how it compares to the other queries.

As shown in the following listing, a `query_string` search can be performed either from the URL of the request or sent in a request body. In this example, you search for documents that contain "nosql." The query should return one document.

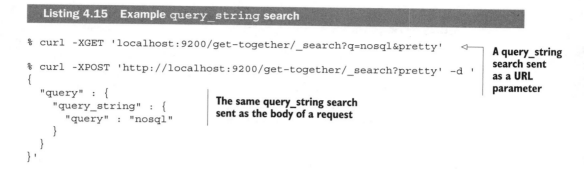

Listing 4.15   Example `query_string` **search**

```
% curl -XGET 'localhost:9200/get-together/_search?q=nosql&pretty'
% curl -XPOST 'http://localhost:9200/get-together/_search?pretty' -d '
{
  "query" : {
    "query_string" : {
      "query" : "nosql"
    }
  }
}'
```

A query_string search sent as a URL parameter

The same query_string search sent as the body of a request

By default, a `query_string` query searches the `_all` field, which, if you recall from chapter 3, is made up of all the fields combined. You can change this by either specifying a field with the query, such as `description:nosql`, or by specifying a `default_field` with the request, as shown in the next listing.

Listing 4.16   Specifying a `default_field` **for a** `query_string` **search**

```
% curl -XPOST 'localhost:9200/_search' -d '
{
  "query" : {
    "query_string" : {
      "default_field" : "description",
      "query" : "nosql"
    }
  }
}'
```

Because no field is specified in the query, the default field (description) is used.

As you may have guessed, this syntax offers more than searching for a single word. Under the hood, this is the entire Lucene query syntax, which allows combining searching different terms with Boolean operators like AND and OR, as well as excluding documents from the results using the minus sign (-) operator. The following query searches for all groups with "nosql" in the name but without "mongodb" in the description:

```
name:nosql AND -description:mongodb
```

To search for all search and Lucene groups created between 1999 and 2001, you could use the following:

```
(tags:search OR tags:lucene) AND created_on:[1999-01-01 TO 2001-01-01]
```

> **NOTE**   Refer to www.lucenetutorial.com/lucene-query-syntax.html for a full example of syntax the `query_string` query supports.

Query_string cautions

Although the `query_string` query is one of the most powerful queries available to you in Elasticsearch, it can sometimes be one of the hardest to read and extend. It may be tempting to allow your users the ability to specify their own queries with this syntax, but consider the difficulty in explaining the meaning of complex queries such as this:

```
name:search^2 AND (tags:lucene OR tags:"big data"~2) AND -
description:analytics AND created_on:[2006-05-01 TO 2007-03-29]
```

One big disadvantage with the `query_string` query is that it has great power. Giving your website users this power might put your Elasticsearch cluster at risk. If users start entering queries with the wrong format, they'll get back exceptions; it's also possible to make combinations that would return the world and that way put your cluster at risk. See the previous note for an example.

Suggested replacements for the `query_string` query include the `term`, `terms`, `match`, or `multi_match` queries, all of which allow you to search for strings within a field or fields in a document. Another good replacement is the `simple-query-string` query; this is meant to be a replacement with easy access to a query syntax using +, -, `AND`, `OR`. More on these queries in the sections that follow.

TERM QUERY AND TERM FILTER

`term` queries and filters are some of the simplest queries that can be performed, allowing you to specify a field and term to search for within your documents. Note that because the term being searched for isn't analyzed, it must match a term in the document *exactly* for the result to be found. We'll cover how exactly *tokens*, which are individual pieces of text indexed by Elasticsearch, get analyzed in chapter 5. If you're familiar with Lucene, it might be helpful to know that the `term` query maps directly to Lucene's `TermQuery`.

The following listing shows a `term` query that searches for groups with the elasticsearch tag.

Listing 4.17   Example `term` query

```
% curl 'localhost:9200/get-together/group/_search' -d '
{
  "query": {
    "term": {
      "tags": "elasticsearch"
    }
  },
  "_source": ["name", "tags"]
}'
{
    ...
      "hits": [
          {
              "_id": "3",
```

```
                    "_index": "get-together",
                    "_score": 1.0769258,
                    "_type": "group",
                    "_source": {
                        "name": "Elasticsearch San Francisco",
                        "tags": [
                            "elasticsearch",              ◁────┐
                            "big data",                        │
                            "lucene",                          │
                            "open source"                      │
                        ]                                      │
                    }                                          │
                },                                             │      Because these two
                {                                              │      results contain the
                                                               │      word "elasticsearch"
                    "_id": "2",                                │      in the tags, they're
                    "_index": "get-together",                 │      returned.
                    "_score": 0.8948604,                      │
                    "_type": "group",                         │
                    "_source": {                              │
                        "name": "Elasticsearch Denver",       │
                        "tags": [                             │
                            "denver",                         │
                            "elasticsearch",          ◁───────┘
                            "big data",
                            "lucene",
                            "solr"
                        ]
                    }
                }
            ],
        ...
}
```

Like the term query, a term filter can be used when you want to limit the results to documents that contain the term but without affecting the score. Compare the scores of the documents in the previous listing with the scores in the following listing: you'll notice that the filter doesn't bother calculating and therefore influencing the score; due to the match_all query, the score for all documents is 1.0.

Listing 4.18   Example term filter

```
% curl 'localhost:9200/get-together/_search' -d '
{
  "query": {
    "filtered": {
      "query": {
        "match_all": {}
      },
      "filter": {                        The same query as
        "term": {                        before but using a
          "tags": "elasticsearch"        filter this time
        }
      }
    }
  }
}
```

```
      },
    "_source": ["name", "tags"]
  }'
  {
      ...
          "hits": [
              {
                  "_id": "3",
                  "_index": "get-together",
                  "_score": 1.0,
                  "_type": "group",
                  "_source": {
                      "name": "Elasticsearch San Francisco",
                      "tags": [
                          "elasticsearch",
                          "big data",
                          "lucene",
                          "open source"
                      ]
                  }
              },
              {
                  "_id": "2",
                  "_index": "get-together",
                  "_score": 1.0,
                  "_type": "group",
                  "_source": {
                      "name": "Elasticsearch Denver",
                      "tags": [
                          "denver",
                          "elasticsearch",
                          "big data",
                          "lucene",
                          "solr"
                      ]
                  }
              }
          ]
      ...
  }
```

The document scores are now constant because a filter was used instead of a query.

TERMS QUERY

Similar to the term query, the terms query (note the *s*!) can search for multiple terms in a document's field. For example, the following listing searches for groups by a tag matching either "jvm" or "hadoop."

Listing 4.19 Searching for multiple terms with the terms query

```
% curl 'localhost:9200/get-together/group/_search' -d '
{
  "query": {
    "terms": {
      "tags": ["jvm", "hadoop"]
    }
```

Multiple terms to search for

```
    },
    "_source": ["name", "tags"]
}'
{
    ...
        "hits": [
            {
                "_id": "1",
                "_index": "get-together",
                "_score": 0.33779633,
                "_type": "group",
                "_source": {
                    "name": "Denver Clojure",
                    "tags": [
                        "clojure",
                        "denver",
                        "functional programming",
                        "jvm",
                        "java"
                    ]
                }
            },
            {
                "_id": "4",
                "_index": "get-together",
                "_score": 0.22838624,
                "_type": "group",
                "_source": {
                    "name": "Boulder/Denver big data get-together",
                    "tags": [
                        "big data",
                        "data visualization",
                        "open source",
                        "cloud computing",
                        "hadoop"
                    ]
                }
            }
        ...
}
```

Found one of the matching tags

To force a minimum number of matching terms to be in a document before it matches the query, specify the `minimum_should_match` parameter:

```
% curl 'localhost:9200/get-together/group/_search' -d '
{
    "query": {
        "terms": {
            "tags": ["jvm", "hadoop", "lucene"],
            "minimum_should_match": 2
        }
    }
}'
```

If you're thinking, "Wait! That's pretty limited!" you're probably also wondering what happens when you need to combine multiple queries into a single query. More information about combining multiple term queries is discussed in section 4.3 about compound queries.

4.2.3 *Match query and term filter*

Similar to the term query, the match query is a hash map containing the field you'd like to search as well as the string you want to search for, which can be either a field or the special _all field to search all fields at once. Here's an example match query, searching for groups where name contains "elasticsearch":

```
% curl 'localhost:9200/get-together/group/_search' -d '
{
  "query": {
    "match": {
      "name": "elasticsearch"
    }
  }
}'
```

The match query can behave in a number of different ways; the two most important behaviors are *boolean* and *phrase*.

BOOLEAN QUERY BEHAVIOR

By default, the match query uses Boolean behavior and the OR operator. For example, if you search for the text "Elasticsearch Denver," Elasticsearch searches for "Elasticsearch OR Denver," which would match get-together groups from both "Elasticsearch Amsterdam" and "Denver Clojure Group."

To search for results that contain both "Elasticsearch" and "Denver," change the operator by modifying the match field name into a map and setting the operator field to and:

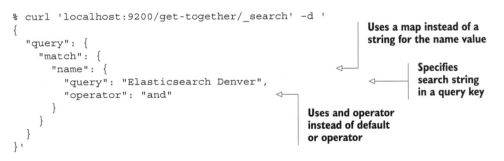

```
% curl 'localhost:9200/get-together/_search' -d '
{
  "query": {
    "match": {
      "name": {
        "query": "Elasticsearch Denver",
        "operator": "and"
      }
    }
  }
}'
```

> Uses a map instead of a string for the name value
>
> Specifies search string in a query key
>
> Uses and operator instead of default or operator

The second important way a match query can behave is as a phrase query.

PHRASE QUERY BEHAVIOR

A phrase query is useful when searching for a specific phrase within a document, with some amount of leeway between the positions of each word. This leeway is called *slop*, which is a number representing the distance between tokens in a phrase. Say you're trying to remember the name of a get-together group; you remember it had the words "Enterprise" and "London" in it, but you don't remember the rest of the name. You could search for the phrase "enterprise london" with `slop` set to 1 or 2 instead of the default of 0 to find results containing that phrase without having to know the exact title of the group:

```
% curl 'localhost:9200/get-together/group/_search' -d'
{
  "query": {
    "match": {
      "name": {
        "type": "phrase",
        "query": "enterprise london",
        "slop": 1
      }
    }
  },
  "_source": ["name", "description"]
}'
...
{
    "_id": "5",
    "_index": "get-together",
    "_score": 1.7768369,
    "_type": "group",
    "_source": {      "description": "Enterprise search get-togethers are an
    opportunity to get together with other people doing search.",
        "name": "Enterprise search London get-together"
    }
}
...
```

Instead of a regular match query, use a match phrase query.

Specifies a slop of 1 to tell Elasticsearch to have leeway with the distance between the terms

The matching field with "enterprise" and "london" separated by a word

4.2.4 Phrase_prefix query

Similar to the `match_phrase` query, the `match_phrase_prefix` query allows you to go one step further and search for a phrase, but it allows prefix matching on the last term in the phrase. This behavior is extremely useful for providing a running autocomplete for a search box, where the user gets search suggestions while typing a search term. When using the search for this kind of behavior, it's a good idea to set the maximum number of expansions for the prefix by setting the `max_expansions` setting so the search returns in a reasonable amount of time.

In the following example, "elasticsearch den" is used as the `phrase_prefix` query. Elasticsearch takes the "den" text and looks across all the values of the `name` field to check for those that start with "den" ("Denver," for example). Because this could potentially be a large set, the number of expansions should be limited:

```
% curl 'localhost:9200/get-together/group/_search' -d '
{
  "query": {
    "match": {
      "name": {
```

```
        "type": "phrase_prefix",
        "query": "Elasticsearch den",
        "max_expansions": 1
      }
    }
  },
  "_source": ["name"]
}'
...
{
    "_id": "2",
    "_index": "get-together",
    "_score": 2.7294521,
    "_type": "group",
    "_source": {
        "name": "Elasticsearch Denver"
    }
}
...
```

Uses a phrase_prefix
instead of a regular
phrase query

Matches fields containing
"Elasticsearch" and another
term that starts with "den"

Specifies the maximum
number of prefix
expansions to try

The `Boolean` and `phrase` queries are a great choice for accepting user input; they allow you to pass in user input in a much less error-prone way, and unlike a `query_string` query, a `match` query won't choke on reserved characters like +, -, ?, and !.

MATCHING MULTIPLE FIELDS WITH MULTI_MATCH

Although it might be tempting to think that the `multi_match` query behaves like the `terms` query by searching for multiple matches in a field, its behavior is slightly different. Instead, it allows you to search for a value across multiple fields. This can be helpful in the get-together example where you may want to search for a string across both the name of the group and the description:

```
% curl 'localhost:9200/get-together/_search' -d'
{
  "query": {
    "multi_match": {
      "query": "elasticsearch hadoop",
      "fields": [ "name", "description" ]
    }
  }
}'
```

Just as the `match` query can be turned into a `phrase` query, a `prefix` query, or a `phrase_prefix` query, the `multi_match` query can be turned into a `phrase` query or `phrase_prefix` query as well by specifying the type key. Consider the `multi_match` query exactly like the `match` query, except that you can specify multiple fields for searching instead of a single field only.

With all the different `match` queries, it's possible to find a way to search for almost anything, which is why the `match` query and its relatives are considered the go-to query type for most uses. We highly recommended that you use them whenever possible. For everything else, however, we'll cover some of the other types of queries that Elasticsearch supports.

4.3 Combining queries or compound queries

After learning about and using different types of queries, you'll likely find yourself needing to combine query types; this is where Elasticsearch's `bool` query comes in.

4.3.1 bool query

The `bool` query allows you to combine any number of queries into a single query by specifying a query clause that indicates which parts `must`, `should`, or `must_not` match the data in your Elasticsearch index:

- If you specify that part of a `bool` query `must` match, only results matching that query (or queries) are returned.
- Specifying that a part of a query `should` match means that a specified number of the clauses must match for a document to be returned.
- If no `must` clauses are specified, at least one `should` clause has to match for the document to be returned.
- Finally, the `must_not` clause causes matching documents to be excluded from the result set.

Table 4.1 lists the three clauses and their binary counterparts.

Table 4.1 `bool` query clause types

`bool` query clause	Binary equivalent	Meaning
`must`	To combine multiple clauses, use a binary `and` (`query1 AND query2 AND query3`).	Any searches in the `must` clause must match the document; lowercase `and` is a function; uppercase `AND` is an operator.
`must_not`	Combines multiple clauses with a binary `not`.	Any searches in the `must_not` clause must not be part of the document; multiple clauses are combined in a binary `not` manner (`NOT query1 AND NOT query2 AND NOT query3`).
`Should`	Combines multiple clauses with a binary `or` (`query 1 OR query2 OR query3`).	Searches in the `should` clause may or may not match a document, but at least the `minimum_should_match` parameter number of them should match (defaults to 1 if `must` is not present and 0 if `must` is present); similar to a binary `OR` (`query1 OR query2 OR query3`).

Understanding the difference between `must`, `should`, and `must_not` may be easier through an example. In the following listing, you search for events that were attended by David, must be attended by either Clint or Andy, and must not be older than June 30, 2013.

Listing 4.20 Combining queries with a `bool` query

```
% curl 'localhost:9200/get-together/_search' -d'
{
  "query": {
    "bool": {
      "must": [
        {
          "term": {
            "attendees": "david"
          }
        }
      ],
      "should": [
        {
          "term": {
            "attendees": "clint"
          }
        },
        {
          "term": {
            "attendees": "andy"
          }
        }
      ],
      "must_not": [
        {
          "range" :{
            "date": {
              "lt": "2013-06-30T00:00"
            }
          }
        }
      ],
      "minimum_should_match": 1
    }
  }
}'
{
    "_shards": {
        "failed": 0,
        "successful": 2,
        "total": 2
    },
"max_score": 0.56109595,
    "total": 1,
    "hits": {
        "hits": [
            {
                "_id": "110",
                "_index": "get-together",
                "_score": 0.56109595,
  "_type": "event",
                "_source": {
                    "attendees": [
```

Query that must match resulting documents

First query that should match documents

Second query that should match documents

Query that must not match resulting documents

Minimum number of should clauses that have to match a document to return it as a result

```
                                  "Andy",
                                  "Michael",
                                  "Ben",
                                  "David"
                            ],
                            "date": "2013-07-31T18:00",
                            "description": "Discussion about the Microsoft
                             Azure cloud and HDInsight.",
                            "host": "Andy",
                            "location": {
                                "geolocation": "40.018528,-105.275806",
                                "name": "Bing Boulder office"
                            },
                            "title": "Big Data and the cloud at Microsoft"
                     }
                 }
            ],
        },
        "timed_out": false,
        "took": 67
}
```

4.3.2   *bool filter*

The filter version of the `bool` query acts almost exactly like the query version, but instead of combining queries, it combines filters. The filter equivalent of the previous example is shown in the following listing.

Listing 4.21   Combining filters with the `bool` filter

```
% curl 'localhost:9200/get-together/_search' -d'
{
  "query": {
    "filtered": {
      "query": {
        "match_all": {}
      },
      "filter": {
        "bool": {
          "must": [
            {
              "term": {
                "attendees": "david"
              }
            }
          ],
          "should": [
            {
              "term": {
                "attendees": "clint"
              }
            },
            {
              "term": {
                "attendees": "andy"
```

```
            }
          }
        ],
        "must_not": [
          {
            "range" :{
              "date": {
                "lt": "2013-06-30T00:00"
              }
            }
          }
        ]
      }
    }
  }
}'
```

As you saw in the `bool` query (listing 4.20), the `minimum_should_match` setting of the query version lets you specify the minimum number of `should` clauses that have to match for a result to be returned. In listing 4.21, the default value of 1 is used; the `bool` filter does not support this property.

IMPROVING THE BOOL QUERY

The provided `bool` query is slightly contrived, but it includes all three of the `bool` query options: `must`, `should`, and `must_not`. You could rewrite this bool query in a better form like this:

```
% curl 'localhost:9200/get-together/_search' -d'
{
  "query": {
    "bool": {
      "must": [
        {
          "term": {
            "attendees": "david"
          }
        },
        {
          "range" :{
            "date": {
              "gte": "2013-06-30T00:00"        ◁─── gte stands for
            }                                        greater than or
          }                                          equal to.
        },
        {
          "terms": {
            "attendees": ["clint", "andy"]
          }
        }
      ]
    }
  }
}'... same results as the previous query ...
```

Note that this query is smaller than the previous query. By inverting the `range` query from `lt` (less than) to `gte` (greater than or equal to), you can move it from the `must_not` section to the `must` section. You can also collapse the two separate `should` queries into a single `terms` query instead of two `term` queries. Now you can replace the `minimum_should_match` of 1 and the `should` clause by moving the `terms` query into the `must` clause as well. Elasticsearch has a flexible query language, so don't be afraid to experiment with how queries are formed as you're sending them to Elasticsearch!

With the `bool` query and filter under your belt, you can combine any number of queries and filters. We can now return to the other types of queries that Elasticsearch supports. You already know about the `term` query, but what if you want Elasticsearch to analyze the data you're sending it? The `match` query is exactly what you need.

> **NOTE** The option `minimum_should_match` has some hidden features for default values. If you specify a `must` clause, the `minimum_should_match` has a default value of 0. If there's no `must` clause, the default value is 1.

4.4 Beyond match and filter queries

General-purpose queries that we've discussed so far, such as the `query_string` and the `match` queries, are particularly useful when the user is faced with a search box because you can run such a query with the words the user types in.

To narrow the scope of a search, some user interfaces also include other elements next to the search box, such as a calendar widget that allows you to search for newly created groups or a check box for filtering events that have a location already established.

4.4.1 Range query and filter

The `range` query and filter are self-explanatory; they're used to query for values between a certain range and can be used for numbers, dates, and even strings.

To use the `range` query, you specify the top and bottom values for a field. For example, to search for all groups created after June 1 and before September 1, 2012 in the index, use the following query:

```
% curl 'localhost:9200/get-together/_search' -d '
{
  "query": {
    "range": {
      "created_on": {
        "gt": "2012-06-01",          Specifies a date range
        "lt": "2012-09-01"           using gt (greater than)
      }                              and lt (less than)
    }
  }
}'
```

Or you could use a filter instead:

```
% curl 'localhost:9200/get-together/_search' -d '
{
  "query": {
    "filtered": {
      "query": {
        "match_all": {}
      },
      "filter": {
        "range": {
          "created_on": {
            "gt": "2012-06-01",
            "lt": "2012-09-01"
          }
        }
      }
    }
  }
}'
```

By using match_all, you
could leave out the query
part; this is the default.

Searches for a
created_on date
after June 1...

... as well as a
created_on date
before September 1

See table 4.2 for the meaning of the parameters gt, gte, lt, and lte.

Table 4.2   Range query parameters

Parameter	Meaning
gt	Search for fields greater than the value, not including the value.
gte	Search for fields greater than the value, including the value.
lt	Search for fields less than the value, not including the value.
lte	Search for fields less than the value, including the value.

The range query also supports ranges of strings, so if you wanted to search for all the groups in get-togethers between "c" and "e", you could search using the following:

```
% curl 'localhost:9200/get-together/_search' -d '
{
  "query": {
    "range": {
      "name": {
        "gt": "c",
        "lt": "e"
      }
    }
  }
}'
```

When you use the range query, think long and hard about whether a filter would be a better choice. Because documents that fall into the range of the query have a binary match ("Yes, this document is in the range" or "No, this document isn't in the range"), the range query doesn't need to be a query. For better performance, it should be a filter. If you're unsure whether to make it a query or a filter, make it a filter. In 99% of cases, making a `range` query a filter is the right thing to do.

4.4.2 *Prefix query and filter*

Similar to the `term` query, the `prefix` query and filter allow you to search for a term containing the given prefix, where the prefix isn't analyzed before searching. For example, to search the index for all events that start with "liber," the following query is used:

```
% curl 'localhost:9200/get-together/event/_search' -d '
{
  "query": {
    "prefix": {
      "title": "liber"
    }
  }
}'
```

And, similarly, you can use a filter instead of a regular query, which has almost the same syntax:

```
% curl 'localhost:9200/get-together/event/_search' -d '
{
  "query": {
    "filtered": {
      "query": {
        "match_all": {}
      },
      "filter": {
        "prefix": {
          "title": "liber"
        }
      }
    }
  }
}'
```

But wait! What happens if you were to send the same request but with "Liber" instead of "liber"? Because the search prefix isn't analyzed before being sent, it won't find the terms that have been lowercased in the index. This is because of the way Elasticsearch analyzes documents and queries, which we cover in much more depth in chapter 5. Because of this behavior, the `prefix` query is a good choice for autocompletion of a partial term that a user enters if the term is part of the index. For example, you could provide a categories input box when existing categories are already known. If a user was typing terms that were part of an index, you could take the text entered into a search box by the user, lowercase it, and then use a `prefix` query to see what other results show up. Once you have matching results from a prefix query, you can offer them as suggestions while the user is typing. But if you need to analyze the term or want an amount of fuzziness in the results, it's probably better to stick with the `match_phrase_prefix` query for autocomplete functionality. We'll talk more about suggestions and suggesters in appendix F.

4.4.3   *Wildcard query*

You may be tempted to think of the `wildcard` query as a way to search with regular expressions, but in truth, the `wildcard` query is closer to the way shell wildcard *globbing* works; for example, running

```
ls *foo?ar
```

matches words such as "myfoobar," "foocar," and "thefoodar."

Using a string, you can allow Elasticsearch to substitute either any number of characters (including none of them) for the * wildcard or a single character for the ? wildcard.

For example, a query for "ba*n" would match "bacon," "barn," "ban," and "baboon" because the * can be any character sequence, whereas a query for "ba?n" would match only "barn" because ? must match a single character at all times. Listing 4.22 demonstrates these `wildcard` queries using a new index called wildcard-test.

You can also mix and match with multiple * and ? characters to match a more complex wildcard pattern, but keep in mind that when a string is analyzed, spaces are stripped out by default, so ? can't match a space if spaces aren't indexed.

Listing 4.22   Example `wildcard` query

```
% curl -XPOST 'localhost:9200/wildcard-test/doc/1' -d '
{"title":"The Best Bacon Ever"}'
% curl -XPOST 'localhost:9200/wildcard-test/doc/2' -d'
{"title":"How to raise a barn"}'

% curl 'localhost:9200/wildcard-test/_search' -d'
{
  "query": {
    "wildcard": {
      "title": {
        "wildcard": "ba*n"          ⟵  "ba*n" matches both
      }                                 bacon and barn.
    }
  }
}'
{
  ...
    "hits" : [ {
      "_index" : "wildcard-test",
      "_type" : "doc",
      "_id" : "1",
      "_score" : 1.0, "_source" : {"title":"The Best Bacon Ever"}
    }, {
```

```
      "_index" : "wildcard-test",
      "_type" : "doc",
      "_id" : "2",
      "_score" : 1.0, "_source" : {"title":"How to raise a barn"}
  } ]
  ...
}

% curl 'localhost:9200/wildcard-test/_search' -d '
{
  "query": {
    "wildcard": {
      "title": {                          ┌─ "ba?n" matches only
        "wildcard": "ba?n"                 │  barn, not bacon.
      }                              ◁─────┘
    }
  }
}'
{
    ...
    "hits" : [ {
      "_index" : "wildcard-test",
      "_type" : "doc",
      "_id" : "2",
      "_score" : 1.0, "_source" : {"title":"How to raise a barn"}
    } ]
    ...
}
```

Something to note when using this query is that the `wildcard` query isn't as light-weight as other queries like the `match` query; the sooner a wildcard character (`*` or `?`) occurs in the query term, the more work Lucene and Elasticsearch have to do to match it. Take, for example, the search term "h*"; Elasticsearch must now match every term starting with "h". If the term was "hi*", Elasticsearch would only have to search through every term starting with "hi", which is a smaller subset of all terms starting with "h". Because of this overhead and performance considerations, be careful to test the `wildcard` query on a copy of your data before putting these queries into production! We'll talk more about a similar query, the `regexp` query, in chapter 6, where we discuss searching with relevancy.

4.5 Querying for field existence with filters

Sometimes when querying Elasticsearch, it can be helpful to search for all the documents that don't have a field or are missing a value in the field. In the get-together index, for example, you might want to search for all groups that don't have a review. On the other hand, you may also want to search for all the documents that have a field, regardless of what the content of the field is. This is where the `exists` and `missing` filters come in, both of which act only as filters, not as regular queries.

4.5.1   *Exists filter*

As the name suggests, the `exists` filter allows you to filter any query to documents that have a value in a particular field, whatever that value may be. Here's what the exists filter looks like:

```
% curl 'localhost:9200/get-together/_search' -d '
{
  "query": {
    "filtered": {
      "query": {
        "match_all": {}
      },
      "filter": {
        "exists": { "field": "location.geolocation" }
      }
    }
  }
}'
... only documents with the location.geolocation field are returned ...
```

On the opposite side, you can use the `missing` filter.

4.5.2   *Missing filter*

The `missing` filter allows you to search for documents that have no value or where the value is a default value (also called the null value, or `null_value` in the mapping) that was specified during the mapping. To search for documents that are missing the reviews field, you'd use a filter like this:

```
% curl 'localhost:9200/get-together/_search' -d '
{
  "query": {
    "filtered": {
      "query": {
        "match_all": {}
      },
      "filter": {
        "missing": {                          Finds documents
          "field": "reviews",          ◁──── missing the reviews
          "existence": true,                  field entirely
          "null_value": true
        }
      }
    }
  }
}'
```

If you wanted to expand that filter to also match documents that are missing the field entirely and that might have the `null_value` field, you can specify a Boolean value for the `existence` and `null_value` fields. The response includes documents that have `null_value` set in the field, as shown in the next listing.

Listing 4.23 Specify `existence` and `null_value` fields as Boolean values

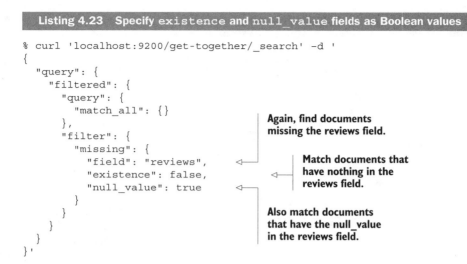

```
% curl 'localhost:9200/get-together/_search' -d '
{
  "query": {
    "filtered": {
      "query": {
        "match_all": {}
      },
      "filter": {
        "missing": {
          "field": "reviews",
          "existence": false,
          "null_value": true
        }
      }
    }
  }
}'
```

Again, find documents missing the reviews field.

Match documents that have nothing in the reviews field.

Also match documents that have the null_value in the reviews field.

Both the `missing` and `exists` filters are cached by default.

4.5.3 Transforming any query into a filter

So far, we've talked about the different types of queries and filters that Elasticsearch supports, but we've been limited to using only the filters that are already provided. Sometimes you may want to take a query such as `query_string`, which has no filter equivalent, and turn it into a filter. You rarely need this, but if you need full-text search within the filter context, you can use this. Elasticsearch allows you to do this with the `query` filter, which takes any query and turns it into a filter.

To transform a `query_string` query that searches for a name matching "denver clojure" to a filter, you'd use a search like this:

```
% curl 'localhost:9200/get-together/_search' -d '
{
  "query": {
    "filtered": {
      "query": {
        "match_all": {}
      },
      "filter": {
        "query" : {
          "query_string" : {
            "query" : "name:\"denver clojure\""
          }
        }
      }
    }
  }
}'
```

Using the query filter to wrap a query that doesn't have a filter equivalent

Using this, you can get some of the benefits of a filter (such as not having to calculate a score for that part of the query). You can also choose to cache this filter if it turns out to be used many times; the syntax for caching looks slightly different than adding the _cache key, as shown in the next listing.

Listing 4.24   Caching query filter

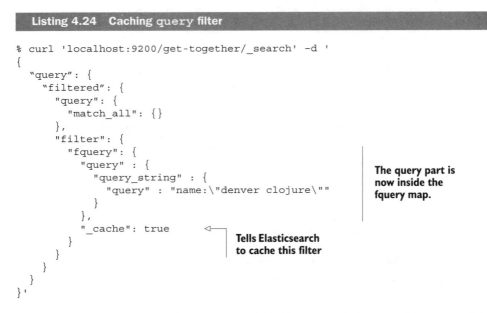

```
% curl 'localhost:9200/get-together/_search' -d '
{
  "query": {
    "filtered": {
      "query": {
        "match_all": {}
      },
      "filter": {
        "fquery": {
          "query" : {
            "query_string" : {
              "query" : "name:\"denver clojure\""
            }
          }
        },
        "_cache": true
      }
    }
  }
}'
```

The query part is now inside the fquery map.

Tells Elasticsearch to cache this filter

The query part of the query has moved inside a new key named fquery, which is where the _cache key now resides. If you find yourself often using a particular query that doesn't have a filter equivalent (like one of the match queries or a query_string query), you may want to cache it, assuming the score for that particular part of the query isn't important.

4.6   *Choosing the best query for the job*

Now that we've covered some of the most popular Elasticsearch queries, let's look at how to decide which queries to use and when. Although there's no hard-and-fast rule for which query to use for what, table 4.3 helps you determine which query to use for the general case.

Table 4.3   Which type of query to use for general use cases

Use case	Query type to use
You want to take input from a user, similar to a Google-style interface, and search for documents with the input.	Use a match query or the simple_query_string query if you want to support +/- and search in specific fields.
You want to take input as a phrase and search for documents containing that phrase, perhaps with some amount of leniency (slop).	Use a match_phrase query with an amount of slop to find phrases similar to what the user is searching for.

Table 4.3 Which type of query to use for general use cases

Use case	Query type to use
You want to search for a single word in a `not_analyzed` field, knowing exactly how the word should appear.	Use a `term` query because query terms aren't analyzed.
You want to combine many different searches or types of searches, creating a single search out of them.	Use the `bool` query to combine any number of sub-queries into a single query.
You want to search for certain words across many fields in a document.	Use the `multi_match` query, which behaves similarly to the `match` query but on multiple fields.
You want to return every document from a search.	Use the `match_all` query to return all documents from a search.
You want to search a field for values that are between two specified values.	Use a `range` query to search within documents with values between a certain range.
You want to search a field for values that start with a specified string.	Use a `prefix` query to search for terms starting with a given string.
You want to autocomplete the value of a single word based on what the user has already typed in.	Use a `prefix` query to send what the user has typed in and get back exact matches starting with the text.
You want to search for all documents that have no value for a specified field.	Use the `missing` filter to filter out documents that are missing fields.

4.7   Summary

Filters can speed up queries by skipping over the scoring calculations and by caching. In this chapter you learned the following:

- Human-language type queries, such as the `match` and `query_string` queries, are suitable for search boxes.
- The `match` query is the go-to query for full-text search, but the `query_string` query is both more flexible and more complex because it exposes the full Lucene query syntax.
- The `match` query has multiple subtypes: `boolean`, `phrase`, and `phrase_prefix`. The main difference is that `boolean` matches individual words, whereas the `phrase` types take the order of words into account, as if they were in a phrase.
- Specialized queries such as the `prefix` and `wildcard` queries are also supported.
- To filter documents where a field doesn't exist, use the `missing` filter.
- The `exists` filter does the exact opposite; it returns only documents having the specified field value.

Other types of queries are available that allow you to tune your relevance. We'll discuss them in chapter 6. Matching results and their relevance is heavily influenced by how the text is analyzed. Chapter 5 covers the details of analysis.

Analyzing your data 5

So far we've covered indexing and searching your data, but what actually happens when you send data to Elasticsearch? What happens to the text sent in a document to Elasticsearch? How can Elasticsearch find specific words within sentences, even when the case changes? For example, when a user searches for "nosql," generally you'd like a document containing the sentence "share your experience with NoSql & big data technologies" to match, because it contains the word *NoSql*. You can use the information you learned in the previous chapter to do a `query_string` search for "nosql" and find the document. In this chapter you'll learn why using the `query string` query will return the document. Once you finish this chapter you'll have a better idea how Elasticsearch's analysis allows you to search your document set in a more flexible manner.

5.1   What is analysis?

Analysis is the process Elasticsearch performs on the body of a document before the document is sent off to be added to the inverted index. Elasticsearch goes through a number of steps for every analyzed field before the document is added to the index:

- *Character filtering*—Transforms the characters using a character filter
- *Breaking text into tokens*—Breaks the text into a set of one or more tokens
- *Token filtering*—Transforms each token using a *token* filter
- *Token indexing*—Stores those tokens into the index

We'll talk about each step in more detail next, but first let's look at the entire process summed up in a diagram. Figure 5.1 shows the text "share your experience with NoSql & big data technologies" transformed into the analyzed tokens: share, your, experience, with, nosql, big, data, tools, and technologies. The presented analyzer

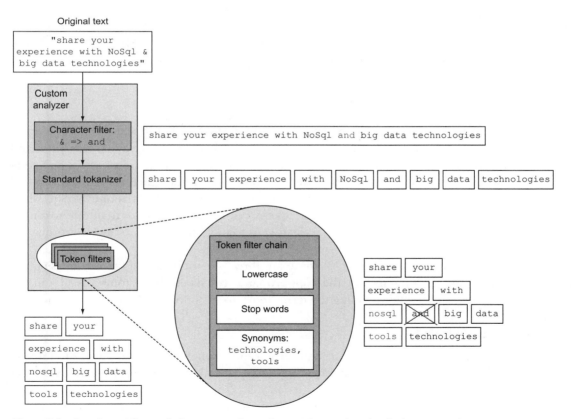

Figure 5.1   Overview of the analysis process of a custom analyzer using standard components

is a custom analyzer created using provided character filters, tokenizers, and token filters. Later in this chapter we discuss the custom analyzer in more depth.

5.1.1   Character filtering

As you can see in the upper left of the figure, Elasticsearch first runs the character filters; these filters are used to transform particular character sequences into other character sequences. This can be used for things like stripping HTML out of text or converting an arbitrary number of characters into other characters (perhaps correcting the text-message shortening of "I love u 2" into "I love you too"). In figure 5.1 we use the character filter to replace "&" with the word "and."

5.1.2   Breaking into tokens

After the text has had the character filters applied, it needs to be split into pieces that can be operated on. Lucene itself doesn't act on large strings of data; instead, it acts on what are known as *tokens*. Tokens are generated out of a piece of text, which results in any number (even zero!) of tokens. In English, for example, a common tokenization that can be used is the standard tokenizer, which splits text into tokens, based on whitespace like spaces and newlines, but also on some characters like the dash. In figure 5.1 this is represented by breaking the string "share your experience with NoSql and big data technologies" into the tokens share, your, experience, with, NoSql, and, big, data, and technologies.

5.1.3   Token filtering

Once the block of text has been converted into tokens, Elasticsearch will then apply what are called *token filters* to each token. These token filters take a token as input and can modify, add, or remove more tokens as needed. One of the most useful and common examples of a token filter is the lowercase token filter, which takes in a token and lowercases it to ensure that you will be able to find a get-together about "NoSql" when searching for the term "nosql." The tokens can go through more than one token filter, each doing different things to the tokens to mold the data into the best format for your index.

In the example in figure 5.1 there are three token filters: the first lowercasing the tokens, the second removing the stopword "and" (we'll talk about stopwords later in this chapter), and the third adding the term "tools" to "technologies," using synonyms.

5.1.4   Token indexing

After the tokens have gone through zero or more token filters, they're sent to Lucene to be indexed for the document. These tokens make up the inverted index we discussed back in chapter 1.

Together, these different parts make up an *analyzer*, which can also be defined as zero or more character filters, a tokenizer, and zero or more token filters. There are some prebuilt analyzers we'll talk about later on in this chapter that you can use without having to construct your own, but first we'll talk about the individual components of an analyzer.

Analysis while executing a search

Depending on what kind of query you use, this analysis can also be applied to the search text before the search is performed against the index. In particular, queries such as the `match` and `match_phrase` queries perform analysis before searching, and queries like the `term` and `terms` query do not. It's important to keep this in mind when debugging why a particular search matches or doesn't match a document—it might be analyzed differently than what you expect! There's even a configuration option to configure a different analyzer for the searched text than for the indexed text. More on this when we discuss the ngram analyzer. Check section 4.2.1 for more details on the match and term queries.

Now that you have an understanding of what goes on during Elasticsearch's analysis phase, let's talk about how analyzers are specified for fields in your mapping and how custom analyzers are specified.

5.2   *Using analyzers for your documents*

Knowing about the different types of analyzers and token filters is fine, but before they can actually be used, Elasticsearch needs to know how you want to use them. For instance, you can specify in the mapping which individual tokenizer and token filters to use for an analyzer and which analyzer to use for which field.

There are two ways to specify analyzers that can be used by your fields:

- When the index is created, as settings for that particular index
- As global analyzers in the configuration file for Elasticsearch

Generally, to be more flexible, it's easier to specify analyzers at the index-creation time, which is also when you want to specify your mappings. This allows you to create new indices with updated or entirely different analyzers. On the other hand, if you find yourself using the same set of analyzers across your indices without changing them very often, you can also save some bandwidth by putting the analyzers into the configuration file. Examine how you're using Elasticsearch and pick the option that works best for you. You could even combine the two and put the analyzers that are used by all of your indices into the configuration file and specify additional analyzers for added stability when you create indices.

Regardless of the way you specify your custom analyzers, you'll need to specify which field uses which analyzer in the mapping of your index, either by specifying the mapping when the index is created or using the "put mapping API" to specify it at a later time.

5.2.1 *Adding analyzers when an index is created*

In chapter 3 you saw some of the settings when an index is created, notably settings for the number of primary and replica shards for an index, which look something like the following listing.

Listing 5.1   Setting the number of primary and replica shards

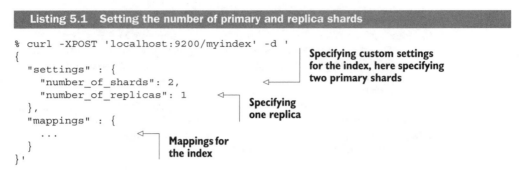

```
% curl -XPOST 'localhost:9200/myindex' -d '
{
  "settings" : {
    "number_of_shards": 2,
    "number_of_replicas": 1
  },
  "mappings" : {
    ...
  }
}'
```

Specifying custom settings for the index, here specifying two primary shards

Specifying one replica

Mappings for the index

Adding a custom analyzer is done by specifying another map in the settings configuration under the index key. This key should specify the custom analyzer you want to use, and it can also contain the custom tokenizer, token filters, and char filters that the index can use. The next listing shows a custom analyzer that specifies custom parts for all the analysis steps. This is a complex example, so we've added some headings to show the different parts. Don't worry about all the code details yet because we'll go through them later on in this chapter.

Listing 5.2   Adding a custom analyzer during index creation

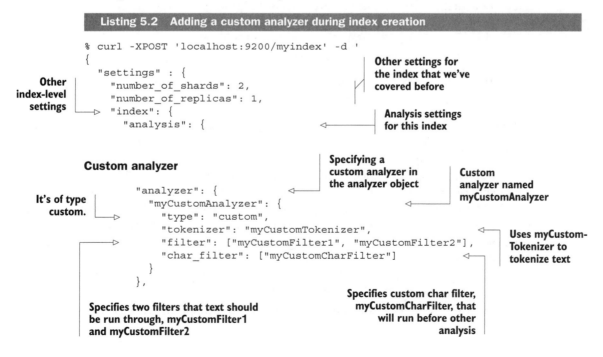

```
% curl -XPOST 'localhost:9200/myindex' -d '
{
  "settings" : {
    "number_of_shards": 2,
    "number_of_replicas": 1,
    "index": {
      "analysis": {
```

Other index-level settings

Other settings for the index that we've covered before

Analysis settings for this index

Custom analyzer

It's of type custom.

```
      "analyzer": {
        "myCustomAnalyzer": {
          "type": "custom",
          "tokenizer": "myCustomTokenizer",
          "filter": ["myCustomFilter1", "myCustomFilter2"],
          "char_filter": ["myCustomCharFilter"]
        }
      },
```

Specifying a custom analyzer in the analyzer object

Custom analyzer named myCustomAnalyzer

Uses myCustom-Tokenizer to tokenize text

Specifies two filters that text should be run through, myCustomFilter1 and myCustomFilter2

Specifies custom char filter, myCustomCharFilter, that will run before other analysis

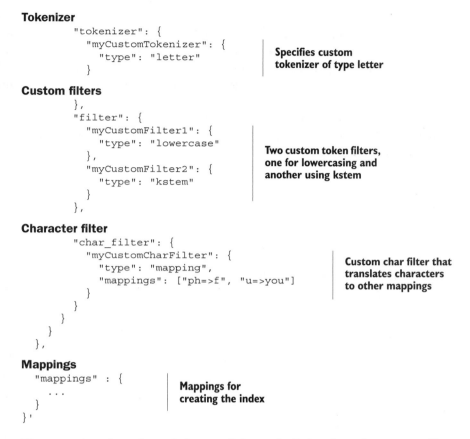

Tokenizer

```
"tokenizer": {
  "myCustomTokenizer": {
    "type": "letter"
  }
}
```
Specifies custom tokenizer of type letter

Custom filters

```
},
"filter": {
  "myCustomFilter1": {
    "type": "lowercase"
  },
  "myCustomFilter2": {
    "type": "kstem"
  }
},
```
Two custom token filters, one for lowercasing and another using kstem

Character filter

```
"char_filter": {
  "myCustomCharFilter": {
    "type": "mapping",
    "mappings": ["ph=>f", "u=>you"]
  }
    }
   }
  }
 },
```
Custom char filter that translates characters to other mappings

Mappings

```
"mappings" : {
  ...
  }
}'
```
Mappings for creating the index

The mappings have been left out of the code listing here because we'll cover how to specify the analyzer for a field in section 5.2.3. In this example you create a custom analyzer called myCustomAnalyzer, which uses the custom tokenizer myCustomTokenizer, two custom filters named myCustomFilter1 and myCustomFilter2, and a custom character filter named myCustomCharFilter (notice a trend here?). Each of these separate analysis parts is given in its respective JSON submaps. You can specify multiple analyzers with different names and combine them into custom analyzers to give you flexible analysis options when indexing and searching.

Now that you have a sense of what adding custom analyzers looks like when an index is created, let's look at the same analyzers added to the Elasticsearch configuration itself.

5.2.2 Adding analyzers to the Elasticsearch configuration

In addition to specifying analyzers with settings during index creation, adding analyzers into the Elasticsearch configuration file is another supported way to specify custom analyzers. But there are tradeoffs to this method; if you specify the analyzers during index creation, you'll always be able to make changes to the analyzers without restarting Elasticsearch. But if you specify the analyzers in the Elasticsearch configuration, you'll need to restart Elasticsearch to pick up any changes you make to the analyzers. On the flip side, you'll have less data to send when creating indices. Although it's generally easier to specify them at index creation for a larger degree of flexibility, if you plan to never change your analyzers, you can go ahead and put them into the configuration file.

Specifying analyzers in the elasticsearch.yml configuration file is similar to specifying them as JSON; here are the same custom analyzers from the previous section but specified in the configuration YAML file:

```
index:
  analysis:
    analyzer:
      myCustomAnalyzer:
        type: custom
        tokenizer: myCustomTokenizer
        filter: [myCustomFilter1, myCustomFilter2]
        char_filter: myCustomCharFilter
    tokenizer:
      myCustomTokenizer:
        type: letter
    filter:
      myCustomFilter1:
        type: lowercase
      myCustomFilter2:
        type: kstem
    char_filter:
      myCustomCharFilter:
        type: mapping
        mappings: ["ph=>f", "u =>you"]
```

5.2.3   *Specifying the analyzer for a field in the mapping*

There's one piece of the puzzle left to solve before you can analyze fields with custom analyzers: how to specify that a particular field in the mapping should be analyzed using one of your custom analyzers. It's simple to specify the analyzer for a field by setting the analyzer field on a mapping. For instance, if you had the mapping for a field called description, specifying the analyzer would look like this:

```
{
  "mappings" : {
    "document" : {
      "properties" : {
        "description" : {
          "type" : "string",
          "analyzer" : "myCustomAnalyzer"     ⊲──  Specifying the analyzer
        }                                           myCustomAnalyzer for
      }                                             the description field
    }
  }
}
```

If you want a particular field to not be analyzed at all, you need to specify the `index` field with the `not_analyzed` setting. This keeps the text as a single token without any kind of modification (no lowercasing or anything). It looks something like this:

```
{
  "mappings" : {
    "document" : {
      "properties" : {
        "name" : {
          "type" : "string",
          "index" : "not_analyzed"      ⟵  Specifying that the
        }                                   name field is not
      }                                     to be analyzed
    }
  }
}
```

A common pattern for fields where you may want to search on both the analyzed and verbatim text of a field is to place them in multi-fields.

USING MULTI-FIELD TYPE TO STORE DIFFERENTLY ANALYZED TEXT

Often it's helpful to be able to search on both the analyzed version of a field as well as the original, non-analyzed text. This is especially useful for things like aggregations or sorting on a string field. Elasticsearch makes this simple to do by using multi-fields, which you first saw in chapter 3. Take the `name` field of groups in the get-together index, for example; you may want to be able to sort on the `name` field but search through it using analysis. You can specify a field that does both like this:

```
% curl -XPOST 'localhost:9200/get-together' -d '

{
    "mappings": {
        "group": {
            "properties": {
                "name": {
                    "type": "string",
                    "analyzer": "standard",      ⟵  The original analysis,
                    "fields": {                     using the standard
                        "raw": {                    analyzer, can be left out
                            "index": "not_analyzed",   and is the default.
                            "type": "string"    ⟵  A raw version of the
                        }                           field, which isn't
                    }                               analyzed
                }
            }
        }
    }
}'
```

We've covered how to specify analyzers; now we'll show you a neat way to check how any arbitrary text can be analyzed: the analyze API.

5.3   *Analyzing text with the analyze API*

Using the analyze API to test the analysis process can be extremely helpful when tracking down how information is being stored in your Elasticsearch indices. This API allows you to send any text to Elasticsearch, specifying what analyzer, tokenizer, or token filters to use, and get back the analyzed tokens. The following listing shows an example of what the analyze API looks like, using the standard analyzer to analyze the text "share your experience with NoSql & big data technologies."

Listing 5.3   Example of using the analyze API

```
% curl -XPOST 'localhost:9200/_analyze?analyzer=standard' -d 'share your
experience with NoSql & big data technologies'
"tokens" : [ {
    "token" : "share",
    "start_offset" : 0,
    "end_offset" : 5,
    "type" : "<ALPHANUM>",
    "position" : 1
}, {
    "token" : "your",
    "start_offset" : 6,
    "end_offset" : 10,
    "type" : "<ALPHANUM>",
    "position" : 2
}, {
    "token" : "experience",
    "start_offset" : 11,
    "end_offset" : 21,
    "type" : "<ALPHANUM>",
    "position" : 3
}, {
    "token" : "with",
    "start_offset" : 22,
    "end_offset" : 26,
    "type" : "<ALPHANUM>",
    "position" : 4
}, {
    "token" : "nosql",
    "start_offset" : 27,
    "end_offset" : 32,
    "type" : "<ALPHANUM>",
    "position" : 5
}, {
    "token" : "big",
    "start_offset" : 35,
    "end_offset" : 38,
    "type" : "<ALPHANUM>",
    "position" : 6
}, {
    "token" : "data",
    "start_offset" : 39,
    "end_offset" : 43,
```

The analyzed tokens: share, your, experience, with, nosql, big, data, and technologies

```
      "type" : "<ALPHANUM>",
      "position" : 7
    }, {
      "token" : "technologies",          The analyzed
      "start_offset" : 44,                tokens: share, your,
      "end_offset" : 56,           ◁────  experience, with,
      "type" : "<ALPHANUM>",              nosql, big, data,
      "position" : 8                      and technologies
    } ]
}
```

The most important output from the analysis API is the token key. The output is a list of these maps, which gives you a representation of what the processed tokens (the ones that are going to actually be written to the index) look like. For example, with the text "share your experience with NoSql & big data technologies," you get back eight tokens: share, your, experience, with, nosql, big, data, and technologies. Notice that in this case, with the standard analyzer, each token was lowercased and the punctuation at the end of the sentence was removed. This is a great way to test documents to see how Elasticsearch will analyze them, and it has quite a few ways to customize the analysis that's performed on the text.

5.3.1 Selecting an analyzer

If you already have an analyzer in mind and want to see how it handles some text, you can set the analyzer parameter to the name of the analyzer. We'll go over the different built-in analyzers in the next section, so keep this in mind if you want to try out any of them!

  If you configured an analyzer in your elasticsearch.yml file, you can also reference it by name in the analyzer parameter. Additionally, if you've created an index with a custom analyzer similar to the example in listing 5.2, you can still use this analyzer by name, but instead of using the HTTP endpoint of /_search, you'll need to specify the index first. An example using the index named get-together and an analyzer called myCustomAnalyzer is shown here:

```
% curl -XPOST 'localhost:9200/get-together/_analyze?analyzer=myCustomAnalyzer'
-d 'share your experience with NoSql & big data technologies'
```

5.3.2 Combining parts to create an impromptu analyzer

Sometimes you may not want to use a built-in analyzer but instead try out a combination of tokenizers and token filters—for instance, to see how a particular tokenizer breaks up a sentence without any other analysis. With the analysis API you can specify a tokenizer and a list of token filters to be used for analyzing the text. For example, if you wanted to use the whitespace tokenizer (to split the text on spaces) and then use the lowercase and reverse token filters, you could do so as follows:

```
% curl -XPOST 'localhost:9200/
_analyze?tokenizer=whitespace&filters=lowercase,reverse' -d 'share your
experience with NoSql & big data technologies'
```

You'd get back the following tokens:

```
erahs, ruoy, ecneirepxe, htiw, lqson, &, gib, atad, seigolonhcet
```

This tokenizer first tokenized the sentence "share your experience with NoSql & big data technologies" into the tokens share, your, experience, with, NoSql, &, big, data, technologies. Next, it lowercased the tokens, and finally, it reversed each token to get the provided terms.

5.3.3 *Analyzing based on a field's mapping*

One more helpful thing about the analysis API once you start creating mappings for an index is that Elasticsearch allows you to analyze based on a field where the mapping has already been created. If you create a mapping with a field description that looks like this snippet

```
… other mappings …
"description": {
    "type": "string",
    "analyzer": "myCustomAnalyzer"
}
```

you can then use the analyzer associated with the field by specifying the field parameter with the request:

```
% curl -XPOST 'localhost:9200/get-together/_analyze?field=description' -d '
share your experience with NoSql & big data technologies'
```

The custom analyzer will automatically be used because it's the analyzer associated with the description field. Keep in mind that in order to use this, you'll need to specify an index, because Elasticsearch needs to be able to get the mappings for a particular field from an index.

Now that we've covered how to test out different analyzers using cURL, we'll jump into all the different analyzers that Elasticsearch provides for you out of the box. Keep in mind that you can always create your own analyzer by combining the different parts (tokenizers and token filters).

5.3.4 *Learning about indexed terms using the terms vectors API*

When thinking about the right analyzer, the _analyze endpoint of the previous section is a fine method. But if you want to learn more about the terms in a certain document, there's a more effective way than going over all the separate fields. You can use the endpoint _termvector to get more information about all the terms. Using the endpoint you can learn about the terms, how often they occur in the document, the index, and where they occur in the document.

The basic usage of the _termvector endpoint looks like this:

```
% curl 'localhost:9200/get-together/group/1/_termvector?pretty=true'
{
  "_index" : "get-together",
  "_type" : "group",
```

```
                            "_id" : "1",
                            "_version" : 1,
Sum the                     "found" : true,
documents                   "term_vectors" : {
each term in                  "description" : {
this field                      "field_statistics" : {
occurs in.                        "sum_doc_freq" : 197,
                                  "doc_count" : 12,
                                  "sum_ttf" : 209
Number of                       },
documents                       "terms" : {
that contain                      "about" : {
this field                          "term_freq" : 1,
                                    "tokens" : [ {
                                      "position" : 16,
Array                                 "start_offset" : 90,
containing the                        "end_offset" : 95
location(s) that                    } ]
the term can                      },
be found in                       "and" : {
the field                           "term_freq" : 1,
                                    "tokens" : [ {
                                      "position" : 13,
                                      "start_offset" : 75,
                                      "end_offset" : 78
                                    } ]
                                  },
                                  "clojure" : {
                                    "term_freq" : 2,
                                    "tokens" : [ {
                                      "position" : 2,
                                      "start_offset" : 9,
                                      "end_offset" : 16
                                    }, {
                                      "position" : 17,
                                      "start_offset" : 96,
                                      "end_offset" : 103
                                    } ]
                                  },
                          … More terms omitted
                                }
                            }
                        }
```

- The field for which the terms information is returned
- The statistics for the terms in this field
- Sum of all term frequencies in this field; will be more than 0 if a term occurs multiple times in one document.
- Object containing all the terms in the field description
- The term that belongs with the provided data
- The number of times the term occurs in the field

There are some things you can configure, one of them being the term statistics; be aware that this is a heavy operation. The following command shows how to change this request. Now you request the terms statistics as well and mention the fields you want statistics for:

```
% curl 'localhost:9200/get-together/group/1/_termvector?pretty=true' -d '{
    "fields" : ["description","tags"],
    "term_statistics" : true
}'
```

Here's part of the response. Only one term is shown, and the structure is the same as the previous code sample:

```
"about" : {
        "doc_freq" : 2,
        "ttf" : 2,
        "term_freq" : 1,
        "tokens" : [ {
          "position" : 16,
          "start_offset" : 90,
          "end_offset" : 95
        } ]
      }
```

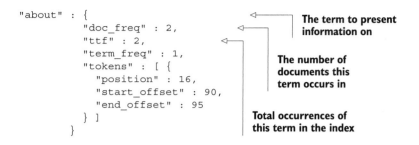

The term to present information on

The number of documents this term occurs in

Total occurrences of this term in the index

By now you've learned a lot about what analyzers do and how you can explore the outcome of analyzers. You'll keep using the _analyze and _termvector APIs when exploring built-in analyzers in the next section.

5.4   Analyzers, tokenizers, and token filters, oh my!

In this section we'll discuss the built-in analyzers, tokenizers, and token filters that Elasticsearch provides. Elasticsearch provides a large number of them, such as lowercasing, stemming, language-specific, synonyms, and so on, so you have a lot of flexibility to combine them in different ways to get your desired tokens.

5.4.1   Built-in analyzers

This section provides a rundown of the analyzers that Elasticsearch comes with out of the box. Remember that an analyzer consists of an optional character filter, a single tokenizer, and zero or more token filters. Figure 5.2 is a visualization of an analyzer.

We'll be referencing tokenizers and token filters, which we'll cover in more detail in the following sections. With each analyzer, we'll include an example of some text that demonstrates what analysis using that analyzer looks like.

STANDARD

The *standard analyzer* is the default analyzer for text when no analyzer is specified. It combines sensible defaults for most European languages by combining the standard tokenizer, the standard token filter, the lowercase token filter, and the stop token filter. There isn't much to say about the standard analyzer. We'll talk about what the standard tokenizer and standard token filter do in sections 5.4.2

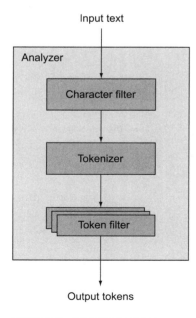

Input text

Analyzer

Character filter

Tokenizer

Token filter

Output tokens

Figure 5.2   Analyzer overview

and 5.4.3; just keep in mind that if you don't specify an analyzer for a field, the standard analyzer will be used.

SIMPLE

The *simple analyzer* is just that—simple! It uses the lowercase tokenizer, which means tokens are split at nonletters and automatically lowercased. This analyzer doesn't work well for Asian languages that don't separate words with whitespace, though, so use it only for European languages.

WHITESPACE

The *whitespace* analyzer does nothing but split text into tokens around whitespace—very simple!

STOP

The *stop* analyzer behaves like the simple analyzer but additionally filters out stopwords from the token stream.

KEYWORD

The *keyword* analyzer takes the entire field and generates a single token on it. Keep in mind that rather than using the keyword tokenizer in your mappings, it's better to set the index setting to not_analyzed.

PATTERN

The *pattern* analyzer allows you to specify a pattern for tokens to be broken apart. But because the pattern would have to be specified regardless, it often makes more sense to use a custom analyzer and combine the existing pattern tokenizer with any needed token filters.

LANGUAGE AND MULTILINGUAL

Elasticsearch supports a wide variety of language-specific analyzers out of the box. There are analyzers for arabic, armenian, basque, brazilian, bulgarian, catalan, chinese, cjk, czech, danish, dutch, english, finnish, french, galician, german, greek, irish, hindi, hungarian, indonesian, italian, norwegian, persian, portuguese, romanian, russian, sorani, spanish, swedish, turkish, and thai. You can specify the language-specific analyzer by using one of those names, but make sure you use the lowercase name! If you want to analyze a language not included in this list, there may be a plugin for it as well.

SNOWBALL

The *snowball* analyzer uses the standard tokenizer and token filter (like the standard analyzer), with the lowercase token filter and the stop filter; it also stems the text using the snowball stemmer. Don't worry if you aren't sure what stemming is; we'll discuss it in more detail near the end of this chapter.

Before you can fully comprehend these analyzers, you need to understand the parts that make up an analyzer, so we'll now discuss the tokenizers that Elasticsearch supports.

5.4.2 *Tokenization*

As you may recall from earlier in the chapter, tokenization is taking a string of text and breaking it into smaller chunks called tokens. Just as Elasticsearch includes analyzers out of the box, it also includes a number of built-in tokenizers.

STANDARD TOKENIZER

The *standard* tokenizer is a grammar-based tokenizer that's good for most European languages; it also handles segmenting Unicode text but with a default max token length of 255. It also removes punctuation like commas and periods:

```
% curl -XPOST 'localhost:9200/_analyze?tokenizer=standard' -d 'I have,
potatoes.'
```

The tokens are I, have, and potatoes.

KEYWORD

Keyword is a simple tokenizer that takes the entire text and provides it as a single token to the token filters. This can be useful when you only want to apply token filters without doing any kind of tokenization:

```
% curl -XPOST 'localhost:9200/_analyze?tokenizer=keyword' -d 'Hi, there.'
```

The tokens are Hi and there.

LETTER

The *letter* tokenizer takes the text and divides it into tokens at things that are not letters. For example, with the sentence "Hi, there." the tokens would be Hi and there because the comma, space, and period are all nonletters:

```
% curl -XPOST 'localhost:9200/_analyze?tokenizer=letter' -d 'Hi, there.'
```

The tokens are Hi and there.

LOWERCASE

The *lowercase* tokenizer combines both the regular letter tokenizer's action as well as the action of the lowercase token filter (which, as you can imagine, lowercases the entire token). The main reason to do this with a single tokenizer is that you gain better performance by doing both at once:

```
% curl -XPOST 'localhost:9200/_analyze?tokenizer=letter' -d 'Hi, there.'
```

The tokens are hi and there.

WHITESPACE

The *whitespace* tokenizer separates tokens by whitespace: space, tab, line break, and so on. Note that this tokenizer doesn't remove any kind of punctuation, so tokenizing the text "Hi, there." results in two tokens: Hi and there:

```
% curl -XPOST 'localhost:9200/_analyze?tokenizer=whitespace' -d 'Hi, there.'
```

The tokens are Hi and there.

PATTERN

The *pattern* tokenizer allows you to specify an arbitrary pattern where text should be split into tokens. The pattern that's specified should match the spacing characters; for example, if you wanted to split text on any two-digit number, you could create a custom analyzer that breaks tokens at wherever the text .-. occurs, which would look like this:

```
% curl -XPOST 'localhost:9200/pattern' -d '{
  "settings": {
    "index": {
      "analysis": {
        "tokenizer": {
          "pattern1": {
            "type": "pattern",
            "pattern": "\\.-\\."
          }
        }
      }
    }
  }
}'
% curl -XPOST 'localhost:9200/pattern/_analyze?tokenizer=pattern1' \
-d 'breaking.-.some.-.text'
```

The tokens are breaking, some, and text.

UAX URL EMAIL

The standard tokenizer is pretty good at figuring out English words, but these days there's quite a bit of text that ends up containing website addresses and email addresses. The standard analyzer breaks these apart in places where you may not intend; for example, if you take the example email address john.smith@example.com and analyze it with the standard tokenizer, it gets split into multiple tokens:

```
% curl -XPOST 'localhost:9200/_analyze?tokenizer=standard' \
-d 'john.smith@example.com'
```

The tokens are john.smith and example.com.

Here you see it's been split into the john.smith part and the example.com part. It also splits URLs into separate parts:

```
% curl -XPOST 'localhost:9200/_analyze?tokenizer=standard' \
-d 'http://example.com?q=foo'
```

The tokens are http, example.com, q, and foo.

The UAX URL email tokenizer will preserve both emails and URLs as single tokens:

```
% curl -XPOST 'localhost:9200/_analyze?tokenizer=uax_url_email' \
-d 'john.smith@example.com http://example.com?q=bar'
{
  "tokens" : [ {
    "token" : "john.smith@example.com",
    "start_offset" : 1,
```

```
    "end_offset" : 23,
    "type" : "<EMAIL>",
    "position" : 1
}, {
    "token" : "http://example.com?q=bar",
    "start_offset" : 24,
    "end_offset" : 48,
    "type" : "<URL>",
    "position" : 2
} ]
}
```

> The output is shown;
> notice the type of
> the fields. There's a
> default maximum of
> 255 chars.

This can be extremely helpful when you want to search for exact URLs or email addresses in a text field. In this case we included the response to make it visible that the type of the fields is also set to email and url.

PATH HIERARCHY

The *path hierarchy* tokenizer allows you to index filesystem paths in a way where searching for files sharing the same path will return results. For example, let's assume you have a filename you want to index that looks like /usr/local/var/log/elasticsearch.log. Here's what the path hierarchy tokenizer tokenizes this into:

```
% curl 'localhost:9200/_analyze?tokenizer=path_hierarchy' \
-d '/usr/local/var/log/elasticsearch.log'
```

The tokens are /usr, /usr/local, /usr/local/var, /usr/local/var/log, and /usr/local/var/log/elasticsearch.log.

This means a user querying for a file sharing the same path hierarchy (hence the name!) as this file will find a match. Querying for "/usr/local/var/log/es.log" will still share the same tokens as "/usr/local/var/log/elasticsearch.log," so it can still be returned as a result.

Now that we've touched on the different ways of splitting a block of text into different tokens, let's talk about what you can do with each of those tokens.

5.4.3 *Token filters*

There are a lot of token filters included in Elasticsearch; we'll cover only the most popular ones in this section because enumerating all of them would make this section much too verbose. Like figure 5.1, figure 5.3 provides an example of three token filters: the lowercase filter, the stopword filter, and the synonym filter.

STANDARD

Don't be fooled into thinking that the *standard* token filter performs complex calculation; it actually does nothing at all! In the older versions of Lucene it used to remove the "'s" characters from the end of words, as well as some extraneous period characters, but these are now handled by some of the other token filters and tokenizers.

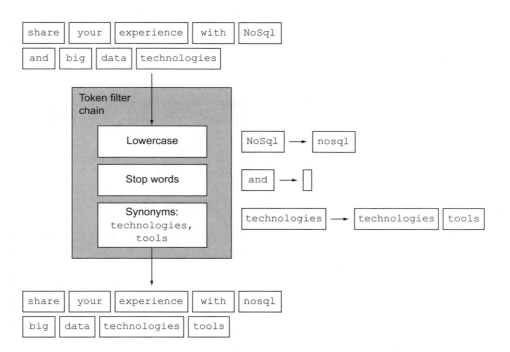

Figure 5.3 Token filters accept tokens from tokenizer and prep data for indexing.

LOWERCASE

The *lowercase* token filter does just that: it lowercases any token that gets passed through it. This should be simple enough to understand:

```
% curl 'localhost:9200/_analyze?tokenizer=keyword&filters=lowercase' -d 'HI
THERE!'
```

The token is hi there!.

LENGTH

The *length* token filter removes words that fall outside a boundary for the minimum and maximum length of the token. For example, if you set the min setting to 2 and the max setting to 8, any token shorter than two characters will be removed and any token longer than eight characters will be removed:

```
% curl -XPUT 'localhost:9200/length' -d '{
  "settings": {
    "index": {
      "analysis": {
        "filter": {
          "my-length-filter": {
            "type": "length",
            "max": 8,
            "min": 2
          }
```

```
          }
        }
      }
    }
  }'
```

Now you have the index with the configured custom filter called `my-length-filter`. In the next request you use this filter to filter out all tokens smaller than 2 or bigger than 8.

```
% curl 'localhost:9200/length/_analyze?tokenizer=standard&filters=my-length-
filter&pretty=true' -d 'a small word and a longerword'
```

The tokens are `small`, `word`, and `and`.

STOP

The *stop* token filter removes stopwords from the token stream. For English, this means all tokens that fall into this list are entirely removed. You can also specify a list of words to be removed for this filter.

What are the stopwords? Here's the default list of stopwords for the English language:

a, an, and, are, as, at, be, but, by, for, if, in, into, is, it, no, not, of, on, or, such, that, the, their, then, there, these, they, this, to, was, will, with

To specify the list of stopwords, you can create a custom token filter with a list of words like this:

```
% curl -XPOST 'localhost:9200/stopwords' -d'{
  "settings": {
    "index": {
      "analysis": {
        "analyzer": {
          "stop1": {
            "type": "custom",
            "tokenizer": "standard",
            "filter": ["my-stop-filter"]
          }
        },
        "filter": {
          "my-stop-filter": {
            "type": "stop",
            "stopwords": ["the", "a", "an"]
          }
        }
      }
    }
  }
}'
```

To read the list of stopwords from a file, using either a path relative to the configuration location or an absolute path, each word should be on a new line and the file must be UTF-8 encoded. You'd use the following to use the stop word filter configured with a file:

```
% curl -XPOST 'localhost:9200/stopwords' -d'{
  "settings": {
    "index": {
      "analysis": {
        "analyzer": {
          "stop1": {
            "type": "custom",
            "tokenizer": "standard",
            "filter": ["my-stop-filter"]
          }
        },
        "filter": {
          "my-stop-filter": {
            "type": "stop",
            "stopwords_path": "config/stopwords.txt"
          }
        }
      }
    }
  }
}'
```

A final option would be to use a predefined language list of stop words. In that case the value for stopwords could be "_dutch_", or any of the other predefined languages.

TRUNCATE, TRIM, AND LIMIT TOKEN COUNT

The next three token filters deal with limiting the token stream in some way:

- The *truncate* token filter allows you to truncate tokens over a certain length by settings the `length` parameter in the custom configuration; by default it truncates to 10 characters.
- The *trim* token filter removes all of the whitespace around a token; for example, the token " foo " will be transformed into the token foo.
- The *limit token count* token filter limits the maximum number of tokens that a particular field can contain. For example, if you create a customized token count filter with a limit of 8, only the first eight tokens from the stream will be indexed. This is set using the `max_token_count` parameter, which defaults to 1 (only a single token will be indexed).

REVERSE

The *reverse* token filter allows you to take a stream of tokens and reverse each one. This is particularly useful if you're using the edge ngram filter or want to do leading wildcard searches. Instead of doing a leading wildcard search for "*bar," which is very slow for Lucene, you can search using "rab*" on a field that has been reversed, resulting in a much faster query. The following listing shows an example of reversing a stream of tokens.

Listing 5.4   Example of the reverse token filter

```
% curl 'localhost:9200/_analyze?tokenizer=standard&filters=reverse' \
-d 'Reverse token filter'
{
  "tokens" : [ {
    "token" : "esreveR",
    "start_offset" : 0,
    "end_offset" : 7,
    "type" : "<ALPHANUM>",
    "position" : 1
  }, {
    "token" : "nekot",
    "start_offset" : 8,
    "end_offset" : 13,
    "type" : "<ALPHANUM>",
    "position" : 2
  }, {
    "token" : "retlif",
    "start_offset" : 14,
    "end_offset" : 20,
    "type" : "<ALPHANUM>",
    "position" : 3
  } ]
}
```

The word "Reverse" that has been reversed

The word "token" that has been reversed

The word "filter" that has been reversed

You can see that each token has been reversed, but the order of the tokens has been preserved.

UNIQUE

The *unique* token filter keeps only unique tokens; it keeps the metadata of the first token that matches, removing all future occurrences of it:

```
% curl 'localhost:9200/_analyze?tokenizer=standard&filters=unique' \
-d 'foo bar foo bar baz'
{
  "tokens" : [ {
    "token" : "foo",
    "start_offset" : 0,
    "end_offset" : 3,
    "type" : "<ALPHANUM>",
    "position" : 1
  }, {
    "token" : "bar",
    "start_offset" : 4,
    "end_offset" : 7,
    "type" : "<ALPHANUM>",
    "position" : 2
  }, {
    "token" : "baz",
    "start_offset" : 16,
    "end_offset" : 19,
    "type" : "<ALPHANUM>",
    "position" : 3
```

```
  } ]
}
```

ASCII FOLDING

The *ascii folding* token filter converts Unicode characters that aren't part of the regular ASCII character set into the ASCII equivalent, if one exists for the character. For example, you can convert the Unicode "ü" into an ASCII "u" as shown here:

```
% curl 'localhost:9200/_analyze?tokenizer=standard&filters=asciifolding' -d
'ünicode'
{
  "tokens" : [ {
    "token" : "unicode",
    "start_offset" : 0,
    "end_offset" : 7,
    "type" : "<ALPHANUM>",
    "position" : 1
  } ]
}
```

SYNONYM

The *synonym* token filter replaces synonyms for words in the token stream at the same offset as the original tokens. For example, let's take the text "I own that automobile" and the synonym for "automobile," "car." Without the synonym token filter you'd produce the following tokens:

```
% curl 'localhost:9200/_analyze?analyzer=standard' -d'I own that automobile'
{
  "tokens" : [ {
    "token" : "i",
    "start_offset" : 0,
    "end_offset" : 1,
    "type" : "<ALPHANUM>",
    "position" : 1
  }, {
    "token" : "own",
    "start_offset" : 2,
    "end_offset" : 5,
    "type" : "<ALPHANUM>",
    "position" : 2
  }, {
    "token" : "that",
    "start_offset" : 6,
    "end_offset" : 10,
    "type" : "<ALPHANUM>",
    "position" : 3
  }, {
    "token" : "automobile",
    "start_offset" : 11,
    "end_offset" : 21,
    "type" : "<ALPHANUM>",
    "position" : 4
  } ]
}
```

You can define a custom analyzer that specifies a synonym for "automobile" like this:

```
% curl -XPOST 'localhost:9200/syn-test' -d'{
  "settings": {
    "index": {
      "analysis": {
        "analyzer": {
          "synonyms": {
            "type": "custom",
            "tokenizer": "standard",
            "filter": ["my-synonym-filter"]
          }
        },
        "filter": {
          "my-synonym-filter": {
            "type": "synonym",
            "expand": true,
            "synonyms": ["automobile=>car"]
          }
        }
      }
    }
  }
}'
```

When you use it, you can see that the automobile token has been replaced by the car token in the results:

```
% curl 'localhost:9200/syn-test/_analyze?analyzer=synonyms' -d'I own that
automobile'
{
  "tokens" : [ {
    "token" : "i",
    "start_offset" : 0,
    "end_offset" : 1,
    "type" : "<ALPHANUM>",
    "position" : 1
  }, {
    "token" : "own",
    "start_offset" : 2,
    "end_offset" : 5,
    "type" : "<ALPHANUM>",
    "position" : 2
  }, {
    "token" : "that",
    "start_offset" : 6,
    "end_offset" : 10,
    "type" : "<ALPHANUM>",
    "position" : 3
  }, {
    "token" : "car",
    "start_offset" : 11,          <─── Notice that the start_offset
    "end_offset" : 21,                 and end_offset are the ones
    "type" : "SYNONYM",                from automobile.
    "position" : 4
```

```
      } ]
    }
```

In the example you configure the synonym filter to replace the token, but it's also possible to add the `synonym` token to the tokens using the filter. In that case you should replace `automobile=>car` with `automobile,car`.

5.5 Ngrams, edge ngrams, and shingles

Ngrams and edge ngrams are two of the more unique ways of tokenizing text in Elasticsearch. Ngrams are a way of splitting a token into multiple subtokens for each part of a word. Both the ngram and edge ngram filters allow you to specify a `min_gram` as well as a `max_gram` setting. These settings control the size of the tokens that the word is being split into. This might be confusing, so let's look at an example. Assuming you want to analyze the word "spaghetti" with the ngram analyzer, let's start with the simplest case, 1-grams (also known as unigrams).

5.5.1 1-grams

The 1-grams for "spaghetti" are `s`, `p`, `a`, `g`, `h`, `e`, `t`, `t`, `i`. The string has been split into smaller tokens according to the size of the ngram. In this case, each item is a single character because we're talking about unigrams.

5.5.2 Bigrams

If you were to split the string into bigrams (which means a size of two), you'd get the following smaller tokens: `sp`, `pa`, `ag`, `gh`, `he`, `et`, `tt`, `ti`.

5.5.3 Trigrams

Again, if you were to use a size of three (which are called trigrams), you'd get the tokens `spa`, `pag`, `agh`, `ghe`, `het`, `ett`, `tti`.

5.5.4 Setting min_gram and max_gram

When using this analyzer, you need to set two different sizes: one specifies the smallest ngrams you want to generate (the `min_gram` setting), and the other specifies the largest ngrams you want to generate. Using the previous example, if you specified a `min_gram` of 2 and a `max_gram` of 3, you'd get the combined tokens from our two previous examples:

```
sp, spa, pa, pag, ag, agh, gh, ghe, he, het, et, ett, tt, tti, ti
```

If you were to set the `min_gram` setting to 1 and leave `max_gram` at 3, you'd get even more tokens, starting with `s`, `sp`, `spa`, `p`, `pa`, `pag`, `a`, ...

Analyzing text in this way has an interesting advantage. When you query for text, your query is going to be split into text the same way, so say you're looking for the incorrectly spelled word "spaghety." One way of searching for this is to do a *fuzzy query*, which allows you to specify an edit distance for words to check matches. But you can get a similar sort of behavior by using ngrams. Let's compare the bigrams generated for the original word ("spaghetti") with the misspelled one ("spaghety"):

- Bigrams for "spaghetti": sp, pa, ag, gh, he, et, tt, ti
- Bigrams for "spaghety": sp, pa, ag, gh, he, et, ty

You can see that six of the tokens overlap, so words with "spaghetti" in them would still be matched when the query contained "spaghety." Keep in mind that this means that more words that you may not intend match the original "spaghetti" word, so always make sure to test your query relevancy!

Another useful thing ngrams do is allow you to analyze text when you don't know the language beforehand or when you have languages that combine words in a different manner than other European languages. This also has an advantage in being able to handle multiple languages with a single analyzer, rather than having to specify different analyzers or using different fields for documents in different languages.

5.5.5   *Edge ngrams*

A variant to the regular ngram splitting called edge ngrams builds up ngrams only from the front edge. In the "spaghetti" example, if you set the `min_gram` setting to 2 and the `max_gram` setting to 6, you'd get the following tokens:

```
sp, spa, spag, spagh, spaghe
```

You can see that each token is built from the edge. This can be helpful for searching for words sharing the same prefix without actually performing a prefix query. If you need to build ngrams from the back of a word, you can use the side property to take the edge from the back instead of the default front.

5.5.6   *Ngram settings*

Ngrams turn out to be a great way to analyze text when you don't know what the language is because they can analyze languages that don't have spaces between words. An example of configuring an edge ngram analyzer with min and max grams would look like the following listing.

Listing 5.5   Ngram analysis

```
% curl -XPOST 'localhost:9200/ng' -d'{
  "settings": {
    "number_of_shards": 1,
    "number_of_replicas": 0,
    "index": {
      "analysis": {
        "analyzer": {
          "ng1": {
            "type": "custom",
            "tokenizer": "standard",
            "filter": ["reverse", "ngf1", "reverse"]    ◁─┐ Configures an
          }                                                │ analyzer for reversing,
        },                                                 │ edge ngrams, and
                                                           │ reversing again
```

```
          "filter": {
            "ngf1": {
              "type": "edgeNgram",        Sets the minimum
              "min_gram": 2,              and maximum sizes
              "max_gram": 6               for the edge ngram
            }                             token filter
          }
        }
      }
    }
  }
}'
% curl -XPOST 'localhost:9200/ng/_analyze?analyzer=ng1' -d'spaghetti'
{
  "tokens" : [ {
    "token" : "ti",                  ◁——
    "start_offset" : 0,
    "end_offset" : 9,
    "type" : "word",
    "position" : 1
  }, {
    "token" : "tti",                 ◁——
    "start_offset" : 0,
    "end_offset" : 9,
    "type" : "word",
    "position" : 1
  }, {                                         The analyzed
    "token" : "etti",                ◁——       tokens from the
    "start_offset" : 0,                         right side of the
    "end_offset" : 9,                           word "spaghetti"
    "type" : "word",
    "position" : 1
  }, {
    "token" : "hetti",               ◁——
    "start_offset" : 0,
    "end_offset" : 9,
    "type" : "word",
    "position" : 1
  }, {
    "token" : "ghetti",              ◁——
    "start_offset" : 0,
    "end_offset" : 9,
    "type" : "word",
    "position" : 1
  } ]
}
```

5.5.7 Shingles

Along the same lines as ngrams and edge ngrams, there is a filter known as the
shingles filter (no, not the disease!). The shingles token filter is basically ngrams at
the token level instead of the character level.

Think of our favorite word, "spaghetti." Using ngrams with a min and max set to 1
and 3, Elasticsearch will generate the tokens s, sp, spa, p, pa, pag, a, ag, and so on. A
shingle filter does this at the token level instead, so if you had the text "foo bar baz"

and used, again, a `min_shingle_size` of 2 and a `max_shingle_size` of 3, you'd generate the following tokens:

```
foo, foo bar, foo bar baz, bar, bar baz, baz
```

Why is the single-token output still included? This is because by default the `shingles` filter includes the original tokens, so the original tokenizer produces the tokens foo, bar, and baz, which are then passed to the `shingles` token filter, which generates the tokens foo bar, foo bar baz, and bar baz. All of these tokens are combined to form the final token stream. You can disable this behavior by setting the `output_unigrams` option to `false`.

The next listing shows an example of a `shingles` token filter; note that the `min_shingle_size` option must be larger than or equal to 2.

Listing 5.6 Shingle token filter example

```
% curl -XPOST 'localhost:9200/shingle' -d '{
  "settings": {
    "index": {
      "analysis": {
        "analyzer": {
          "shingle1": {
            "type": "custom",
            "tokenizer": "standard",
            "filter": ["shingle-filter"]
          }
        },
        "filter": {
          "shingle-filter": {
            "type": "shingle",
            "min_shingle_size": 2,          Specifies the
            "max_shingle_size": 3,          minimum and
            "output_unigrams": false        maximum shingle size
          }                                 Tells the shingle token
        }                                   filter not to keep the
      }                                     original single tokens
    }
  }
}'
% curl -XPOST 'localhost:9200/shingle/_analyze?analyzer=shingle1' -d 'foo bar
    baz'
{
  "tokens" : [ {
    "token" : "foo bar",
    "start_offset" : 0,
    "end_offset" : 7,                       The analyzed
    "type" : "shingle",                     shingle tokens
    "position" : 1
  }, {
    "token" : "foo bar baz",
    "start_offset" : 0,
    "end_offset" : 11,
```

```
        "type" : "shingle",
        "position" : 1
    }, {
        "token" : "bar baz",          ◁─┐   The analyzed
        "start_offset" : 4,             │   shingle tokens
        "end_offset" : 11,              │
        "type" : "shingle",
        "position" : 2
    } ]
}
```

5.6   Stemming

Stemming is the act of reducing a word to its base or root word. This is extremely handy when searching because it means you're able to match things like the plural of a word as well as words sharing the root or stem of the word (hence the name *stemming*). Let's look at a concrete example. If the word is "administrations," the root of the word is "administr." This allows you to match all of the other roots for this word, like "administrator," "administration," and "administrate." Stemming is a powerful way of making your searches more flexible than rigid exact matching.

5.6.1   Algorithmic stemming

Algorithmic stemming is applied by using a formula or set of rules for each token in order to stem it. Elasticsearch currently offers three different algorithmic stemmers: the `snowball` filter, the `porter stem` filter, and the `kstem` filter. They behave in almost the same way but have some slight differences in how aggressive they are with regard to stemming. By *aggressive* we mean that the more aggressive stemmers chop off more of the word than the less aggressive stemmers. Table 5.1 shows a comparison of the different algorithmic stemmers.

Table 5.1   Comparing stemming of `snowball`, `porter stem`, and `kstem`

stemmer	administrations	administrators	Administrate
snowball	administr	administr	Administer
porter_stem	administr	administr	Administer
kstem	administration	administrator	Administrate

To see how a stemmer stems a word, you can specify it as a token filter with the analyze API:

```
curl -XPOST 'localhost:9200/_analyze?tokenizer=standard&filters=kstem' -d
'administrators'
```

Use either `snowball`, `porter_stem`, or `kstem` for the filter to test it out.

As an alternative to algorithmic stemming, you can stem using a dictionary, which is a one-to-one mapping of the original word to its stem.

5.6.2   *Stemming with dictionaries*

Sometimes algorithmic stemmers can stem words in a strange way because they don't know any of the underlying language. Because of this, there's a more accurate way to stem words that uses a dictionary of words. In Elasticsearch you can use the hunspell token filter, combined with a dictionary, to handle the stemming. Because of this, the quality of the stemming is directly related to the quality of the dictionary that you use. The stemmer will only be able to stem words it has in the dictionary.

When creating a hunspell analyzer, the dictionary files should be in a directory called hunspell in the same directory as elasticsearch.yml. Inside the hunspell directory dictionary for each language should be a folder named after its associated locale. Here's how to create an index with a hunspell analyzer:

```
% curl -XPOST 'localhost:9200/hspell' -d'{
    "analysis" : {
        "analyzer" : {
            "hunAnalyzer" : {
                "tokenizer" : "standard",
                "filter" : [ "lowercase", "hunFilter" ]
            }
        },
        "filter" : {
            "hunFilter" : {
                "type" : "hunspell",
                "locale" : "en_US",
                "dedup" : true
            }
        }
    }
}
```

The hunspell dictionary files should be inside <es-config-dir>/hunspell/en_US (replace <es-config-dir> with the location of your Elasticsearch configuration directory). The en_US folder is used because this hunspell analyzer is for the English language and corresponds to the locale setting in the previous example. You can also change where Elasticsearch looks for hunspell dictionaries by setting the indices.analysis .hunspell.dictionary.location setting in elasticsearch.yml. To test that your analyzer is working correctly, you can use the analyze API again:

```
% curl -XPOST 'localhost:9200/hspell/_analyze?analyzer=hunAnalyzer' -
d'administrations'
```

5.6.3   *Overriding the stemming from a token filter*

Sometimes you may not want to have words stemmed because either the stemmer treats them incorrectly or you want to do exact matches on a particular word. You can accomplish this by placing a *keyword marker* token filter before the stemming filter in the chain of token filters. In this keyword marker token filter, you can specify either a list of words or a file with a list of words that shouldn't be stemmed.

Other than preventing a word from being stemmed, it may be useful for you to manually specify a list of rules to be used for stemming words. You can achieve this with the `stemmer override` token filter, which allows you to specify rules like `cats =>` `cat` to be applied. If the `stemmer override` finds a rule and applies it to a word, that word can't be stemmed by any other stemmer.

Keep in mind that both of these token filters must be placed before any other stemming filters because they'll protect the term from having stemming applied by any other token filters later in the chain.

5.7 Summary

You should now understand how Elasticsearch breaks apart a field's text before indexing or querying. Text is broken into different tokens, and then filters are applied to create, delete, or modify these tokens:

- Analysis is the process of making tokens out of the text in fields of your documents. The same process is applied to your search string in queries such as the `match` query. A document matches when its tokens match tokens from the search string.
- Each field is assigned an analyzer through the mapping. That analyzer can be defined in your Elasticsearch configuration or index settings, or it could be a default analyzer.
- Analyzers are processing chains made up by a tokenizer, which can be preceded by one or more char filters and succeeded by one or more token filters.
- Char filters are used to process strings before passing them to the tokenizer. For example, you can use the mapping char filter to change "&" to "and."
- Tokenizers are used for breaking strings into multiple tokens. For example, the whitespace tokenizer can be used to make a token out of each word delimited by a space.
- Token filters are used to process tokens coming from the tokenizer. For example, you can use stemming to reduce a word to its root and make your searches work across both plural and singular versions of that word.
- Ngram token filters make tokens out of portions of words. For example, you can make a token out of every two consecutive letters. This is useful when you want your searches to work even if the search string contains typos.
- Edge ngrams are like ngrams, but they work only from the beginning or the end of the word. For example, you can take "event" and make e, ev, and eve tokens.
- Shingles are like ngrams at the phrase level. For example, you can generate terms out of every two consecutive words from a phrase. This is useful when you want to boost the relevance of multiple-word matches, like in the short description of a product. We'll talk more about relevancy in the next chapter.

Searching with relevancy

6

In the world of free text, being able match a document to a query is a feature touted by many different storage and search engines. What really makes an Elasticsearch query different from doing a `SELECT * FROM users WHERE name LIKE 'bob%'` is the ability to assign a *relevancy*, also known as a *score*, to a document. From this score you know how relevant the document is to the original query.

When users type a query into a search box on a website, they expect to find not only results matching their query but also those results ranked based on how closely they match the query's criteria. As it turns out, Elasticsearch is quite flexible when it comes to determining the relevancy of a document, and there are a lot of ways to customize your searches to provide more relevant results.

Don't fret if you find yourself in a position where you don't particularly care about how well a document matches a query but only that it does or does not match. This chapter also deals with some flexible ways to filter out documents, and it's important to understand the field data cache, which is the in-memory cache where Elasticsearch stores the values of the fields from documents in the index when it comes to sorting, scripting, or aggregating on the values inside these fields.

We'll start the chapter by talking about the scoring Elasticsearch does, as well as an alternative to the default scoring algorithm, move on to affecting the scoring directly using boosting, and then talk about understanding how the score was computed using the explain API. After that we'll cover how to reduce the impact of scoring using query rescoring, extending queries to have ultimate control over the scoring with the function score query, and custom sorting using a script. Finally, we'll talk about the in-memory field data cache, how it affects and impacts your queries, and an alternative to it called doc values.

Before we get to the field data cache, though, let's start at the beginning with how Elasticsearch calculates the score for documents.

6.1 How scoring works in Elasticsearch

Although it may make sense to first think about documents matching queries in a binary sense, meaning either "Yes, it matches" or "No, it doesn't match," it makes much more sense to think about documents matching in a *relevancy* sense. Whereas before you could speak of a document either matching or not matching (the binary method), it's more accurate to be able to say that document A is a better match for a query than document B. For example, when you use your favorite search engine to search for "elasticsearch," it's not enough to say that a particular page contains the term and therefore matches; instead, you want the results to be ranked according to the best and most relevant results.

The process of determining how relevant a document is to a query is called *scoring*, and although it isn't necessary to understand exactly how Elasticsearch calculates the score of a document in order to use Elasticsearch, it's quite useful.

6.1.1 How scoring documents works

Scoring in Lucene (and by extension, Elasticsearch) is a formula that takes the document in question and uses a few different pieces to determine the score for that document. We'll first cover each piece and then combine them in the formula to better explain the overall scoring. As we mentioned previously, we want documents that are more relevant to be returned first, and in Lucene and Elasticsearch this relevancy is called the score.

To begin calculating the score, Elasticsearch uses the frequency of the term being searched for as well as how common the term is to influence the score. A short explanation is that the more times a term occurs in a document, the more relevant it is. But the more times the term appears across all the documents, the less relevant that term is. This is called TF-IDF (TF = term frequency, IDF = inverse document frequency), and we'll talk about each of these types of frequency in more detail now.

6.1.2   *Term frequency*

The first way to think of scoring a document is to look at how often a term occurs in the text. For example, if you were searching for get-togethers in your area that are about Elasticsearch, you would want the groups that mention Elasticsearch more frequently to show up first. Consider the following text snippets, shown in figure 6.1.

> "We will discuss Elasticsearch at the next Big Data group."
>
> "Tuesday the Elasticsearch team will gather to answer questions about Elasticsearch."

Figure 6.1   Term frequency is how many times a term appears in a document.

The first sentence mentions Elasticsearch a single time, and the second mentions Elasticsearch twice, so a document containing the second sentence should have a higher score than a document containing the first. If we were to speak in absolute numbers, the first sentence would have a term frequency (TF) of 1, and the second sentence would have a term frequency of 2.

6.1.3   *Inverse document frequency*

Slightly more complicated than the term frequency for a document is the *inverse document frequency* (IDF). What this fancy-sounding description means is that a token (usually a word, but not always) is less important the more times it occurs across all of the documents in the index. This is easiest to explain with a few examples. Consider the three documents shown in figure 6.2.

> "We use Elasticsearch to power the search for our website."
>
> "The developers like Elasticsearch so far."
>
> "The scoring of documents is calculated by the scoring formula."

Figure 6.2   Inverse document frequency checks to see if a term occurs in a document, not how often it occurs.

In the three documents in the figure, note the following:

- The term "Elasticsearch" has a document frequency of 2 (because it occurs in two documents). The inverse part of the document frequency comes from the score being multiplied by 1/DF, where DF is the document frequency of the term. This means that because the term has a higher document frequency, its weight decreases.
- The term "the" has a document frequency of 3 because it occurs in all three documents. Note that the frequency of "the" is still 3, even though "the" occurs twice in the last document, because the inverse document frequency only checks for a term occurring in the document, not how often it occurs in the document; that's the job of the term frequency!

Inverse document frequency is an important factor in balancing out the frequency of a term. For instance, consider a user who searches for the term "the score"; the word *the* is likely to be in almost all regular English text, so if it were not balanced out, the frequency of it would totally overwhelm the frequency of the word *score*. The IDF balances the relevancy impact of common words like *the*, so the actual relevancy score gives a more accurate sense of the query's terms.

Once the TF and the IDF have been calculated, you're ready to calculate the score of a document using the TF-IDF formula.

6.1.4 *Lucene's scoring formula*

Lucene's default scoring formula, known as TF-IDF, as discussed in the previous section, is based on both the term frequency and the inverse document frequency of a term. First let's look at the formula, shown in figure 6.3, and then we'll tackle each part individually.

$$score_{query,\,document} = \sum_{t}^{q} \sqrt{TF_{t,d}} * IDF_{t,d}^{2} * norm(d,\,field) * boost(t)$$

Figure 6.3   Lucene's scoring formula for a score given a query and document

Reading this in human English, we would say "The score for a given query q and document d is the sum (for each term t in the query) of the square root of the term frequency of the term in document d, times the inverse document frequency of the term squared, times the normalization factor for the field in the document, times the boost for the term."

Whew, that's a mouthful! Don't worry; you don't need to have this formula memorized to use Elasticsearch. We're providing it here so you can understand how the formula is computed. The important part is to understand how the term frequency and the inverse document frequency of a term affect the score of the document and how they're integral in determining the score for a document in an Elasticsearch index.

The higher the term frequency, the higher the score; similarly, the inverse document frequency is higher the rarer a term is in the index. Although we're now finished with TF-IDF, we're not finished with the default scoring function of Lucene. Two things are missing: the coordination factor and the query normalization. The coordination factor takes into account how many documents were searched and how many terms were found. The query norm is an attempt to make the results of queries comparable. It turns out that this is difficult, and in reality you shouldn't compare scores among different queries. This default scoring method is a combination of the TF-IDF and the vector space model.

If you're interested in learning more about this, we recommend checking out the Javadocs for the `org.apache.lucene.search.similarities.TFIDFSimilarity` Java class in the Lucene documentation.

6.2   *Other scoring methods*

Although the practical scoring model from the previous section, a combination of TF-IDF and the vector space model, is arguably the most popular scoring mechanism for Elasticsearch and Lucene, that doesn't mean it's the only model. From now on we'll call the default scoring model TF-IDF, though we mean the practical scoring model based on TF-IDF. Other models include the following:

- Okapi BM25
- Divergence from randomness, or DFR similarity
- Information based, or IB similarity
- LM Dirichlet similarity
- LM Jelinek Mercer similarity

We'll briefly cover one of the most popular alternative options here (BM25) and how to configure Elasticsearch to use it. When we talk about scoring methods, we're talking about changing the similarity module inside Elasticsearch.

Before we talk about the alternate scoring method to TF-IDF (known as BM25, a probabilistic scoring framework), let's talk about how to configure Elasticsearch to use it. There are two different ways to specify the similarity for a field; the first is to change the `similarity` parameter in a field's mapping, as shown in the following listing.

Listing 6.1   Changing the `similarity` parameter in a field's mapping

```
{
  "mappings": {
    "get-together": {
      "properties": {
        "title": {
          "type": "string",
          "similarity": "BM25"          ⟵  Similarity to use for
        }                                    this field; in this
      }                                      case, BM25
```

```
        }
      }
    }
}
```

The second way to configure Elasticsearch to use an alternate scoring method is an extension of specifying it in the field's mapping. The similarity is defined in the settings, similarly to how an analyzer is, and then referenced in the mappings for a field by name. This approach allows you to configure the settings for a similarity algorithm. The next listing shows an example of configuring advanced settings for the BM25 similarity and using that scoring algorithm for a field in the mappings.

> **Listing 6.2 Configuring advanced settings for BM25 similarity**

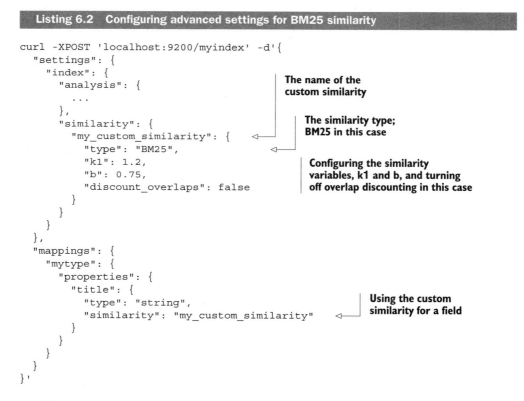

```
curl -XPOST 'localhost:9200/myindex' -d'{
  "settings": {
    "index": {
      "analysis": {
        ...
      },
      "similarity": {
        "my_custom_similarity": {          <──┐   The name of the
          "type": "BM25",                  <──┘   custom similarity
          "k1": 1.2,                           The similarity type;
          "b": 0.75,                           BM25 in this case
          "discount_overlaps": false
        }                                    Configuring the similarity
      }                                      variables, k1 and b, and turning
    }                                        off overlap discounting in this case
  },
  "mappings": {
    "mytype": {
      "properties": {
        "title": {
          "type": "string",
          "similarity": "my_custom_similarity"    <──┐   Using the custom
        }                                             │   similarity for a field
      }
    }
  }
}'
```

Additionally, if you've decided you want to always use a particular scoring method, you can configure it globally by adding the following setting to your elasticsearch.yml configuration file:

```
index.similarity.default.type: BM25
```

Great! Now that you've seen how to specify an alternative similarity, let's talk about this alternate similarity and how it differs from TF-IDF.

6.2.1 *Okapi BM25*

Okapi BM25 is probably the second most popular scoring method behind TF-IDF for Lucene and is a probabilistic relevance algorithm, which means the score can be thought of as the probability that a given document matches the query. BM25 is also reputed to be better for shorter fields, though you should always test to ensure it remains true for your dataset! BM25 maps each document into an array of values corresponding to each term in the dictionary and uses a probabilistic model to determine the document's ranking.

While discussing the full scoring formula for BM25 is beyond the scope of this book, you can read more about how BM25 is implemented in Lucene at http://arxiv.org/pdf/0911.5046.pdf.

BM25 has three main settings—k1, b, and discount_overlaps:

- k1 and b are numeric settings used to tweak how the scoring is calculated.
- k1 controls how important term frequency is to the score (how often the term occurs in the document, or TF from earlier in this chapter).
- b is a number between 0 and 1 that controls what degrees of impact the length of the document has on the score.
- k1 is set to 1.2 and b is set to 0.75 by default.
- The discount_overlaps setting can be used to tell Elasticsearch that multiple tokens occurring at the same position within a field should or should not influence how the length is normalized. It defaults to true.

> **Testing your scoring**
>
> Keep in mind that if you do tweak these settings, you need to be sure to have a good testing infrastructure with which to judge changes in the ranking and scoring of your documents. It makes no sense at all to change relevancy algorithm settings without a way to evaluate your changes in a reproducible manner; anything less is just guessing!

Now that you've seen the default TF-IDF scoring formula as well as an alternative, BM25, let's talk about how you can influence the scoring of documents in a more fine-grained manner, with boosting.

6.3 *Boosting*

Boosting is the process by which you can modify the relevance of a document. There are two different types of boosting. You can boost a document while you are indexing it or when you query for the document. Because changing the boosting of a document at index time stores data in the index, and the only way to change that boosting value is to re-index the document, we definitely recommend you use the query-time boosting because it's the most flexible and allows you to change your mind about what fields or terms are important without having to re-index your data.

Let's take the example from the get-together index. In the example, if you're searching for a group, it makes sense that matching a group's title is more important than matching the description of the group. Take the Elasticsearch Berlin group. The title contains only the most important information that the group is focused on, Elasticsearch in the Berlin area, versus the description of the group, which may contain many more terms. The title of a group should have more weight than the description, and to accomplish this, you'll use boosting.

Before you start, though, it's important to mention that boost numbers are not exact multipliers. This means that the boost value is normalized when computing the scores. For example, if you specify a boost of 10 for every single field, it will end up *normalized* to 1 for every field, meaning no boost is applied. You should think of boost numbers as relative; boosting the name field by 3 means that the name field is roughly three times as important as the other fields.

6.3.1 Boosting at index time

As we mentioned, in addition to boosting a document during a query, you can also boost it at index time. Even though we don't recommend this type of boosting, as you'll see shortly, it can still be useful in some cases, so let's talk about how to set it up.

When doing this type of boosting, you need to specify the mapping for your field with the boost parameter. For example, to boost the name field for the group type, you'd create an index with mappings that look like those in the next listing.

Listing 6.3   Boosting the name field in the group type at index time

```
curl -XPUT 'localhost:9200/get-together' -d'{
  "mappings": {
    "group": {
      "properties": {
        "name": {               ┐  Index-time boosting value for
          "boost": 2.0,         ◁─┘  the name field
          "type": "string"
        },
        ... rest of the mappings ...
      }
    }
  }
}'
```

After specifying this mapping for the index, any document that's indexed automatically has a boost applied to the terms in the name field (stored with the document in the Lucene index). Again, remember that this boost value is *fixed*, which means if you decide you want to change it, you'll need to re-index.

Another reason to not do index-time boosting is that boost values are stored as low-precision values in Lucene's internal index structure; only a single byte is used to store the floating-point number, so it's possible to lose precision when calculating the final score of a document.

The final reason to not use index-time boosting is that the boost is applied to all terms. Therefore, matching multiple terms in the boosted field implies a multiplied boost, increasing the weight for the field even more.

Because of these issues with boosting at index time, it's much better to boost when performing the queries, as you'll see next.

6.3.2   Boosting at query time

There are quite a few ways to perform boosting when searching. If you're using the basic match, multi_match, simple_query_string, or query_string queries, you control the boost either on a per-term or per-field basis. Almost all of Elasticsearch's query types support boosting. If this isn't flexible enough, you can control the boosting in a more fine-grained manner with the function_score query, which we'll cover a little later in the chapter.

With the match query, you can boost the query by using the additional boost parameter, as shown in the next listing. Boosting the query means that each found term in the configured field you query for gets a boost.

Listing 6.4   Query-time boosting using the match query

```
curl -XPOST 'localhost:9200/get-together/_search?pretty' -d'{
  "query": {
    "bool": {
      "should": [
        {
          "match": {
            "description": {
              "query": "elasticsearch big data",        Query-time boosting
              "boost": 2.5                                of this match query
            }
          }
        },
        {
          "match": {
            "name": {
              "query": "elasticsearch big data"          No boosting for the
            }                                             second match query
          }
        }]
    }
  }
}'
```

This also works for other queries that Elasticsearch provides, such as the term query, prefix query, and so on. In the previous example, notice that a boost was added only to the first match query. Now the first match query has a bigger impact on the final score than the second match query. It only makes sense to boost a query when you're combining multiple queries using the bool or and/or/not queries.

6.3.3   *Queries spanning multiple fields*

For queries that span multiple fields, such as the `multi_match` query, you also have access to an alternative syntax. You can specify the boost for the entire `multi_match`, similar to the `match` query with the `boost` parameter you've already seen, as shown in the next listing.

Listing 6.5   Specify a boost for the entire `multi_match` query

```
curl -XPOST 'localhost:9200/get-together/_search?pretty' -d'{
  "query": {
    "multi_match": {
      "query": "elasticsearch big data",
      "fields": ["name", "description"],
      "boost": 2.5
    }
  }
}'
```

Or you can specify a boost for only particular fields by using a special syntax. By appending the field name with a caret (^) and the boost value, you tell Elasticsearch to boost only that field. The following listing shows an example of the previous query, but instead of boosting the entire query, you boost only the name field.

Listing 6.6   Boosting on the `name` field only

```
curl -XPOST 'localhost:9200/get-together/_search?pretty' -d'{
  "query": {
    "multi_match": {
      "query": "elasticsearch big data",
      "fields": ["name^3", "description"]    ⟵  The name field being
    }                                            boosted by 3 with
  }                                              the ^3 suffix
}'
```

In the `query_string` query, you can boost individual terms using a special syntax, appending the term with a caret (^) and the boost value. An example searching for "elasticsearch" and "big data" and boosting "elasticsearch" by 3 would look like the next listing.

Listing 6.7   Boosting individual terms in `query_string` queries

```
curl -XPOST 'localhost:9200/get-together/_search?pretty' -d'{
  "query": {
    "query_string": {
      "query": "elasticsearch^3 AND \"big data\""    ⟵  Boosting a specific
    }                                                    term by 3 with a
  }                                                      ^3 suffix
}'
```

As we mentioned before, keep in mind when boosting either fields or terms that a boost is a relative value and not an absolute multiplier. If you boost all of the terms you're searching for by the same amount, it's the same as though you boosted none of them because Lucene normalizes the boost values. Remember that boosting a field by 4 doesn't automatically mean that the score for that field will be multiplied by 4, so don't worry if the score isn't an exact multiplication.

Because boosting during query time is highly flexible, play around with it! Don't be afraid to experiment with the dataset until you get the desired relevancy from your results. Changing the boosting is as easy as adjusting a number in the query you send to Elasticsearch.

6.4   Understanding how a document was scored with explain

Before we go much further into customizing the scoring of documents, we should cover how you can break down the scoring of a document on a result-by-result basis, with the actual numbers Lucene is using under the hood. This is helpful in understanding why one document matches a query better than another from Elasticsearch's perspective.

This is called *explaining* the score, and you can tell Elasticsearch to do it by specifying the explain=true flag, either on the URL when sending the request or by setting the explain flag to true in the body of the request itself. This can be useful in explaining why a document was scored a particular way, but it has another use: explaining why a document didn't match a query. This turns out to be useful if you expect a document to match a query but it isn't returned in the results.

Before we get to that, though, let's take a look at an example of explaining the results of a query in the next listing.

Listing 6.8   Setting the `explain` flag in the request body

```
curl -XPOST 'localhost:9200/get-together/_search?pretty' -d'
{
  "query": {
    "match": {
      "description": "elasticsearch"
    }
  },
  "explain": true            ⟵   Setting the
}'                                explain flag in
                                  the request body
```

You can see in this listing how to add the explain parameter. This, in turn, produces verbose output. Let's take a look at the first result returned from this request:

```
{
  "hits" : {
    "total" : 9,
    "max_score" : 0.4809364,
    "hits" : [ {
```

```
         "_shard" : 0,
         "_node" : "Kwc3QxdsT7m23T_gb4l3pw",
         "_index" : "get-together",
         "_type" : "group",
         "_id" : "3",
         "_score" : 0.4809364,
         "_source":{
    "name": "Elasticsearch San Francisco",
    "organizer": "Mik",
    "description": "Elasticsearch group for ES users of all knowledge levels",
    "created_on": "2012-08-07",
    "tags": ["elasticsearch", "big data", "lucene", "open source"],
    "members": ["Lee", "Igor"],
    "location": "San Francisco, California, USA"
    },
         "_explanation" : {
           "value" : 0.4809364,
           "description" : "weight(description:elasticsearch in 1)
           [PerFieldSimilarity], result of:",
           "details" : [ {
             "value" : 0.4809364,
             "description" : "fieldWeight in 1, product of:",
             "details" : [ {
               "value" : 1.0,
               "description" : "tf(freq=1.0), with freq of:",
               "details" : [ {
                 "value" : 1.0,
                 "description" : "termFreq=1.0"
               } ]
             }, {
               "value" : 1.5389965,
               "description" : "idf(docFreq=6, maxDocs=12)"
             }, {
               "value" : 0.3125,
               "description" : "fieldNorm(doc=1)"
             } ]
           } ]
         }
       } ]
     }
   }
```

Top-level score for this document →

Human-readable explanation for the score value →

_explanation contains an explanation for the document's score ←

Composite parts combined to make the final score ←

The added part of this response is the new _explanation key, which contains a breakdown of each of the different parts of the score. In this case, you're searching the description for "elasticsearch," and the term "elasticsearch" occurs once in the description of the document, so the term frequency (TF) for that term is 1.

Likewise, the inverse document frequency (IDF) explanation shows that the term "elasticsearch" occurs in 6 out of the 12 documents in this index. Finally, you can also see the normalization for this field, which Lucene uses internally. These scores multiplied together determine the final score:

```
1.0 x 1.5389965 x 0.3125 = 0.4809364.
```

Keep in mind that this is only a simple example with a single query term, and we looked only at the explanation for a single document. The explanation can be extremely verbose and much more difficult to understand when used for more complex queries. It's also important to mention that using the explain feature adds additional overhead to Elasticsearch when querying, so make sure you use it only to debug a query, rather than specifying it with every request by default.

6.4.1   *Explaining why a document did not match*

We mentioned earlier that explain has another use. Just as you can get an explanation of how the score was calculated for a particular matching document, you can also use the special explain API to tell why a document did *not* match a query.

But in this case, because you can't simply add the explain parameter, there's a different API to use it, as shown in the next listing.

Listing 6.9   Explain API to discover why a document didn't match a query

```
curl -XPOST 'localhost:9200/get-together/group/4/_explain' -d'
{
  "query": {
    "match": {
      "description": "elasticsearch"
    }
  }
}'
{
  "_id": "4",
  "_index": "get-together",
  "_type": "group",
  "explanation": {
    "description": "no matching term",        ⟵ Explanation of why
    "value": 0.0                                   the document didn't
  },                                               match the query
  "matched": false        ◁
}
```

Flag indicating whether the
document matched the query

In this example, because the term "elasticsearch" doesn't occur in the description field for this document, the explanation is a simple "no matching term." You can also use this API to get the score of a single document if you know the document's ID.

Armed with this tool, which allows you to determine how documents are scored, experiment. Play around. Don't be afraid to use the tools in this book to modify your scoring.

Next, before we get into more meat about tweaking the score, we'll talk about the impact of scoring and what you can do if you find that scoring is taking too long.

6.5   *Reducing scoring impact with query rescoring*

Something we haven't talked about yet is the impact of scoring on the speed of the system. In most regular querying, computing the score of a document requires a small amount of overhead. This is because TF-IDF has been heavily optimized by the Lucene team to be efficient.

In some cases, however, scoring can be more resource-intensive:

- Scoring with a script runs a script to calculate the score for each document in the index
- Doing a `phrase` query searches for words within a certain distance from each other, with a large slop (discussed in section 4.2.1)

In those cases, you may want to lessen the impact of the scoring algorithm running on millions or billions of documents.

To address this, Elasticsearch has a feature called rescoring. *Rescoring* means that an initial query is performed, and then a second round of scoring is computed on the results that are returned; hence the name. This means that for a potentially expensive query that uses a script, you can execute it on only the top 1,000 hits retrieved, using a much cheaper `match` query. Let's look at an example of using `rescore` in the next listing.

Listing 6.10 Using `rescore` to score a subset of matching documents

```
curl -XPOST 'localhost:9200/get-together/_search?pretty' -d'{
  "query": {
    "match": {
      "title": "elasticsearch"          Original query to execute
    }                                    on all documents
  },
  "rescore": {
    "window_size": 20,          Number of results on which
    "query": {                  to perform the rescore
      "rescore_query": {
        "match": {
          "title":{
            "type": "phrase",            Query that will run
            "query": "elasticsearch hadoop",   on the top 20 results
            "slop": 5                    of the original query
          }
        }
      },
      "query_weight": 0.8,            Weight of the scores from
      "rescore_query_weight": 1.3     the original query
    }
  }
}'                                Weight of the scores from
                                  the rescored query
```

In this example you search for all the documents that have "elasticsearch" in the title and then take the top 20 results and rescore them, using a `phrase` query with a high level of slop. Even though a `phrase` query with a high slop value can be expensive to run, you don't have to worry, because the query will run on only the top 20 documents instead of potentially millions or billions of documents. You can use the `query_weight` and `rescore_query_weight` parameters to weigh each of the different queries, depending on how much you want the score to be determined by the initial query and the `rescore` query. You can use multiple `rescore` queries in sequence, each one taking the previous one as the input.

6.6   *Custom scoring with function_score*

Finally, we come to one of the coolest queries that Elasticsearch has to offer: `function_score`. The `function_score` query allows you to take control over the relevancy of your results in a fine-grained manner by specifying any number of arbitrary functions to be applied to the score of the documents matching an initial query.

Each *function* in this case is a small snippet of JSON that influences the score in some way. Sound confusing? Well, we'll clear it up by the end of this section. We'll start with the basic structure of the `function_score` query; the next listing an example that doesn't perform any fancy scoring.

Listing 6.11   `Function_score` query basic structure

```
curl -XPOST 'localhost:9200/get-together/_search?pretty' -d'{
  "query": {
    "function_score": {
      "query": {
        "match": {
          "description": "elasticsearch"
        }
      },
      "functions": []          ←┤ Empty
    }                            functions list
  }
}'
```

Simple enough—it looks just like a regular `match` query inside a `function_score` wrapper. There's a new key, `functions`, that's currently empty, but don't worry about that yet; you'll put things into that array in just a second. This listing is intended to show that the results of this query are going to be the documents that the `function_score` functions operate on. For example, if you have 30 total documents in the index and the `match` query for "elasticsearch" in the `description` field matches 25 of them, the functions inside the array will be applied to those 25 documents.

The `function_score` query has a number of different functions, and in addition to the original query, each function can take another filter element. You'll see examples of this as we go into the details about each function in the next sections.

6.6.1   *weight*

The `weight` function is the simplest of the bunch; it multiplies the score by a constant number. Note that instead of a regular `boost` field, which increases the score by a value that gets normalized, `weight` really does multiply the score by the value.

In the previous example, you're already matching all of the documents that have "elasticsearch" in the description, so you'll boost documents that contain "hadoop" in the description as well in the next listing.

Listing 6.12 Using `weight` function to boost documents containing "hadoop"

```
curl -XPOST 'localhost:9200/get-together/_search?pretty' -d'{
  "query": {
    "function_score": {
      "query": {
        "match": {
          "description": "elasticsearch"
        }
      },
      "functions": [
        {
          "weight": 1.5,
          "filter": {"term": {"description": "hadoop"}}
        }
      ]
    }
  }
}'
```

weight function
boosting documents
with "hadoop" in
the description
by 1.5

The only change to the example was adding the following snippet to the `functions` array:

```
{
 "weight": 1.5,
 "filter": {"term": {"description": "hadoop"}}
}
```

This means that documents that match the term query for "hadoop" in the description will have their score multiplied by 1.5.

You can have as many of these as you'd like. For example, to also increase the score of get-together groups that mention "logstash," you could specify two different `weight` functions, as in the following listing.

Listing 6.13 Specifying two `weight` functions

```
curl -XPOST 'localhost:9200/get-together/_search?pretty' -d'{
  "query": {
    "function_score": {
      "query": {
        "match": {
          "description": "elasticsearch"
        }
      },
      "functions": [
        {
          "weight": 2,
          "filter": {"term": {"description": "hadoop"}}
        },
```

Boosting
documents
containing
"hadoop" in the
description by 2

```
    {
      "weight": 3,
      "filter": {"term": {"description": "logstash"}}
    }
  ]
 }
}
}'
```

> Boosting documents containing "logstash" in the description by 3

6.6.2   *Combining scores*

Let's talk about how these scores get combined. There are two different factors we need to discuss when talking about scores:

- How the scores from each of the individual functions should be combined, called the `score_mode`
- How the score of the functions should be combined with the original query score (searching for "elasticsearch" in the description in our example), known as `boost_mode`

The first factor, known as the `score_mode` parameter, deals with how each of the different functions' scores are combined. In the previous cURL request you have two functions: one with a weight of 2, the other with a weight of 3. You can set the `score_mode` parameter to `multiply`, `sum`, `avg`, `first`, `max`, or `min`. If not specified, the scores from each function will be multiplied together.

If `first` is specified, only the first function with a matching filter will have its score taken into account. For example, if you set `score_mode` to `first` and had a document with both "hadoop" and "logstash" in the description, only a boost factor of 2 would be applied, because that's the first function that matches the document.

The second score-combining setting, known as `boost_mode`, controls how the score of the original query is combined with the scores of the functions themselves. If not specified, the new score will be the original query score and the combined function's score multiplied together. You can change this to `sum`, `avg`, `max`, `min`, or `replace`. Setting this to `replace` means that the original query's score is replaced by the score of the functions.

Armed with these settings, you can tackle the next function score function, which is used for modifying the score based on a field's value. The functions we'll cover are `field_value_factor`, `script_score`, and `random_score`, as well as the three decay functions: `linear`, `gauss`, and `exp`. We'll start with the `field_value_factor` function.

6.6.3   *field_value_factor*

Modifying the score based on other queries is quite useful, but a lot of people want to use the data inside their documents to influence the score of a document. In this example, you might want to use the number of reviews an event has received to increase the score for that event; this is possible to do by using the `field_value_factor` function inside a `function_score` query.

The `field_value_factor` function takes the name of a field containing a numeric field, optionally multiplies it by a constant number, and then finally applies a math function such as taking the logarithm of the value. Look at the example in the next listing.

Listing 6.14 Using `field_value_factor` inside a `function_score` query

```
curl -XPOST 'localhost:9200/get-together/event/_search?pretty' -d'{
  "query": {
    "function_score": {
      "query": {
        "match": {
          "description": "elasticsearch"
        }
      },
      "functions": [
        {
          "field_value_factor": {
            "field": "reviews",
            "factor": 2.5,
            "modifier": "ln"
          }
        }
      ]
    }
  }
}'
```

- Numeric field to use as a value
- Factor the reviews field will be multiplied by
- Optional modifier to calculate the score with

The score that comes out of the `field_value_factor` function here will be

```
ln(2.5 * doc['reviews'].value)
```

For a document with a value of 7 in the `reviews` field, the score would be

```
ln(2.5 * 7) -> ln(17.5) -> 2.86
```

Besides `ln` there are other modifiers: `none` (default), `log`, `log1p`, `log2p`, `ln1p`, `ln2p`, `square`, `sqrt`, and `reciprocal`. One more thing to remember when using `field_value_factor`: it loads all the values of whichever field you've specified into memory, so the scores can be calculated quickly; this is part of the field data, which we'll discuss in section 6.10. But before we talk about that, we'll cover another function, which can give you finer-grained control over influencing the score by specifying a custom script.

6.6.4 *Script*

Script scoring gives you complete control over how to change the score. You can perform any sort of scoring inside a script.

As a brief refresher, scripts are written in the Groovy language, and you can access the original score of the document by using `_score` inside a script. You can access the values of a document using `doc['fieldname']`. An example of scoring using a slightly more complex script is shown in the next listing.

Listing 6.15   Scoring using a complex script

```
curl -XPOST 'localhost:9200/get-together/event/_search?pretty' -d'{
  "query": {
    "function_score": {
      "query": {
        "match": {
          "description": "elasticsearch"
        }
      },
      "functions": [
        {
          "script_score": {
            "script": "Math.log(doc['attendees'].values.size() *
myweight)",
            "params": {
              "myweight": 3
            }
          }
        }
      ],
      "boost_mode": "replace"
    }
  }
}'
```

Script that will be run on each document to determine a value

The variable myweight will be replaced by the parameters in the request.

The original document's score will be replaced by the score generated in the script.

In this example, you're using the size of the attendee list to influence the score by multiplying it by a weight and taking the logarithm of it.

Scripting is extremely powerful because you can do anything you'd like inside it, but keep in mind that scripts will be much slower than regular scoring because they must be executed dynamically for each document that matches your query. When using the parameterized script as in listing 6.15, caching the script helps performance.

6.6.5   *random*

The `random_score` function gives you the ability to assign random scores to your documents. The advantage of being able to sort documents randomly is the ability to introduce a bit of variation into the first page of results. When searching for get-togethers, sometimes it is nice to not always see the same result at the top.

You can also optionally specify a *seed*, which is a number passed with the query that will be used to generate the randomness with the function; this lets you sort documents in a random manner, but by using the same random seed, the results will be sorted the same way if the same request is performed again. That's the only option it supports, so that makes this a simple function.

The next listing shows an example of using it to sort get-togethers randomly.

Listing 6.16 Using `random_score` function to sort documents randomly

```
curl -XPOST 'localhost:9200/get-together/event/_search?pretty' -d'{
  "query": {
    "function_score": {
      "query": {
        "match": {
          "description": "elasticsearch"
        }
      },
      "functions": [
        {
          "random_score": {              Optional seed for the
            "seed": 1234        ◁────┐   random_score function
          }
        }
      ]
    }
  }
}'
```

Don't worry if this doesn't seem useful yet. Once we've covered all of the different functions, we'll come up with an example that ties them all together at the end of this section. Before we do that, though, there's one more set of functions we need to discuss: decay functions.

6.6.6 Decay functions

The last set of functions for `function_score` is the decay functions. They allow you to apply a gradual decay in the score of a document based on some field. There are a number of ways this can be useful. For example, you may want to make get-togethers that occurred more recently have a higher score, with the score gradually tapering off as the get-togethers get older. Another example is with geolocation data; using the decay functions, you can increase the score of results that are closer to a geo point (a user's location, for example) and decrease the score the farther the group is from the point.

There are three types of decay functions: `linear`, `gauss`, and `exp`. Each decay function follows the same sort of syntax:

```
{
  "TYPE": {
    "origin": "...",
    "offset": "...",
    "scale": "...",
    "decay": "..."
  }
}
```

The `TYPE` can be one of the three types. Each of the types corresponds to a differently shaped curve, shown in figures 6.4, 6.5, and 6.6.

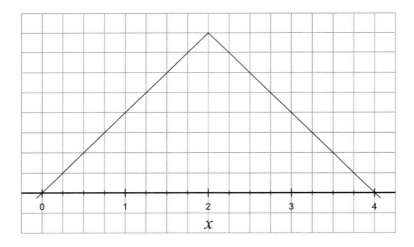

Figure 6.4   Linear curve—scores decrease from the origin at the same rate.

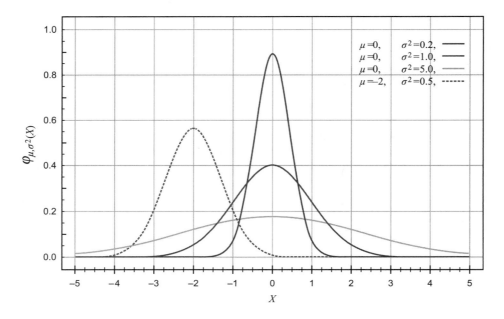

Figure 6.5   Gauss curve—scores decrease more slowly until the scale point is reached and then they decrease faster.

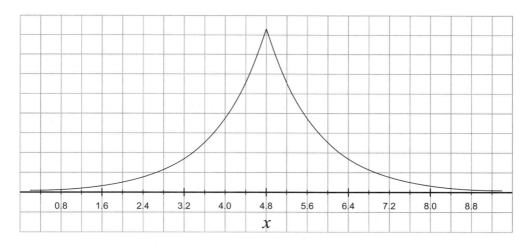

0.8   1.6   2.4   3.2   4.0   4.8   5.6   6.4   7.2   8.0   8.8

x

Figure 6.6   Exponential curve—scores drastically drop from the origin.

6.6.7   Configuration options

The configuration options define what the curve will look like; there are four configuration options for each of the three decay curves:

- The origin is the center point of the curve, so it's the point where you'd like the score to be the highest. In the geo-distance example, the origin is most like a person's current location. In other situations the origin can also be a date or a numeric field.
- The offset is the distance away from the originating point, before the score starts to be reduced. In our example, if the offset is set to 1km, it means the score will not be reduced for points within one kilometer from the origin point. It defaults to 0, meaning that scores immediately start to decay as the numeric value moves away from the origin.
- The scale and decay options go hand in hand; by setting them, you can say that at the scale value for a field, the score should be reduced to the decay. Sound confusing? It's much simpler to think of it with actual values. If you set the scale to 5km and the decay to 0.25, it's the same as saying "at 5 kilometers from my origin point, the score should be 0.25 times the score at the origin."

The next listing shows an example of Gaussian decay with the get-together data.

Listing 6.17   Using Gaussian decay on the geo point location

```
curl -XPOST 'localhost:9200/get-together/event/_search?pretty' -d'{
  "query": {
    "function_score": {
      "query": {"match_all": {}},
```

```
            "functions": [
              {
                "gauss": {
                  "geolocation": {
                    "origin": "40.018528,-105.275806",
                    "offset": "100m",
                    "scale": "2km",
                    "decay": 0.5
                  }
                }
              }
            ]
          }
        }
      }'
```

Point of origin for the decay to start at →

Scores will remain the same within 100 meters from the origin point.

At 2 kilometers from the origin point, the score will be reduced by half.

Let's look at what's going on in this listing:

- You use a `match_all` query, which will return all results.
- Then you score each result using a Gaussian decay on the score.
- The origin point is set in Boulder, Colorado, so the results that come back have the get-togethers in Boulder scored the highest, then results in Denver (a city near Boulder), and so on, as the different get-togethers get farther and farther away from the point of origin.

6.7   *Tying it back together*

We promised we'd show an example that used multiple functions, and we didn't lie. The next listing shows a query for all of the get-together events, where

- A particular term is weighted higher.
- The reviews are taken into account.
- Events with more attendees rank higher.
- Events nearer to a geo point are boosted.

Seeing the example will make more sense, so take a look at the next listing.

Listing 6.18   Tying all the `function_score` functions together

```
curl -XPOST 'localhost:9200/get-together/event/_search?pretty' -d'{
  "query": {
    "function_score": {
      "query": {"match_all": {}},
      "functions": [
        {
          "weight: 1.5,
          "filter": {"term": {"description": "hadoop"}}
        },
        {
          "field_value_factor": {
            "field": "reviews",
            "factor": 10.5,
            "modifier": "log1p"
```

The original query matches all documents.

Boost documents with descriptions containing "hadoop" by 1.5 using the weight function.

Score documents with higher reviews higher.

```
          }
        },
        {
          "script_score": {
            "script": "Math.log(doc['attendees'].values.size() *
myweight)",
            "params": {
              "myweight": 3
            }
          }
        },
        {
          "gauss": {
            "geolocation": {
              "origin": "40.018528,-105.275806",
              "offset": "100m",
              "scale": "2km",
              "decay": 0.5
            }
          }
        }
      ],
      "score_mode": "sum",
      "boost_mode": "replace"
    }
  }
}'
```

> **Use the number of attendees to influence the score.**

> **Decay the score the farther it is from the geo point 40.018528,-105.275806.**

> **Add each function's score together to produce the total value for the functions.**

> **Replace the original match_all query's score with the score from the functions.**

In this example, the following occurs:

1 You start by matching all events in the index due to the match_all.
2 You then boost events that have the term "hadoop" in their description using the weight function.
3 Next, you use the number of reviews an event received to modify the score with the field_value_factor function.
4 Then you take the number of attendees into account using the script_score.
5 Finally, you make the score gradually decay as it gets farther from your origin point with the gauss decay.

6.8 Sorting with scripts

Along with modifying the score of a document with a script, Elasticsearch allows you to use a script to sort documents before they're returned to you. This can be useful if you need to sort on a field that doesn't exist as a field in the document.

For example, imagine you're searching for events about "elasticsearch" but you want to sort the groups by the number of people who attended; you can easily do this with the request shown in the following listing.

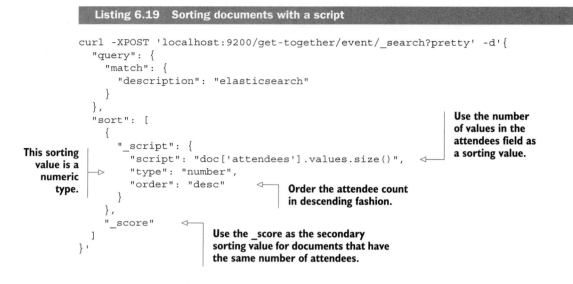

Listing 6.19   Sorting documents with a script

```
curl -XPOST 'localhost:9200/get-together/event/_search?pretty' -d'{
  "query": {
    "match": {
      "description": "elasticsearch"
    }
  },
  "sort": [
    {
      "_script": {
        "script": "doc['attendees'].values.size()",
        "type": "number",
        "order": "desc"
      }
    },
    "_score"
  ]
}'
```

Use the number of values in the attendees field as a sorting value.

This sorting value is a numeric type.

Order the attendee count in descending fashion.

Use the _score as the secondary sorting value for documents that have the same number of attendees.

You should notice that you will get back a field in each matching document that looks like `"sort": [5.0, 0.28856182]`; these are the values that Elasticsearch has used to sort the documents. Notice that the `5.0` is a number; that's because you specified to Elasticsearch that the output of your script was a number (as opposed to a string). The second value in the sort array is the original score of the document because you specified it as the next sort field in case the numbers of attendees match for multiple documents.

Although this is powerful, it's much easier and faster to instead use the `function _score` query to influence the score of your document and sort by the `_score` instead of sorting using a custom script; that way all of your relevancy changes are in a single place (the query) instead of inside the sorting.

Another option is to have the number of attendees as another numeric field in the document that's indexed. That makes sorting or changing the score using a function a lot easier to do.

Next, let's take a little detour and talk about something that's somewhat related to scripting but a little different: field data.

6.9   *Field data detour*

The inverted index is great when you want to look for a term and get back the matching documents. But when you need to sort on a field or return some aggregations, Elasticsearch needs to quickly figure out, for each matching document, the terms that will be used for sorting or aggregations.

Inverted indices don't perform well for such tasks, and this is where field data becomes useful. When we talk about *field data*, we're talking about all of the unique values for a field. These values are loaded by Elasticsearch into memory. If you have three documents that look like these

```
{"body": "quick brown fox"}
{"body": "fox brown fox"}
{"body": "slow turtle"}
```

the terms that would get loaded into memory would be quick, brown, fox, slow, and turtle. Elasticsearch loads these in a compressed manner into the field data cache, which we'll look at next.

6.9.1 *The field data cache*

The *field data cache* is an in-memory cache that Elasticsearch uses for a number of things. This cache is usually (but not always) built the first time the data is needed and then kept around to be used for various operations. This loading can take a lot of time and CPU if you have lots of data, slowing down that first search.

This is where *warmers,* queries that Elasticsearch runs automatically to make sure internal caches are filled, can come in handy to preload data used for queries before it's needed. We'll discuss warmers more in chapter 10.

> **Why the field data cache is so necessary**
> Elasticsearch needs this cache because a lot of comparison and analytic operations operate on a large amount of data, and the only way these operations can be accomplished in a reasonable amount of time is if the data is accessible in memory. Elasticsearch goes to great lengths to minimize the amount of memory that this cache takes up, but it still ends up being one of the largest users of heap space in the Java virtual machine.

Not only should you be aware of the memory used by the cache, but you should also be aware that the initial loading of this cache can take a nontrivial amount of time. You may notice this when performing aggregations and seeing that the first aggregation takes 2–3 seconds to complete, whereas subsequent aggregation requests return in 30 milliseconds.

If this loading time becomes problematic, you can pay the price at index time and make Elasticsearch load the field data automatically when making a new segment available for search. To do this for a field you sort or aggregate on, you have to set fielddata.loading to eager in the mapping. By your setting this to eager, Elasticsearch won't wait until the first search to load the field data but will do it as soon as it's available to be loaded.

For example, to make the verbatim tags of a get-together group (on which you run a terms aggregation to get the top 10 tags) eagerly loaded, you can have the mapping shown in the following listing.

Listing 6.20   Eager loaded field data for the `title` field

```
curl -XPOST 'localhost:9200/get-together' -d '
{
  "mappings": {
    "group": {
      "properties": {
        "title": {
          "type": "string",
          "fielddata": {                          Configuring the field data
            "loading": "eager"                    for the title field to be
          }                                        loaded eagerly
        }
      }
    }
  }
}'
```

6.9.2   What field data is used for

As previously mentioned, field data is used for a number of things in Elasticsearch. Here are some of the uses of field data:

- Sorting by a field
- Aggregating on a field
- Accessing the value of a field in a script with the `doc['fieldname']` notation
- Using the `field_value_factor` function in the `function_score` query
- Using the `decay` functions in the `function_score` query
- Returning fields from field data using `fielddata_fields` in a search request
- Caching the IDs of a parent/child document relationship

Probably the most common of these uses is sorting or aggregating on a field. For example, if you sort the get-together results by the `organizer` field, all of the unique values of that field must be loaded into memory in order for them to be efficiently compared to provide a sorting order.

Right behind sorting on a field is aggregating on a field. When a `terms` aggregation is performed, Elasticsearch needs to be able to count each unique term, so those unique terms and their counts must be held in memory in order to generate these sorts of analytic results. Likewise in the case of a statistical aggregation, the numeric data for a field has to be loaded in order to calculate the resulting values.

Not to fear, though; as I mentioned, although this may sound like a lot of data to load (and it certainly can be), Elasticsearch does its best to load the data in a compressed manner. That said, you do need to be aware of it, so let's talk about how to manage field data in your cluster.

6.9.3   Managing field data

There are a few ways to manage field data in an Elasticsearch cluster. Now, what do we mean when we say "manage"? Well, *managing* field data means avoiding issues in the cluster where JVM garbage collection is taking a long time or so much memory is being loaded that you get an OutOfMemoryError; it would also be beneficial to avoid cache churn, so data isn't constantly being loaded and unloaded from memory.

We're going to talk about three different ways to do such management:

- Limiting the amount of memory used by field data
- Using the field data circuit breaker
- Bypassing memory altogether with doc values

LIMITING THE AMOUNT OF MEMORY USED BY FIELD DATA

One of the easiest ways to make sure your data doesn't take up too much space in memory is to limit the field data cache to a certain size. If you don't specify this, Elasticsearch doesn't limit the cache at all, and data isn't automatically expired from the cache after a set time.

There are two different options when it comes to limiting the field data cache: you can limit by a size amount, or you can set an expiration time after which the field data in the cache will be invalidated.

To set these options, specify the following in your elasticsearch.yml file; these settings can't be updated through the cluster update settings API and therefore require a restart when changed:

```
indices.fielddata.cache.size: 400mb
indices.fielddata.cache.expire: 25m
```

But when setting these, it makes more sense to set the indices.fielddata.cache .size option instead of the expire option. Why? Because when field data is loaded into the cache, it will stay there until the limit is reached, and then it will be evicted in a last-recently-used (LRU) manner. By setting just the size limit, you're also removing only the oldest data from the cache once the limit has been reached.

When setting the size, you can also use a relative size instead of an absolute, so instead of the 400mb from our example, you can specify 40% to use 40% of the JVM's heap size for the field data cache. This can be useful if you have machines with differing amounts of physical memory but want to unify the elasticsearch.yml configuration file between them without specifying absolute values.

USING THE FIELD DATA CIRCUIT BREAKER

What happens if you don't set the size of the cache? Well, in order to protect against loading too much data into memory, Elasticsearch has the concept of a *circuit breaker*, which monitors the amount of data being loaded into memory and "trips" if a certain limit is reached.

In the case of field data, every time a request happens that would load field data (sorting on a field, for example), the circuit breaker estimates the amount of memory required for the data and checks whether loading it would exceed the maximum size. If it does exceed the size, an exception is returned and the operation is prevented.

This has a number of benefits: when applying a limit to the field data cache, the size of field data can be calculated only *after* the data has been loaded into memory, so it's possible to load too much data and run out of memory; the circuit breaker, on the other hand, estimates the size of the data *before* it's loaded so as to avoid loading it if it would cause the system to run out of memory.

Another benefit of this approach is that the circuit breaker limit can be dynamically adjusted while the node is running, whereas the size of the cache must be set in the configuration file and requires restarting the node to change. The circuit breaker is configured by default to limit the field data size to 60% of the JVM's heap size. You can configure this by sending a request like this:

```
curl -XPUT 'localhost:9200/_cluster/settings'
{
  "transient": {
    "indices.breaker.fielddata.limit": "350mb"
  }
}
```

Again, this setting supports either an absolute value like 350mb or a percentage such as 45%. Once you've set this, you can see the limit and how much memory is currently tracked by the breaker with the Nodes Stats API, which we'll talk about in chapter 11.

> **NOTE** As of version 1.4, there is also a request circuit breaker, which helps you make sure that other in-memory data structures generated by a request don't cause an OutOfMemoryError by limiting them to a default of 40%. There's also a parent circuit breaker, which makes sure that the field data and the request breakers together don't exceed 70% of the heap. Both limits can be updated via the Cluster Update Settings API through indices.breaker .request.limit and indices.breaker.total.limit, respectively.

BYPASSING MEMORY AND USING THE DISK WITH DOC VALUES

So far you've seen that you should use circuit breakers to make sure outstanding requests don't crash your nodes, and if you fall consistently short of field data space, you should either increase your JVM heap size to use more RAM or limit the field data size and live with bad performance. But what if you're consistently short on field data space, don't have enough RAM to increase the JVM heap, and can't live with bad performance caused by field data evictions? This is where doc values come in.

Doc values take the data that needs to be loaded into memory and instead prepare it when the document is indexed, storing it on disk alongside the regular index data. This means that when field data would normally be used and read out of memory, the data can be read from disk instead. This provides a number of advantages:

- *Performance degrades smoothly*—Unlike default field data, which needs to live in the JVM heap all at once, doc values are read from the disk, like the rest of the index. If the OS can't fit everything in its RAM caches, more disk seeks will be needed, but there are no expensive loads and evictions, no risk of OutOfMemory-Errors, and no circuit-breaking exceptions because the circuit breaker prevented the field data cache from using too much memory.

- *Better memory management*—When used, doc values are cached in memory by the kernel, avoiding the cost of garbage collection associated with heap usage.
- *Faster loading*—With doc values, the uninverted structure is calculated at index time, so even when you run the first query, Elasticsearch doesn't have to uninvert on the fly. This makes the initial requests faster, because the uninverting process has already been performed.

As with everything in this chapter, there's no such thing as free lunch. Doc values come with disadvantages, too:

- *Bigger index size*—Storing all doc values on disk inflates the index size.
- *Slightly slower indexing*—The need to calculate doc values at index time slows down the process of indexing.
- *Slightly slows requests that use field data*—Disk is also slower than memory, so some requests that would usually use an already-loaded field data cache in memory will be slightly slower when reading doc values from disk. This includes sorting, facets, and aggregations.
- *Works only on non-analyzed fields*—As of version 1.4, doc values don't support analyzed fields. If you want to build a word cloud of the words in event titles, for example, you can't take advantage of doc values. Doc values can be used for numeric, date, Boolean, binary, and geo-point fields, though, and work well for large datasets on non-analyzed data, such as the `timestamp` field of log messages that are indexed into Elasticsearch.

The good news is that you can mix and match fields that use doc values with those that use the in-memory field data cache, so although you may want to use doc values for the `timestamp` field in your events, you can still keep the event's `title` field in memory.

How are doc values used? Because they're written out at indexing time, configuring doc values has to happen in the mapping for a particular field. If you have a string field that's not analyzed and you'd like to use field values on it, you can configure the mapping when creating an index, as shown in the next listing.

Listing 6.21 Using `doc-values` in the mapping for the `title` field

```
curl -XPOST 'localhost:9200/myindex' -d'
{
  "mappings": {
    "document": {
      "properties": {
        "title": {
          "type": "string",
          "index": "not_analyzed",
          "doc_values": true          ⤆ Configuring the title
        }                                field to use doc_values
      }                                  for its field data
    }
  }
}'
```

Once the mapping has been configured, indexing and searching will work as normal without any additional changes.

6.10 *Summary*

You now have a better understanding of how scoring works inside Elasticsearch as well as how documents interact with the field data cache, so let's review what this chapter was about:

- The frequency of a term and the number of times that term occurs in a document are used to calculate the score of a term inside a query.
- Elasticsearch has a lot of tools to customize and modify scoring.
- Scoring impact can be lessened by rescoring a subset of documents.
- Use the explain API to understand how a document has been scored.
- The `function_score` query gives you ultimate control over scoring your documents.
- Understanding the field data cache can help you understand how your Elasticsearch cluster uses memory.
- Alternatives like `doc_values` can be used if the field data cache is using too much memory.

In chapter 7 we'll move on to how you can not only get the results of a query but also explore data from a different angle using aggregations.

Exploring your data
with aggregations

This chapter covers

- Metrics aggregations
- Single and multi-bucket aggregations
- Nesting aggregations
- Relations among queries, filters, and aggregations

So far in this book, we've concentrated on the use case of indexing and searching: you have many documents and the user wants to find the most relevant matches to some keywords. There are more and more use cases where users aren't interested in specific results. Instead, they want to get statistics from a set of documents. These statistics might be hot topics for news, revenue trends for different products, the number of unique visitors to your website, and much more.

Aggregations in Elasticsearch solve this problem by loading the documents matching your search and doing all sorts of computations, such as counting the terms of a string field or calculating the average on a numeric field. To look at how aggregations work, we'll use an example from the get-together site you've worked with in previous chapters: a user entering your site may not know what groups to look for. To give the user something to start with, you could make the

179

Tags

☐ open source (7)

☑ elasticsearch (3)

☐ big data (2)

Figure 7.1   Example use case of aggregations: top tags for get-together groups

UI show the most popular tags for existing groups of your get-together site, as illustrated in figure 7.1.

Those tags would be stored in a separate field of your group documents. The user could then select a tag and filter down to only documents containing that tag. This makes it easier for users to find groups relevant to their interests.

To get such a list of popular tags in Elasticsearch, you'd use aggregations, and in this specific case, you'd use the `terms` aggregation on the `tags` field, which counts occurrences of each term in that field and returns the most frequent terms. Many other types of aggregations are also available, and we'll discuss them later in this chapter. For example, you can use a `date_histogram` aggregation to show how many events happened in each month of the last year, use the `avg` aggregation to show you the average number of attendees for each event, or even find out which users have similar taste for events as you do by using the `significant_terms` aggregation.

What about facets?

If you've used Lucene, Solr, or even Elasticsearch for some time, you might have heard about facets. *Facets* are similar to aggregations, because they also load the documents matching your query and perform computations in order to return statistics. Facets are still supported in versions 1.x but are deprecated and will be removed in version 2.0.

The main difference between aggregations and facets is that you can't nest multiple types of facets in Elasticsearch, which limits the possibilities for exploring your data. For example, if you had a blogging site, you could use the `terms` facet to find out the hot topics this year, or you could use the `date histogram` facet to find out how many articles are posted each day, but you couldn't find the number of posts per day, separately for each topic (at least not in one request). You'd be able to do that if you could nest the `date histogram` facet under the `terms` facet.

Aggregations were born to remove this limit and allow you to get deeper insights from your documents. For example, if you store your online shop logs in Elasticsearch, you can use aggregations to find not only the best-selling products but also the best-selling products in each country, the trends for each product in each country, and so on.

In this chapter, we'll first discuss the common traits of all aggregations: how you run them and how they relate to the queries and filters you learned in previous chapters. Then we'll dive into the particularities of each type of aggregation, and in the end, we'll show you how to combine different aggregation types.

Aggregations are divided in two main categories: metrics and bucket. *Metrics* aggregations refer to the statistical analysis of a group of documents, resulting in metrics such as the minimum value, maximum value, standard deviation, and much more. For example, you can get the average price of items from an online shop or the number of unique users logging on to it.

Bucket aggregations divide matching documents into one or more containers (buckets) and then give you the number of documents in each bucket. The `terms` aggregation, which would give you the most popular tags in figure 7.1, makes a bucket of documents for each tag and gives you the document count for each bucket.

Within a bucket aggregation, you can nest other aggregations, making the sub-aggregation run on each bucket of documents generated by the top-level aggregation. You can see an example in figure 7.2.

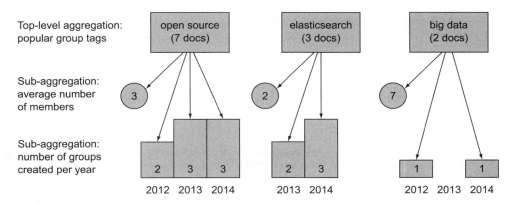

Figure 7.2   The `terms` bucket aggregation allows you to nest other aggregations within it.

Looking at the figure from the top down, you can see that if you're using the `terms` aggregation to get the most popular group tags, you can also get the average number of members for groups matching each tag. You could also ask Elasticsearch to give you, per tag, the number of groups created per year.

As you may imagine, you can combine many types of aggregations in many ways. To get a better view of the available options, we'll go through metrics and bucket aggregations and then discuss how you can combine them. But first, let's see what's common for all types of aggregations: how to write them and how they relate to your queries.

7.1 Understanding the anatomy of an aggregation

All aggregations, no matter their type, follow some rules:

- You define them in the same JSON request as your queries, and you mark them by the key `aggregations`, or `aggs`. You need to give each one a name and specify the type and the options specific to that type.
- They run on the results of your query. Documents that don't match your query aren't accounted for unless you include them with the `global` aggregation, which is a bucket aggregation that will be covered later in this chapter.
- You can further filter down the results of your query, without influencing aggregations. To do that, we'll show you how to use post filters. For example, when searching for a keyword in an online shop, you can build statistics on all items matching the keyword but use post filters to show only results that are in stock.

Let's take a look at the popular `terms` aggregation, which you've already seen in the intro to this chapter. The example use case was getting the most popular subjects (tags) for existing groups of your get-together site. We'll use this same `terms` aggregation to explore the rules that all aggregations must follow.

7.1.1 Structure of an aggregation request

In listing 7.1, you'll run a `terms` aggregation that will give you the most frequent tags in the get-together groups. The structure of this `terms` aggregation will apply to every other aggregation.

> **NOTE** For this chapter's listing to work, you'll need to index the sample dataset from the code samples that come with the book, located at https://github.com/dakrone/elasticsearch-in-action.

Listing 7.1   Using the `terms` aggregation to get top tags

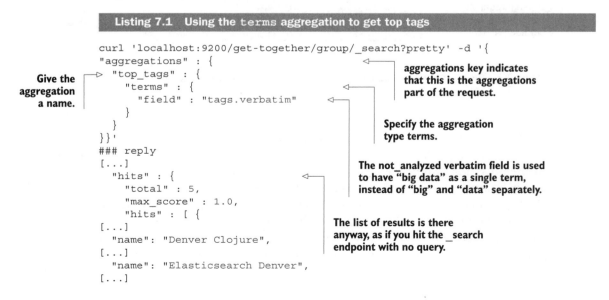

```
curl 'localhost:9200/get-together/group/_search?pretty' -d '{
"aggregations" : {
  "top_tags" : {
    "terms" : {
      "field" : "tags.verbatim"
    }
  }
}}'
### reply
[...]
  "hits" : {
    "total" : 5,
    "max_score" : 1.0,
    "hits" : [ {
[...]
  "name": "Denver Clojure",
[...]
  "name": "Elasticsearch Denver",
[...]
```

Give the aggregation a name.

aggregations key indicates that this is the aggregations part of the request.

Specify the aggregation type terms.

The not_analyzed verbatim field is used to have "big data" as a single term, instead of "big" and "data" separately.

The list of results is there anyway, as if you hit the _search endpoint with no query.

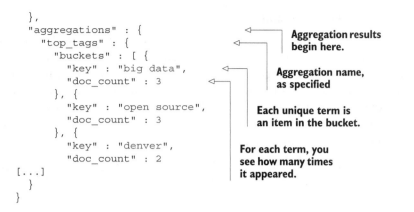

- At the top level there's the `aggregations` key, which can be shortened to `aggs`.
- On the next level, you have to give the aggregation a name. You can see that name in the reply. This is useful when you use multiple aggregations in the same request, so you can easily see the meaning of each set of results.
- Finally, you have to specify the aggregation type `terms` and the specific option. In this case, you'll have the `field` name.

The aggregation request from listing 7.1 hits the `_search` endpoint, just like the queries you've seen in previous chapters. In fact, you also get back 10 group results. This is all because no query was specified, which will effectively run the `match_all` query you saw in chapter 4, so your aggregation will run on all the group documents. Running a different query will make the aggregation run through a different set of documents. Either way, you get 10 such results because `size` defaults to `10`. As you saw in chapters 2 and 4, you can change `size` from either the URI or the JSON payload of your query.

Field data and aggregations

When you run a regular search, it goes fast because of the nature of the inverted index: you have a limited number of terms to look for, and Elasticsearch will identify documents containing those terms and return the results. An aggregation, on the other hand, has to work with the terms of each document matching the query. It needs a mapping between document IDs and terms—opposite of the inverted index, which maps terms to documents.

By default, Elasticsearch un-inverts the inverted index into *field data*, as we explained in chapter 6, section 6.10. The more terms it has to deal with, the more memory the field data will use. That's why you have to make sure you give Elasticsearch a large enough heap, especially when you're doing aggregations on large numbers of documents or if you're analyzing fields and you have more than one term per document. For `not_analyzed` fields, you can use doc values to have this un-inverted data structure built at index time and stored on disk. More details about field data and doc values can be found in chapter 6, section 6.10.

7.1.2 *Aggregations run on query results*

Computing metrics over the whole dataset is just one of the possible use cases for aggregations. Often you want to compute metrics in the context of a query. For example, if you're searching for groups in Denver, you probably want to see the most popular tags for those groups only. As you'll see in the next listing, this is the default behavior for aggregations. Unlike in listing 7.1, where the implied query was `match_all`, in the following listing you query for "Denver" in the `location` field, and aggregations will only be about groups from Denver.

```
Listing 7.2   Getting top tags for groups in Denver
```

```
curl 'localhost:9200/get-together/group/_search?pretty' -d '{
"query": {
  "match": {
    "location": "Denver"          ◁──┐  In this query you
  }                                    look only for groups
},                                     in Denver.
"aggregations" : {
  "top_tags" : {
    "terms" : {
      "field" : "tags.verbatim"
    }
  }
}
}}'
### reply
[...]
  "hits" : {
    "total" : 2,                  ◁──┐  Fewer results than in
    "max_score" : 1.44856,             listing 7.1 because
    "hits" : [ {                       you look only for
[...]                                  Denver groups
  "name": "Denver Clojure",
[...]
  "name": "Elasticsearch Denver",
[...]
  },
  "aggregations" : {
    "top_tags" : {
      "buckets" : [ {
        "key" : "denver",
        "doc_count" : 2              Tags are counted only for
      }, {                           Denver groups, so they
        "key" : "big data",          look different than in
        "doc_count" : 1              listing 7.1.
[...]
```

Recall from chapter 4 that you can use the `from` and `size` parameters of your query to control the pagination of results. These parameters have no influence on aggregations because aggregations always run on all the documents matching a query.

If you want to restrict query results more without also restricting aggregations, you can use post filters. We'll discuss post filters and the relationship between filters and aggregations in general in the next section.

7.1.3 *Filters and aggregations*

In chapter 4 you saw that for most query types there's a filter equivalent. Because filters don't calculate scores and are cacheable, they're faster than their query counterparts. You've also learned that you should wrap filters in a `filtered` query, like this:

```
% curl 'localhost:9200/get-together/group/_search?pretty' -d '{
"query": {
  "filtered": {
    "filter": {
      "term": {
        "location": "denver"
      }
    }
  }
}}'
```

Using the filter this way is good for overall query performance because the filter runs first. Then the query—which is typically more performance-intensive—runs only on documents matching the filter. As far as aggregations are concerned, they run only on documents matching the overall `filtered` query, as shown in figure 7.3.

"Nothing new so far," you might say. "The `filtered` query behaves like any other query when it comes to aggregations," and you'd be right. But there's also another way of running filters: by using a *post filter,* which will run after the query and independent of the aggregation. The following request will give the same results as the previous filtered query:

```
% curl 'localhost:9200/get-together/group/_search?pretty' -d '{
"post_filter": {
  "term": {
    "location": "denver"
  }
}}'
```

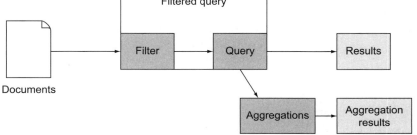

Figure 7.3 A filter wrapped in a `filtered` query runs first and restricts both results and aggregations.

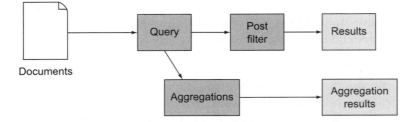

Figure 7.4   Post filter runs after the query and doesn't affect aggregations.

As illustrated in figure 7.4, the post filter differs from the filter in the `filtered` query in two ways:

- *Performance*—The post filter runs after the query, making sure the query will run on all documents, and the filter runs only on those documents matching the query. The overall request is typically slower than the `filtered` query equivalent, where the filter runs first.
- *Document set processed by aggregations*—If a document doesn't match the post filter, it will still be accounted for by aggregations.

Now that you understand the relationships between queries, filters, and aggregations, as well as the overall structure of an aggregation request, we can dive deeper into Aggregations Land and explore different aggregation types. We'll start with metrics aggregations and then go to bucket aggregations, and then we'll discuss how to combine them to get powerful insights from your data in real time.

7.2   *Metrics aggregations*

Metrics aggregations extract statistics from groups of documents, or, as we'll explore in section 7.4, buckets of documents coming from other aggregations.

   These statistics are typically done on numeric fields, such as the minimum or average price. You can get each such statistic separately or you can get them together via the `stats` aggregation. More advanced statistics, such as the sum of squares or the standard deviation, are available through the `extended_stats` aggregation.

   For both numeric and non-numeric fields you can get the number of unique values using the `cardinality` aggregation, which will be discussed in section 7.2.3.

7.2.1   *Statistics*

We'll begin looking at metrics aggregations by getting some statistics on the number of attendees for each event.

   From the code samples, you can see that event documents contain an array of attendees. You can calculate the number of attendees at query time through a script, which we'll show in listing 7.3. We discussed scripting in chapter 3, when you used scripts for updating documents. In general, with Elasticsearch queries you can build a script field, where you put a typically small piece of code that returns a value for each document. In this case, the value will be the count of elements of the attendees array.

> ### The flexibility of scripts comes with a price
>
> Scripts are flexible when it comes to querying, but you have to be aware of the caveats in terms of performance and security.
>
> Even though most aggregation types allow you to use them, scripts slow down aggregations because they have to be run on every document. To avoid the need of running a script, you can do the calculation at index time. In this case, you can extract the number of attendees for every event and add it to a separate field before indexing it. We'll talk more about performance in chapter 10.
>
> In most Elasticsearch deployments, the user specifies a query string, and it's up to the server-side application to construct the query out of it. But if you allow users to specify any kind of query, including scripts, someone might exploit this and run malicious code. That's why, depending on your Elasticsearch version, running scripts inline like in listing 7.3 (called *dynamic scripting*) is disabled. To enable it, set script.disable_dynamic: false in elasticsearch.yml.

In the following listing, you'll request statistics on the number of attendees for all events. To get the number of attendees in the script, you'll use doc['attendees'].values to get the array of attendees. Adding the length property to that will return their number.

Listing 7.3 Getting stats for the number of event attendees

```
URI=localhost:9200/get-together/event/_search
curl "$URI?pretty&search_type=count" -d '{     <-- When you care only about
"aggregations": {                                  aggregations, you shouldn't ask
  "attendees_stats": {                             for any result, just their count.
    "stats": {
      "script": "doc['"'attendees'"'].values.length"  <-- Script to generate the
    }                                                      number of attendees.
  }                                                        Use field instead of script
}}'                                                        to point to a real field.
### reply
[...]
  "aggregations" : {
    "attendees_stats" : {
      "count" : 15,
      "min" : 3.0,
      "max" : 5.0,
      "avg" : 3.8666666666666667,
      "sum" : 58.0
    }
  }
}
```

You can see that you get back the minimum number of attendees per event, as well as the maximum, the sum, and the average. You also get the number of documents these statistics were computed on.

If you need only one of those statistics, you can get it separately. For example, you'll calculate the average number of attendees per event through the avg aggregation in the next listing.

Listing 7.4   Getting the average number of event attendees

```
URI=localhost:9200/get-together/event/_search
curl "$URI?pretty&search_type=count" -d '{
"aggregations": {
  "attendees_avg": {
    "avg": {
      "script": "doc['"'attendees'"'].values.length"
    }
  }
}}'
### reply
[...]
  "aggregations" : {
    "attendees_avg" : {
      "value" : 3.8666666666666667
    }
  }
}
```

Similar to the avg aggregation, you can get the other metrics through the min, max, sum, and value_count aggregations. You'd have to replace avg from listing 7.4 with the needed aggregation name. The advantage of separate statistics is that Elasticsearch won't spend time computing metrics that you don't need.

7.2.2   *Advanced statistics*

In addition to statistics gathered by the stats aggregation, you can get the sum of squares, variance, and standard deviation of your numeric field by running the extended_stats aggregation, as shown in the next listing.

Listing 7.5   Getting extended statistics on the number of attendees

```
URI=localhost:9200/get-together/event/_search
curl "$URI?pretty&search_type=count" -d '{
"aggregations": {
  "attendees_extended_stats": {
    "extended_stats": {
      "script": "doc['"'attendees'"'].values.length"
    }
  }
}}'
### reply
  "aggregations" : {
    "attendees_extended_stats" : {
```

```
        "count" : 15,
        "min" : 3.0,
        "max" : 5.0,
        "avg" : 3.8666666666666667,
        "sum" : 58.0,
        "sum_of_squares" : 230.0,
        "variance" : 0.38222222222222135,
        "std_deviation" : 0.6182412330330462
      }
  }
```

All these statistics are calculated by looking at all the values in the document set matching the query, so they're 100% accurate all the time. Next we'll look at some statistics that use approximation algorithms, trading some of the accuracy for speed and less memory consumption.

7.2.3 *Approximate statistics*

Some statistics can be calculated with good precision—though not 100%—by looking at some of the values from your documents. This will limit both their execution time and their memory consumption.

Here we'll look at how to get two types of such statistics from Elasticsearch: percentiles and cardinality. *Percentiles* are values below which you can find x% of the total values, where x is the given percentile. This is useful, for example, when you have an online shop: you log the value of each shopping cart and you want to see in which price range are most shopping carts. Perhaps most of your users only buy an item or two, but the upper 10% buy a lot of items and generate most of your revenue.

Cardinality is the number of unique values in a field. This is useful, for example, when you want the number of unique IP addresses accessing your website.

PERCENTILES

For percentiles, think about the number of attendees for events once again and determine the maximum number of attendees you'll consider normal and the number you'll consider high. In listing 7.6, you'll calculate the 80th percentile and the 99th. You'll consider numbers under the 80th to be normal and numbers under the 99th high, and you'll ignore the upper 1%, because they're exceptionally high.

To accomplish this, you'll use the percentiles aggregation, and you'll set the percents array to 80 and 99 in order to get these specific percentiles.

Listing 7.6 Getting the 80th and the 99th percentiles from the number of attendees

```
URI=localhost:9200/get-together/event/_search
curl "$URI?pretty&search_type=count" -d '{
"aggregations": {
  "attendees_percentiles": {
    "percentiles": {
      "script": "doc['"'attendees'"'].values.length",
      "percents": [80, 99]
    }
```

```
      }
  }}'
  ### reply
    "aggregations" : {
      "attendees_percentiles" : {          80% of values
        "values" : {                       are at most 4.
          "80.0" : 4.0,            ◄──────
          "99.0" : 5.0          ◄─
        }
      }                              99% of values
    }                                are at most 5.
```

For small data sets like the code samples, you have 100% accuracy, but this may not happen with large data sets in production. With the default settings, you have over 99.9% accuracy for most data sets for most percentiles. The specific percentile matters, because accuracy is at its worst for the 50th percentile, and as you go toward 0 or 100 it gets better and better.

You can trade memory for accuracy by increasing the `compression` parameter from the default `100`. Memory consumption increases proportionally to the compression, which in turn controls how many values are taken into account when approximating percentiles.

There's also a `percentile_ranks` aggregation that allows you to do the opposite—specify a set of values—and you'll get back the corresponding percentage of documents having up to those values:

```
% curl "$URI?pretty&search_type=count" -d '{
"aggregations": {
  "attendees_percentile_ranks": {
    "percentile_ranks": {
      "script": "doc['"'attendees'"'].values.length",
      "values": [4, 5]
    }
  }
}}'
```

CARDINALITY

For cardinality, let's imagine you want the number of unique members of your get-together site. The following listing shows how to do that with the `cardinality` aggregation.

> **Listing 7.7 Getting the number of unique members through the `cardinality` aggregation**

```
URI=localhost:9200/get-together/group/_search
curl "$URI?pretty&search_type=count" -d '{
"aggregations": {
  "members_cardinality": {
    "cardinality": {
      "field": "members"
    }
  }
```

```
}}'
### reply
  "aggregations" : {
    "members_cardinality" : {
      "value" : 8
    }
  }
}
```

Like the `percentiles` aggregation, the `cardinality` aggregation is approximate. To understand the benefit of such approximation algorithms, let's take a closer look at the alternative. Before the `cardinality` aggregation was introduced in version 1.1.0, the common way to get the cardinality of a field was by running the `terms` aggregation you saw in section 7.1. Because the `terms` aggregation will get the counts of each term for top N terms, where N is the configurable `size` parameter, if you specify a `size` large enough, you could get all the unique terms back. Counting them will give you the cardinality.

Unfortunately, this approach only works for fields with relatively low cardinality and a low number of documents. Otherwise, running a `terms` aggregation with a huge size requires a lot of resources:

- *Memory*—All the unique terms need to be loaded in memory in order to be counted.
- *CPU*—Those terms have to be returned in order; by default the order is on how many times each term occurs.
- *Network*—From each shard, the large array of sorted unique terms has to be transferred to the node that received the client request. That node also has to merge per-shard arrays into one big array and transfer it back to the client.

This is where approximation algorithms come into play. The `cardinality` field works with an algorithm called HyperLogLog++ that hashes values from the field you want to examine and uses the hashes to approximate the cardinality. It loads only some of those hashes into memory at once, so the memory usage will be constant no matter how many terms you have.

> **NOTE** For more details on the HyperLogLog++ algorithm, have a look at the original paper from Google: http://static.googleusercontent.com/external _content/untrusted_dlcp/research.google.com/en/us/pubs/archive/ 40671.pdf.

MEMORY AND CARDINALITY

We said that the memory usage of the `cardinality` aggregation is constant, but how large would that constant be? You can configure it through the `precision_threshold` parameter. The higher the threshold, the more precise the results, but more memory is consumed. If you run the `cardinality` aggregation on its own, it will take about `precision_threshold` times 8 bytes of memory for each shard that gets hit by the query.

The `cardinality` aggregation, like all other aggregations, can be nested under a bucket aggregation. When that happens, the memory usage is further multiplied by the number of buckets generated by the parent aggregations.

> **TIP** For most cases, the default `precision_threshold` will work well, because it provides a good tradeoff between memory usage and accuracy, and it adjusts itself depending on the number of buckets.

Next, we'll look at the choice of multi-bucket aggregations. But before we go there, table 7.1 gives you a quick overview of each metrics aggregation and the typical use case.

Table 7.1 Metrics aggregations and typical use cases

Aggregation type	Example use case
`stats`	Same product sold in multiple stores. Gather statistics on the price: how many stores have it and what the minimum, maximum, and average prices are.
individual stats (`min`, `max`, `sum`, `avg`, `value_count`)	Same product sold in multiple stores. Show "prices starting from" and then the minimum price.
`extended_stats`	Documents contain results from a personality test. Gather statistics from that group of people, such as the variance and the standard deviation.
`percentiles`	Access times on your website: what the usual delays are and how long the longest response times are.
`percentile_ranks`	Checking if you meet SLAs: if 99% of requests have to be served under 100ms, you can check what's the actual percentage.
`cardinality`	Number of unique IP addresses accessing your service.

7.3 *Multi-bucket aggregations*

As you saw in the previous section, metrics aggregations are about taking all your documents and generating one or more numbers that describe them. Multi-bucket aggregations are about taking those documents and putting them into buckets—like the group of documents matching each tag. Then, for each bucket, you'll get one or more numbers that describe the bucket, such as counting the number of groups for each tag.

So far you've run metrics aggregations on all documents matching the query. You can think of those documents as one big bucket. Other aggregations generate such buckets: for example, if you're indexing logs and have a country code field, you can do a `terms` aggregation on it to create one bucket of documents for each country. As you'll see in section 7.4, you can nest aggregations: for example, a `cardinality` aggregation could run on the buckets created by the `terms` aggregation to give you the number of unique visitors per country.

For now, let's see what kinds of multi-bucket aggregations are available and where they're typically useful:

- *Terms aggregations* let you figure out the frequency of each term in your documents. There's the `terms` aggregation, which you've seen a couple of times already, that gives you back the number of times each term appears. It's useful for figuring out things like frequent posters on a blog or popular tags. There's also the `significant_terms` aggregation, which gives you back the difference between the occurrence of a term in the whole index and its occurrence in your query results. This is useful for suggesting terms that are significant for the search context, like "elasticsearch" would be for the context of "search engine."

- *Range aggregations* create buckets based on how documents fall into which numerical, date, or IP address range. This is useful when analyzing data where the user has fixed expectations. For example, if someone is searching for a laptop in an online shop, you know the price ranges that are most popular.

- *Histogram aggregations*, either numerical or date, are similar to range aggregations, but instead of requiring you to define each range, you have to define an interval, and Elasticsearch will build buckets based on that interval. This is useful when you don't know where the user is likely to look. For example, you could show a chart of how many events occur each month.

- *Nested, reverse nested, and children aggregations* allow you to perform aggregations across document relationships. We'll discuss them in chapter 8 when we talk about nested and parent-child relations.

- *Geo distance and geohash grid aggregations* allow you to create buckets based on geolocation. We'll show them in appendix A, which is focused on geo search.

Figure 7.5 shows an overview of the types of multi-bucket aggregations we'll discuss here.

Next, let's zoom into each of these multi-bucket aggregations and see how you can use them.

7.3.1 Terms aggregations

We first looked at the `terms` aggregation in section 7.1 as an example of how all aggregations work. The typical use case is to get the *top frequent X*, where *X* would be a field in your document, like the name of a user, a tag, or a category. Because the `terms` aggregation counts every term and not every field value, you'll normally run this aggregation on a non-analyzed field, because you want "big data" to be counted once and not once for "big" and once for "data."

Terms aggregation:
most frequent tags

Significant terms aggregation:
tags appearing more often when searching
for "search engine" than they appear overall

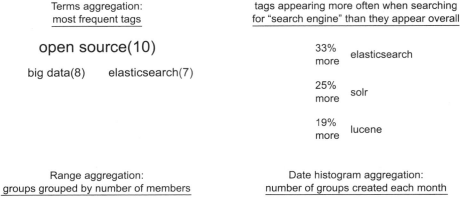

Range aggregation:
groups grouped by number of members

Date histogram aggregation:
number of groups created each month

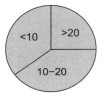

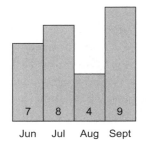

Figure 7.5   Major types of multi-bucket aggregations

You could use the `terms` aggregation to extract the most frequent terms from an analyzed field, like the description of an event. You can use this information to generate a word cloud, like the one in figure 7.6. Just make sure you have enough memory for loading all the fields in memory if you have many documents or the documents contain many terms.

By default, the order of terms is by their count, descending, which fits all the top frequent X use cases. But you can order terms ascending, or by other criteria, such as the term name itself. The following listing shows how to list the group tags ordered alphabetically by using the `order` property.

> introduction
>
> elasticsearch   hadoop
>   use-case
> talk

Figure 7.6   A `terms` aggregation can be used to get term frequencies and generate a word cloud.

Listing 7.8   Ordering tag buckets by name

```
URI=localhost:9200/get-together/group/_search
curl "$URI?pretty&search_type=count" -d '{
```

```
"aggregations": {
  "tags": {
    "terms": {
      "field": "tags.verbatim",
      "order": {
        "_term": "asc"                    ◁─┐  Criterion to sort on (the
      }                                     │  term for that bucket)
    }                                       │  and order (ascending)
  }
}
}}'
### reply
  "aggregations" : {
    "tags" : {
      "buckets" : [ {
        "key" : "apache lucene",
        "doc_count" : 1
      }, {
        "key" : "big data",
        "doc_count" : 3
      }, {
        "key" : "clojure",
        "doc_count" : 1
```

If you're nesting a metric aggregation under your terms aggregation, you can order terms by the metric, too. For example, you could use the average metric aggregation under your tags aggregation from listing 7.8 to get the average number of group members per tag. And you can order tags by the number of members by referring your metric aggregation name, like avg_members: desc (instead of _term: asc as in listing 7.8).

WHICH TERMS TO INCLUDE IN THE REPLY
By default, the terms aggregation will return only the top 10 terms by the order you selected. You can, however, change that number though the size parameter. Setting size to 0 will get you all the terms, but it's dangerous to use with a high-cardinality field, because returning a very large result is CPU-intensive to sort and might saturate your network.

To get back the top 10 terms—or the number of terms you configure with size—Elasticsearch has to get a number of terms (configurable through shard_size) from each shard and aggregate the results. The process is shown in figure 7.7, with shard_size and size set to 2 for clarity.

This mechanism implies that you might get inaccurate counters for some terms if those terms don't make it to the top of each individual shard. This can even result in missing terms, like in figure 7.7 where lucene, with a total value of 7, isn't returned in the top 2 overall tags because it didn't make the top 2 for each shard.

You can get more accurate results by setting a large shard_size, as shown in figure 7.8. But this will make aggregations more expensive (especially if you nest them) because there are more buckets that need to be kept in memory.

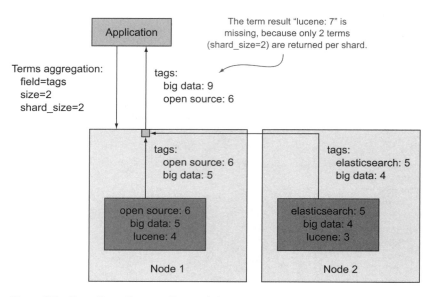

Figure 7.7   Sometimes the overall top *X* is inaccurate, because only the top *X* terms are returned per shard.

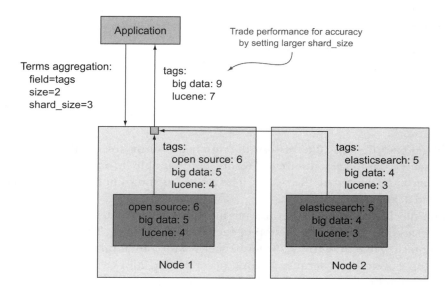

Figure 7.8   Reducing inaccuracies by increasing `shard_size`

To get an idea of how accurate results are, you can check the values at the beginning of the aggregation response:

```
"tags" : {
  "doc_count_error_upper_bound" : 0,
  "sum_other_doc_count" : 6,
```

The first number is the worst-case scenario error margin. For example, if the minimum count for a term returned by a shard is 5, it could be that a term occurring four times in that shard has been missed. If that term should have appeared in the final results, that's a worst-case error of 4. The total of these numbers for all shards makes up `doc_count_error_upper_bound`. For our code samples, that number is always 0, because we have only one shard—the top terms for that shard are the same as the global top terms.

The second number is the total count of the terms that didn't make the top.

You can get a `doc_count_error_upper_bound` value for each term by setting `show_term_doc_count_error` to `true`. This will take the worst-case scenario error per term: for example if "big data" is returned by a shard, you know that it's the exact value. But if another shard doesn't return "big data" at all, the worst-case scenario is that "big data" actually exists with a value just below the last returned term. Adding up these error numbers for shards not returning that term make up `doc_count_error _upper_bound` per term.

At the other end of the accuracy spectrum, you could consider terms with low frequency irrelevant and exclude them from the result set entirely. This is especially useful when you sort terms by something other than frequency, which makes it likely that low-frequency terms will appear, but you don't want to pollute the results with irrelevant results like typos. To do that, you'll need to change the `min_doc_count` setting from the default value of 1. If you want to cut these low-frequency terms at the shard level, you use `shard_min_doc_count`.

Finally, you can include and exclude specific terms from the result. You'd do that by using the `include` and `exclude` options and providing regular expressions as values. Using `include` alone will include only terms matching the pattern; using `exclude` alone will include terms that don't match. Using both will have `exclude` take precedence: included terms will match the `include` pattern but won't match the `exclude` pattern.

The following listing shows how to only return counters for tags containing "search."

Listing 7.9 Creating buckets only for terms containing "search"

```
URI=localhost:9200/get-together/group/_search
curl "$URI?pretty&search_type=count" -d '{
"aggregations": {
  "tags": {
    "terms": {
      "field": "tags.verbatim",
      "include": ".*search.*"
```

```
      }
    }
  }}'
### reply
   "aggregations" : {
     "tags" : {
       "buckets" : [ {
         "key" : "elasticsearch",
         "doc_count" : 2
       }, {
         "key" : "enterprise search",
         "doc_count" : 1
```

Collect mode

By default, Elasticsearch does all aggregations in a single pass. For example, if you had a `terms` aggregation and a `cardinality` aggregation nested in it, Elasticsearch would make a bucket for each term, calculate the cardinality for each bucket, sort those buckets, and return the top *X*.

This works well for most use cases, but it will take lots of time and memory if you have lots of buckets and lots of sub-aggregations, especially if a sub-aggregation is also a multi-bucket aggregation with lots of buckets. In such cases, a two-pass approach will be better: first create the buckets of the top-level aggregation, sort and cache the top *X*, and then calculate sub-aggregations on only those top *X*.

You can control which approach Elasticsearch uses by setting `collect_mode`. The default is `depth_first`, and the two-pass approach is `breadth_first`.

SIGNIFICANT TERMS

The `significant_terms` aggregation is useful if you want to see which terms have higher frequencies than normal in your current search results. Let's take the example of get-together groups: in all the groups out there, the term `clojure` may not appear frequently enough to count. Let's assume that it appears 10 times out of 1,000,000 terms (0.0001%). If you restrict your search for Denver, let's say it appears 7 times out of 10,000 terms (0.007%). The percentage is significantly higher than before and indicates a strong Clojure community in Denver, compared to the rest of the search area. It doesn't matter that other terms such as `programming` or `devops` have a much higher absolute frequency.

The `significant_terms` aggregation is much like the `terms` aggregation in the sense that it's counting terms. But the resulting buckets are ordered by a score, which represents the difference in percentage between the foreground documents (that 0.007% in the previous example) and the background documents (0.0001%). The foreground documents are those matching your query, and the background documents are all the documents from the index.

In the following listing, you'll try to find out which users of the get-together site have a similar preference to Lee for events. To do that, you'll query for events where

Lee attends and use the `significant_terms` aggregation to see which event attendees participate in more, compared to the overall set of events they attend.

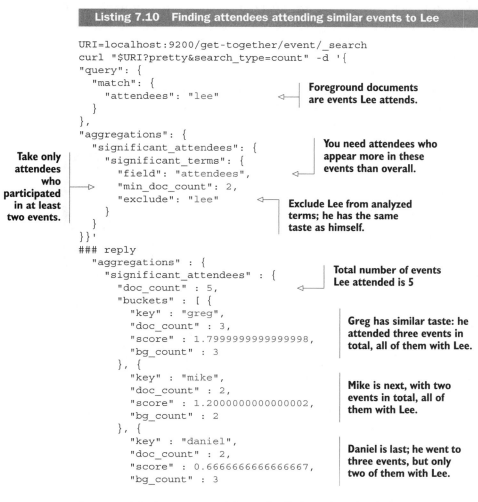

Listing 7.10 Finding attendees attending similar events to Lee

```
URI=localhost:9200/get-together/event/_search
curl "$URI?pretty&search_type=count" -d '{
"query": {
  "match": {
    "attendees": "lee"          ◄─── Foreground documents
  }                                   are events Lee attends.
},
"aggregations": {
  "significant_attendees": {        You need attendees who
    "significant_terms": {          appear more in these
      "field": "attendees",    ◄─── events than overall.
      "min_doc_count": 2,
      "exclude": "lee"         ◄─── Exclude Lee from analyzed
    }                               terms; he has the same
  }                                 taste as himself.
}}'
### reply
  "aggregations" : {
    "significant_attendees" : {     Total number of events
      "doc_count" : 5,         ◄─── Lee attended is 5
      "buckets" : [ {
        "key" : "greg",             Greg has similar taste: he
        "doc_count" : 3,            attended three events in
        "score" : 1.7999999999999998,  total, all of them with Lee.
        "bg_count" : 3
      }, {
        "key" : "mike",             Mike is next, with two
        "doc_count" : 2,            events in total, all of
        "score" : 1.2000000000000002,  them with Lee.
        "bg_count" : 2
      }, {
        "key" : "daniel",           Daniel is last; he went to
        "doc_count" : 2,            three events, but only
        "score" : 0.6666666666666667,  two of them with Lee.
        "bg_count" : 3
```

Take only attendees who participated in at least two events.

As you might have guessed from the listing, the `significant_terms` aggregation has the same `size`, `shard_size`, `min_doc_count`, `shard_min_doc_count`, `include`, and `exclude` options as the `terms` aggregation, which lets you control the terms you get back. In addition to those, it allows you to change the background documents from all the documents in the index to only those matching a defined filter in the `background_filter` parameter. For example, you may know that Lee participates only in technology events, so you can filter those to make sure that events irrelevant to him aren't taken into account.

Both the `terms` and `significant_terms` aggregations work well for string fields. For numeric fields, `range` and `histogram` aggregations are more relevant, and we'll look at them next.

7.3.2 *Range aggregations*

The `terms` aggregation is most often used with strings, but it works with numeric values, too. This is useful when you have low cardinality, like when you want to give counts on how many laptops have two years of warranty, how many have three, and so on.

With high-cardinality fields, such as ages or prices, you're most likely looking for ranges. For example, you may want to know how many of your users are between 18 and 39, how many are between 40 and 60, and so on. You can still do that with the `terms` aggregation, but it's going to be tedious: in your application, you'd have to add up counters for ages 18, 19, and so on until you get to 39 to get the first bucket. And if you want to add sub-aggregations, like the ones you'll see later in this chapter, things will get even more complicated.

To solve this problem for numerical values, you have the `range` aggregation. As the name suggests, you give the numerical ranges you want, and it will count the documents with values that fall into each bucket. You can use those counters to represent the data in a graphical way—for example, with a pie chart, as shown in figure 7.9.

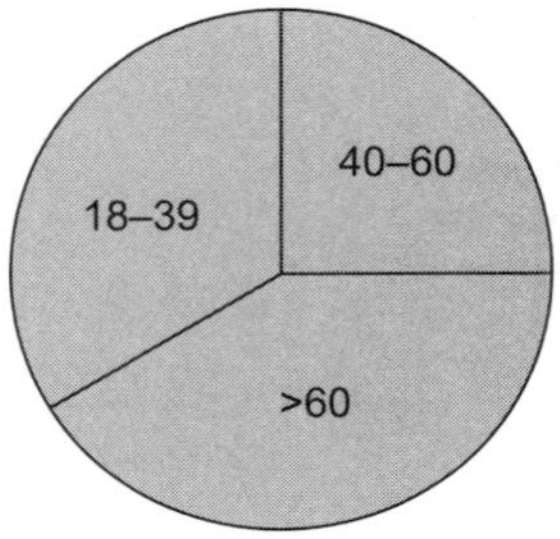

Recall from chapter 3 that date strings are stored as type `long` in Elasticsearch, representing the UNIX time in milliseconds. To work with date ranges, you have a variant of the `range` aggregation called the `date_range` aggregation.

Figure 7.9 `range` aggregations give you counts of documents for each range. This is good for pie charts.

RANGE AGGREGATION

Let's get back to our get-together site example and do a breakdown of events by their number of attendees. You'll do it with the `range` aggregation and give it an array of ranges. The thing to keep in mind here is that the minimum value from the range (the key `from`) is included in the bucket, whereas the maximum value (`to`) is excluded. In listing 7.11, you'll have three categories:

- Events with fewer than four members
- Events with at least four members but fewer than six
- Events with at least six members

NOTE Ranges don't have to be adjacent; they can be separated or they can overlap. In most cases it makes sense to cover all values, but you don't need to.

Listing 7.11 Using a range aggregation to divide events by the number of attendees

```
URI=localhost:9200/get-together/event/_search
curl "$URI?pretty&search_type=count" -d '{
"aggregations": {
  "attendees_breakdown": {
    "range": {
      "script": "doc['"'attendees'"'].values.length",
```

Use a script to get the number, like in previous examples.

```
        "ranges": [
            { "to": 4 },
            { "from": 4, "to": 6 },     ┤ The ranges to
            { "from": 6 }                 use for counting
        ]
    }
  }
}
}}'
### reply
    "aggregations" : {
        "attendees_breakdown" : {
            "buckets" : [ {
                "key" : "*-4.0",
                "to" : 4.0,                      For each range, you
                "to_as_string" : "4.0",          get the document
                "doc_count" : 4         ◄─┤      count...
            }, {
                "key" : "4.0-6.0",
                "from" : 4.0,
                "from_as_string" : "4.0",
                "to" : 6.0,
                "to_as_string" : "6.0",
                "doc_count" : 11
            }, {
                "key" : "6.0-*",
                "from" : 6.0,                     even if that
                "from_as_string" : "6.0",         value is 0.
                "doc_count" : 0         ◄─┤
```

You can see from the listing that you don't have to specify both `from` and `to` for every range in the aggregation. Omitting one of these parameters will remove the respective boundary, and this enables you to search for all events with fewer than four members or with at least six.

DATE RANGE AGGREGATION

As you might imagine, the `date_range` aggregation works just like the `range` aggregation, except you put date strings in your range definitions. And because of that, you should define the date format so Elasticsearch will know how to translate the string you give it into the numerical UNIX time, which is how date fields are stored.

In the following listing, you'll divide events into two categories: before July 2013 and starting with July 2013. You can use a similar approach to count future events and past events, for example.

> **Listing 7.12 Using a `date range` aggregation to divide events by scheduled date**

```
URI=localhost:9200/get-together/event/_search
curl "$URI?pretty&search_type=count" -d '{
"aggregations": {
  "dates_breakdown": {
    "date_range": {                    Define a format to
      "field": "date",                 parse the date
      "format": "YYYY.MM",     ◄─┤     strings.
```

```
        "ranges": [
            { "to": "2013.07" },              Ranges are defined
            { "from": "2013.07"}              in date strings, too.
        ]
    }
  }
}}'
### reply
  "aggregations" : {
    "dates_breakdown" : {
      "buckets" : [ {
        "key" : "*-2013.07",
        "to" : 1.3726368E12,                  For each range, you
        "to_as_string" : "2013.07",           get the document
        "doc_count" : 8                ◄──     count.
      }, {
        "key" : "2013.07-*",
        "from" : 1.3726368E12,
        "from_as_string" : "2013.07",
        "doc_count" : 7
```

If the value of the format field looks familiar, it's because it's the same Joda Time annotation that you saw in chapter 3 when you defined date formats in the mapping. For the complete syntax, you can look at the DateTimeFormat documentation: http://joda-time.sourceforge.net/apidocs/org/joda/time/format/DateTimeFormat.html.

7.3.3 *Histogram aggregations*

For dealing with numeric ranges, you also have histogram aggregations. These are much like the range aggregations you just saw, but instead of manually defining each range, you'd define a fixed interval, and Elasticsearch would build the ranges for you. For example, if you want age groups from people documents, you can define an interval of 10 (years) and you'll get buckets like 0–10 (excluding 10), 10–20 (excluding 20), and so on.

Like the range aggregation, the histogram aggregation has a variant that works with dates, called the date_histogram aggregation. This is useful, for example, when building histogram charts of how many emails were sent on a mailing list each day.

HISTOGRAM AGGREGATION

Running a histogram aggregation is similar to running a range aggregation. You just replace the ranges array with an interval, and Elasticsearch will build ranges starting with the minimum value, adding the interval until the maximum value is included. For example, in the following listing, you specify an interval of 1 and show how many events have three attendees, how many have four, and how many have five.

Listing 7.13 Histogram showing the number of events for each number of attendees

```
URI=localhost:9200/get-together/event/_search
curl "$URI?pretty&search_type=count" -d '{
"aggregations": {
```

```
  "attendees_histogram": {
    "histogram": {
      "script": "doc['"'attendees'"'].values.length",
      "interval": 1                    ◄─┐  interval used for building
    }                                     │  ranges. Here you want to
  }                                       │  see every value.
}}'
### reply
  "aggregations" : {
    "attendees_histogram" : {          ┌─  Keys show the from
      "buckets" : [ {                  │   value of the range;
        "key" : 3,                   ◄─┘   "to" is key+interval.
        "doc_count" : 4
      }, {
        "key" : 4,                   ◄─┐  Next "from" is the
        "doc_count" : 9               │  previous "to".
      }, {
        "key" : 5,
        "doc_count" : 2
```

Like the `terms` aggregation, the `histogram` aggregation lets you specify a `min_doc`
`_count` value, which is helpful if you want buckets with few documents to be ignored.
`min_doc_count` is also useful if you want to show empty buckets. By default, if there's
an interval between the minimum and maximum values that has no documents, that
interval will be omitted altogether. Set `min_doc_count` to `0` and those intervals will still
appear with a document count of `0`.

DATE HISTOGRAM AGGREGATION

As you might expect, you'd use the `date_histogram` aggregation like the `histogram`
one, but you'd insert a date in the `interval` field. That date would be specified in the
same Joda Time annotation as the `date_range` aggregation, with values such as `1M` or
`1.5h`. For example, the following listing gives the breakdown of events happening in
each month.

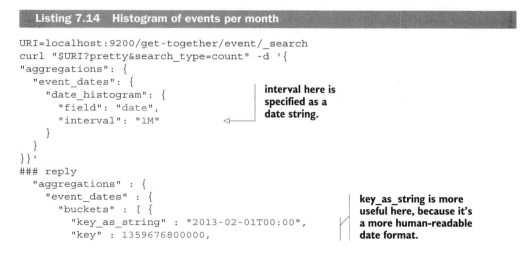

> **Listing 7.14   Histogram of events per month**

```
URI=localhost:9200/get-together/event/_search
curl "$URI?pretty&search_type=count" -d '{
"aggregations": {
  "event_dates": {
    "date_histogram": {
      "field": "date",
      "interval": "1M"          ◄─┐  interval here is
    }                             │  specified as a
  }                               │  date string.
}
}}'
### reply
  "aggregations" : {
    "event_dates" : {
      "buckets" : [ {                         ┌─  key_as_string is more
        "key_as_string" : "2013-02-01T00:00", │   useful here, because it's
        "key" : 1359676800000,              ◄─┘   a more human-readable
                                                  date format.
```

```
        "doc_count" : 1
    }, {
      "key_as_string" : "2013-03-01T00:00",
      "key" : 1362096000000,
      "doc_count" : 1
    }, {
      "key_as_string" : "2013-04-01T00:00",
      "key" : 1364774400000,
      "doc_count" : 2
[...]
```

Like the regular `histogram` aggregation, you can use the `min_doc_count` option to either show empty buckets or omit buckets containing just a few documents.

You probably noticed that the `date_histogram` aggregation has two things in common with all the other multi-bucket aggregations:

- It counts documents having certain terms.
- It creates buckets of documents falling into each category.

The buckets themselves are useful only when you nest other aggregations under a multi-bucket aggregation. This allows you to have deeper insights into your data, and we'll look at nesting aggregations in the next section. First, take time to look at table 7.2, which gives you a quick overview of the multi-bucket aggregations and what they're typically used for.

Table 7.2 Multi-bucket aggregations and typical use cases

Aggregation type	Example use case
`terms`	Show top tags on a blogging site; hot topics this week on a news site.
`significant_terms`	Identify new technology trends by looking at what's used/downloaded a lot this month compared to overall.
`range` and `date_range`	Show entry-level, medium-priced, and expensive laptops. Show archived events, events this week, upcoming events.
`histogram` and `date_histogram`	Show distributions: how much people of each age exercise. Or show trends: items bought each day.

The list isn't exhaustive, but it does include the most important aggregation types and their options. You can check the documentation[1] for a complete list. Also, geo aggregations are dealt with in appendix A, and nested and children aggregations in chapter 8.

7.4 Nesting aggregations

The real power of aggregations is the fact that you can combine them. For example, if you have a blog and you record each access to your posts, you can use the `terms`

---

[1] www.elastic.co/guide/en/elasticsearch/reference/master/search-aggregations.html

aggregation to show the most-viewed posts. But you can also nest a `cardinality` aggregation under this `terms` aggregation and show the number of unique visitors for each post; you can even change the sorting in the `terms` aggregation to show posts with the most unique visitors.

As you may imagine, nesting aggregations opens a whole new range of possibilities for exploring data. Nesting is the main reason aggregations emerged in Elasticsearch as a replacement for facets, because facets couldn't be combined.

Multi-bucket aggregations are typically the point where you start nesting. For example, the `terms` aggregation allows you to show the top tags for get-together groups; this means you'll have a bucket of documents for each tag. You can use sub-aggregations to show more metrics for each bucket. For example, you can show how many groups are being created each month, for each tag, as illustrated in figure 7.10.

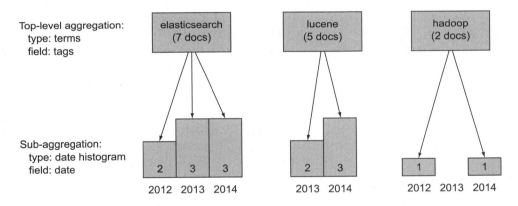

Figure 7.10 Nesting a `date histogram` aggregation under a `terms` aggregation

Later in this section, we'll discuss one particular use case for nesting: *result grouping*, which, unlike a regular search that gives you the top *N* results by relevance, gives you the top *N* results for each bucket of documents generated by the parent aggregation. Say you have an online shop and someone searches for "Windows." Normally, relevance-sorted results will show many versions of the Windows operating system first. This may not be the best user experience, because at this point it's not 100% clear whether the user is looking to buy a Windows operating system, some software built for Windows, or some hardware that works with Windows. This is where result grouping, illustrated in figure 7.11, comes in handy: you can show the top three results from each of the operating systems, software, and hardware categories and give the user a broader range of results. The user may also want to click on the category name to narrow the search to that category only.

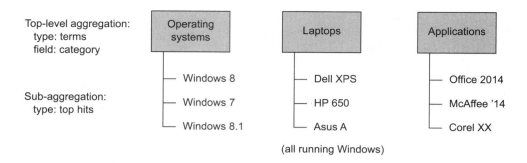

Figure 7.11   Nesting the `top_hits` aggregation under a `terms` aggregation to get result grouping

In Elasticsearch, you'll be able to get result grouping by using a special aggregation called `top_hits`. It retrieves the top *N* results, sorted by score or a criterion of your choice, for each bucket of a parent aggregation. That parent aggregation can be a `terms` aggregation that's running on the `category` field, as suggested in the online shop example of figure 7.11; we'll go over this special aggregation in the next section.

The last nesting use case we'll talk about is controlling the document set on which your aggregations run. For example, regardless of the query, you might want to show the top tags for get-together groups created in the last year. To do this, you'd use the `filter` aggregation, which creates a bucket of documents that match the provided filter, in which you can nest other aggregations.

7.4.1   *Nesting multi-bucket aggregations*

To nest an aggregation within another one, you just have to use the `aggregations` or `aggs` key on the same level as the parent aggregation type and then put the sub-aggregation definition as the value. For multi-bucket aggregations, this can be done indefinitely. For example, in the following listing you'll use the `terms` aggregation to show the top tags. For each tag, you'll use the `date_histogram` aggregation to show how many groups were created each month, for each tag. Finally, for each bucket of such groups, you'll use the `range` aggregation to show how many groups have fewer than three members and how many have at least three.

Listing 7.15   Nesting multi-bucket aggregations three times

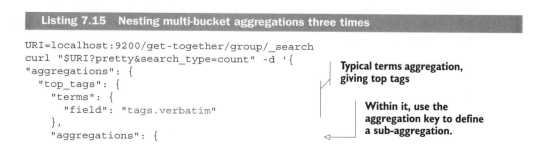

```
URI=localhost:9200/get-together/group/_search
curl "$URI?pretty&search_type=count" -d '{
"aggregations": {
  "top_tags": {
    "terms": {
      "field": "tags.verbatim"
    },
    "aggregations": {
```

Typical terms aggregation, giving top tags

Within it, use the aggregation key to define a sub-aggregation.

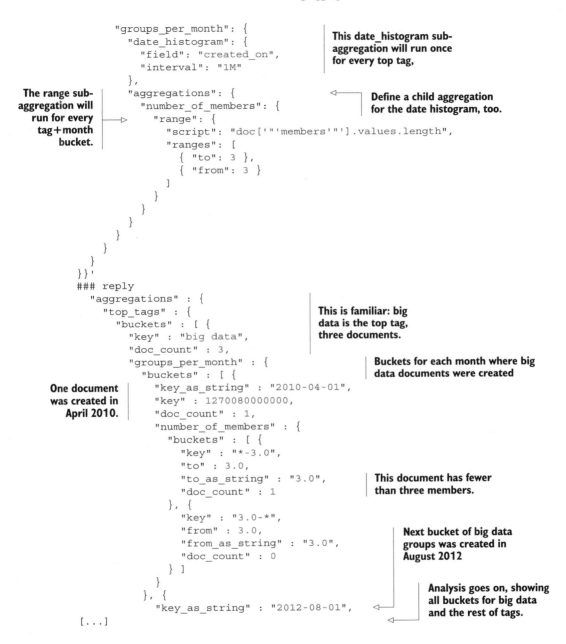

```
        "groups_per_month": {
          "date_histogram": {                    This date_histogram sub-
            "field": "created_on",               aggregation will run once
            "interval": "1M"                      for every top tag,
          },
          "aggregations": {              ◁────   Define a child aggregation
            "number_of_members": {                for the date histogram, too.
              "range": {
                "script": "doc['"'members'"'].values.length",
                "ranges": [
                  { "to": 3 },
                  { "from": 3 }
                ]
              }
            }
          }
        }
      }
    }
  }
}}'
### reply
  "aggregations" : {
    "top_tags" : {                    This is familiar: big
      "buckets" : [ {                 data is the top tag,
        "key" : "big data",           three documents.
        "doc_count" : 3,
        "groups_per_month" : {                    Buckets for each month where big
          "buckets" : [ {                          data documents were created
            "key_as_string" : "2010-04-01",
            "key" : 1270080000000,
            "doc_count" : 1,
            "number_of_members" : {
              "buckets" : [ {
                "key" : "*-3.0",
                "to" : 3.0,
                "to_as_string" : "3.0",           This document has fewer
                "doc_count" : 1                    than three members.
              }, {
                "key" : "3.0-*",
                "from" : 3.0,                                  Next bucket of big data
                "from_as_string" : "3.0",                      groups was created in
                "doc_count" : 0                                August 2012
              } ]
            }
          }, {                                               Analysis goes on, showing
            "key_as_string" : "2012-08-01",   ◁──────┘       all buckets for big data
[...]                                          ◁──────        and the rest of tags.
```

The range sub-aggregation will run for every tag+month bucket.

One document was created in April 2010.

You can always nest a metrics aggregation within a bucket aggregation. For example, if you wanted the average number of group members instead of the 0–2 and 3+ ranges that you had in the previous listing, you could use the avg or stats aggregation.

One particular type of aggregation we promised to cover in the last section is top_hits. It will get you the top N results, sorted by the criteria you like, for each bucket of its parent aggregation. Next, we'll look at how you'll use the `top_hits` aggregation to get result grouping.

7.4.2   *Nesting aggregations to get result grouping*

Result grouping is useful when you want to show the top results grouped by a certain category. Like in Google, when you have many results from the same site, you sometimes see only the top three or so, and then it moves on to the next site. You can always click the site's name to get all the results from it that match your query.

That's what result grouping is for: it allows you to give the user a better idea of what else is in there. Say you want to show the user the most recent events, and to make results more diverse you'll show the most recent event for the most frequent attendees. You'll do this in the next listing by running the `terms` aggregation on the attendees field and nesting the `top_hits` aggregation under it.

Listing 7.16   Using the `top hits` aggregation to get result grouping

```
URI=localhost:9200/get-together/event/_search
curl "$URI?pretty&search_type=count" -d '{
"aggregations": {
  "frequent_attendees": {
    "terms": {                              This terms aggregation
      "field": "attendees",                 gives the two users
      "size": 2                             going to most events.
    },
    "aggregations": {
      "recent_events": {                    The top_hits aggregation
        "top_hits": {                 ◄──── gives the actual events.
          "sort": {
            "date": "desc"          ◄───    You get the most
          },                               recent first.
          "_source": {                      You can select the
            "include": [ "title" ]          fields to include.
          },
          "size": 1          ◄───    Use size to select the
        }                           number of results
      }                            per bucket.
    }
  }
}
}}'
### reply
  "aggregations" : {
    "frequent_attendees" : {
      "buckets" : [ {
        "key" : "lee",                       Lee is the most frequent,
        "doc_count" : 5,                      with five events.
        "recent_events" : {
          "hits" : {
            "total" : 5,                             Results look exactly
            "max_score" : 1.0,                       like the ones you get
            "hits" : [ {                             while querying.
              "_index" : "get-together",
```

```
                  "_type" : "event",
                  "_id" : "100",
                  "_score" : 1.0,
                  "_source":{"title":"Liberator and Immutant"},
                  "sort" : [ 1378404000000 ]
                } ]
              }
           }
        }, {
          "key" : "shay",
          "doc_count" : 4,
          "recent_events" : {
            "hits" : {
[...]
                "_source":{"title":"Piggyback on Elasticsearch training in San
      Francisco"},
[...]
```

Results look exactly like the ones you get while querying.

At first, it may seem strange to use aggregations for getting results grouping. But now that you've learned what aggregations are all about, you can see that these concepts of buckets and nesting are powerful and enable you to do much more than gather some statistics on query results. The top_hits aggregation is an example of a non-statistic outcome of aggregations.

You're not limited to only query results when you run aggregations; this is the default behavior, as you learned in section 7.1, but you can work around that if you need to. For example, let's say that you want to show the most popular blog post tags on your blog somewhere on a sidebar. And you want to show that sidebar no matter what the user is searching for. To achieve this, you'd need to run your terms aggregation on all blog posts, independent of your query. Here's where the global aggregation becomes useful: it produces a bucket with all the documents of your search context (the indices and types you're searching in), making all other aggregations nested under it work with all these documents.

The global aggregation is one of the single-bucket aggregations that you can use to change the document set other aggregations run on, and that's what we'll explore next.

7.4.3 Using single-bucket aggregations

As you saw in section 7.1, Elasticsearch will run your aggregations on the query results by default. If you want to change this default, you'll have to use single-bucket aggregations. Here we'll discuss three of them:

- global creates a bucket with all the documents of the indices and types you're searching on. This is useful when you want to run aggregations on all documents, no matter the query.
- filter and filters aggregations create buckets with all the documents matching one or more filters. This is useful when you want to further restrict the document set—for example, to run aggregations only on items that are in stock, or separate aggregations for those in stock and those that are promoted.

- `missing` creates a bucket with documents that don't have a specified field. It's useful when you have another aggregation running on a field, but you want to do some computations on documents that aren't covered by that aggregation because the field is missing. For example, you want to show the average price of items across multiple stores and also want to show the number of stores not listing a price for those items.

GLOBAL

Using your get-together site from the code samples, assume you're querying for events about Elasticsearch, but you want to see the most frequent tags overall. For example, as we described earlier, you want to show those top tags somewhere on a sidebar, independent of what the user is searching for. To achieve this, you need to use the `global` aggregation, which can alter the flow of data from query to aggregations, as shown in figure 7.12.

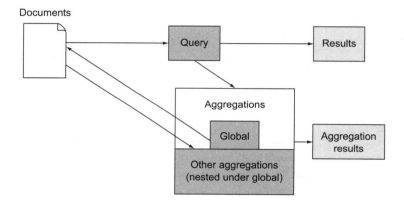

Figure 7.12 Nesting aggregations under the `global` aggregation makes them run on all documents.

In the following listing you'll nest the `terms` aggregation under the `global` aggregation to get the most frequent tags on all documents, even if the query looks for only those with "elasticsearch" in the title.

Listing 7.17 Global aggregation helps show top tags overall regardless of the query

```
URI=localhost:9200/get-together/group/_search
curl "$URI?pretty&search_type=count" -d '{
"query": {
  "match": {
    "name": "elasticsearch"
  }
},
"aggregations": {
  "all_documents": {
    "global": {},
    "aggregations": {
```

> The global aggregation is the parent.

```
      "top_tags": {
        "terms": {                    │ The terms aggregation is nested
          "field": "tags.verbatim"    │ under it, to work on all data.
        }
      }
    }
  }
}
}}'
### reply
[...]
  "hits" : {                    │ The query returns
    "total" : 2,                │ two documents...
[...]
  "aggregations" : {
    "all_documents" : {         │ but aggregations
      "doc_count" : 5,          │ run on all five.
      "top_tags" : {
        "buckets" : [ {
          "key" : "big data",   │ The terms aggregation results
          "doc_count" : 3       │ are as if there was no query.
[...]
```

When we say "all documents," we mean all the documents from the search context defined in the search URI. In this case you're searching in the group type of the get-together index, so all the groups will be taken into account. If you searched in the whole get-together index, both groups and events would be included in the aggregation.

FILTER

Remember the post filter from section 7.1? It's used when you define a filter directly in the JSON request, instead of wrapping it in a filtered query; the post filter restricts the results you get without affecting the aggregations.

The filter aggregation does the opposite: it restricts the document set your aggregations run on, without affecting the results. This is illustrated in figure 7.13.

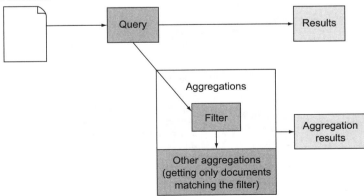

Figure 7.13   The filter **aggregation restricts query results for aggregations nested under it.**

If you're searching for events with "elasticsearch" in the title, you want to create a word cloud from words within the description, but you want to only account for documents that are recent enough—let's say after July 1, 2013.

To do that, in the following listing you'd run a query as usual, but with aggregations. You'll first have a `filter` aggregation restricting the document set to those after July 1, and under it you'll nest the `terms` aggregation that generates the word-cloud information.

Listing 7.18   `filter` aggregation restricts the document set coming from the query

```
URI=localhost:9200/get-together/event/_search
curl "$URI?pretty&search_type=count" -d '{
"query": {
  "match": {
    "title": "elasticsearch"
  }
},
"aggregations": {
  "since_july": {
    "filter": {
      "range": {
        "date": {
          "gt": "2013-07-01T00:00"
        }
      }
    },
    "aggregations": {
      "description_cloud": {
        "terms": {
          "field": "description"
        }
      }
    }
  }
}}'
### reply
[...]
  "hits" : {
    "total" : 7,
[...]
  "aggregations" : {
    "since_july" : {
      "doc_count" : 2,
      "description_cloud" : {
        "buckets" : [ {
          "key" : "we",
          "doc_count" : 2
        }, {
          "key" : "with",
          "doc_count" : 2
[...]
```

Filter query defines the bucket on which its sub-aggregations will run

The query returns seven results.

The description_cloud aggregation runs only on the two results matching the filter.

NOTE There's also a `filters` (plural) aggregation, which allows you to define multiple filters. It works similarly to the `filter` aggregation, except that it generates multiple buckets, one for each filter—like the `range` aggregation generates multiple buckets, one for each range. For more information about the `filters` aggregation, go to www.elastic.co/guide/en/elasticsearch/reference/current/search-aggregations-bucket-filters-aggregation.html.

MISSING

Most of the aggregations we've looked at so far make buckets of documents and get metrics from values of a field. If a document is missing that field, it won't be part of the bucket and it won't contribute to any metrics.

For example, you might have a `date_histogram` aggregation on event dates, but some events have no date set yet. You can count them, too, through the `missing` aggregation:

```
% curl "$URI?pretty&search_type=count" -d '{
"aggregations": {
  "event_dates": {
    "date_histogram": {
      "field": "date",
      "interval": "1M"
    }
  },
  "missing_date": {
    "missing": {
      "field": "date"
    }
  }
}}'
```

As with other single-bucket aggregations, the `missing` aggregation allows you to nest other aggregations under it. For example, you can use the `max` aggregation to show the maximum number of people who intend to participate in a single event that doesn't have a date set yet.

There are other important single-bucket aggregations that we didn't cover here, like the `nested` and `reverse_nested` aggregations, which allow you to use all the power of aggregations with nested documents.

Using nested documents is one of the ways to work with relational data in Elasticsearch. The next chapter provides all you need to know about relations among documents, including nested documents and nested aggregations.

7.5 Summary

In this chapter, we covered the major aggregation types and how you can combine them to get insights about documents matching a query:

- Aggregations help you get an overall view of query results by counting terms and computing statistics from resulting documents.

- Aggregations are the new facets in Elasticsearch because there are more types of aggregations, and you can also combine them to get deeper insights into the data.
- There are two main types of aggregations: bucket and metrics.
- Metrics aggregations calculate statistics over a set of documents, such as the minimum, maximum, or average value of a numeric field.
- Some metrics aggregations are calculated with approximation algorithms, which allows them to scale a lot better than exact metrics. The `percentiles` and `cardinality` aggregations work like this.
- Bucket aggregations put documents into one or more buckets and return counters for those buckets—for example, the most frequent posters in a forum. You can nest sub-aggregations under bucket aggregations, making these sub-aggregations run one time for each bucket generated by the parent. You can use this nesting, for example, to get the average number of comments for blog posts matching each tag.
- The `top_hits` aggregation can be used as a sub-aggregation to implement result grouping.
- The `terms` aggregation is typically used for top frequent users/locations/ items/... kinds of use cases. Other multi-bucket aggregations are variations of the `terms` aggregation, such as the `significant_terms` aggregation, which returns those words that appear more often in the query results than in the overall index.
- The `range` and `date_range` aggregations are useful for categorizing numeric and date fields. The `histogram` and `date_histogram` aggregations are similar, but they use fixed intervals instead of manually defined ranges.
- Single-bucket aggregations, such as the `global`, `filter`, `filters`, and `missing` aggregations, are used to change the document set on which other aggregations run, which defaults to the documents returned by the query.

Relations among documents

- Objects and arrays of objects
- Nested mapping, queries, and filters
- Parent mapping, `has_parent`, and `has_child` queries and filters
- Denormalization techniques

Some data is inherently relational. For example, with the get-together site we've used throughout the book, there are groups of people with the same interests and events organized by those groups. How might you search for groups that host events about a certain topic?

If your data is flat structured, then you might as well skip this chapter and move on to scaling out, which will be discussed in chapter 9. This is typically the case for logs, where you have independent fields, such as timestamp, severity, and message. If, on the other hand, you have related entities in your data, such as blog posts and comments, users and products, and so on, then by now you may wonder how you should best represent those relationships in your documents so you can run queries and aggregations across those relationships.

With Elasticsearch you don't have joins like in an SQL database. As we'll discuss in section 8.4 on denormalizing (duplicating data), that's because having query-time joins in a distributed system is typically slow, and Elasticsearch strives to be real time and return query results in milliseconds. On the upside, there are multiple ways to define relationships in Elasticsearch. You can, for example, search for events based on their locations or search for groups based on properties of the events they host. We'll explore all the possibilities for defining relationships among documents in Elasticsearch—object types, nested documents, parent-child relationships, and denormalizing—and we'll explore the advantages and disadvantages of each in this chapter.

8.1 Overview of options for defining relationships among documents

First, let's quickly define each of these approaches:

- *Object type*—This allows you to have an object (with its own fields and values) as the value of a field in your document. For example, your `address` field for an event could be an object with its own fields: `city`, `postal code`, `street name`, and so on. You could even have an array of addresses if the same event happens in multiple cities.

- *Nested documents*—The problem you may have with the object type is that all the data is stored in the same document, so matches for a search can go across subdocuments. For example, `city=Paris AND street_name=Broadway` could return an event that's hosted in New York and Paris at the same time, even though there's no Broadway street in Paris. Nested documents allow you to index the same JSON document but will keep your addresses in separate Lucene documents, making only searches like `city=New York AND street_name=Broadway` return the expected result.

- *Parent-child relationships between documents*—This method allows you to use completely separate Elasticsearch documents for different types of data, like events and groups, but still define a relationship between them. For example, you can have groups as parents of events to indicate which event hosts which group. This will allow you to search for events hosted by groups in your area or for groups that host events about Elasticsearch.

- *Denormalizing*—This is a general technique for duplicating data in order to represent relationships. In Elasticsearch, you're likely to employ it to represent many-to-many relationships because other options work only on one-to-many. For example, all groups have members, and members could belong to multiple groups. You can duplicate one side of the relationship by including all the members of a group in that group's document.

- *Application-side joins*—This is another general technique where you deal with relationships from your application. It works well when you have less data and can afford to keep it normalized. For example, instead of duplicating members for all groups they're part of, you could store them separately and include only their IDs in the groups. Then you'd run two queries: first, on members to filter those matching member criteria. Then you'd take their IDs and include them in the search criteria for groups.

Before we dive into all the details of working with each possibility, we'll provide an overview of them and their typical use cases.

8.1.1   Object type

The easiest way to represent a common interest group and the corresponding events is to use the *object type*. This allows you to put a JSON object or an array of JSON objects as the value of your field, like the following example:

```
{
  "name": "Denver technology group",
  "events": [
    {
      "date": "2014-12-22",
      "title": "Introduction to Elasticsearch"
    },
    {
      "date": "2014-06-20",
      "title": "Introduction to Hadoop"
    }
  ]
}
```

If you want to search for a group with events that are about Elasticsearch, you can search in the events.title field.

Under the hood, Elasticsearch (or rather, Lucene) isn't aware of the structure of each object; it only knows about fields and values. The document ends up being indexed as if it looked like this:

```
{
  "name": "Denver technology group",
  "events.date": ["2014-12-22", "2014-06-20"],
  "events.title": ["Introduction to Elasticsearch", "Introduction to Hadoop"]
}
```

Because of how they're indexed, objects work brilliantly when you need to query only one field of the object at a time (generally one-to-one relationships), but when querying multiple fields (as is generally the case with one-to-many relationships), you might get unexpected results. For example, let's say you want to filter groups hosting Hadoop meetings in December 2014. Your query can look like this:

```
"bool": {
  "must": [
    {
      "term": {
        "events.title": "hadoop"
      }
    },
```

```
   {
     "range": {
       "events.date": {
         "from": "2014-12-01",
         "to": "2014-12-31"
       }
     }
   }
 ]
}
```

This will match the sample document because it has a title that matches hadoop and a date that's in the specified range. But this isn't what you want: it's the Elasticsearch event that's in December; the Hadoop event is in June. Sticking with the default object type is the fastest and easiest approach to relations, but Elasticsearch is unaware of the boundaries between documents, as illustrated in figure 8.1.

8.1.2   Nested type

If you need to make sure such cross-object matches don't happen, you can use the *nested type*, which will index your events in separate Lucene documents. In both cases, the group's JSON document will look exactly the same, and applications will index each in the same way. The difference is in the mapping, which triggers Elasticsearch to index nested inner objects in adjacent but separate Lucene documents, as illustrated in figure 8.2. When searching, you'll need to use nested filters and queries, which will be explored in section 8.2; those will search in all those Lucene documents.

   In some use cases, it's not a good idea to mash all the data in the same document as objects and nested types do. Take the case of groups and events: if a new event is organized by a group and all of that group's data is in the same document, you'll

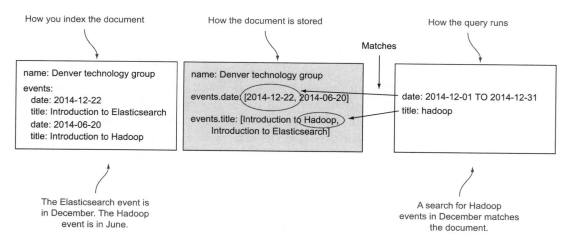

Figure 8.1   Inner object boundaries aren't accounted for when storing, leading to unexpected results.

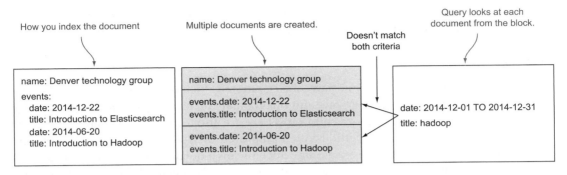

Figure 8.2   The nested type makes Elasticsearch index objects as separate Lucene documents.

have to re-index the whole document for that event. This can hurt performance and concurrency, depending on how big those documents get and how often those operations are done.

8.1.3   *Parent-child relationships*

With parent-child relationships, you can use completely different Elasticsearch documents by putting them in different types and defining their relationship in the mapping of each type. For example, you can have events in one mapping type and groups in another and you can specify in the mapping that groups are parents of events. Also, when you index an event, you can point it to the group that it belongs to, as in figure 8.3. At

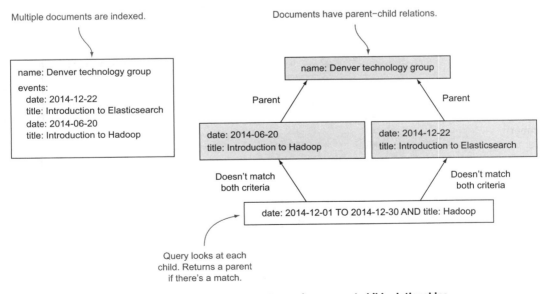

Figure 8.3   Different types of Elasticsearch documents can have parent-child relationships.

search time, you can use has_parent or has_child queries and filters to take the other part of the relationship into account. We'll discuss them later in this chapter as well.

8.1.4 *Denormalizing*

For any relational work, you have objects, nested documents, and parent-child relations. These work for one-to-one and one-to-many relationships—the kinds that have one parent with one or more children. There are also techniques that are not specific to Elasticsearch but are methods often employed by NoSQL data stores to overcome the lack of joins: one is *denormalizing,* which means a document will include data that's related to it, even if the same data will have to be duplicated in another document. Another is doing joins in your application.

For example, let's take groups and their members. A group can have more than one member, and a user can be a member of more than one group. Both have their own set of properties. To represent this relationship, you can have groups as parents of the members. For users who are members of multiple groups, you can *denormalize* their data: once for each group they belong to, like in figure 8.4.

Alternatively, you can keep groups and members separated and include only member IDs in group documents. You'd join groups and their members by using member IDs in your application, which works well if you have a small number of member IDs to query by, as shown in figure 8.5.

In the rest of this chapter, we'll take a deeper look at each of these techniques: objects and arrays, and nested, parent-child, denormalizing, and application-side joins. You'll learn how they work internally, how to define them in the mapping, how to index them, and how to search those documents.

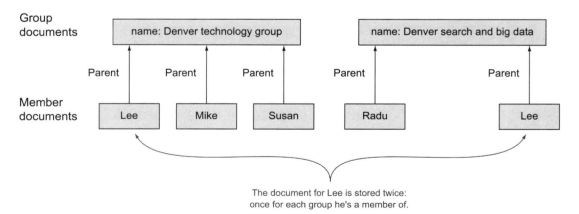

The document for Lee is stored twice:
once for each group he's a member of.

Figure 8.4   Denormalizing is the technique of multiplying data to avoid costly relations.

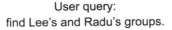

User query:
find Lee's and Radu's groups.

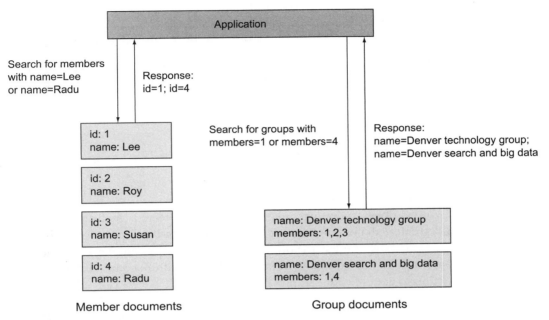

Figure 8.5 **You can keep your data normalized and do the joins in your application.**

8.2 *Having objects as field values*

As you saw back in chapter 2, documents in Elasticsearch can be hierarchical. For example, in the code samples, an event of the get-together site has its location as an object with two fields—name and geolocation:

```
{
  "title": "Using Hadoop with Elasticsearch",
  "location": {
    "name": "SkillsMatter Exchange",
    "geolocation": "51.524806,-0.099095"
  }
}
```

If you're familiar with Lucene, you may ask yourself, "How can Elasticsearch documents be hierarchical when Lucene supports only flat structures?" With objects, Elasticsearch flattens hierarchies internally by putting each inner field with its full path as a separate field in Lucene. You can see the process in figure 8.6.

Typically, when you want to search in an event's location name, you'll refer to it as location.name. We'll look at that in section 8.2.2, but before we go into searching, let's define a mapping and see how to index some documents.

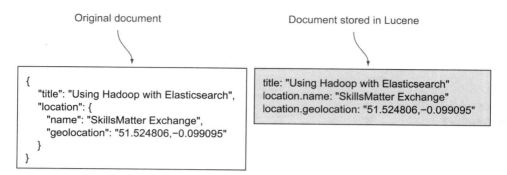

Original document   Document stored in Lucene

```
{
   "title": "Using Hadoop with Elasticsearch",
   "location": {
     "name": "SkillsMatter Exchange",
     "geolocation": "51.524806,-0.099095"
   }
}
```

```
title: "Using Hadoop with Elasticsearch"
location.name: "SkillsMatter Exchange"
location.geolocation: "51.524806,-0.099095"
```

Figure 8.6   JSON hierarchical structure stored as a flat structure in Lucene

8.2.1 *Mapping and indexing objects*

By default, inner object mappings are automatically detected. In listing 8.1 you'll index a hierarchical document and see how the detected mapping looks. If those events documents look familiar to you, it's because the code samples store the location of an event in an object, too. You can go to https://github.com/dakrone/elastic-search-in-action to get the code samples now if you haven't done so already.

Listing 8.1   Inner JSON objects mapped as the object type

```
curl -XPUT 'localhost:9200/get-together/event-object/1' -d '{
   "title": "Introduction to objects",
   "location": {
     "name": "Elasticsearch in Action book",        An object within the
     "address": "chapter 8"                          JSON document
   }
}'
curl 'localhost:9200/get-together/_mapping/event-object?pretty'
# expected reply:
{
   "get-together" : {
     "mappings": {
       "event-object" : {
         "properties" : {
           "location" : {
             "properties" : {
               "address" : {
                 "type" : "string"
               },                                    Object's mapping
               "name" : {                            is automatically
                 "type" : "string"                   detected with its
               }                                      properties, like
             }                                        the root object
           },
           "title" : {
             "type" : "string"
           }
```

```
            }
          }
        }
      }
    }
```

You can see that the inner object has a list of `properties` just like the root JSON object has. You configure field types from inner objects in the same way you do for fields in the root object. For example, you can upgrade `location.address` to have multiple `fields`, as you saw in chapter 3. This will allow you to index the address in different ways, such as having a `not_analyzed` version for exact matches in addition to the default `analyzed` version.

> **TIP** If you need to look at core types or how to use multi-fields, you can revisit chapter 3. For more details on analysis, go back to chapter 5.

The mapping for a single inner object will also work if you have multiple such objects in an array. For example, if you index the following document, the mapping from listing 8.1 will stay the same:

```
{
  "title": "Introduction to objects",
  "location": [
    {
      "name": "Elasticsearch in Action book",
      "address": "chapter 8"
    },
    {
      "name": "Elasticsearch Guide",
      "address": "elasticsearch/reference/current/mapping-object-type.html"
    }
  ]
}'
```

To summarize, working with objects and arrays of objects in the mapping is very much like working with the fields and arrays you saw in chapter 3. Next we'll look at searches, which also work like the ones you saw in chapters 4 and 6.

8.2.2 Searching in objects

By default, Elasticsearch will recognize and index hierarchical JSON documents with inner objects without defining anything up front. As you can see in figure 8.7, the same goes for searching. By default, you have to refer to inner objects by specifying the path to the field you're looking at, such as `location.name`.

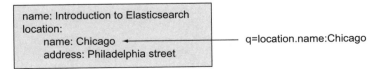

Figure 8.7 You can search in an object's field by specifying that field's full path.

As you worked through chapters 2 and 4, you indexed documents from the code samples. You can now search through events happening in offices, as in listing 8.2, where you'll specify the full path of `location.name` as the field to search on.

> **TIP**   If you didn't index the documents from the code samples yet, you can do it now by cloning the repository at https://github.com/dakrone/elastic-search-in-action and running the populate.sh script.

Listing 8.2   Searching in `location.name` from events indexed by the code samples

```
EVENT_PATH="localhost:9200/get-together/event"
curl "$EVENT_PATH/_search?q=location.name:office&pretty"
# reply: [...]  "title": "Hortonworks, the future of Hadoop and big data",
[...]  "location": {    "name": "SendGrid Denver office",
    "geolocation": "39.748477,-104.998852"[...]
        "title": "Big Data and the cloud at Microsoft",
[...]  "location": {    "name": "Bing Boulder office",
    "geolocation": "40.018528,-105.275806"[...]
```

Two events matching office in the name field within the location object

AGGREGATIONS

While searching, treat object fields like `location.name` in the same way as any other field. This also works with the aggregations that you saw in chapter 7. For example, the following `terms` aggregation gets the most-used words in the `location.name` field to help you build a word cloud:

```
% curl "localhost:9200/get-together/event/_search?pretty" -d '{
"aggregations" : {
  "location_cloud" : {
    "terms" : {
      "field" : "location.name"
    }
  }
}}'
```

OBJECTS WORK BEST FOR ONE-TO-ONE RELATIONSHIPS

One-to-one relationships are the perfect use case for objects: you can search in the inner object's fields as if they were fields in the root document. That's because they are! At the Lucene level, `location.name` is another field in the same flat structure.

You can also have one-to-many relationships with objects by putting them in arrays. For example, take a group with multiple members. If each member had its own object, you'd represent them like this:

```
"members": [
  {
    "first_name": "Lee",
    "last_name": "Hinman"
  },
  {
    "first_name": "Radu",
    "last_name": "Gheorghe"
  }
]
```

You can still search for `members.first_name:lee` and it will match "Lee" as expected. But you need to keep in mind that in Lucene the structure of the document looks more like this:

```
"members.first_name": ["Lee", "Radu"],
"members.last_name": ["Hinman", "Gheorghe"]
```

It only works well if you search in one field, even if you have multiple criteria. If you search for `members.first_name:lee AND members.last_name:gheorghe`, the document will still match because it matches each of those two criteria. This happens even though there's no member named Lee Gheorghe because Elasticsearch throws everything in the same document and it's not aware of boundaries between objects. To have Elasticsearch understand those boundaries, you can use the nested type, covered next.

Using objects to define document relationships: pros and cons

Before moving on, here's a quick recap of why you should (or shouldn't) use objects. The plus points:

- They're easy to use. Elasticsearch detects them by default; in most cases you don't have to define anything special up front to index objects.
- You can run queries and aggregations on objects as you would do with flat documents. That's because at the Lucene level they are flat documents.
- No joins are involved. Because everything is in the same document, using objects will give you the best performance of any of the options discussed in this chapter.

The downsides:

- There are no boundaries between objects. If you need such functionality, you need to look at other options—nested, parent-child, and denormalizing—and eventually combine them with objects if it suits your use case.
- Updating a single object will re-index the whole document.

8.3 Nested type: connecting nested documents

The nested type is defined in the mapping in much the same way as the object type, which we've already discussed. Internally, nested documents are indexed as different Lucene documents. To indicate that you want to use the nested type instead of the object type, you have to set `type` to `nested`, as you'll see in section 8.3.1.

From an application's perspective, indexing nested documents is the same as indexing objects because the JSON document indexed as an Elasticsearch document looks the same. For example:

```
{
  "name": "Elasticsearch News",
  "members": [
```

```
    {
      "first_name": "Lee",
      "last_name": "Hinman"
    },
    {
      "first_name": "Radu",
      "last_name": "Gheorghe"
    }
  ]
}
```

At the Lucene level, Elasticsearch will index the root document and all the `members` objects in separate documents. But it will put them in a single *block*, as shown in figure 8.8.

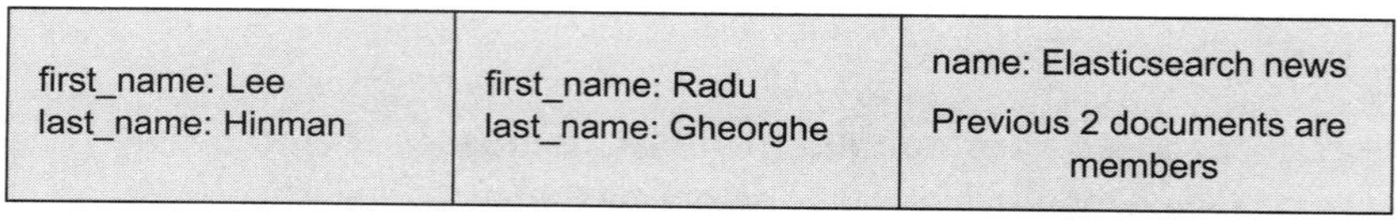

first_name: Lee last_name: Hinman	first_name: Radu last_name: Gheorghe	name: Elasticsearch news Previous 2 documents are members

Figure 8.8   A block of documents in Lucene storing the Elasticsearch document with nested-type objects

Documents of a block will always stay together, ensuring they get fetched and queried with the minimum number of operations.

Now that you know how nested documents work, let's see how to make Elasticsearch use them. You have to specify that you want them nested at index time and at search time:

- Inner objects must have a nested mapping, to get them indexed as separate documents in the same block.
- Nested queries and filters must be used to make use of those blocks while searching.

We'll discuss how you can do each in the next two sections.

8.3.1   Mapping and indexing nested documents

The nested mapping looks similar to the object mapping, except instead of the `type` being `object`, you have to make it `nested`. In the following listing you'll define a mapping with a `nested` type field and index a document that contains an array of nested objects.

Listing 8.3   Mapping and indexing `nested` documents

```
curl -XPUT localhost:9200/get-together/_mapping/group-nested -d '{
  "group-nested": {
    "properties": {
      "name": { "type": "string" },
```

```
        "members": {
          "type": "nested",
          "properties": {
            "first_name": { "type": "string" },
            "last_name": { "type": "string" }
          }
        }
      }
    }
  }
}'
curl -XPUT localhost:9200/get-together/group-nested/1 -d '{
  "name": "Elasticsearch News",
  "members": [
    {
      "first_name": "Lee",
      "last_name": "Hinman"
    },
    {
      "first_name": "Radu",
      "last_name": "Gheorghe"
    }
  ]
}'
```

> This signals Elasticsearch to index members objects in separate documents of the same block.

> This property goes in the main document.

> These objects go into their own documents, part of the same block as the root document.

JSON objects with the nested mapping, like the ones you indexed in this listing, allow you to search them with `nested` queries and filters. We'll explore those searches in a bit, but the thing to remember now is that nested queries and filters allow you to search within the boundaries of such documents. For example, you'll be able to search for groups with members with the first name "Lee" and the last name "Hinman." Nested queries won't do cross-object matches, thus avoiding unexpected matches such as "Lee" with the last name "Gheorghe."

ENABLING CROSS-OBJECT MATCHES

In some situations, you might need cross-object object matches as well. For example, if you're searching for a group that has both Lee and Radu, a query like this would work for the regular JSON objects we discussed in the section on object type:

```
    "query": {
      "bool": {
        "must": [
          {
            "term": {
              "members.first_name": "lee"
            }
          },
          {
            "term": {
              "members.first_name": "radu"
            }
          }
        ]
      }
    }
```

This query would work because when you have everything in the same document, both criteria will match.

With nested documents, a query structured this way won't work because `members` objects would be stored in separate Lucene documents. And there's no `members` object that will match both criteria: there's one for Lee and one for Radu, but there's no document containing both.

In such situations, you might want to have both: objects for when you want cross-object matches and nested documents for when you want to avoid them. Elasticsearch lets you do that through a couple of mapping options: `include_in_root` and `include_in_parent`.

INCLUDE_IN_ROOT

Adding `include_in_root` to your nested mapping will index the inner `members` objects twice: one time as a nested document and one time as an object within the root document, as shown in figure 8.9.

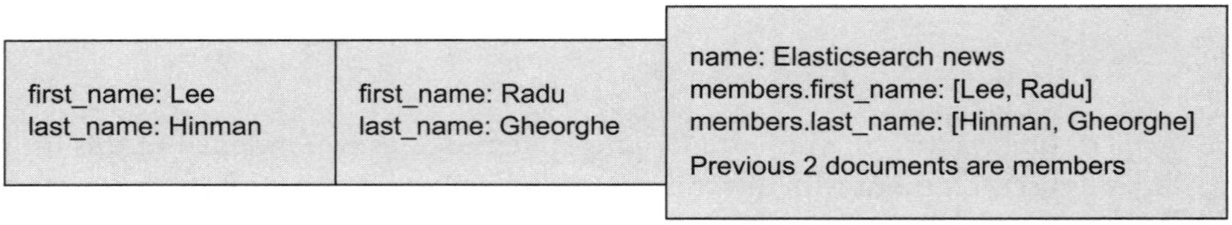

first_name: Lee last_name: Hinman	first_name: Radu last_name: Gheorghe	name: Elasticsearch news members.first_name: [Lee, Radu] members.last_name: [Hinman, Gheorghe] Previous 2 documents are members

Figure 8.9 With `include_in_root`, fields of nested documents are indexed in the root document, too.

The following mapping will let you use nested queries for the nested documents and regular queries for when you need cross-object matches:

```
"members": {
  "type": "nested",
  "include_in_root": true,
  "properties": {
    "first_name": { "type": "string" },
    "last_name": { "type": "string" }
  }
}
```

INCLUDE_IN_PARENT

Elasticsearch allows you to have multiple levels of nested documents. For example, if your group can have members as its nested children, members can have children of their own, such as the comments they posted on that group. Figure 8.10 illustrates this hierarchy.

With the `include_in_root` option you just saw, you can add the fields at any level to the root document—in this case, the grandparent. There's also an `include_in _parent` option, which allows you to index the fields of one nested document into the

Figure 8.10 `include_in_parent` **indexes a nested document's field into the immediate parent, too.**

immediate parent document. For example, the following listing will include the `comments` in the `members` documents.

Listing 8.4 Using `include_in_parent` **when there are multiple nested levels**

```
curl -XPUT localhost:9200/get-together/_mapping/group-multinested -d '{
  "group-multinested": {
    "properties": {
      "name": { "type": "string" },
      "members": {
        "type": "nested",
        "properties": {
          "first_name": { "type": "string" },
          "last_name": { "type": "string" },
          "comments": {
            "type": "nested",
            "include_in_parent": true,
            "properties": {
              "date": {
                "type": "date",
                "format": "dateOptionalTime"
              },
              "comment": { "type": "string" }
            }
          }
        }
      }
    }
  }
}'
```

members are nested documents
relative to the root group-multinested
document. No inclusion here.

comments are nested documents
of the members. Contents are
also indexed as objects for the
parent members documents.

By now you're probably wondering how you'd query these nested structures. This is exactly what we'll look at next.

8.3.2 Searches and aggregations on nested documents

As with mappings, when you run searches and aggregations on nested documents you'll need to specify that the objects you're looking at are nested. There are `nested` queries, filters, and aggregations that help you achieve this. Running these special queries and aggregations will trigger Elasticsearch to join the different Lucene documents within the same block and treat the resulting data as the same Elasticsearch document.

The way to search within nested documents is to use the `nested` query or `nested` filter. As you might expect after chapter 4, these are equivalent, with the traditional differences between queries and filters:

- Queries calculate score; thus they're able to return results sorted by relevance.
- Filters don't calculate score, making them faster and easier to cache.

TIP In particular, the `nested` filter isn't cached by default. You can change this by setting `_cache` to `true`, as you can do in all filters.

If you want to run aggregations on nested fields—for example, to get the most frequent group members—you'll have to wrap them in a `nested` aggregation. If sub-aggregations have to refer to the parent Lucene document—like showing top group tags for each member—you can go up the hierarchy with the `reverse_nested` aggregation.

NESTED QUERY AND FILTER

When you run a `nested` query or filter, you need to specify the `path` argument to tell Elasticsearch where in the Lucene block those nested objects are located. In addition to that, your `nested` query or filter will wrap a regular query or filter, respectively. In the next listing, you'll search for members with the first name "Lee" and the last name "Gheorghe," and you'll see that the document indexed in listing 8.3 won't match because you have only Lee Hinman and Radu Gheorghe and no member called Lee Gheorghe.

Listing 8.5   Nested query example

```
curl 'localhost:9200/get-together/group-nested/_search?pretty' -d '{
  "query": {
    "nested": {
      "path": "members",              ◄──┐ Look for nested documents
      "query": {                          │ under members.
        "bool": {
          "must": [                       ◄── The query would be the one that
            {                               │ you'd normally run on objects
              "term": {                     │ within the same document.
                "members.first_name": "lee"
              }
            },
            {                                   ┌ There's no member Lee
              "term": {                         │ Gheorghe. Change this
                "members.last_name": "gheorghe" ◄── to hinman and it will
              }}]}}}}                            │ match Lee Hinman.
}'
```

A `nested` filter would look exactly the same as the `nested` query you just saw. You'll have to replace the word `query` with `filter`.

SEARCHING IN MULTIPLE LEVELS OF NESTING

Elasticsearch also allows you to have multiple levels of nesting. For example, back in listing 8.4, you added a mapping that nests on two levels: members and their comments. To search in the comments-nested documents, you'd have to specify `members.comments` as the path, as shown in the following listing.

Listing 8.6   Indexing and searching multiple levels of nested documents

```
curl -XPUT localhost:9200/get-together/group-multinested/1 -d '{
  "name": "Elasticsearch News",
  "members": {
    "first_name": "Radu",
    "last_name": "Gheorghe",               comments object is nested under
    "comments": {            ◁──────       the members object, also nested,
      "date": "2013-12-22",                as configured in listing 8.4
      "comment": "hello world"
    }
  }
}'
curl 'localhost:9200/get-together/group-multinested/_search' -d '{
  "query": {
    "nested": {                            Look in comments,
      "path": "members.comments",  ◁──┤    which is under
      "query": {                          members.
        "term": {
          "members.comments.comment": "hello"   ◁──   The query still provides
        }                                             the full path to the field
      }                                               to look at.
    }
  }
} '
```

AGGREGATING SCORES OF NESTED OBJECTS

The `nested` query calculates the score, but we didn't mention how. Let's say you have three members in a group: Lee Hinman, Radu Gheorghe, and another guy called Lee Smith. If you have a `nested` query for "Lee," it will match two members. Each inner member document will get its own score, depending on how well it matches the criteria. But the query coming from the application is for group documents, so Elasticsearch will need to give back a score for the whole group document. At this point, there are four options, which can be specified with the `score_mode` option:

- `avg`—This is the default option, which will take the scores of the matching inner documents and return their average score.
- `total`—This will sum up the matching inner documents' scores and return it, which is useful when the number of matches counts.
- `max`—The maximum inner document score is returned.
- `none`—No score is kept or counted toward the total document score.

If you're thinking that there are too many options for including the nested type in the root or parent and the score options, see table 8.1 for a quick references on all those options and when they're useful.

Table 8.1   Nested type options

Option	Description	Example
`include_in_parent: true`	Indexes the nested document in the parent document, too.`"first_name:Lee AND last_name:Hinman"`, for which you need the nested type, as well as `"first_name:Lee AND first_name:Radu"`, for which you need the object type.	
`include_in_root: true`	Indexes the nested document in the root document.	Same scenario as previously, but you have multiple layers; for example, `event>members>comments`.
`score_mode: avg`	Average score of matching nested documents count.	Search for groups hosting events about Elasticsearch.
`score_mode: total`	Sums up nested document scores.	Search for groups hosting most events that have to do with Elastic-search.
`score_mode: max`	Maximum nested document score.	Search for groups hosting top events about Elasticsearch.
`score_mode: none`	No score counts towards the total score.	Filter groups hosting events about Elasticsearch. Use the `nested` filter instead.

GETTING WHICH INNER DOCUMENT MATCHED

When you index big documents with many nested subdocuments in them, you might wonder which of the nested documents matched a specific nested query—in this case, which of the group members matched a query looking for lee in first_name. Starting with Elasticsearch 1.5, you can add an inner_hits object within your nested query or filter to show the matching nested documents. Like your main search request, it supports options such as from and size:

```
"query": {
  "nested": {
    "path": "members",
    "query": {
      "term": {
        "members.first_name": "lee"
      }
    }
  },
  "inner_hits": {
    "from": 0,
```

```
        "size": 1
      }
    }
  }
```

The reply will contain an `inner_hits` object for each matching document, looking much like a regular query reply, except that each document is a nested subdocument:

```
    "_source":{
      "name": "Elasticsearch News",
[...]
    "inner_hits" : {
      "members" : {
        "hits" : {
          "total" : 1,
          "max_score" : 1.4054651,
          "hits" : [ {
            "_index" : "get-together",
            "_type" : "group-nested",
            "_id" : "1",
            "_nested" : {
              "field" : "members",
              "offset" : 0
            },
            "_score" : 1.4054651,
            "_source":{"first_name":"Lee","last_name":"Hinman"}
          } ]
        }
      }
    }
```

In order to identify the subdocument, you can look at the `_nested` object. `field` is the path of the nested object, and `offset` shows the location of that nested document in the array. In this case, Lee is the first `member`.

NESTED SORTING

In most use cases you'd sort root documents by score, but you can also sort them based on numeric values of inner nested documents. This would be done in a similar way to sorting on other fields, as you saw in chapter 6. For example, if you have a price aggregator site with products as root documents and offers from various shops as nested documents, you can sort on the minimum price of each offer. Similar to the `score_mode` option you've seen before, you can specify a `mode` option and take the min, max, sum, or avg value of nested documents as the sort value for the root document:

```
"sort": [
  {
  "offers.price": {
      "mode":  "min",
      "order": "asc"
    }
  }
]
```

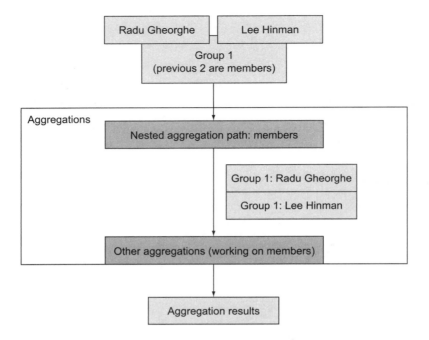

Figure 8.11   Nested aggregation doing necessary joins for other aggregations to work on the indicated path

Elasticsearch will be smart about it and figure out that offers.price is located in the offers object (if that's what you defined in the mapping) and access the price field under those nested documents for sorting.

NESTED AND REVERSE NESTED AGGREGATIONS

In order to do aggregations on nested type objects, you have to use the nested aggregation. This is a single-bucket aggregation, where you indicate the path to the nested object containing your field. As shown in figure 8.11, the nested aggregation triggers Elasticsearch to do the necessary joins in order for other aggregations to work properly on the indicated path.

For example, you'd normally run a terms aggregation on a member name field in order to get the top users by the number of groups they're part of. If that name field is stored within the members nested type object, you'll wrap that terms aggregation in a nested aggregation that has the path set to members:

```
% curl "localhost:9200/get-together/group/_search?pretty" -d '{
  "aggregations" : {
    "members" : {
      "nested" : {
        "path" : "members"
      },
```

```
    "aggregations" : {
      "frequent_members" : {
        "terms" : {
          "field" : "members.name"
        }
      }
    }
  }
}
}'
```

You can put more aggregations under the `members` nested aggregation and Elasticsearch will know to look in the `members` type for all of them.

There are use cases where you'd need to navigate back to the parent or root document. For example, you want each of the obtained frequent members to show the top group `tags`. To do that, you'll use the `reverse_nested` aggregation, which will tell Elasticsearch to go up the nested hierarchy:

```
"frequent_members" : {
  "terms" : {
    "field" : "members.name"
  },
  "aggregations": {
    "back_to_group": {
      "reverse_nested": {},
      "aggregations": {
        "tags_per_member": {
          "terms": {
            "field": "tags"
          }
        }
      }
    }
  }
}
```

The `nested` and `reverse_nested` aggregations can effectively be used to tell Elasticsearch in which Lucene document to look for the fields of the next aggregation. This gives you the flexibility to use all the aggregation types you saw in chapter 7 for nested documents, just as you could use them for objects. The only downside of this flexibility is the performance ópenalty.

PERFORMANCE CONSIDERATIONS

We'll cover performance in more detail in chapter 10, but in general you can expect nested queries and aggregations to be slower than their object counterparts. That's because Elasticsearch needs to do some extra work to join multiple documents within a block. But because of the underlying implementation using blocks, these queries and aggregations are much faster than they would be if you had to join completely separate Elasticsearch documents.

This block implementation also has its drawbacks. Because nested documents are stuck together, updating or adding one inner document requires re-indexing the whole ensemble. Applications also work with nested documents in a single JSON.

If your nested documents become big, as they would in a get-together site if you had one document per group and all its events nested, a better option might be to use separate Elasticsearch documents and define parent-child relations between them.

Using nested type to define document relationships: pros and cons

Before moving on, here's a quick recap of why you should (or shouldn't) use nested documents. The plus points:

- Nested types are aware of object boundaries: no more matches for "Radu Hinman"!
- You can index the whole document at once, as you would with objects, after you define your nested mapping.
- Nested queries and aggregations join the parent and child parts, and you can run any query across the union. No other option described in this chapter provides this feature.
- Query-time joins are fast because all Lucene documents making the Elasticsearch document are together in the same block in the same segment.
- You can include child documents in parents to get all the functionality from objects if you need it. This functionality is transparent for your application.

The downsides:

- Queries will be slower than their object equivalents. If objects provide you all the needed functionality, they're the better option because they're faster.
- Updating a child will re-index the whole document.

8.4   *Parent-child relationships: connecting separate documents*

Another option for defining relationships among data in Elasticsearch is to define a type within an index as a child of another type of the same index. This is useful when documents or relations need to be updated often. You'd define the relationship in the mapping through the _parent field. For example, you can see in the mapping.json file from the book's code samples that events are children of groups, as illustrated in figure 8.12.

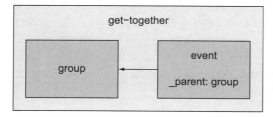

Figure 8.12   The relationship between events and groups as it's defined in the mapping

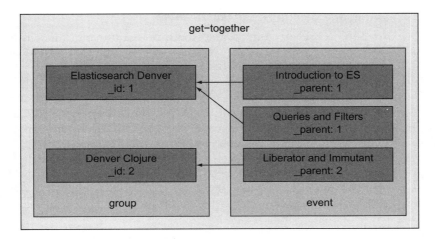

Figure 8.13   The `_parent` **field of each child document is pointing to the** `_id` **field of its parent.**

Once you have this relationship defined in the mapping, you can start indexing documents. The parents (group documents in this case) are indexed normally. For children (events in this example) you need to specify the parent's ID in the `_parent` field. This will basically point the event to its group and allow you to search for groups that include some event's criteria or the other way around, like figure 8.13.

Compared to the nested approach, searches are slower. With nested documents, the fact that all inner objects are Lucene documents in the same block pays dividends because they can be joined easily into the root document. Parent and child documents are completely different Elasticsearch documents, so they have to be searched for separately.

The parent-child approach shines when it comes to indexing, updating, and deleting documents. Because parent and child documents are different Elasticsearch documents, they can be managed separately. For example, if a group has many events and you need to add a new one, you add that new event document. Using the nested-type approach, Elasticsearch will have to re-index the group documents with the new event and all existing events, which is much slower.

A parent document can already be indexed or not when you index its child. This is useful when you have lots of new documents and you want to index them asynchronously. For example, you can index events on your website generated by users and also index the users. Events may come from your logging system, and users may be synchronized from a database. You don't need to worry about making sure a user exists before you can index an event that will have that user as a parent. If the user doesn't exist, the event is indexed anyway.

But how would you index parent and child documents in the first place? This is what we'll explore next.

8.4.1   Indexing, updating, and deleting child documents

We'll only worry about child documents here because parents are indexed like any other document you've indexed so far. It's the child documents that must point to their parents via the _parent field.

> **NOTE** Parents of a document type can be children of another type. You can have multiple levels of such relationships, just as you can with nested type. You can even combine them. For example, a group can have its members stored as nested type and events separately stored as their children.

When it comes to child documents, you have to define the _parent field in the mapping, and when indexing, you must specify the parent's ID in the _parent field. The parent's ID and type will also serve as the child's routing value.

Routing and routing values

You may recall from chapter 2 how indexing operations get distributed to shards by default: each document you index has an ID, and that ID gets hashed. At the same time, each shard of the index has an equal slice of the total range of hashes. The document you index goes to the shard that has that document's hashed ID in its range.

The hashed ID is called the *routing value*, and the process of assigning a document to a shard is called *routing*. Because each ID is different and you hash them all, the default routing mechanism will evenly balance documents between shards.

You can also specify a custom routing value. We'll go into the details of using custom routing in chapter 9, but the basic idea is that Elasticsearch hashes that routing value and not the document's ID to determine the shard. You'd use custom routing when you wanted to make sure multiple documents are in the same shard because hashing the same routing value will always give you the same hash.

Custom routing becomes useful when you start searching because you can provide a routing value to your query. When you do, Elasticsearch goes only to the shard that corresponds to that routing value, instead of querying all the shards. This reduces the load in your cluster a lot and is typically used for keeping each user's documents together.

The _parent field provides Elasticsearch with the ID and type of the parent document, which lets it route the child documents to the same hash as the parent document. _parent is essentially a routing value, and you benefit from it when searching. Elasticsearch will automatically use this routing value to query only the parent's shard to get its children or the child's shard to get its parent.

The common routing value makes all the children of the same parent land in the same shard as the parent itself. When searching, all the correlations that Elasticsearch has to do between a parent and its children happen on the same node. This is much faster than broadcasting all the child documents over the network in search of a parent. Another implication of routing is that when you update or delete a child document, you need to specify the _parent field.

Next we'll look at how you'd practically do all those things:

- Define the _parent field in the mapping.
- Index, update, and delete child documents by specifying the _parent field.

MAPPING

The next listing shows the relevant part of the events mapping from the code samples. The _parent field has to point to the parent type—in this case, group.

Listing 8.7 _parent mapping from the code samples

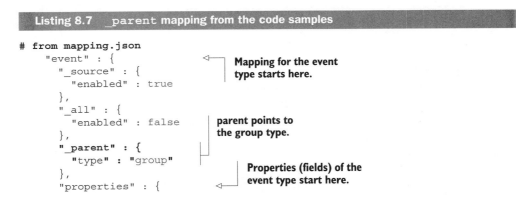

```
# from mapping.json
    "event" : {                          ⟵  Mapping for the event
      "_source" : {                          type starts here.
        "enabled" : true
      },
      "_all" : {                          parent points to
        "enabled" : false                 the group type.
      },
      "_parent" : {
        "type" : "group"
      },                                  Properties (fields) of the
      "properties" : {                 ⟵  event type start here.
```

INDEXING AND RETRIEVING

With the mapping in place, you can start indexing documents. Those documents have to contain the parent value in the URI as a parameter. For your events, that value is the document ID of the groups they belong to, such as where you have 2 for the Elasticsearch Denver group:

```
% curl -XPOST 'localhost:9200/get-together/event/1103?parent=2' -d '{
  "host": "Radu,
  "title": "Yet another Elasticsearch intro in Denver"
}'
```

The _parent field is stored so you can retrieve it later, and it's also indexed so you can search on its value. If you look at the contents of _parent for a group, you'll see the type you defined in the mapping as well as the group ID you specified when indexing.

To retrieve an event document, you run a normal index request, and you also have to specify the _parent value:

```
% curl 'localhost:9200/get-together/event/1103?parent=2&pretty'
{
  "_index" : "get-together",
  "_type" : "event",
  "_id" : "1103",
  "_version" : 1,
  "found" : true, "_source" : {
  "host": "Radu",
  "title": "Yet another Elasticsearch intro in Denver"
  }
}
```

The _parent value is required because you can have multiple events with the same ID pointing to different groups. But the _parent and _id combination is unique. If you try to get the child document without specifying its parent, you'll get an error saying that a routing value is required. The _parent value is that routing value Elasticsearch is waiting for:

```
% curl 'localhost:9200/get-together/event/1103?pretty'
{
  "error" : "RoutingMissingException[routing is required for [get-together]/
    [event]/[1103]]",
  "status" : 400
}
```

UPDATING

You'd update a child document through the update API, in a similar way to what you did in chapter 3, section 3.5. The only difference here is that you have to provide the parent again. As in the case of retrieving an event document, the parent is needed to get the routing value of the event document you're trying to change. Otherwise, you'd get the same RoutingMissingException you had earlier when trying to retrieve the document without specifying a parent.

The following snippet adds a description to the document you just indexed:

```
curl -XPOST 'localhost:9200/get-together/event/1103/_update?parent=2' -d '{
  "doc": {
    "description": "Gives an overview of Elasticsearch"
  }
}'
```

DELETING

To delete a single event document, run a delete request like in chapter 3, section 3.6.1, and add the parent parameter:

```
curl -XDELETE 'localhost:9200/get-together/event/1103?parent=2'
```

Deleting by query works as before: documents that match get deleted. This API doesn't need parent values and it doesn't take them into account, either:

```
curl -XDELETE 'http://localhost:9200/get-together/event/_query?q=host:radu'
```

Speaking of queries, let's look at how you can search across parent-child relations.

8.4.2 *Searching in parent and child documents*

With parent-child relations, like those you have with groups and their events, you can search for groups and add event criteria or the other way around. Let's see what the actual queries and filters are that you'll use:

- has_child queries and filters are useful in searching for parents with criteria from their children—for example, if you need groups hosting events about Elasticsearch.

- has_parent queries and filters are useful when searching for children with criteria from their parents—for example, events that happen in Denver because location is a group property.

HAS_CHILD QUERY AND FILTER

If you want to search in groups hosting events about Elasticsearch, you can use the has_child query or filter. The classic difference here is that filters don't care about scoring.

A has_child filter can wrap another filter or a query. It runs that filter or query against the specified child type and collects the matches. The matching children contain the IDs of their parents in the _parent field. Elasticsearch collects those parent IDs and removes the duplicates—because the same parent ID can appear multiple times, once for each child—and returns the list of parent documents. The whole process is illustrated in figure 8.14.

In Phase 1 of the figure, the following actions take place:

- The application runs a has_child filter, requesting group documents with children of type event that have "Elasticsearch" in their title.
- The filter runs on the event type for documents matching "Elasticsearch."
- The resulting event documents point to their respective parents. Multiple events can point to the same group.

In Phase 2, Elasticsearch gathers all the unique group documents and returns them to the application.

The filter from figure 8.14 would look like this:

```
% curl 'localhost:9200/get-together/group/_search?pretty' -d '{
"query": {
  "filtered": {
    "filter": {
      "has_child": {
        "type": "event",
        "filter": {
          "term": {
            "title": "elasticsearch"
          }
        }
      }
    }
  }
}}'
```

The has_child query runs in a similar way to the filter, except it can give a score to each parent by aggregating child document scores. You'd do that by setting score_mode to max, sum, avg, or none, as you can do with nested queries.

NOTE If the has_child filter can wrap a filter or a query, the has_child query can only wrap another query.

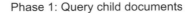

Phase 1: Query child documents

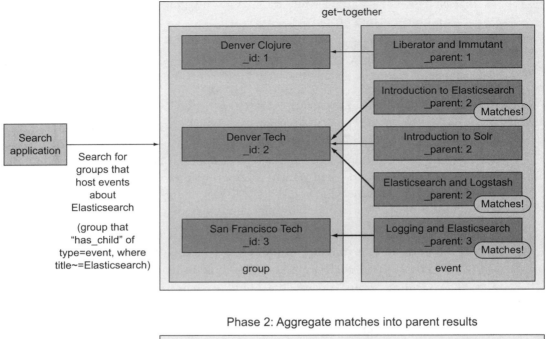

Phase 2: Aggregate matches into parent results

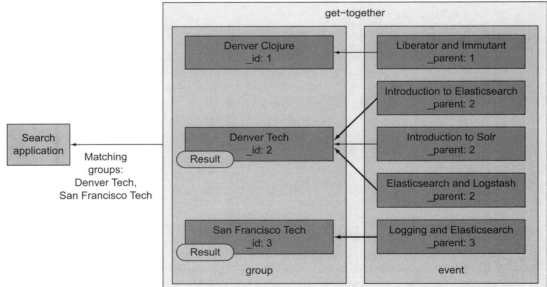

Figure 8.14   The `has_child` filter first runs on children and then aggregates the results into parents, which are returned.

For example, you can set `score_mode` to `max` and get the following query to return groups ordered by which one hosts the most relevant event about Elasticsearch:

```
% curl 'localhost:9200/get-together/group/_search?pretty' -d '{
"query": {
  "has_child": {
    "type": "event",
    "score_mode": "max",
    "query": {
      "term": {
        "title": "elasticsearch"
      }
    }
  }
}}'
```

> **WARNING** In order for `has_child` queries and filters to remove parent duplicates quickly, it caches their IDs in the field cache we introduced in chapter 6. This may take a lot of JVM heap if you have lots of parent matches for your queries. This will be less of a problem once you can have doc values for the `_parent` field, as described for this issue: https://github.com/elastic/elasticsearch/issues/6107.

GETTING THE CHILD DOCUMENTS IN THE RESULTS

By default, only the parent documents are returned by the `has_child` query, not the children that match. You can get the children as well by adding the `inner_hits` option you saw earlier for nested documents:

```
"query": {
  "has_child": {
    "type": "event",
    "query": {
      "term": {
        "title": "elasticsearch"
      }
    },
    "inner_hits": {}
  }
}
```

As with nested documents, the reply for each matching group will also contain matching events, except that now events are separate documents and have their own ID instead of an offset:

```
  "name": "Elasticsearch Denver",
[...]
      "inner_hits" : {
        "event" : {
          "hits" : {
            "total" : 2,
            "max_score" : 0.9581454,
            "hits" : [ {
              "_index" : "get-together",
```

```
              "_type" : "event",
              "_id" : "103",
              "_score" : 0.9581454,
              "_source":{
  "host": "Lee",
  "title": "Introduction to Elasticsearch",
```

HAS_PARENT QUERY AND FILTER

has_parent is, as you might expect, the opposite of has_child. You use it when you want to search for events but include criteria from the groups they belong to.

The has_parent filter can wrap a query or a filter. It runs on the "type" that you provide, takes the parent results, and returns the children, pointing to their IDs from their _parent field.

The following listing shows how to search for events about Elasticsearch, but only if they happen in Denver.

Listing 8.8   `has_parent` query to find Elasticsearch events in Denver

```
curl 'localhost:9200/get-together/event/_search?pretty' -d '{
"query": {
  "bool": {                            The main query contains
    "must": [                          two must-have queries.
      {
        "term": {                           This runs on the events
          "title": "elasticsearch"          to make sure they have
        }                                    "elasticsearch" in their title.
      },
      {
        "has_parent": {
          "type": "group",
          "query": {
            "term": {                        This runs on each event's
              "location": "denver"           group to make sure events
            }                                happen in Denver.
          }
        }
      }
    ]
  }
}}'
```

Because a child only has a parent, there are no scores to aggregate, as would be the case with has_child. By default, has_parent has no influence on the child's score ("score_mode": "none"). You can change "score_mode" to "score" to make events inherit the score of their parent groups.

Like the has_child queries and filters, has_parent queries and filters have to load parent IDs in field data to support fast lookups. That being said, you can expect all those parent/child queries to be slower than the equivalent nested queries. It's the price you pay for being able to index and search all the documents independently.

Another similarity with has_child queries and filters is the fact that has_parent returns, by default, only one side of the relationship—in this case, the child documents.

From Elasticsearch 1.5, you can fetch the parents as well by adding the `inner_hits` object to the query.

CHILDREN AGGREGATION

With version 1.4, a `children` aggregation was introduced, which allows you to nest aggregations on child documents under those you make on parent documents. Let's say that you already get the most popular tags for your get-together groups through the `terms` aggregation. For each of those tags, you also need the most frequent attendees to events belonging to each tag's groups. In other words, you want to see the people with strong preferences toward specific categories of events.

You'll get these people in the following listing by nesting a `children` aggregation under your top-tags `terms` aggregation. Under the `children` aggregation, you'll nest another `terms` aggregation that will count the number of attendees for each tag.

Listing 8.9 Combining parent and child aggregations

```
curl "localhost:9200/get-together/_search?pretty" -d '{
  "aggs": {
    "top-tags": {
      "terms": {
        "field": "tags.verbatim"
      },
      "aggs": {
        "to-events": {
          "children": {
            "type" : "event"
          },
          "aggs": {
            "frequent-attendees": {
              "terms": {
                "field": "attendees"
              }
            }
          }
        }
      }
    }
  }
}'
```

top-tags aggregation creates one bucket of groups for each tag.

to-events creates one bucket of events for the groups in each tag.

frequent-attendees counts attendees within each of the event buckets.

```
### reply
  "aggregations" : {
    "top-tags" : {
      "buckets" : [ {
        "key" : "big data",
        "doc_count" : 3,
        "to-events" : {
          "doc_count" : 9,
          "frequent-attendees" : {
            "buckets" : [ {
              "key" : "andy",
              "doc_count" : 3
            }, {
              "key" : "greg",
              "doc_count" : 3
[...]
        "key" : "open source",
        "doc_count" : 3,
        "to-events" : {
          "doc_count" : 9,
          "frequent-attendees" : {
            "buckets" : [ {
              "key" : "shay",
              "doc_count" : 4
            }, {
              "key" : "andy",
              "doc_count" : 3
[...]
```

There are three groups with the big data tag.

The three groups have a total of nine event child documents.

Andy and Greg go to three big data events each.

Shay goes to four open-source events.

NOTE You may have noticed that the children aggregation is similar to the nested aggregation—it passes child documents to the aggregations within it. Unfortunately, at least up to version 1.4, Elasticsearch doesn't provide a parent-child equivalent of the reverse nested aggregation to allow you to do the opposite: pass parent documents to the aggregations within it.

You can think of nested documents as index-time joins and parent-child relations as query-time joins. With nested, a parent and all its children are joined in a single Lucene block when indexing. By contrast, the _parent field allows different types of documents to be correlated at query time.

Nested and parent-child structures are good for one-to-many relationships. For many-to-many relationships, you'll have to employ a technique common in the NoSQL space: denormalizing.

Using parent-child designation to define document relationships: pros and cons

Before moving on, here's a quick recap of why you should or shouldn't use parent-child relationships. The plus points:

- Children and parents can be updated separately.
- Query-time join performance is better than if you did joins in your application because all related documents are routed to the same shard and joins are done at the shard level without adding network hops.

The downsides:

- Queries are more expensive than the nested equivalent and need more memory than field data.
- Aggregations can only join child documents to their parents and not the other way around, at least up to version 1.4.

8.5 *Denormalizing: using redundant data connections*

Denormalizing is about multiplying data in order to avoid expensive joins. Let's take an example we've already discussed: groups and events. It's a one-to-many relationship because an event can be hosted by only one group, and one group can host many events.

With parent-child or nested structures, groups and events are stored in different Lucene documents, as shown in figure 8.15.

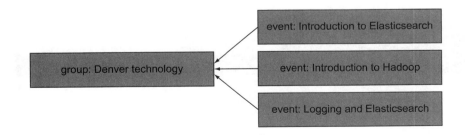

Figure 8.15   Hierarchical relationship (nested or parent-child) between different Lucene documents

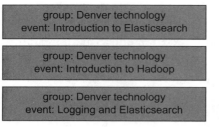

Figure 8.16 Hierarchical relationship denormalized by copying group information to each event

This relationship can be denormalized by adding the group info to all the events, as shown in figure 8.16.

Next we'll look at how and when denormalizing helps and how you'd concretely index and query denormalized data.

8.5.1 Use cases for denormalizing

Let's start with the disadvantages: denormalized data takes more space and is more difficult to manage than normalized data. In the example from figure 8.16, if you change the group's details, you have to update three documents because those details appear three times.

On the positive side, you don't have to join different documents when you query. This is particularly important in distributed systems because having to join documents across the network introduces big latencies, as you can see in figure 8.17.

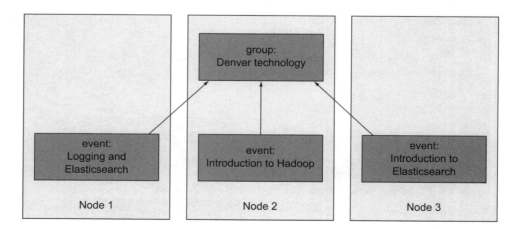

Figure 8.17 Joining documents across nodes is difficult because of network latency.

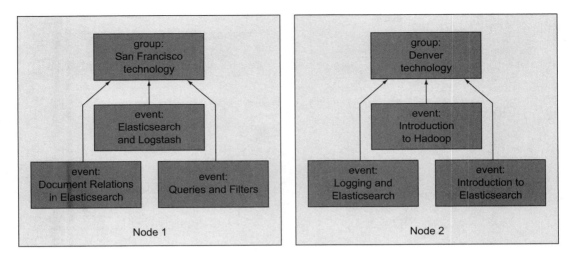

Figure 8.18   Nested/parent-child relations make sure all joins are local.

Nested and parent-child documents get around this by making sure a parent and all its children are stored in the same node, as shown in figure 8.18:

- Nested documents are indexed in Lucene blocks, which are always together in the same segment of the same shard.
- Child documents are indexed with the same routing value as their parents, making them belong to the same shard.

DENORMALIZING ONE-TO-MANY RELATIONS

Local joins done with nested and parent-child structures are much, much faster than remote joins could be. Still, they're more expensive than having no joins at all. This is where denormalizing can help, but it implies that there's more data. Your indexing operations will cause more load because you'll index more data and queries will run on larger indices, making them slower.

You can see that there's a tradeoff when it comes to choosing among nested, parent-child, and denormalizing. Typically, you'll denormalize for one-to-many relations if your data is fairly small and static and you have lots of queries. This way, disadvantages hurt less—index size is acceptable and there aren't too many indexing operations—and avoiding joins should make queries faster.

> **TIP**   If performance is important to you, take a look at chapter 10, which is all about indexing and searching fast.

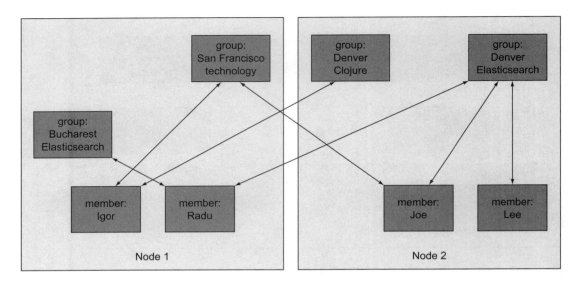

Figure 8.19 Many-to-many relationships can contain a huge amount of data, making local joins impossible.

DENORMALIZING MANY-TO-MANY RELATIONSHIPS

Many-to-many relationships are dealt with differently than one-to-many relationships in Elasticsearch. For example, a group can contain multiple members, and a person could be a member of multiple groups.

Here denormalizing is a much better proposition because unlike one-to-many implementations of nested and parent-child, Elasticsearch can't promise to contain many-to-many relationships in a single node. As shown in figure 8.19, a single relationship may expand to your whole dataset. This would make expensive, cross-network joins inevitable.

Because of how slow cross-network joins would be, as of version 1.5, denormalizing is the only way to represent many-to-many relationships in Elasticsearch. Figure 8.20 shows how the structure of figure 8.19 looks when members are denormalized as children of each group they belong to. We denormalize one side of the many-to-many relationship into more one-to-many relationships.

Next we'll look at how you can index, update, and query a structure like the one in figure 8.20.

8.5.2 *Indexing, updating, and deleting denormalized data*

Before you start indexing, you have to decide how you want to denormalize your many-to-many into one-to-many, and there are two big decision points: which side of the relationship you should denormalize and how you want to represent the resulting one-to-many relationship.

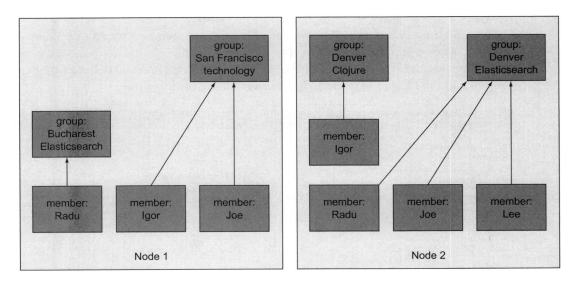

Figure 8.20   Many-to-many relation denormalized into multiple one-to-many relations, allowing local joins

WHICH SIDE WILL BE DENORMALIZED?

Will members be multiplied as children of groups or the other way around? To pick one you have to understand how data is indexed, updated, deleted, and queried. The part that's denormalized—the child—will be more difficult to manage in all aspects:

- You index those documents multiple times, once for each of its parents.
- When you update, you have to update all instances of that document.
- When you delete, you have to delete all instances.
- When you query for children separately, you'll get more hits with the same content, so you have to remove duplicates on the application side.

Based on these assumptions, it looks like it makes more sense to make members children of groups. Member documents are smaller in size, change less often, and are queried less often than groups are with their events. As a result, managing cloned member documents should be easier.

HOW DO YOU WANT TO REPRESENT THE ONE-TO-MANY RELATIONSHIP?

Will you have parent-child or nested documents? You'd choose here based on how often groups and members are searched and retrieved together. Nested queries perform better than `has_parent` or `has_child` queries.

Another important aspect is how often membership changes. Parent-child structures perform better here because they can be updated separately.

For this example, let's assume that searching and retrieving groups and members together is rare and that members often join and leave groups, so we'll go with parent-child.

INDEXING

Groups and their events would be indexed as before, but members have to be indexed once for every group they belong to. The following listing will first define a mapping for the new member type and then index Mr. Hinman as a member of both the Denver Clojure and the Denver Elasticsearch groups from the code samples.

Listing 8.10   Indexing denormalized members

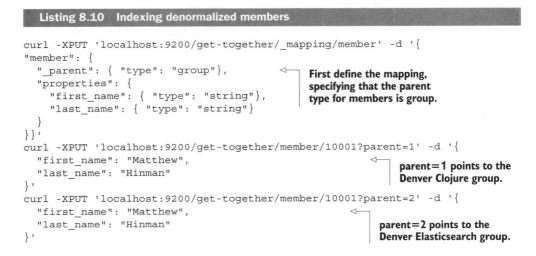

```
curl -XPUT 'localhost:9200/get-together/_mapping/member' -d '{
"member": {
  "_parent": { "type": "group"},          ◁─┐  First define the mapping,
  "properties": {                              specifying that the parent
    "first_name": { "type": "string"},         type for members is group.
    "last_name": { "type": "string"}
  }
}}'
curl -XPUT 'localhost:9200/get-together/member/10001?parent=1' -d '{
  "first_name": "Matthew",                ◁─┐  parent=1 points to the
  "last_name": "Hinman"                        Denver Clojure group.
}'
curl -XPUT 'localhost:9200/get-together/member/10001?parent=2' -d '{
  "first_name": "Matthew",               ◁─┐   parent=2 points to the
  "last_name": "Hinman"                        Denver Elasticsearch group.
}'
```

NOTE   Multiple indexing operations can be done in a single HTTP request by using the bulk API. We'll discuss the bulk API in chapter 10, which is all about performance.

UPDATING

Once again, groups get lucky and you update them just as you saw in chapter 3, section 3.5. But if a member changes its details because it's denormalized, you'll first have to search for all its duplicates and then update each one. In listing 8.11, you'll search for all the documents that have an _id of "10001" and update his first name to Lee because that's what he likes to be called.

You're searching for IDs instead of names because IDs tend to be more reliable than other fields, such as names. You may recall from the parent-child section that when you're using the _parent field, multiple documents within the same type within the same index can have the same _id value. Only the _id and _parent combination is guaranteed to be unique. When denormalizing, you can use this feature and intentionally use the same _id for the same person, once for each group they belong to. This allows you to quickly and reliably retrieve all the instances of the same person by searching for their ID.

> **Listing 8.11 Updating denormalized members**

```
curl 'localhost:9200/get-together/member/_search?pretty' -d '{
"query": {
  "filtered": {
    "filter": {
      "term": {
        "_id": "10001"
      }
    }
  }
},
"fields": ["_parent"]
}'
curl -XPOST 'localhost:9200/get-together/member/10001/_update?parent=1' -d '{
"doc": {
  "first_name": "Lee"
}
}'
curl -XPOST 'localhost:9200/get-together/member/10001/_update?parent=2' -d '{
"doc": {
  "first_name": "Lee"
}
}'
```

Searching for all the members with the same ID, which will return all the duplicates of this person

You need only the _parent field from each document, so you know how to update.

For each of the returned documents, update the name to "Lee."

NOTE Multiple updates can also be done in a single HTTP request over the bulk API. As with bulk indexing, we'll discuss bulk updates in chapter 10.

DELETING
Deleting a denormalized member requires you to identify all the copies again. Recall from the parent-child section that in order to delete a specific document, you have to specify both the _id and the _parent; that's because the combination of the two is unique in the same index and type. You'd have to identify members first through a term filter like the one in listing 8.11. Then you'd delete each member instance:

```
% curl -XDELETE 'localhost:9200/get-together/member/10001?parent=1'
% curl -XDELETE 'localhost:9200/get-together/member/10001?parent=2'
```

Now that you know how to index, update, and delete in denormalized members, let's look at how you can run queries on them.

8.5.3 Querying denormalized data

If you need to query groups, there's nothing denormalizing-specific because groups aren't denormalized. If you need search criteria from their members, use the has_child query as you did in section 8.4.2.

Members got the shortest straw with queries, too, because they're denormalized. You can search for them, even including criteria from the groups they belong to, with the has_parent query. But there's a problem: you'll get back identical members. In the following listing, you'll index another two members, and when you search, you'll get them both back.

Listing 8.12 Querying for denormalized data returns duplicate results

```
curl -XPUT 'localhost:9200/get-together/member/10002?parent=1' -d '{
  "first_name": "Radu",
  "last_name": "Gheorghe"
}'
curl -XPUT 'localhost:9200/get-together/member/10002?parent=2' -d '{
  "first_name": "Radu",
  "last_name": "Gheorghe"
}'
curl -XPOST 'localhost:9200/get-together/_refresh'
curl 'localhost:9200/get-together/member/_search?pretty' -d '{
"query": {
  "term": {
    "first_name": "radu"
  }
}}'
# reply    "hits" : [ {        "_index" : "get-together",        "_type" :
"member",      "_id" : "10002",        "_score" : 2.871802, "_source" : {
"first_name": "Radu","last_name": "Gheorghe"}      }, {        "_index" :
"get-together",        "_type" : "member",        "_id" : "10002",
"_score" : 2.5040774, "_source" : {
"first_name": "Radu","last_name": "Gheorghe"}        } ]
```

Indexing a person twice, once for each group

Searching for the person by name

The same person is returned twice, once for each group.

As of version 1.5, you can only remove those duplicate members from your application. Once again, if the same person always has the same ID, you can use that ID to make this task easier: two results with the same ID are identical.

The same problem occurs with aggregations: if you want to count some properties of the members, those counts will be inaccurate because the same member appears in multiple places.

The workaround for most searches and aggregations is to maintain a copy of all members in a separate index. Let's call it "members." Querying that index will return just that one copy of each member. The problem with this workaround is that it only helps when you query members alone, unless you're doing application-side joins, which we'll discuss next.

Using denormalization to define relationships: pros and cons

As we did with the other methods, we provide a quick overview of the strengths and weaknesses of denormalizing. The plus points:

- It allows you to work with many-to-many relationships.
- No joins are involved, making querying faster if your cluster can handle the extra data caused by duplication.

> The downsides:
>
> - Your application has to take care of duplicates when indexing, updating, and deleting.
> - Some searches and aggregations won't work as expected because data is duplicated.

8.6 Application-side joins

Instead of denormalizing, another option for the groups and members relationship is to keep them in separate indices and do the joins from your application. Much like Elasticsearch does with parent-child, it requires you to store IDs to indicate which member belongs to which group, and you have to query both.

For example, if you have a query for groups with "Denver" in the name, where "Lee" or "Radu" is a member, you can run a `bool` query on members first to find out which ones are Lee and Radu. Once you get the IDs, you can run a second query on groups, where you add the member IDs in a `terms` filter next to the Denver query. The whole process is illustrated in figure 8.21.

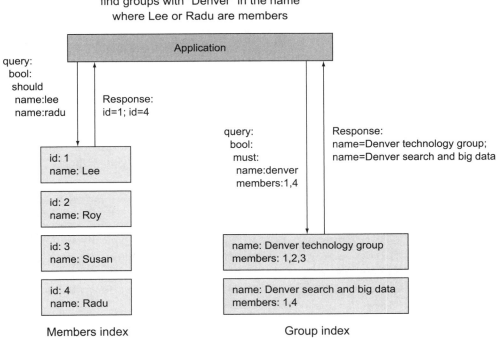

Figure 8.21 Application-side joins require you to run two queries.

This works well when there aren't many matching members. But if you want to include all members from a city, for example, the second query will have to run a `terms` filter with possibly thousands of members, making it expensive. Still, there are some things you can do:

- When you run the first query, if you need only member IDs, you can disable retrieving the _source field to reduce traffic:

```
"query": {
  "filtered": {
[...]
  }
},
"_source": false
```

- In the second query, if you have lots of IDs, it might be faster to execute the `terms` filter on field data:

```
"query": {
  "filtered": {
    "filter": {
      "terms": {
        "members": [1, 4],
        "execution": "fielddata"
      }
    }
  }
}
```

We'll cover more about performance in chapter 10, but when you model document relations, it ultimately comes down to picking your battles.

8.7   *Summary*

Lots of use cases have to deal with relational data, and in this chapter you saw how you can deal with these:

- Object mapping, mostly useful for one-to-one relationships
- Nested documents and parent-child structures, which deal with one-to-many relationships
- Denormalizing and application-side joins, which are mostly helpful with many-to-many relationships

Joining hurts performance, even when it's local, so it's typically a good idea to put as many properties as you can in a single document. Object mapping helps with this because it allows hierarchies in your documents. Searches and aggregations work here as they do with a flat-structured document; you have to refer to fields using their full path, like `location.name`.

When you need to avoid cross-object matches, nested and parent/child documents are available to help:

- Nested documents are basically index-time joins, putting multiple Lucene documents in a single block. To the application, the block looks like a single Elasticsearch document.
- The _parent field allows you to point a document to another document of another type in the same index to be its parent. Elasticsearch will use routing to make sure a parent and all its children land in the same shard so that it can perform a local join at query time.

You can search nested and parent-child documents with the following queries and filters:

- nested query and filter
- has_child query and filter
- has_parent query and filter

Aggregations work across the relationship only with nested documents through the nested and reverse_nested aggregation types.

Objects, nested and parent-child documents, and the generic technique of denormalizing can be combined in any way so you can get a good mix of performance and functionality.

Part 2

In this part, we'll shift the focus from development to production. There are three chapters that focus on scaling Elasticsearch, tuning it for better performance, and maintaining it. You'll also get a deeper understanding of the functionality we covered in part 1 as we explore how various features perform. This information is valuable for both development and operations, as they typically have to work together to set up Elasticsearch in a way that can scale out to the production requirements and be easy to maintain.

Scaling out 9

This chapter covers

- Adding nodes to your Elasticsearch cluster
- Master election in your Elasticsearch cluster
- Removing and decommissioning nodes
- Using the _cat API to understand your cluster
- Planning and scaling strategies
- Aliases and custom routing

Now that you have a good understanding of what Elasticsearch is capable of, you're ready to hear about Elasticsearch's next killer feature: the ability to scale—that is, to be able to handle more indexing and searching or to handle indexing and searching faster. These days, scaling is an important factor when dealing with millions or billions of documents. You won't always be able to support the amount of traffic you'd like to on a single running instance of Elasticsearch, or *node*, without scaling in some form. Fortunately, Elasticsearch is easy to scale. In this chapter we'll take a look at the scaling capabilities that Elasticsearch has at its disposal and how you can use those features to give Elasticsearch more performance and, at the same time, more reliability.

Having already seen how Elasticsearch handles the get-together data we introduced in chapters 2 and 3, we're now ready to talk about how to scale your search system to handle all the traffic you can throw at it. Imagine you're sitting in your office, and in comes your boss to announce that your site has been featured in *Wired* magazine as the hot new site everyone should use for booking social get-togethers. Your job: make sure Elasticsearch can handle the influx of new groups and events, as well as all the new searches expected to hit the site once that *Wired* article gets published! You have 24 hours. How are you going to scale up your Elasticsearch server to handle this traffic in this time frame? Thankfully, Elasticsearch makes scaling a breeze by adding nodes to your existing Elasticsearch cluster.

9.1 *Adding nodes to your Elasticsearch cluster*

Even if you don't end up in a situation at work like the one just described, during the course of your experimentation with Elasticsearch you'll eventually come to the point where you need to add more processing power to your Elasticsearch cluster.

You need to be able to search and index data in your indices faster, with more parallelization; you've run out of disk space on your machine, or perhaps your Elasticsearch node is now running out of memory when performing queries against your data. In these cases, the easiest way to add performance to your Elasticsearch node is usually to turn it into an Elasticsearch cluster by adding more nodes, which you first learned about in chapter 2. Elasticsearch makes it easy to scale horizontally by adding nodes to your cluster so they can share the indexing and searching workload. By adding nodes to your Elasticsearch cluster, you'll soon be able to handle indexing and searching the millions of groups and events headed your way.

9.1.1 *Adding nodes to your cluster*

The first step in creating an Elasticsearch cluster is to add another node (or nodes) to the single node to make it a cluster of nodes. Adding a node to your local development environment is as simple as extracting the Elasticsearch distribution to a separate directory, entering the directory, and running the `bin/elasticsearch` command, as the following code snippet shows. Elasticsearch will automatically pick the next port available to bind to—in this case, 9201—and automatically join the existing node like magic! If you want to go one step further, there's no need to even extract the Elasticsearch distribution again; multiple instances of Elasticsearch can run from the same directory without interfering with one another:

```
% bin/elasticsearch

[in another terminal window or tab]
% mkdir elasticsearch2
% cd elasticsearch2
% tar zxf elasticsearch-1.5.0.tar.gz
% cd elasticsearch-1.5.0
% bin/elasticsearch
```

The originally running Elasticsearch node from chapter 2

The newly started Elasticsearch node

Now that you have a second Elasticsearch node added to the cluster, you can run the `health` command from before and see how the status of the cluster has changed, as shown in the following listing.

Listing 9.1 Getting cluster health for a two-node cluster

```
% curl -XGET 'http://localhost:9200/_cluster/health?pretty'
{
  "cluster_name" : "elasticsearch",
  "status" : "green",                          The cluster is now green
  "timed_out" : false,                         instead of yellow.
  "number_of_nodes" : 2,
  "number_of_data_nodes" : 2,                  Two nodes that can handle
  "active_primary_shards" : 5,                 data are now in the cluster.
  "active_shards" : 10,
  "relocating_shards" : 0,                     All 10 shards
  "initializing_shards" : 0,                   are now active.
  "unassigned_shards" : 0
}                                              There are no longer any
                                               unassigned shards.
```

There are now no unassigned shards in this cluster, as you can see from the `unassigned_shards` count, which is zero. How exactly did the shards end up on the other node? Take a look at figure 9.1 and see what happens to the test index before and after adding a node to the cluster. On the left side, the primary shards for the test index have all been assigned to `Node1`, whereas the replica shards are unassigned. In

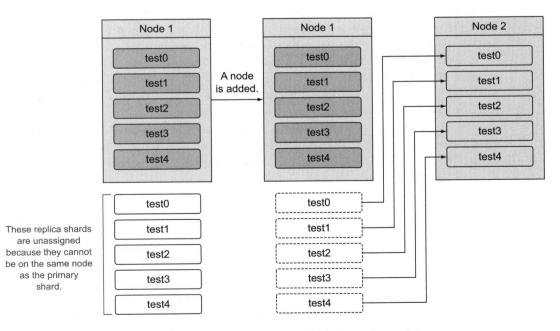

Figure 9.1 Shard allocation for the test index for one node transitioning to two nodes

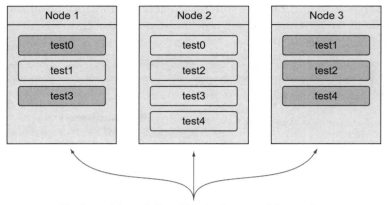

Elasticsearch has rebalanced the shards across all three nodes.

Figure 9.2   Shard allocation for the test index with three Elasticsearch nodes

this state, the cluster is yellow because all primary shards have a home, but the replica shards don't. Once a second node is added, the unassigned replica shards are assigned to the new Node2, which causes the cluster to move to the green state.

When another node is added, Elasticsearch will automatically try to balance out the shards among all nodes. Figure 9.2 shows how the same shards are distributed across three Elasticsearch nodes in the same cluster. Notice that there's no ban on having primary and replica shards on the same node as long as the primary and replica shards for the same shard number aren't on the same node.

If even more nodes are added to this cluster, Elasticsearch will try to balance the number of shards evenly across all nodes because each node added in this way shares the burden by taking a portion of the data (in the form of shards). Congratulations, you just horizontally scaled your Elasticsearch cluster!

Adding nodes to your Elasticsearch cluster comes with substantial benefits, the primary being high availability and increased performance. When replicas are enabled (which they are by default), Elasticsearch will automatically promote a replica shard to a primary in the event the primary shard can't be located, so even if you lose the node where the primary shards for your index are, you'll still be able to access the data in your indices. This distribution of data among nodes also increases performance because search and get requests can be handled by both primary and replica shards, as you'll recall from figure 2.9. Scaling this way also adds more memory to the cluster as a whole, so if memory-intensive searches and aggregations are taking too long or causing your cluster to run out of memory, adding more nodes is almost always an easy way to handle more numerous and complex operations.

Now that you've turned your Elasticsearch node into a true cluster by adding a node, you may be wondering how each node was able to discover and communicate with the other node or nodes. In the next section, we'll talk about Elasticsearch's node discovery methods.

9.2 *Discovering other Elasticsearch nodes*

You might be wondering exactly how the second node you added to your cluster discovered the first node and automatically joined the cluster. Out of the box, Elasticsearch nodes can use two different ways to discover one another: multicast or unicast. Elasticsearch can use both at once but by default is configured to use only multicast because unicast requires a list of known nodes to connect to.

9.2.1 *Multicast discovery*

When Elasticsearch starts up, it sends a *multicast* ping to the address 224.2.2.4 on port 54328, which in turn is responded to by other Elasticsearch nodes with the same cluster name, so if you notice a coworker's local copy of Elasticsearch running and joining your cluster, make sure to change the `cluster.name` setting inside your elasticsearch.yml configuration file from the default `elasticsearch` to a more specific name. Multicast discovery has a few options that you can change or disable entirely by setting the following options in elasticsearch.yml, shown with their default values:

```
discovery.zen.ping.multicast:
  group: 224.2.2.4
  port: 54328
  ttl: 3
  address: null
  enabled: true
```

An address of null means to bind to all network interfaces.

Generally, multicast discovery is a decent option when dealing with very flexible clusters on the same network, where the IP address of nodes being added changes frequently. Think of *multicast discovery* as shouting "Hey, are there any other nodes out there running an Elasticsearch cluster named 'xyz'?" and then waiting for a response. Figure 9.3 shows what multicast discovery looks like graphically.

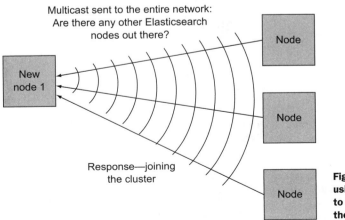

Multicast sent to the entire network:
Are there any other Elasticsearch nodes out there?

New node 1

Node

Node

Response—joining the cluster

Node

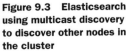
Figure 9.3   Elasticsearch using multicast discovery to discover other nodes in the cluster

Although multicast discovery is great for local development and a quick proof-of-concept test, when developing a production cluster, a more stable way of having Elasticsearch discover other nodes is to use some or all of the nodes as "gossip routers" to discover more information about the cluster. This can prevent the situation where nodes accidentally connect to a cluster they shouldn't have when someone connects a laptop to the same network. Unicast helps combat this by not sending a message to everyone on a network but connecting to a specific list of nodes.

9.2.2   *Unicast discovery*

Unicast discovery uses a list of hosts for Elasticsearch to connect to and attempt to find more information about the cluster. This is ideal for cases where the IP address of the node won't change frequently or for production Elasticsearch systems where only certain nodes should be communicated with instead of the entire network. Unicast is used by telling Elasticsearch the IP address and, optionally, the port or range of ports for other nodes in the cluster. An example of a unicast configuration would be setting `discovery.zen.ping.unicast.hosts: ["10.0.0.3", "10.0.0.4:9300", "10.0.0.5[9300-9400]"]` inside elasticsearch.yml for the Elasticsearch nodes on your network. Not all of the Elasticsearch nodes in the cluster need to be present in the unicast list to discover all the nodes, but enough addresses must be configured for each node to know about a gossip node that's available. For example, if the first node in the unicast list knows about three out of seven nodes in a cluster, and the second node in the unicast list knows about the other four out of the seven nodes, the node performing the discovery will still be able to find all seven nodes in the cluster. Figure 9.4 shows a graphical representation of unicast discovery.

There's no need to disable unicast discovery. If you'd like to use only multicast discovery to find other Elasticsearch nodes, leave the list unset (or empty) in the configuration file. After discovering other nodes that are part of the cluster, the Elasticsearch nodes will hold a master election.

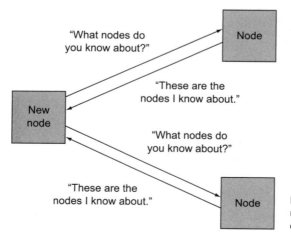

Figure 9.4   **Elasticsearch using unicast discovery to discover other nodes in the cluster**

9.2.3 *Electing a master node and detecting faults*

Once the nodes in your cluster have discovered each other, they'll negotiate who becomes the master. The master node is in charge of managing the *state* of the cluster—that is, the current settings and state of the shards, indices, and nodes in the cluster. After the master node has been elected, it sets up a system of internal pings to make sure each node stays alive and healthy while in the cluster; this is called *fault detection,* which we'll talk more about at the end of this section. Elasticsearch considers all nodes eligible to become the master node unless the `node.master` setting is set to `false`. We'll talk more in this chapter about why you may want to set the `node.master` setting, and the different types of Elasticsearch nodes, when we talk about how to search faster. In the event that your cluster has only a single node, that node will elect itself as the master after a timeout period if it doesn't detect any other nodes in the cluster.

For production clusters with more than a couple of nodes, it's a good idea to set the minimum number of master nodes. Although this setting may make it seem like Elasticsearch can have multiple master nodes, it actually tells Elasticsearch how many nodes in a cluster must be eligible to become a master before the cluster is in a healthy state. Setting the minimum number of eligible master nodes can be helpful in making sure your cluster doesn't try to perform potentially dangerous operations without first having a complete view of the state of your cluster. You can either set the minimum number to the total number of nodes in your cluster if the number of nodes doesn't change over time or set it according to a common rule, which is the number of nodes in your cluster divided by 2, plus 1. Setting the `minimum_master_nodes` setting to a number higher than 1 can help prevent what's called a *split brain* in the cluster. Following the common rule for a three-node cluster, you'd set `minimum_master_nodes` to 2, or for a 14-node cluster, you'd set the value to 8. To change this setting, change `discovery.zen.minimum_master_nodes` in elasticsearch.yml to the number that fits your cluster.

What's a split brain?

The term *split brain* describes a scenario where (usually under heavy load or network issues) one or more of the nodes in your Elasticsearch cluster loses communication to the master node, elects a new master, and continues to process requests. At this point, you may have two different Elasticsearch clusters running independently of each other—hence the term *split brain*, because a single cluster has split into two distinct parts, similar to the hemispheres in a brain. To prevent this from happening, you should set `discovery.zen.minimum_master_nodes` depending on the number of nodes in your cluster. If the number of nodes won't change, set it to the total number of nodes in the cluster; otherwise the number of nodes divided by 2 plus 1 is a good setting, because that means that if one or two nodes lose communication to the other nodes, they won't be able to elect a new master and form a new cluster because they don't meet the required number of master-eligible nodes.

Once your nodes are up and have discovered each other, you can see what node your cluster has elected as master by using the `curl` command shown in the following listing.

Listing 9.2   Getting information about nodes in the cluster with `curl`

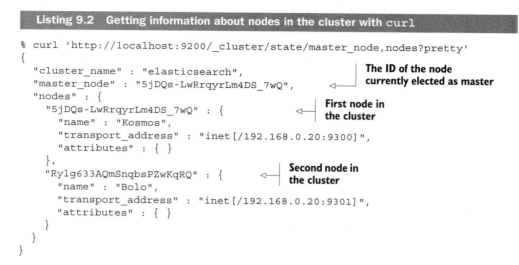

```
% curl 'http://localhost:9200/_cluster/state/master_node,nodes?pretty'
{
    "cluster_name" : "elasticsearch",
    "master_node" : "5jDQs-LwRrqyrLm4DS_7wQ",          The ID of the node
    "nodes" : {                                        currently elected as master
        "5jDQs-LwRrqyrLm4DS_7wQ" : {                   First node in
            "name" : "Kosmos",                         the cluster
            "transport_address" : "inet[/192.168.0.20:9300]",
            "attributes" : { }
        },
        "Rylg633AQmSnqbsPZwKqRQ" : {                   Second node in
            "name" : "Bolo",                           the cluster
            "transport_address" : "inet[/192.168.0.20:9301]",
            "attributes" : { }
        }
    }
}
```

9.2.4   Fault detection

Now that your cluster has two nodes in it, as well as an elected master node, it needs to communicate with all nodes in the cluster to make sure everything is okay within the cluster; this is called the *fault detection* process. The master node pings all other nodes in the cluster and each node pings the master to make sure an election doesn't need to be held, as shown in figure 9.5.

As the figure shows, each node sends a ping every `discovery.zen.fd.ping_interval` (defaulting to 1s), waits for `discovery.zen.fd.ping_timeout` (defaulting to 30s), and

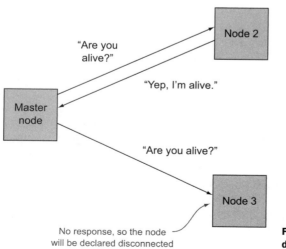

Figure 9.5   Cluster fault detection by the master node

tries a maximum number of `discovery.zen.fd.ping_retries` times (defaulting to 3) before declaring a node disconnected and routing shards or holding a master election as necessary. Be sure to change these values if your environment has higher latency—say, when running on ec2 nodes that may not be in the same Amazon AWS zone.

Inevitably, one of the nodes in your cluster will go down, so in the next section, we'll talk about what happens when nodes are removed from the cluster and how to remove nodes without causing data loss in a distributed system.

9.3   *Removing nodes from a cluster*

Adding nodes is a great way to scale, but what happens when a node drops out of the Elasticsearch cluster or you stop the node? Use the three-node example cluster you created in figure 9.2, containing the test index with five primary shards and one replica spread across the three nodes.

Let's say Joe, the sys admin, accidentally trips over the power cord for `Node1`; what happens to the three shards currently on `Node1`? The first thing that Elasticsearch does is automatically turn the `test0` and `test3` replica shards that are on `Node2` into primary shards, as shown in figure 9.6. This is because indexing first goes to the primary shards, so Elasticsearch tries hard to make sure there are always primaries assigned for an index.

> **NOTE**   Elasticsearch can choose any of the replicas to turn into a primary shard. It just so happens in this example that there's only one replica for each primary shard to choose from: the replicas on `Node2`.

After Elasticsearch turns the replicas for the missing primary shards into primaries, the cluster looks like figure 9.6.

After turning the replica shards into primaries, the cluster is now in a yellow state, meaning that some replica shards aren't allocated to a node. Elasticsearch next needs

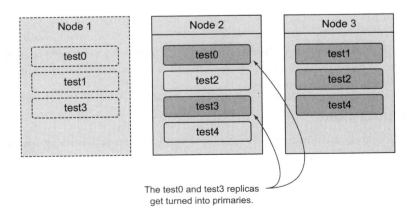

The test0 and test3 replicas
get turned into primaries.

Figure 9.6   Turning replica shards into primaries after node loss

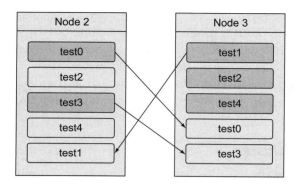

Figure 9.7   Re-creating replica shards after losing a node

to create more replica shards to maintain the high-availability setup for the test index. Because all the primaries are available, the data from the test0 and test3 primary shards on Node2 will be replicated into replicas on Node3, and the data from the test1 primary shard on Node3 will be replicated onto Node2, as shown in figure 9.7.

Once the replica shards have been re-created to account for the node loss, the cluster will be back in the green state with all primary and replica shards assigned to a node. Keep in mind that during this time the entire cluster will be available for searching and indexing because no data was actually lost. If more than a single node is lost or a shard with no replicas is lost, the cluster will be in a red state, meaning that some amount of data has been lost permanently, and you'll need to either reconnect the node that has the data to the cluster or re-index the data that's missing.

It's important to understand how much risk you're willing to take with regard to the number of replica shards. Having a single replica means that one node can disappear from the cluster without data loss; if you use two replicas, two nodes can be lost without data loss, and so on, so make sure you choose the appropriate number of replicas for your usage. It's also always a good idea to back up your indices, which is a subject we'll cover in chapter 11 when we talk about administering your cluster.

You've seen what adding and removing a node looks like, but what about shutting down a node without having the cluster go into a yellow state? In the next section we'll talk about decommissioning nodes so that they can be removed from the cluster with no interruption to the cluster users.

9.3.1   Decommissioning nodes

Having Elasticsearch automatically create new replicas when a node goes down is great, but when maintaining a cluster, you're eventually going to want to shut down a node that has data on it without the cluster going into a yellow state. Perhaps the hardware is degraded or you aren't receiving the same number of requests you previously were and don't need to keep the node around. You could always stop the node by killing the Java process, and Elasticsearch would recover the data to the other nodes, but what about when you have zero replicas for an index? That means you could lose data if you were to shut down a node without moving the data off first!

Thankfully, Elasticsearch has a way to decommission a node by telling the cluster not to allocate any shards to a node or set of nodes. In our three-node example, let's assume that Node1, Node2, and Node3 have the IP addresses of 192.168.1.10, 192.168.1.11, and 192.168.1.12, respectively. If you wanted to shut down Node1 while keeping the cluster in a green state, you could decommission the node first, which would move all shards on the node to other nodes in the cluster. You decommission a node by making a temporary change to the cluster settings, as shown in the following listing.

Listing 9.3   Decommissioning a node in the cluster

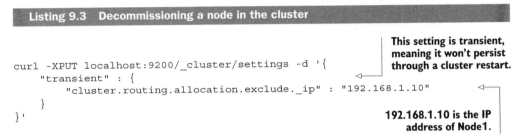

```
curl -XPUT localhost:9200/_cluster/settings -d '{
    "transient" : {
        "cluster.routing.allocation.exclude._ip" : "192.168.1.10"
    }
}'
```

This setting is transient, meaning it won't persist through a cluster restart.

192.168.1.10 is the IP address of Node1.

Once you run this command, Elasticsearch will start moving all the shards from the decommissioned node to other nodes in the cluster. You can check where shards are located in the cluster by first determining the ID of the nodes in the cluster with the _nodes endpoint and then looking at the cluster state to see where each shard in the cluster is currently allocated. See the next listing for example output of these commands.

Listing 9.4   Determining shard location from the cluster state

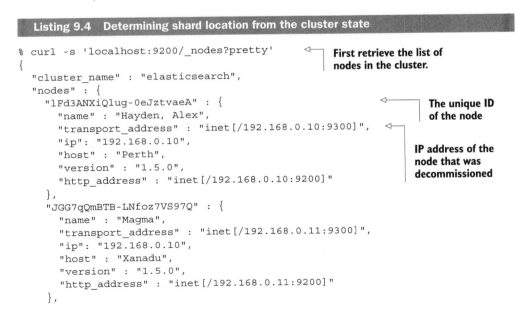

```
% curl -s 'localhost:9200/_nodes?pretty'
{
  "cluster_name" : "elasticsearch",
  "nodes" : {
    "1Fd3ANXiQlug-0eJztvaeA" : {
      "name" : "Hayden, Alex",
      "transport_address" : "inet[/192.168.0.10:9300]",
      "ip": "192.168.0.10",
      "host" : "Perth",
      "version" : "1.5.0",
      "http_address" : "inet[/192.168.0.10:9200]"
    },
    "JGG7qQmBTB-LNfoz7VS97Q" : {
      "name" : "Magma",
      "transport_address" : "inet[/192.168.0.11:9300]",
      "ip": "192.168.0.10",
      "host" : "Xanadu",
      "version" : "1.5.0",
      "http_address" : "inet[/192.168.0.11:9200]"
    },
```

First retrieve the list of nodes in the cluster.

The unique ID of the node

IP address of the node that was decommissioned

```
      "McUL2T6vTSOGEAjSEuI-Zw" : {
        "name" : "Toad-In-Waiting",
        "transport_address" : "inet[/192.168.0.12:9300]",
        "ip": "192.168.0.10",
        "host" : "Corinth",
        "version" : "1.5.0",
        "http_address" : "inet[/192.168.0.12:9200]"
      }
    }
}

% curl 'localhost:9200/_cluster/state/routing_table,routing_nodes?pretty'   ◄─┐
{                                                                             │
  "cluster_name" : "elasticsearch",                          **Retrieving a filtered**
  "routing_table" : {                                              **cluster state**
    "indices" : {
      "test" : {
        "shards" : {
          ...                    ◄─┐  **Shortened to fit**
        }                          │  **on this page**
      }
    }
  },
  "routing_nodes" : {
    "unassigned" : [ ],
    "nodes" : {
      "JGG7qQmBTB-LNfoz7VS97Q" : [ {       ◄─┐  **This key lists each node**
        "state" : "STARTED",                 │  **with the shards currently**
        "primary" : true,                    │  **assigned to it.**
        "node" : "JGG7qQmBTB-LNfoz7VS97Q",
        "relocating_node" : null,
        "shard" : 0,
        "index" : "test"
      }, {
        "state" : "STARTED",
        "primary" : true,
        "node" : "JGG7qQmBTB-LNfoz7VS97Q",
        "relocating_node" : null,
        "shard" : 1,
        "index" : "test"
      }, {
        "state" : "STARTED",
        "primary" : true,
        "node" : "JGG7qQmBTB-LNfoz7VS97Q",
        "relocating_node" : null,
        "shard" : 2,
        "index" : "test"
      }, ...],
      "McUL2T6vTSOGEAjSEuI-Zw" : [ {
        "state" : "STARTED",
        "primary" : false,
        "node" : "McUL2T6vTSOGEAjSEuI-Zw",
        "relocating_node" : null,
        "shard" : 0,
        "index" : "test"
```

```
    }, {
      "state" : "STARTED",
      "primary" : false,
      "node" : "McUL2T6vTSOGEAjSEuI-Zw",
      "relocating_node" : null,
      "shard" : 1,
      "index" : "test"
    }, {
      "state" : "STARTED",
      "primary" : false,
      "node" : "McUL2T6vTSOGEAjSEuI-Zw",
      "relocating_node" : null,
      "shard" : 2,
      "index" : "test"
    }, ...]
  }
 },
 "allocations" : [ ]
}.
```

This is a long and ugly listing! Don't worry, though; later on this chapter we'll talk about a more human-readable version of this API called the _cat API.

Here you can see that there are no shards on the 1Fd3ANXiQlug-0eJztvaeA node, which is the 192.168.1.10 node that was decommissioned, so it's now safe to stop ES on that node without causing the cluster to leave a green state. This process can be repeated one node at a time to decommission each node you want to stop, or you can use a list of comma-separated IP addresses instead of 192.168.1.10 to decommission multiple nodes at once. Keep in mind, however, that the other nodes in the cluster must be able to handle allocating the shard in terms of disk and memory use, so plan accordingly to make sure you have enough headroom before decommissioning nodes!

How much data can an Elasticsearch index handle?

Good question! Unfortunately, the limitations of a single index depend on the type of machine used to store the index, what you're planning to do with the data, and how many shards the index is backed by. Generally, a Lucene index (also known as an Elasticsearch shard) can't have more than 2.1 billion documents or more than 274 billion distinct terms (see https://lucene.apache.org/core/4_9_0/core/org/apache/lucene/codecs/lucene49/package-summary.html#Limitations), but you may be limited in disk space before this point. The best way to tell whether you'll be able to store your data in a single index is to try it out in a nonproduction system, adjusting settings as needed to get the performance characteristics desired. You can't change the number of primary shards once an index has been created; you can only change the number of replica shards, so plan accordingly!

Now that you've seen how nodes are added and removed from the cluster, let's talk about how to upgrade Elasticsearch nodes.

9.4   *Upgrading Elasticsearch nodes*

There comes a point with every installation of Elasticsearch when it's time to upgrade to the latest version. We recommend that you always run the latest version of Elasticsearch because there are always new features being added, as well as bugs being fixed. That said, depending on the constraints of your environment, upgrading may be more or less complex.

Upgrade caveats

Before we get to upgrading instructions, it's important to understand that there are some limitations when upgrading Elasticsearch instances. Once you've upgraded an Elasticsearch server, the server can't be downgraded if any new documents have been written. When you perform upgrades to a production instance, you should always back up your data before performing an upgrade. We'll talk more about backing up your data in chapter 11.

Another important thing to consider is that although Elasticsearch can handle a mixed-version environment easily, there have been cases where different JVM versions serialize information differently, so we recommend that you not mix different JVM versions within the same Elasticsearch cluster.

The simplest way to upgrade an Elasticsearch cluster is to shut down all nodes and then upgrade each Elasticsearch installation with whatever method you originally used—for example, extracting the distribution if you used the .tar.gz distribution or installing the .deb package using dpkg if you're using a Debian-based system. Once each node has been upgraded, you can restart the entire cluster and wait for Elasticsearch to reach the green state. Voila, upgrade done!

This may not always be the case, though; in many situations downtime can't be tolerated, even during off-peak hours. Thankfully, you can perform a rolling restart to upgrade your Elasticsearch cluster while still serving indexing and searching requests.

9.4.1   *Performing a rolling restart*

A *rolling restart* is another way of restarting your cluster in order to upgrade a node or make a nondynamic configuration change without sacrificing the availability of your data. This can be particularly good for production deployments of Elasticsearch. Instead of shutting down the whole cluster at once, you shut nodes down one at a time. This process is slightly more involved than a full restart because of the multiple steps required.

The first step in performing a rolling restart is to decide if you want Elasticsearch to automatically rebalance shards while each individual node is not running. The majority of people don't want Elasticsearch to start its automatic recovery in the event a node leaves the cluster for an upgrade because it means that they'll be rebalancing every single node. In reality the data is still there; the node just needs to be restarted and to rejoin the cluster in order for it to be available.

For most people, it makes sense not to shift data around the cluster while performing the upgrade. You can accomplish this by setting the `cluster.routing.allocation.enable` setting to `none` while performing the upgrade. To clarify, the entire process looks like this:

1 Disable allocation for the cluster.
2 Shut down the node that will be upgraded.
3 Upgrade the node.
4 Start the upgraded node.
5 Wait until the upgraded node has joined the cluster.
6 Enable allocation for the cluster.
7 Wait for the cluster to return to a green state.

Repeat this process for each node that needs to be upgraded. To disable allocation for the cluster, you can use the cluster settings API with the following settings:

```
curl -XPUT 'localhost:9200/_cluster/settings' -d '{
  "transient" : {
    "cluster.routing.allocation.enable" : "none"     ◁──  Setting this to none
  }                                                        means no shards can be
}'                                                         allocated in the cluster.
```

Once you run this command, Elasticsearch will no longer rebalance shards around the cluster. For instance, if a primary shard is lost for an index because the node it resided on is shut down, Elasticsearch will still turn the replica shard into a new primary, but a new replica won't be created. While in this state, you can safely shut down the single Elasticsearch node and perform the upgrade.

After upgrading the node, make sure that you reenable allocation for the cluster; otherwise you'll be wondering why Elasticsearch doesn't automatically replicate your data in the future! You can reenable allocation by setting the `cluster.routing.allocation.enable` setting to `all` instead of `none`, like this:

```
curl -XPUT 'localhost:9200/_cluster/settings' -d '{
  "transient" : {
    "cluster.routing.allocation.enable" : "all"      ◁──  Setting this to all means all
  }                                                        shards can be allocated,
}'                                                         both primaries and replicas.
```

You need to perform these two book-ending steps, disabling allocation and reenabling allocation, for every node in the cluster being upgraded. If you were to perform them only once at the beginning and once at the end, Elasticsearch wouldn't allocate the shards that exist on the upgraded node every time you upgraded a node, and your cluster would be red once you upgraded multiple nodes. By reenabling allocation and waiting for the cluster to return to a green state after each node is upgraded, your data is allocated and available when you move to the next node that needs to be upgraded. Repeat these steps for each node that needs to be upgraded until you have a fully upgraded cluster.

There's one more thing to mention in this section, and that's indices that don't have replicas. The previous examples all take into account the data having at least a single replica so that a node going down doesn't remove access to the data. If you have an index that has no replicas, you can use the decommissioning steps we covered in section 9.3.1 to decommission the node by moving all the data off it before shutting it down to perform the upgrade.

9.4.2 *Minimizing recovery time for a restart*

You may notice that even with the disable and enable allocation steps, it can still take a while for the cluster to return to a green state when upgrading a single node. Unfortunately, this is because the replication that Elasticsearch uses is for each shard segment, rather than document-level. This means that the Elasticsearch node sending data to be replicated is saying, "Do you have segments_1?" If it doesn't have the file or the file isn't the same, the entire segment file is copied. A larger amount of data may be copied in the event that the documents are the same. Until Elasticsearch has a way of verifying the last document written in a segment file, it has to copy over any differing files when replicating data between the primary shard and the replica shard.

There are two different ways to make segment files identical on the primary and replica shards. The first is using the optimize API that we'll talk about in chapter 10 to create a single, large segment for both the primary and the replica. The second is to toggle the number of replicas to 0 and then back to a higher number; this ensures that all replica copies have the same segment files as the primary shard. This means that for a short period you'll have only a single copy of the data, so beware of doing this in a production environment!

Finally, in order to minimize recovery time, you can also halt indexing data into the cluster while you're performing the node upgrade.

Now that we've covered upgrading a node, let's cover a helpful API for getting information out of the cluster in a more human-friendly way: the _cat API.

9.5 *Using the _cat API*

Using the `curl` commands in sections 9.1, 9.2, and 9.3 is a great way to see what's going on with your cluster, but sometimes it's helpful to see the output in a more readable format (if you don't believe us, try curling the http://localhost:9200/ _cluster/state URL on a large cluster and see how much information comes back!). This is where the handy _cat API comes in. The _cat API provides helpful diagnostic and debugging tools that print data in a more human-readable way, rather than trying to page through a giant JSON response. The following listing shows two of its commands for the equivalent health and node listing cURL statements we already covered.

Listing 9.5 Using the _cat API to find cluster health and nodes

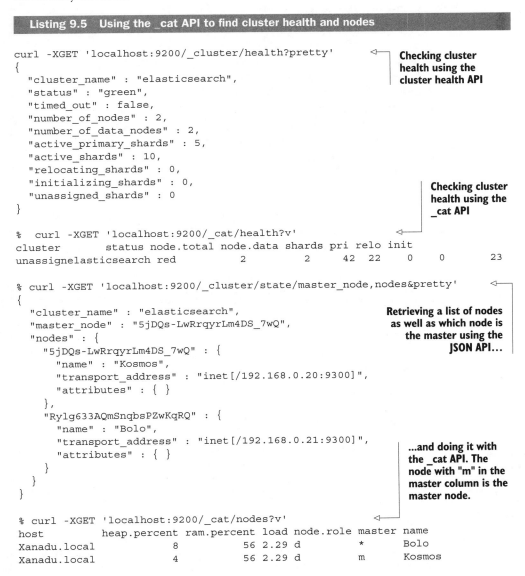

```
curl -XGET 'localhost:9200/_cluster/health?pretty'           Checking cluster
{                                                            health using the
  "cluster_name" : "elasticsearch",                          cluster health API
  "status" : "green",
  "timed_out" : false,
  "number_of_nodes" : 2,
  "number_of_data_nodes" : 2,
  "active_primary_shards" : 5,
  "active_shards" : 10,
  "relocating_shards" : 0,
  "initializing_shards" : 0,                                 Checking cluster
  "unassigned_shards" : 0                                    health using the
}                                                            _cat API

%  curl -XGET 'localhost:9200/_cat/health?v'
cluster         status node.total node.data shards pri relo init
unassignelasticsearch red       2         2     42  22    0    0       23

%  curl -XGET 'localhost:9200/_cluster/state/master_node,nodes&pretty'
{
  "cluster_name" : "elasticsearch",                          Retrieving a list of nodes
  "master_node" : "5jDQs-LwRrqyrLm4DS_7wQ",                  as well as which node is
  "nodes" : {                                                the master using the
    "5jDQs-LwRrqyrLm4DS_7wQ" : {                             JSON API...
      "name" : "Kosmos",
      "transport_address" : "inet[/192.168.0.20:9300]",
      "attributes" : { }
    },
    "Rylg633AQmSnqbsPZwKqRQ" : {
      "name" : "Bolo",
      "transport_address" : "inet[/192.168.0.21:9300]",
      "attributes" : { }                                     ...and doing it with
    }                                                        the _cat API. The
  }                                                          node with "m" in the
}                                                            master column is the
                                                             master node.
%  curl -XGET 'localhost:9200/_cat/nodes?v'
host            heap.percent ram.percent load node.role master name
Xanadu.local              8          56 2.29 d              *    Bolo
Xanadu.local              4          56 2.29 d              m    Kosmos
```

In addition to the health and nodes endpoints, the _cat API has many other features, all of which are useful for debugging different things your cluster may be undergoing. You can see the full list of supported _cat APIs by running curl 'localhost:9200/_cat'.

_cat APIs

At the time of this writing, here are some of the most useful _cat APIs and what they do. Be sure to check out the others!

- allocation—Shows the number of shards allocated to each node
- count—Counts the number of documents in the entire cluster or index
- health—Displays the health of the cluster
- indices—Displays information about existing indices
- master—Shows what node is currently elected master
- nodes—Shows various information about all nodes in the cluster
- recovery—Shows the status of ongoing shard recoveries in the cluster
- shards—Displays count, size, and names of shards in the cluster
- plugins—Displays information about installed plugins

While we're looking at adding nodes to a cluster, why not look at how the shards are distributed across each node using the _cat API in the following code listing. This is a much easier way to see how shards are allocated in your cluster as opposed to the curl command in listing 9.2.

Listing 9.6   Using the _cat API to show shard allocation

The allocation command lists the count of shards across each node.

```
% curl -XGET 'localhost:9200/_cat/allocation?v'
shards disk.used disk.avail disk.total disk.percent host      ip         node
    2    196.5gb    36.1gb    232.6gb          84 Xanadu.local
         192.168.192.16 Molten Man
    2    196.5gb    36.1gb    232.6gb          84 Xanadu.local
         192.168.192.16 Grappler

% curl -XGET 'localhost:9200/_cat/shards?v'
index         shard prirep state   docs store  ip             node
get-together 0     p      STARTED   12 15.1kb 192.168.192.16 Molten Man
get-together 0     r      STARTED   12 15.1kb 192.168.192.16 Grappler
get-together 1     r      STARTED    8 11.4kb 192.168.192.16 Molten Man
get-together 1     p      STARTED    8 11.4kb 192.168.192.16 Grappler
```

Notice all the primary shards are on one node, the replicas on another.

Using the _cat/allocation and _cat/shards APIs is also a great way to determine when a node can be safely shut down after performing the decommission we discussed in section 9.3.1. Compare the output of the curl command from listing 9.2 to the output from the commands in listing 9.6; it's much easier to read the _cat API output!

Now that you can see where the shards are located in your cluster, we should spend some more time discussing how you should plan your Elasticsearch cluster to make the most of your nodes and data.

9.6 Scaling strategies

It might seem easy enough to add nodes to a cluster to increase the performance, but this is actually a case where a bit of planning goes a long way toward getting the best performance out of your cluster.

Every use of Elasticsearch is different, so you'll have to pick the best options for your cluster based on how you'll index data, as well as how you'll search it. In general, though, there are at least three things you'll want to consider when planning for a production Elasticsearch cluster: over-sharding, splitting data between indices and shards, and maximizing throughput.

9.6.1 Over-sharding

Let's start by talking about over-sharding. *Over-sharding* is the process whereby you intentionally create a larger number of shards for an index so you have room to add nodes and grow in the future; this is best illustrated by a diagram, so take a look at figure 9.8.

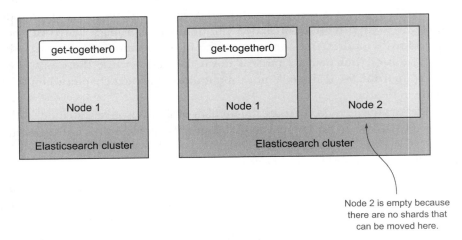

Figure 9.8   A single node with a single shard and two nodes trying to scale a single shard

In figure 9.8, you've created your get-together index with a single shard and no replicas. But what happens when you add another node?

Whoops! You've totally removed any benefit you get from adding nodes to the cluster. By adding another node, you're unable to scale because all of the indexing and querying load will still be handled by the node with the single shard on it. Because a shard is the smallest thing that Elasticsearch can move around, it's a good idea to always make sure you have at least as many primary shards in your cluster as you plan to have nodes; if you currently have a 5-node cluster with 11 primary shards, you have room to grow when you need to add more nodes to handle additional requests. Using the same example, if you suddenly need more than 11 nodes, you won't be able to distribute the primary shards across nodes because you'll have more nodes than shards.

That's easy to fix, you might say: "I'll just create an index with 100 primary shards!" It may seem like a good idea at first, but there's a hidden cost to each shard Elasticsearch has to manage. Because each shard is a complete Lucene index, as you learned in chapter 1, each shard requires a number of file descriptors for each segment of the index, as well as a memory overhead. By creating too large a number of shards for an index, you may be using memory that could be better served to bolster performance, or you could end up hitting the machine's file descriptor or RAM limits. In addition, when compressing your data, you'll end up splitting the data across 100 different things, lowering the compression rate you would have gotten if you had picked a more reasonable size.

It's worth noting that there is no perfect shard-to-index ratio for all use cases; Elasticsearch picks a good default of five shards for the general case, but it's always important to think about how you plan on growing (or shrinking) in the future with regard to the number of shards you create and index with. Don't forget: once an index has been created with a number of shards, the number of primary shards can never be changed for that index! You don't want to be in the position of having to re-index a large portion of your data six months down the line because there wasn't enough planning up front. We'll also talk more about this in the next chapter when we discuss indexing in depth.

Along the same lines as choosing the number of shards to create an index with, you'll also need to decide on how exactly to split your data across indices in Elasticsearch.

9.6.2 *Splitting data into indices and shards*

Unfortunately for now, there's no way to increase or decrease the number of primary shards in an index, but you could always plan your data to span multiple indices. This is another perfectly valid way to split data. Taking our get-together example, there's nothing stopping you from creating an index for every different city an event occurs in. For example, if you expect to have a larger number of events in New York than Sacramento, you could create a sacramento index with two primary shards and a newyork index with four primary shards, or you could segment the data by date, creating an index for each year an event occurs or is created: 2014, 2015, 2016, and so on. Segmenting data in this way can also be helpful when searching because the segmentation is handled by putting the right data in the right place; if the customer wants to search only for events or groups from the year 2014 or 2015, you'll have to search only those indices rather than the entire get-together index.

Another way to plan using indices is with aliases. An *alias* acts like a pointer to an index or a set of indices. An alias also allows you to change the indices that it points to at any time. This is incredibly useful for segmenting your data in a semantic way; you could create an alias called last-year that points to 2015; then, when January 1, 2016 rolls around, you can change the alias to point to the 2015 index. This technique is commonly used when indexing date-based information (like log files) so that data can be segmented by date on a monthly/weekly/daily basis and an alias named current can be used to always point to the data that should be searched without having to change the name of the index being searched every time the segment rolls over. Again, aliases allow an incredible level of flexibility and have almost zero overhead, so experimentation is encouraged. We'll talk in more depth about aliases later on in this chapter.

When creating indices, don't forget that because each index has its own shards, you'll still incur the overhead of creating a shard, so make sure not to create too many shards by creating too many indices and using resources that could be better spent handling requests. Once you know how your data will be laid out in the cluster, you can work on tweaking the node configuration to maximize your throughput.

9.6.3 *Maximizing throughput*

Maximizing throughput is one of those fuzzy, hazy terms that can mean an awful lot of things. Are you trying to maximize the indexing throughput? Make searches faster? Execute more searches at once? There are different ways to tweak Elasticsearch to accomplish each task. For example, if you received thousands of new groups and events, how would you go about indexing them as fast as possible? One way to make indexing faster is to temporarily reduce the number of replica shards in your cluster. When indexing data, by default the request won't complete until the data exists on the primary shard as well as all replicas, so it may be advantageous to reduce the number of replicas to one (or zero if you're okay with the risk) while indexing and then increase the number back to one or more once the period of heavy indexing has completed.

What about searches? Searches can be made faster by adding more replicas because either a primary or a replica shard can be used to search on. To illustrate this, check out figure 9.9, which shows a three-node cluster where the last node can't help with search requests until it has a copy of the data.

But don't forget that creating more shards in an Elasticsearch cluster does come with the small overhead in file descriptors and memory. If the volume of searches is getting too high for the nodes in the cluster to keep up, consider adding nodes with `node.data` and `node.master` both set to `false`. These nodes can then be used to handle incoming requests, distribute the request to the data nodes, and collect the results for responses. This way, the nodes searching the shards don't have to handle connections from search clients; they only need to search shards. We'll talk more about different ways of speeding up both indexing and searching in the next chapter.

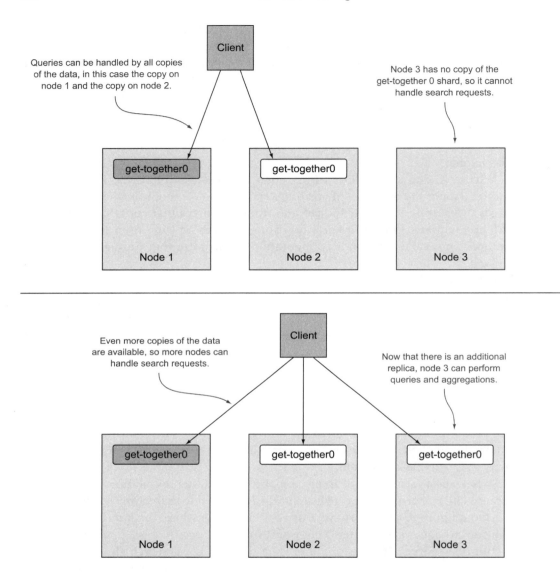

Figure 9.9   Additional replicas handling search and aggregations

9.7   *Aliases*

Now let's talk about one of the easiest and potentially most useful features of Elastic-search: aliases. Aliases are exactly what they sound like; they're a pointer or a name you can use that corresponds to one or more concrete indices. This turns out to be quite useful because of the flexibility it provides when scaling your cluster and managing how data is laid out across your indices. Even when using an Elasticsearch cluster with only a single index, use an alias. You'll thank us later for the flexibility it will give you.

9.7.1 What is an alias, really?

You may be wondering what an alias is exactly and what kind of overhead is involved with Elasticsearch in creating one. An alias spends its life inside the cluster state, managed by the master node; this means that if you have an alias called idaho that points to an index named potatoes, the overhead is an extra key in the cluster state map that maps the name idaho to the concrete index potatoes. This means that compared to additional indices, aliases are much lighter in weight; thousands of them can be maintained without negatively impacting your cluster. That said, we would caution against creating hundreds of thousands or millions of aliases because at that point, even the minimal overhead of a single entry in a map can cause the cluster state to grow to a large size. This means operations that create a new cluster state will take longer because the entire cluster state is sent to each node every time it changes.

WHY ARE ALIASES USEFUL?

We recommend that everyone use an alias for their Elasticsearch indices because it will give a lot more flexibility in the future when it comes to re-indexing. Let's say that you start off by creating an index with a single primary shard and then later decide that you need more capacity on your index. If you were using an alias for the original index, you can now change that alias to point to an additionally created index without having to change the name of the index you're searching (assuming you're using an alias for searching from the beginning).

Another useful feature can be creating windows into different indices; for example, if you create daily indices for your data, you may want a sliding window of the last week's data by creating an alias called last-7-days; then every day when you create a new daily index, you can add it to the alias while simultaneously removing the eight-day-old index.

MANAGING ALIASES

Aliases are created using the dedicated aliases API endpoint and a list of actions. Each action is a map with either an add or remove action followed by the index and alias on which to apply the operation. This will be much clearer with the example shown in the next listing.

Listing 9.7 Adding and removing aliases

```
curl -XPOST 'localhost:9200/_aliases' -d'
{
  "actions": [
    {
      "add" : {
        "index": "get-together",
        "alias": "gt-alias"
```

The operation—in this case, adding an index to an alias

The index get-together will be added to the alias gt-alias.

```
        }
      },
      {
        "remove": {                          ⟵    A remove operation
          "index": "old-get-together",             to remove an index
          "alias": "gt-alias"                       from an alias
        }
                                                   The index old-get-together will be
      }                                             removed from the alias gt-alias.
    ]
  }'
```

In this listing the get-together index is being added to an alias named gt-alias, and the made-up index old-get-together is being removed from the alias gt-alias. The act of adding an index to an alias creates it, and removing all indices that an alias points to removes the alias; there's no manual alias creation and deletion. But the alias operations will fail if the index doesn't exist, so keep that in mind. You can specify as many add and remove actions as you like. It's important to recognize that these actions will all occur atomically, which means in the previous example there'll be no moment of time in which the gt-alias alias points to both the get-together and old-get-together indices. Although the compound Alias API call we just discussed may suit your needs, it's important to note that individual actions can be performed on the Alias API, using the common HTTP methods that Elasticsearch has standardized on. For instance, the following series of calls would have the same effect as the compound actions call shown previously:

```
curl -XPUT 'http://localhost:9200/get-together/_alias/gt-alias'

curl -XDELETE 'http://localhost:9200/old-get-together/_alias/gt-alias'
```

While we're exploring single-call API methods, this section wouldn't be complete without covering the API in more detail, specifically those endpoints that can come in handy in creating and listing operations.

9.7.2   Alias creation

When creating aliases, there are many options available via the API endpoint. For instance, you can create aliases on a specific index, many indices, or a pattern that matches index names:

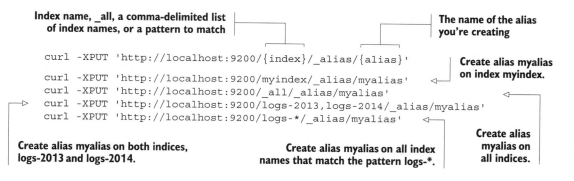

Index name, _all, a comma-delimited list of index names, or a pattern to match | The name of the alias you're creating

```
curl -XPUT 'http://localhost:9200/{index}/_alias/{alias}'
curl -XPUT 'http://localhost:9200/myindex/_alias/myalias'       ⟵  Create alias myalias on index myindex.
curl -XPUT 'http://localhost:9200/_all/_alias/myalias'
curl -XPUT 'http://localhost:9200/logs-2013,logs-2014/_alias/myalias'
curl -XPUT 'http://localhost:9200/logs-*/_alias/myalias'     ⟵
```

Create alias myalias on both indices, logs-2013 and logs-2014.

Create alias myalias on all index names that match the pattern logs-*.

Create alias myalias on all indices.

Alias deletion accepts the same path parameter format:

```
curl -XDELETE 'localhost:9200/{index}/_alias/{alias}'
```

You can retrieve all of the aliases that a concrete index points to by issuing a GET request on an index with _alias, or you can retrieve all indices and the aliases that point to them by leaving out the index name. Retrieving the aliases for an index is shown in the next listing.

Listing 9.8 Retrieving the aliases pointing to a specific index

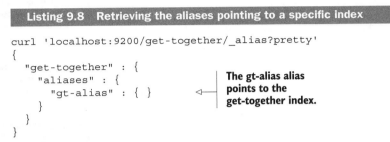

```
curl 'localhost:9200/get-together/_alias?pretty'
{
   "get-together" : {
     "aliases" : {
        "gt-alias" : { }              ◁──  The gt-alias alias
     }                                      points to the
   }                                        get-together index.
}
```

In addition to the _alias endpoint on an index, you have a number of different ways to get the alias information from an index:

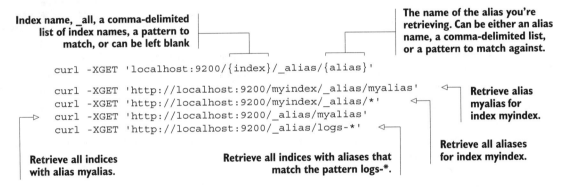

Index name, _all, a comma-delimited list of index names, a pattern to match, or can be left blank

The name of the alias you're retrieving. Can be either an alias name, a comma-delimited list, or a pattern to match against.

```
curl -XGET 'localhost:9200/{index}/_alias/{alias}'

curl -XGET 'http://localhost:9200/myindex/_alias/myalias'    ◁──┐
curl -XGET 'http://localhost:9200/myindex/_alias/*'          ◁──┤   Retrieve alias
curl -XGET 'http://localhost:9200/_alias/myalias'            ◁──┐   myalias for
curl -XGET 'http://localhost:9200/_alias/logs-*'             ◁──┘   index myindex.
```

Retrieve all indices with alias myalias.

Retrieve all indices with aliases that match the pattern logs-*.

Retrieve all aliases for index myindex.

MASKING DOCUMENTS WITH ALIAS FILTERS

Aliases have some other neat features as well; they can be used to automatically apply a filter to queries that are executed. For example, with your get-together data it could be useful to have an alias that points only to the groups that contain the elastic-search tag, so you can create an alias that does this filtering automatically, as shown in the following listing.

Listing 9.9 Creating a filtered alias

```
$ curl -XPOST 'localhost:9200/_aliases' -d'
{
   "actions": [
      {
        "add": {
          "index": "get-together",
```

```
          "alias": "es-groups",
          "filter": {
             "term": {"tags": "elasticsearch"}
          }
        }
      }
    }
  ]
}'
{"acknowledged":true}

$ curl 'localhost:9200/get-together/group/_count' -d'
{
  "query": {
    "match_all": {}
  }
}'
{"count":5,"_shards":{"total":2,"successful":2,"failed":0}}

$ curl 'localhost:9200/es-groups/group/_count' -d'
{
  "query": {
    "match_all": {}
  }
}'
{"count":2,"_shards":{"total":2,"successful":2,"failed":0}}
```

> Adding a filter for the es-groups alias for the elasticsearch tag

> Counting all the groups in the get-together index

> Five groups in the get-together index

> Counting all the groups in the es-groups alias

> Two groups in the es-groups alias; the results have been filtered automatically.

Here you can see that the es-groups alias contains only two groups instead of five. This is because it's automatically applying the term filter for groups that contain the tag elasticsearch. This has a lot of applications; if you're indexing sensitive data, for instance, you can create a filtered alias to ensure that anyone using that alias can't see data they're not meant to see.

There's one more feature that aliases can provide, routing, but before we talk about using it with an alias, we'll talk about using it in general.

9.8   Routing

In chapter 8, we talked about how documents end up in a particular shard; this process is called *routing* the document. To refresh your memory, routing a document occurs when Elasticsearch hashes the ID of the document, either specified by you or generated by Elasticsearch, to determine which shard a document should be indexed into. Elasticsearch also allows you to manually specify the routing of a document when indexing, which is what you do when using parent-child relationships because the child document has to be in the same shard as the parent document.

Routing can also use a custom value for hashing, instead of the ID of the document. By specifying the routing query parameter on the URL, that value will be hashed and used instead of the ID:

```
curl -XPOST 'localhost:9200/get-together/group/9?routing=denver' -d'{
  "title": "Denver Knitting"
}'
```

In this example, `denver` is the value that's hashed to determine which shard the document ends up in, instead of 9, the document's ID. Routing can be useful for scaling strategies, which is why we talk about it in detail in this chapter.

9.8.1 Why use routing?

If you don't use routing at all, Elasticsearch will ensure that your documents are distributed in an even manner across all the different shards, so why would you want to use routing? Custom routing allows you to collect multiple documents sharing a routing value into a single shard, and once these documents are in the same index, it allows you to route certain queries so that they are executed on a subset of the shards for an index. Sound confusing? We'll go over it in more detail to clarify what we mean.

9.8.2 Routing strategies

Routing is a strategy that takes effort in two areas: you'll need to pick good routing values while you're indexing documents, and you'll need to reuse those values when you perform queries. With our get-together example, you first need to decide on a good way to separate each document. In this case, pick the city that a get-together group or event happens to use as the routing value. This is a good choice for a routing value because the cities vary widely enough that you have quite a few values to pick from, and each event and group are already associated with a city, so it's easy to extract that from a document before indexing. If you were to pick something that had only a few different values, you could easily end up with unbalanced shards for the index. If there are only three possible routing values for all documents, all documents will end up routed between a maximum of three shards. It's important to pick a value that will have enough cardinality to spread data among shards in an index.

Now that you've picked what you want to use for the routing value, you need to specify this routing value when indexing documents, as shown in the listing that follows.

Listing 9.10 Indexing documents with custom routing values

```
% curl -XPOST 'localhost:9200/get-together/group/10?routing=denver' -d'      ◄─┐
{
  "name": "Denver Ruby",                                 Indexing a document with
  "description": "The Denver Ruby Meetup"                a routing value of denver
}'

% curl -XPOST 'localhost:9200/get-together/group/11?routing=boulder' -d'      ◄─┐
{
  "name": "Boulder Ruby",                                Indexing a document with
  "description": "Boulderites that use Ruby"             the routing value boulder
}'

% curl -XPOST 'localhost:9200/get-together/group/12?routing=amsterdam' -d'
{
  "name": "Amsterdam Devs that use Ruby",
  "description": "Mensen die genieten van het gebruik van Ruby"
}'
```

In this example, you use three different routing values—denver, boulder, and amsterdam—for three different documents. This means that instead of hashing the IDs 10, 11, and 12 to determine which shard to put the document in, you use the routing values instead. On the index side, this doesn't help you much; the real benefit comes when you combine routing on the query side, as the next listing shows. On the query side, you can combine multiple routing values with a comma.

Listing 9.11 Specifying routing when querying

```
% curl -XPOST 'localhost:9200/get-together/group/
    _search?routing=denver,amsterdam' -d'                    ⟵  Executing a query with a
{                                                                routing value of denver
  "query": {                                                     and amsterdam
    "match": {
      "name": "ruby"
    }
  }
}'
{
    ...
    "hits": {
        "hits": [
            {
                "_id": "10",
                "_index": "get-together",
                "_score": 1.377483,
                "_source": {
                    "description": "The Denver Ruby Meetup",
                    "name": "Denver Ruby"
                },
                "_type": "group"
            },
            {
                "_id": "12",
                "_index": "get-together",
                "_score": 0.9642381,
                "_source": {
                    "description": "Mensen die genieten van het gebruik van
                    Ruby",
                    "name": "Amsterdam Devs that use Ruby"
                },
                "_type": "group"
            }
        ],
        "max_score": 1.377483,
        "total": 2
    }
}
```

Interesting! Instead of returning all three groups, only two were returned. So what actually happened? Internally, when Elasticsearch received the request, it hashed the values of the two provided routing values, denver and amsterdam, and then executed the query on all the shards they hashed to. In this case denver and amsterdam both hash to the same shard, and boulder hashes to a different shard.

Extrapolate this to hundreds of thousands of groups, in hundreds of cities, by specifying the routing for each group both while indexing and while querying, and you're able to limit the scope of where a search request is executed. This can be a great scaling improvement for an index that might have 100 shards; instead of running the query on all 100 shards, it can be limited and thus run faster with less impact to your Elasticsearch cluster.

In the previous example, denver and amsterdam happen to route to the same shard value, but they could have just as easily hashed to different shard values. How can you tell which shard a request will be executed on? Thankfully, Elasticsearch has an API that can show you the nodes and shards a search request will be performed on.

9.8.3 Using the _search_shards API to determine where a search is performed

Let's take the prior example and use the search shards API to see which shards the request is going to be executed on, with and without the routing values, as shown in the following listing.

Listing 9.12 Using the _search_shards API with and without routing

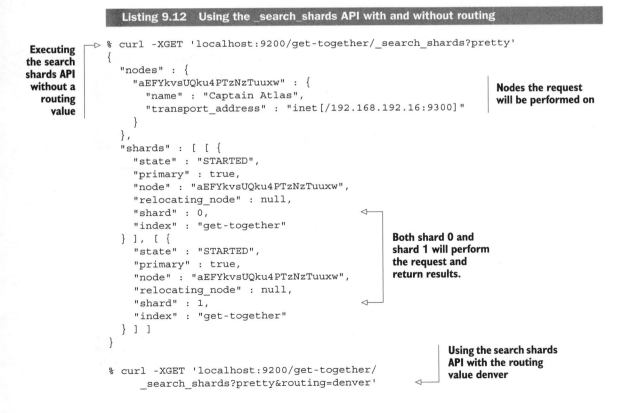

Executing the search shards API without a routing value

```
% curl -XGET 'localhost:9200/get-together/_search_shards?pretty'
{
  "nodes" : {
    "aEFYkvsUQku4PTzNzTuuxw" : {
      "name" : "Captain Atlas",
      "transport_address" : "inet[/192.168.192.16:9300]"
    }
  },
  "shards" : [ [ {
    "state" : "STARTED",
    "primary" : true,
    "node" : "aEFYkvsUQku4PTzNzTuuxw",
    "relocating_node" : null,
    "shard" : 0,
    "index" : "get-together"
  } ], [ {
    "state" : "STARTED",
    "primary" : true,
    "node" : "aEFYkvsUQku4PTzNzTuuxw",
    "relocating_node" : null,
    "shard" : 1,
    "index" : "get-together"
  } ] ]
}

% curl -XGET 'localhost:9200/get-together/
    _search_shards?pretty&routing=denver'
```

Nodes the request will be performed on

Both shard 0 and shard 1 will perform the request and return results.

Using the search shards API with the routing value denver

```
{
  "nodes" : {
    "aEFYkvsUQku4PTzNzTuuxw" : {
      "name" : "Captain Atlas",
      "transport_address" : "inet[/192.168.192.16:9300]"
    }
  },
  "shards" : [ [ {
    "state" : "STARTED",
    "primary" : true,
    "node" : "aEFYkvsUQku4PTzNzTuuxw",
    "relocating_node" : null,
    "shard" : 1,
    "index" : "get-together"
  } ] ]
}
```

Only shard 1 will
perform the
request.

You can see that even though there are two shards in the index, when the routing
value denver is specified, only shard 1 is going to be searched. You've effectively cut
the amount of data the search must execute on by half!

Routing can be useful when dealing with indices that have a large number of
shards, but it's definitely not required for regular usage of Elasticsearch. Think of it as
a way to scale more efficiently in some cases, and be sure to experiment with it.

9.8.4 *Configuring routing*

It can also be useful to tell Elasticsearch that you want to use custom routing for all
documents and to refuse to allow you to index a document without a custom routing
value. You can configure this through the mapping of a type. For example, to create
an index called routed-events and required routing for each event, you can use the
code in the following listing.

Listing 9.13 Defining routing as required in a type's mapping

```
% curl -XPOST 'localhost:9200/routed-events' -d'
{
  "mappings": {
    "event" : {
      "_routing" : {
        "required" : true
      },
      "properties": {
        "name": {
          "type": "string"
        }
      }
    }
  }
}'
{"acknowledged":true}

% curl -XPOST 'localhost:9200/routed-events/event/1' -d'
{"name": "my event"}'
```

Creating an index
named routed-events

Specifying that all
documents for the event
type require routing

Attempted
indexing of a
document without
a routing value

```
{"error":"RoutingMissingException[routing is required for [routed-events]/
[event]/[1]]","status":400}                 ⊲──
```
                                              **Elasticsearch returns an error because
                                              required routing value is missing**

There's one more way to use routing, and that's by associated a routing value with
an alias.

9.8.5 Combining routing with aliases

As you saw in the previous section, aliases are a powerful and flexible abstraction on top
of indices. They can also be used with routing to automatically apply routing values
when querying or when indexing, assuming the alias points to a single index. If you
try to index into an alias that points to more than a single index, Elasticsearch will
return an error because it doesn't know which concrete index the document should
be indexed into.

Reusing the previous example, you can create an alias called denver-events that
automatically filters out events with "denver" in the name and adds "denver" to the
routing when searching and indexing to limit where queries are executed, as shown in
the next listing.

Listing 9.14 Combining routing with an alias

```
% curl -XPOST 'localhost:9200/_aliases' -d'
{
  "actions" : [                                Add an alias to the
    {                                           get-together index.
      "add" : {
        "index": "get-together",    ⊲─────                  The alias will be called
        "alias": "denver-events",          ⊲─────           denver-events.
        "filter": { "term": { "name": "denver" } },  ⊲─
        "routing": "denver"       ⊲─┐                    Filter results by
      }                            │                     documents whose names
    }                              │                     contain "denver".
  ]                     Automatically use the
}'                      routing value denver.
{"acknowledged":true}

% curl -XPOST 'localhost:9200/denver-events/_search?pretty' -d'
{                                                            Query for all
  "query": {                                                 documents, using
    "match_all": {}                                          the denver-events
  },                                                         alias.
  "fields": ["name"]
}'
{
  ...
  "hits" : {
    "total" : 3,
    "max_score" : 1.0,
    "hits" : [ {
      "_index" : "get-together",
```

```
      "_type" : "group",
      "_id" : "2",
      "_score" : 1.0,
      "fields" : {
        "name" : [ "Elasticsearch Denver" ]
      }
    }, {
      "_index" : "get-together",
      "_type" : "group",
      "_id" : "4",
      "_score" : 1.0,
      "fields" : {
        "name" : [ "Boulder/Denver big data get-together" ]
      }
    }, {
      "_index" : "get-together",
      "_type" : "group",
      "_id" : "10",
      "_score" : 1.0,
      "fields" : {
        "name" : [ "Denver Ruby" ]
      }
    } ]
  }
}
```

You can also use the alias you just created for indexing. When indexing with the denver-events alias, it's the same as if documents were indexed with the routing=denver query string parameter. Because aliases are lightweight, you can create as many as you need when using custom routing in order to scale out better.

9.9   *Summary*

You should now have a better understanding of how Elasticsearch clusters are formed and how they're made of multiple nodes, each containing a number of indices, which in turn are made up of a number of shards. Here are some of the other things we talked about in this chapter:

- What happens when nodes are added to an Elasticsearch cluster
- How master nodes are elected
- Removing and decommissioning nodes
- Using the _cat API to understand your cluster
- Over-sharding and how it can be applied to plan for future growth of a cluster
- How to use aliases and routing for cluster flexibility and scaling

In chapter 10 we'll continue talking about scaling from the perspective of improving performance in your Elasticsearch cluster.

Improving performance

Improving performance with the large "10" in the background.

This chapter covers

- Bulk, multiget, and multisearch APIs
- Refresh, flush, merge, and store
- Filter caches and tuning filters
- Tuning scripts
- Query warmers
- Balancing JVM heap size and OS caches

Elasticsearch is commonly referred to as *fast* when it comes to indexing, searching, and extracting statistics through aggregations. *Fast* is a vague concept, making the "How fast?" question inevitable. As with everything, "how fast" depends on the particular use case, hardware, and configuration.

In this chapter, our aim is to show you the best practices for configuring Elasticsearch so you can make it perform well for your use case. In every situation, you need to trade something for speed, so you need to pick your battles:

- *Application complexity*—In the first part of the chapter, we'll show how you can group multiple requests, such as index, update, delete, get, and search, in a single HTTP call. This grouping is something your application needs to be aware of, but it can speed up your overall performance by a huge margin. Think 20 or 30 times better indexing because you'll have fewer network trips.

- *Indexing speed for search speed or the other way around*—In the second section of the chapter, we'll take a deeper look at how Elasticsearch deals with Lucene segments: how refreshes, flushes, merge policies, and store settings work and how they influence index and search performance. Often, tuning for index performance has a negative impact on searches and vice versa.

- *Memory*—A big factor in Elasticsearch's speed is caching. Here's we'll dive into the details of the filter cache and how to use filters to make the best use of it. We'll also look at the shard query cache and how to leave enough room for the operating system to cache your indices, while still leaving enough heap size for Elasticsearch. If running a search on cold caches gets unacceptably slow, you'll be able to keep caches warm by running queries in the background with index warmers.

- *All of the above*—Depending on the use case, the way you analyze the text at index time and the kind of queries you use can be more complicated, slow down other operations, or use more memory. In the last part of the chapter, we'll explore the typical tradeoffs you'll have while modeling your data and your queries: should you generate more terms when you index or look through more terms when you search? Should you take advantage of scripts or try to avoid them? How should you handle deep paging?

We'll discuss all these points and answer these questions in this chapter. By the end, you'll have learned how to make Elasticsearch fast for your use case, and you'll get a deeper understanding of how it works along the way. Grouping multiple operations in a single HTTP request is often the easiest way to improve performance, and it gives the biggest performance gain. Let's start by looking at how you can do that through the bulk, multiget, and multisearch APIs.

10.1 *Grouping requests*

The single best thing you can do for faster indexing is to send multiple documents to be indexed at once via the bulk API. This will save network round-trips and allow for more indexing throughput. A single bulk can accept any indexing operation; for example, you can create documents or overwrite them. You can also add `update` or `delete` operations to a bulk; it's not only for indexing.

If your application needs to send multiple `get` or `search` operations at once, there are bulk equivalents for them, too: the multiget and multisearch APIs. We'll explore them later, but we'll start with the bulk API because in production it's "the way" to index for most use cases.

10.1.1 *Bulk indexing, updating, and deleting*

So far in this book you've indexed documents one at a time. This is fine for playing around, but it implies performance penalties from at least two directions:

- Your application has to wait for a reply from Elasticsearch before it can move on.
- Elasticsearch has to process all data from the request for every indexed document.

If you need more indexing speed, Elasticsearch offers a bulk API, which you can use to index multiple documents at once, as shown in figure 10.1.

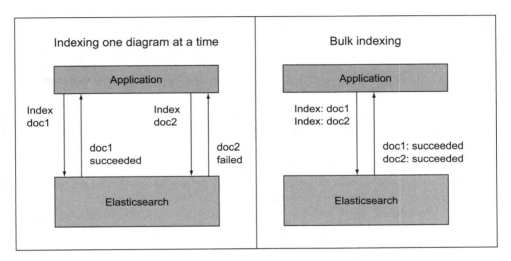

Figure 10.1 Bulk indexing allows you to send multiple documents in the same request.

As the figure illustrates, you can do that using HTTP, as you've used for indexing documents so far, and you'll get a reply containing the results of all the indexing requests.

INDEXING IN BULKS

In listing 10.1 you'll index a bulk of two documents. To do that, you have to do an HTTP POST to the _bulk endpoint, with data in a specific format. The format has the following requirements:

- Each indexing request is composed of two JSON documents separated by a newline: one with the operation (index in your case) and metadata (like index, type, and ID) and one with the document contents.
- JSON documents should be one per line. This implies that each line needs to end with a newline (\n, or the ASCII 10 character), including the last line of the whole bulk of requests.

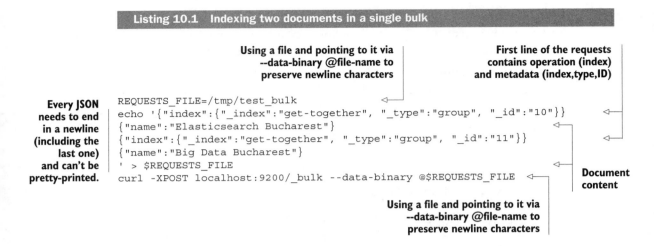

Listing 10.1   Indexing two documents in a single bulk

Using a file and pointing to it via
--data-binary @file-name to
preserve newline characters

First line of the requests
contains operation (index)
and metadata (index,type,ID)

Every JSON
needs to end
in a newline
(including the
last one)
and can't be
pretty-printed.

```
REQUESTS_FILE=/tmp/test_bulk
echo '{"index":{"_index":"get-together", "_type":"group", "_id":"10"}}
{"name":"Elasticsearch Bucharest"}
{"index":{"_index":"get-together", "_type":"group", "_id":"11"}}
{"name":"Big Data Bucharest"}
' > $REQUESTS_FILE
curl -XPOST localhost:9200/_bulk --data-binary @$REQUESTS_FILE
```

Document
content

Using a file and pointing to it via
--data-binary @file-name to
preserve newline characters

For each of the two indexing requests, in the first line you add the operation type and
some metadata. The main field name is the operation type: it indicates what Elasticsearch has to do with the data that follows. For now, you've used index for indexing,
and this operation will overwrite documents with the same ID if they already exist. You
can change that to create, to make sure documents don't get overwritten, or even
update or delete multiple documents at once, as you'll see later.

_index and _type indicate where to index each document. You can put the index
name or both the index and the type in the URL. This will make them the default
index and type for every operation in the bulk. For example:

```
curl -XPOST localhost:9200/get-together/_bulk --data-binary @$REQUESTS_FILE
```

or

```
curl -XPOST localhost:9200/get-together/group/_bulk --data-binary
    @$REQUESTS_FILE
```

You can then omit the _index and _type fields from the request itself. If you specify
them, index and type values from the request override those from the URL.

The _id field indicates the ID of the document you're indexing. If you omit that,
Elasticsearch will automatically generate an ID for you, which is helpful if you don't
already have a unique ID for your documents. Logs, for example, work well with generated IDs because they don't typically have a natural unique ID and you don't need to
retrieve logs by ID.

If you don't need to provide IDs and you index all documents in the same index
and type, the bulk request from listing 10.1 gets quite a lot simpler, as shown in the following listing.

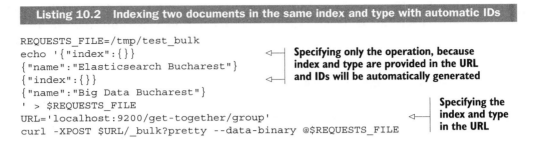

Listing 10.2   Indexing two documents in the same index and type with automatic IDs

```
REQUESTS_FILE=/tmp/test_bulk
echo '{"index":{}}
{"name":"Elasticsearch Bucharest"}
{"index":{}}
{"name":"Big Data Bucharest"}
' > $REQUESTS_FILE
URL='localhost:9200/get-together/group'
curl -XPOST $URL/_bulk?pretty --data-binary @$REQUESTS_FILE
```

Specifying only the operation, because index and type are provided in the URL and IDs will be automatically generated

Specifying the index and type in the URL

The result of your bulk insert should be a JSON containing the time it took to index your bulk and the responses for each operation. There's also an `errors` flag, which indicates whether any of the operations failed. The whole response should look something like this:

```
{
  "took" : 2,
  "errors" : false,
  "items" : [ {
    "create" : {
      "_index" : "get-together",
      "_type" : "group",
      "_id" : "AUyDuQED0pziDTnH-426",
      "_version" : 1,
      "status" : 201
    }
  }, {
    "create" : {
      "_index" : "get-together",
      "_type" : "group",
      "_id" : "AUyDuQED0pziDTnH-426",
      "_version" : 1,
      "status" : 201
    }
  } ]
}
```

Note that because you've used automatic ID generation, the `index` operations were changed to `create`. If one document can't be indexed for some reason, it doesn't mean the whole bulk has failed, because items from the same bulk are independent of each other. That's why you get a reply for each operation, instead of one for the whole bulk. You can use the response JSON in your application to determine which operation succeeded and which failed.

> **TIP**   When it comes to performance, bulk size matters. If your bulks are too big, they take too much memory. If they're too small, there's too much network overhead. The sweet spot depends on document size—you'd put a few big documents or more smaller ones in a bulk—and on the cluster's firepower. A big cluster with strong machines can process bigger bulks faster and still serve searches with decent performance. In the end, you have to test

and find the sweet spot for your use case. You can start with values like 1,000 small documents (such as logs) per bulk and increase until you don't get a significant gain. Be sure to monitor your cluster in the meantime, as we'll discuss in chapter 11.

UPDATING OR DELETING IN BULKS

Within a single bulk, you can have any number of index or create operations and also any number of update or delete operations.

update operations look similar to the index/create operations we just discussed, except for the fact that you must specify the ID. Also, the document content would contain doc or script according to the way you want to update, just as you specified doc or script in chapter 3 when you did individual updates.

delete operations are a bit different than the rest because you have no document content. You just have the metadata line, like with updates, which has to contain the document's ID.

In the next listing you have a bulk that contains all four operations: index, create, update, and delete.

Listing 10.3   Bulk with index, create, update, and delete

```
echo '{"index":{}}
{"title":"Elasticsearch Bucharest"}
{"create":{}}
{"title":"Big Data in Romania"}
{"update":{"_id": "11"}}                Update operation:
{"doc":{"created_on" : "2014-05-06"} }   specify the ID and the
{"delete":{"_id": "10"}}                 partial document.
' > $REQUESTS_FILE
URL='localhost:9200/get-together/group'  ←  Delete operation:
curl -XPOST $URL/_bulk?pretty --data-binary @$REQUESTS_FILE   no document is
# expected reply                              needed, just the ID.
  "took" : 37,
  "errors" : false,
  "items" : [ {
    "create" : {
      "_index" : "get-together",
      "_type" : "group",
      "_id" : "rVPtooieSxqfM6_JX-UCkg",
      "_version" : 1,
      "status" : 201
    }
  }, {
    "create" : {
      "_index" : "get-together",
      "_type" : "group",
      "_id" : "8w3GoNg5T_WEIL5jSTz_Ug",
      "_version" : 1,
      "status" : 201
    }
  }, {
```

```
    "update" : {
      "_index" : "get-together",
      "_type" : "group",
      "_id" : "11",
      "_version" : 2,
      "status" : 200                          ⬅─┐
    }
  }, {                                            Update and delete
    "delete" : {                                  operations increase
      "_index" : "get-together",                  the version, like
      "_type" : "group",                          regular updates
      "_id" : "10",                               and deletes.
      "_version" : 2,
      "status" : 200,                         ⬅─┘
      "found" : true
```

If the bulk APIs can be used to group multiple `index`, `update`, and `delete` operations together, you can do the same for `search` and `get` requests with the multisearch and multiget APIs, respectively. We'll look at these next.

10.1.2 *Multisearch and multiget APIs*

The benefit of using multisearch and multiget is the same as with bulks: when you have to do multiple `search` or `get` requests, grouping them together saves time otherwise spent on network latency.

MULTISEARCH

One use case for sending multiple search requests at once occurs when you're searching in different types of documents. For example, let's assume you have a search box in your get-together site. You don't know whether a search is for groups or for events, so you're going to search for both and offer different tabs in the UI: one for groups and one for events. Those two searches would have completely different scoring criteria, so you'd run them in different requests, or you could group these requests together in a multisearch request.

The multisearch API has many similarities with the bulk API:

- You hit the `_msearch` endpoint, and you may or may not specify an index and a type in the URL.
- Each request has two single-line JSON strings: the first may contain parameters like index, type, routing value, or search type—that you'd normally put in the URI of a single request. The second line contains the query body, which is normally the payload of a single request.

The listing that follows shows an example multisearch request for events and groups about Elasticsearch.

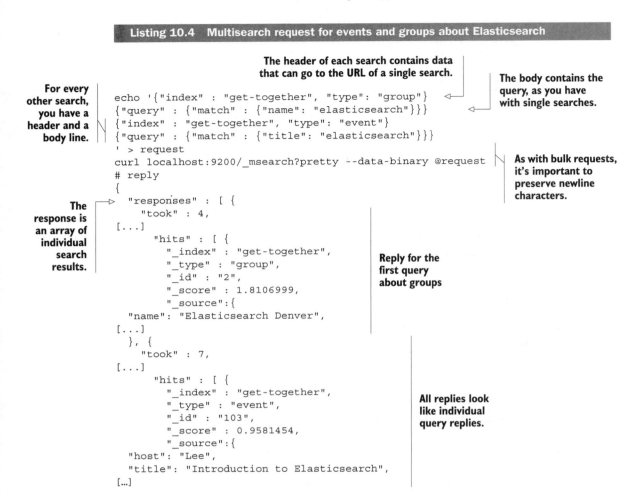

Listing 10.4   Multisearch request for events and groups about Elasticsearch

The header of each search contains data that can go to the URL of a single search.

The body contains the query, as you have with single searches.

For every other search, you have a header and a body line.

```
echo '{"index" : "get-together", "type": "group"}
{"query" : {"match" : {"name": "elasticsearch"}}}
{"index" : "get-together", "type": "event"}
{"query" : {"match" : {"title": "elasticsearch"}}}
' > request
curl localhost:9200/_msearch?pretty --data-binary @request
# reply
{
  "responses" : [ {
    "took" : 4,
[...]
      "hits" : [ {
        "_index" : "get-together",
        "_type" : "group",
        "_id" : "2",
        "_score" : 1.8106999,
        "_source":{
  "name": "Elasticsearch Denver",
[...]
    }, {
    "took" : 7,
[...]
      "hits" : [ {
        "_index" : "get-together",
        "_type" : "event",
        "_id" : "103",
        "_score" : 0.9581454,
        "_source":{
  "host": "Lee",
  "title": "Introduction to Elasticsearch",
[...]
```

As with bulk requests, it's important to preserve newline characters.

The response is an array of individual search results.

Reply for the first query about groups

All replies look like individual query replies.

MULTIGET

Multiget makes sense when some processing external to Elasticsearch requires you to fetch a set of documents without doing any search. For example, if you're storing system metrics and the ID is a timestamp, you might need to retrieve specific metrics from specific times without doing any filtering. To do that, you'd call the _mget endpoint and send a docs array with the index, type, and ID of the documents you want to retrieve, as in the next listing.

Listing 10.5   _mget endpoint and docs array with index, type, and ID of documents

```
curl localhost:9200/_mget?pretty -d '{
    "docs" : [
        {
            "_index" : "get-together",
            "_type" : "group",
            "_id" : "1"
```

The docs array identifies all documents that you want to retrieve.

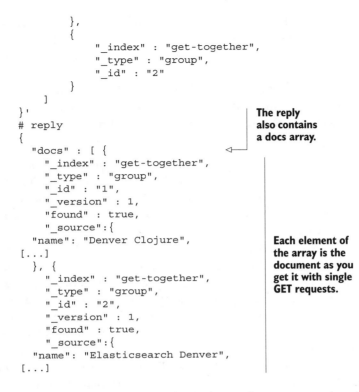

```
          },
          {
              "_index" : "get-together",
              "_type" : "group",
              "_id" : "2"
          }
      ]
}'
# reply                                          The reply
{                                                also contains
  "docs" : [ {                                   a docs array.
    "_index" : "get-together",
    "_type" : "group",
    "_id" : "1",
    "_version" : 1,
    "found" : true,
    "_source":{
    "name": "Denver Clojure",           Each element of
[...]                                    the array is the
    }, {                                document as you
      "_index" : "get-together",        get it with single
      "_type" : "group",                GET requests.
      "_id" : "2",
      "_version" : 1,
      "found" : true,
      "_source":{
    "name": "Elasticsearch Denver",
[...]
```

As with most other APIs, the index and type are optional, because you can also put
them in the URL of the request. When the index and type are common for all IDs, it's
recommended to put them in the URL and put the IDs in an `ids` array, making the
request from listing 10.5 much shorter:

```
% curl localhost:9200/get-together/group/_mget?pretty -d '{
    "ids" : [ "1", "2" ]
}'
```

Grouping multiple operations in the same requests with the multiget API might introduce a little complexity to your application, but it will make such requests faster without significant costs. The same applies to the multisearch and bulk APIs, and to make
the best use of them, you can experiment with different request sizes and see which
size works best for your documents and your hardware.

   Next, we'll look at how Elasticsearch processes documents in bulks internally, in
the form of Lucene segments, and how you can tune these processes to speed up
indexing and searching.

10.2 Optimizing the handling of Lucene segments

Once Elasticsearch receives documents from your application, it indexes them in
memory in inverted indices called *segments*. From time to time, these segments are

written to disk. Recall from chapter 3 that these segments can't be changed—only deleted—to make it easy for the operating system to cache them. Also, bigger segments are periodically created from smaller segments to consolidate the inverted indices and make searches faster.

There are lots of knobs to influence how Elasticsearch handles these segments at every step, and configuring them to fit your use case often gives important performance gains. In this section, we'll discuss these knobs and divide them into three categories:

- *How often to refresh and flush*—*Refreshing* reopens Elasticsearch's view on the index, making newly indexed documents available for search. *Flushing* commits indexed data from memory to the disk. Both refresh and flush operations are expensive in terms of performance, so it's important to configure them correctly for your use case.
- *Merge policies*—Lucene (and by inheritance, Elasticsearch) stores data into immutable groups of files called segments. As you index more data, more segments are created. Because a search in many segments is slow, small segments are merged in the background into bigger segments to keep their number manageable. Merging is performance intensive, especially for the I/O subsystem. You can adjust the merge policy to influence how often merges happen and how big segments can get.
- *Store and store throttling*—Elasticsearch limits the impact of merges on your system's I/O to a certain number of bytes per second. Depending on your hardware and use case, you can change this limit. There are also other options for how Elasticsearch uses the storage. For example, you can choose to store your indices only in memory.

We'll start with the category that typically gives you the biggest performance gain of the three: choosing how often to refresh and flush.

10.2.1 *Refresh and flush thresholds*

Recall from chapter 2 that Elasticsearch is often called near real time; that's because searches are often not run on the very latest indexed data (which would be real time) but close to it.

This near-real-time label fits because normally Elasticsearch keeps a point-in-time view of the index opened, so multiple searches would hit the same files and reuse the same caches. During this time, newly indexed documents won't be visible to those searches until you do a refresh.

Refreshing, as the name suggests, refreshes this point-in-time view of the index so your searches can hit your newly indexed data. That's the upside. The downside is that each refresh comes with a performance penalty: some caches will be invalidated, slowing down searches, and the reopening process itself needs processing power, slowing down indexing.

WHEN TO REFRESH

The default behavior is to refresh every index automatically every second. You can change the interval for every index by changing its settings, which can be done at runtime. For example, the following command will set the automatic refresh interval to 5 seconds:

```
% curl -XPUT localhost:9200/get-together/_settings -d '{
    "index.refresh_interval": "5s"
}'
```

> **TIP** To confirm that your changes were applied, you can get all the index settings by running `curl localhost:9200/get-together/_settings?pretty`.

As you increase the value of `refresh_interval`, you'll have more indexing throughput because you'll spend fewer system resources on refreshing.

Alternatively, you can set `refresh_interval` to `-1` to effectively disable automatic refreshes and rely on manual refresh. This works well for use cases where indices change only periodically in batches, such as for a retail chain where products and stocks are updated every night. Indexing throughput is important because you want to consume those updates quickly, but data freshness isn't, because you don't get the updates in real time, anyway. So you can do nightly bulk index/updates with automatic refresh disabled and refresh manually when you've finished.

To refresh manually, hit the `_refresh` endpoint of the index (or indices) you want to refresh:

```
% curl localhost:9200/get-together/_refresh
```

WHEN TO FLUSH

If you're used to older versions of Lucene or Solr, you might be inclined to think that when a refresh happens, all data that was indexed (in memory) since the last refresh is also committed to disk.

With Elasticsearch (and Solr 4.0 or later) the process of refreshing and the process of committing in-memory segments to disk are independent. Indeed, data is indexed first in memory, but after a refresh, Elasticsearch will happily search the in-memory segments as well. The process of committing in-memory segments to the actual Lucene index you have on disk is called a *flush*, and it happens whether the segments are searchable or not.

To make sure that in-memory data isn't lost when a node goes down or a shard is relocated, Elasticsearch keeps track of the indexing operations that weren't flushed yet in a transaction log. Besides committing in-memory segments to disk, a flush also clears the transaction log, as shown in figure 10.2.

A flush is triggered in one of the following conditions, as shown in figure 10.3:

- The memory buffer is full.
- A certain amount of time passed since the last flush.
- The transaction log hit a certain size threshold.

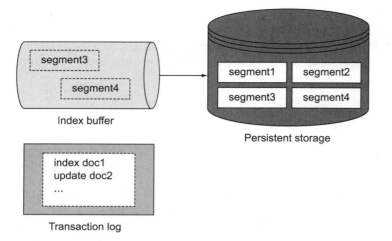

Figure 10.2   A flush moves segments from memory to disk and clears the transaction log.

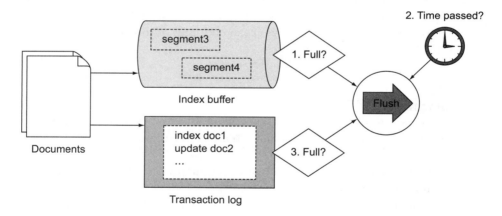

Figure 10.3   A flush is triggered when the memory buffer or transaction log is full or at an interval.

To control how often a flush happens, you have to adjust the settings that control those three conditions.

The memory buffer size is defined in the elasticsearch.yml configuration file through the `indices.memory.index_buffer_size` setting. This controls the overall buffer for the entire node, and the value can be either a percent of the overall JVM heap like 10% or a fixed value like 100 MB.

Transaction log settings are index specific and control both the size at which a flush is triggered (via `index.translog.flush_threshold_size`) and the time since the last flush (via `index.translog.flush_threshold_period`). As with most index settings, you can change them at runtime:

```
% curl -XPUT localhost:9200/get-together/_settings -d '{
  "index.translog": {
    "flush_threshold_size": "500mb",
    "flush_threshold_period": "10m"
  }
}'
```

When a flush is performed, one or more segments are created on the disk. When you run a query, Elasticsearch (through Lucene) looks in all segments and merges the results in an overall shard result. Then, as you saw in chapter 2, per-shard results are aggregated into the overall results that go back to your application.

The key thing to remember here about segments is that the more segments you have to search through, the slower the search. To keep the number of segments at bay, Elasticsearch (again, through Lucene) merges multiple sets of smaller segments into bigger segments in the background.

10.2.2 *Merges and merge policies*

We first introduced segments in chapter 3 as immutable sets of files that Elasticsearch uses to store indexed data. Because they don't change, segments are easily cached, making searches fast. Also, changes to the dataset, such as the addition of a document, won't require rebuilding the index for data stored in existing segments. This makes indexing new documents fast, too—but it's not all good news. Updating a document can't change the actual document; it can only index a new one. This requires deleting the old document, too. Deleting, in turn, can't remove a document from its segment (that would require rebuilding the inverted index), so it's only marked as deleted in a separate .del file. Documents are only actually removed during segment merging.

This brings us to the two purposes of merging segments: to keep the total number of segments in check (and with it, query performance) and to remove deleted documents.

Segment merging happens in the background, according to the defined merge policy. The default merge policy is tiered, which, as illustrated in figure 10.4, divides segments into tiers, and if you have more than the set maximum number of segments in a tier, a merge is triggered in that tier.

There are other merge policies, but in this chapter we'll focus only on the tiered merge policy, which is the default, because it works best for most use cases.

> **TIP** There are some nice videos and explanations of different merge policies on Mike McCandless's blog (he's a co-author of *Lucene in Action*, Second Edition [Manning Publications, 2010]): http://blog.mikemccandless.com/2011/02/visualizing-lucenes-segment-merges.html.

1. Flush operations add segments in the first tier, until there are too many. Let's say four are too many.

2. Small segments are merged into bigger ones. Flushing continues to add new small segments.

3. Eventually, there will be four segments on the bigger tier.

4. The four bigger segments get merged into an even bigger segment, and the process continues...

5. ...until a tier hits a set limit. Only smaller segments get merged; max segments stay the same.

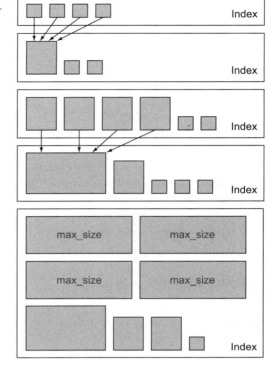

Figure 10.4   Tiered merge policy performs a merge when it finds too many segments in a tier.

TUNING MERGE POLICY OPTIONS

The overall purpose of merging is to trade I/O and some CPU time for search performance. Merging happens when you index, update, or delete documents, so the more you merge, the more expensive these operations get. Conversely, if you want faster indexing, you'll need to merge less and sacrifice some search performance.

In order to have more or less merging, you have a few configuration options. Here are the most important ones:

- `index.merge.policy.segments_per_tier`—The higher the value, the more segments you can have in a tier. This will translate to less merging and better indexing performance. If you have little indexing and you want better search performance, lower this value.

- `index.merge.policy.max_merge_at_once`—This setting limits how many segments can be merged at once. You'd typically make it equal to the `segments_per_tier` value. You could lower the `max_merge_at_once` value to force less merging, but it's better to do that by increasing `segments_per_tier`. Make sure max_merge_at_once isn't higher than segments_per_tier because that will cause too much merging.

- index.merge.policy.max_merged_segment—This setting defines the maximum segment size; bigger segments won't be merged with other segments. You'd lower this value if you wanted less merging and faster indexing because larger segments are more difficult to merge.
- index.merge.scheduler.max_thread_count—Merging happens in the background on separate threads, and this setting controls the maximum number of threads that can be used for merging. This is the hard limit of how many merges can happen at once. You'd increase this setting for an aggressive merge policy on a machine with many CPUs and fast I/O, and you'd decrease it if you had a slow CPU or I/O.

All those options are index-specific, and, as with transaction log and refresh settings, you can change them at runtime. For example, the following snippet forces more merging by reducing segments_per_tier to 5 (and with it, max_merge_at_once), lowers the maximum segment size to 1 GB, and lowers the thread count to 1 to work better with spinning disks:

```
% curl -XPUT localhost:9200/get-together/_settings -d '{
  "index.merge": {
    "policy": {
      "segments_per_tier": 5,
      "max_merge_at_once": 5,
      "max_merged_segment": "1gb"
    },
    "scheduler.max_thread_count": 1
  }
}'
```

OPTIMIZING INDICES
As with refreshing and flushing, you can trigger a merge manually. A forced merge call is also known as *optimize*, because you'd typically run it on an index that isn't going to be changed later to optimize it to a specified (low) number of segments for faster searching.

As with any aggressive merge, optimizing is I/O intensive and invalidates lots of caches. If you continue to index, update, or delete documents from that index, new segments will be created and the advantages of optimizing will be lost. Thus, if you want fewer segments on an index that's constantly changing, you should tune the merge policy.

Optimizing makes sense on a static index. For example, if you index social media data and you have one index per day, you know you'll never change yesterday's index until you remove it for good. It might help to optimize it to a low number of segments, as shown in figure 10.5, which will reduce its total size and speed up queries once caches are warmed up again.

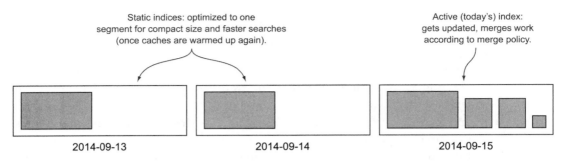

Figure 10.5   Optimizing makes sense for indices that don't get updates.

To optimize, you'd hit the `_optimize` endpoint of the index or indices you need to optimize. The `max_num_segments` option indicates how many segments you should end up with per shard:

```
% curl localhost:9200/get-together/_optimize?max_num_segments=1
```

An optimize call can take a long time on a large index. You can send it to the background by setting `wait_for_merge` to `false`.

One possible reason for an optimize (or any merge) being slow is that Elasticsearch, by default, limits the amount of I/O throughput merge operations can use. This limiting is called *store throttling*, and we'll discuss it next, along with other options for storing your data.

10.2.3 *Store and store throttling*

In early versions of Elasticsearch, heavy merging could slow down the cluster so much that indexing and search requests would take unacceptably long, or nodes could become unresponsive altogether. This was all due to the pressure of merging on the I/O throughput, which would make the writing of new segments slow. Also, CPU load was higher due to I/O wait.

As a result, Elasticsearch now limits the amount of I/O throughput that merges can use through store throttling. By default, there's a node-level setting called `indices.store.throttle.max_bytes_per_sec`, which defaults to 20mb as of version 1.5.

This limit is good for stability in most use cases but won't work well for everyone. If you have fast machines and lots of indexing, merges won't keep up, even if there's enough CPU and I/O to perform them. In such situations, Elasticsearch makes internal indexing work only on one thread, slowing it down to allow merges to keep up. In the end, if your machines are fast, indexing might be limited by store throttling. For nodes with SSDs, you'd normally increase the throttling limit to 100–200 MB.

CHANGING STORE THROTTLING LIMITS

If you have fast disks and need more I/O throughput for merging, you can raise the store throttling limit. You can also remove the limit altogether by setting `indices.store.throttle.type` to `none`. On the other end of the spectrum, you can apply the store throttling limit to all of Elasticsearch's disk operations, not just `merge`, by setting `indices.store.throttle.type` to `all`.

Those settings can be changed from elasticsearch.yml on every node, but they can also be changed at runtime through the Cluster Update Settings API. Normally, you'd tune them while monitoring how much merging and other disk activities are actually happening—we'll show you how to do that in chapter 11.

> **TIP** Elasticsearch 2.0, which will be based on Lucene 5.0, will use Lucene's auto-io-throttle feature,[1] which will automatically throttle merges based on how much indexing is going on. If there's little indexing, merges will be throttled more so they won't affect searches. If there's lots of indexing, there will be less merge throttling, so that merges won't fall behind.

The following command would raise the throttling limit to 500 MB/s but apply it to all operations. It would also make the change persistent to survive full cluster restarts (which is opposed to transient settings that are lost when the cluster is restarted):

```
% curl -XPUT localhost:9200/_cluster/settings -d '{
  "persistent": {
    "indices.store.throttle": {
      "type": "all",
      "max_bytes_per_sec": "500mb"
    }
  }
}'
```

> **TIP** As with index settings, you can also get cluster settings to see if they're applied. You'd do that by running `curl localhost:9200/_cluster/settings?pretty`.

CONFIGURING STORE

When we talked about flushes, merges, and store throttling, we said "disk" and "I/O" because that's the default: Elasticsearch will store indices in the data directory, which defaults to /var/lib/elasticsearch/data if you installed Elasticsearch from a RPM/DEB package, or the data/ directory from the unpacked tar.gz or ZIP archive if you installed it manually. You can change the data directory from the `path.data` property of elasticsearch.yml.

---

[1] For more details, check the Lucene issue, https://issues.apache.org/jira/browse/LUCENE-6119, and the Elasticsearch issue, https://github.com/elastic/elasticsearch/pull/9243.

TIP You can specify multiple directories in `path.data` which—in version 1.5, at least—will put different files in different directories to achieve striping (assuming those directories are on different disks). If that's what you're after, you're often better off using RAID0, in terms of both performance and reliability. For this reason, the plan is to put each shard in the same directory instead of striping it.[2]

The default store implementation stores index files in the file system, and it works well for most use cases. To access Lucene segment files, the default store implementation uses Lucene's `MMapDirectory` for files that are typically large or need to be randomly accessed, such as term dictionaries. For the other types of files, such as stored fields, Elasticsearch uses Lucene's `NIOFSDirectory`.

MMAPDIRECTORY

`MMapDirectory` takes advantage of file system caches by asking the operating system to map the needed files in virtual memory in order to access that memory directly. To Elasticsearch, it looks as if all the files are available in memory, but that doesn't have to be the case. If your index size is larger than your available physical memory, the operating system will happily take unused files out of the caches to make room for new ones that need to be read. If Elasticsearch needs those uncached files again, they'll be loaded in memory while other unused files are taken out and so on. The virtual memory used by `MMapDirectory` works similarly to the system's virtual memory (swap), where the operating system uses the disk to page out unused memory in order to be able to serve multiple applications.

NIOFSDIRECTORY

Memory-mapped files also imply an overhead because the application has to tell the operating system to map a file before accessing it. To reduce this overhead, Elasticsearch uses `NIOFSDirectory` for some types of files. `NIOFSDirectory` accesses files directly, but it has to copy the data it needs to read in a buffer in the JVM heap. This makes it good for small, sequentially accessed files, whereas `MMapDirectory` works well for large, randomly accessed files.

The default store implementation is best for most use cases. You can, however, choose other implementations by changing `index.store.type` in the index settings to values other than `default`:

- `mmapfs`—This will use the `MMapDirectory` alone and will work well, for example, if you have a relatively static index that fits in your physical memory.
- `niofs`—This will use `NIOFSDirectory` alone and would work well on 32-bit systems, where virtual memory address space is limited to 4 GB, which will prevent you from using `mmapfs` or `default` for larger indices.

---

[2] More details can be found on Elasticsearch's bug tracker: https://github.com/elastic/elasticsearch/issues/9498.

Store type settings need to be configured when you create the index. For example, the following command creates an mmap-ed index called unit-test:

```
% curl -XPUT localhost:9200/unit-test -d '{
  "index.store.type": "mmapfs"
}'
```

If you want to apply the same store type for all newly created indices, you can set index.store.type to mmapfs in elasticsearch.yml. In chapter 11 we'll introduce index templates, which allow you to define index settings that would apply to new indices matching specific patterns. Templates can also be changed at runtime, and we recommend using them instead of the more static elasticsearch.yml equivalent if you often create new indices.

> ### Open files and virtual memory limits
> Lucene segments that are stored on disk can spread onto many files, and when a search runs, the operating system needs to be able to open many of them. Also, when you're using the default store type or mmapfs, the operating system has to map some of those stored files into memory—even though these files aren't in memory, to the application it's like they are, and the kernel takes care of loading and unloading them in the cache. Linux has configurable limits that prevent the applications from opening too many files at once and from mapping too much memory. These limits are typically more conservative than needed for Elasticsearch deployments, so it's recommended to increase them. If you're installing Elasticsearch from a DEB or RPM package, you don't have to worry about this because they're increased by default. You can find these variables in /etc/default/elasticsearch or /etc/sysconfig/elasticsearch:
>
> MAX_OPEN_FILES=65535
>
> MAX_MAP_COUNT=262144
>
> To increase those limits manually, you have to run ulimit -n 65535 as the user who starts Elasticsearch for the open files and run sysctl -w vm.max_map_count =262144 as root for the virtual memory.

The default store type is typically the fastest because of the way the operating system caches files. For caching to work well, you need to have enough free memory.

> **TIP**   From Elasticsearch 2.0 on, you'll be able to compress stored fields (and
> _source) further by setting index.codec to best_compression.[3] The default
> (named default, as with store types) still compresses stored fields by using

---

[3]   For more details, check the Elasticsearch issue, https://github.com/elastic/elasticsearch/pull/8863, and the main Lucene issue, https://issues.apache.org/jira/browse/LUCENE-5914.

LZ4, but `best_compression` uses deflate.[4] Higher compression will slow down operations that need `_source`, like fetching results or highlighting. Other operations, such as aggregations, should be at least equally fast because the overall index will be smaller and easier to cache.

We mentioned how `merge` and `optimize` operations invalidate caches. Managing caches for Elasticsearch to perform well deserves more explanation, so we'll discuss that next.

10.3 *Making the best use of caches*

One of Elasticsearch's strong points—if not the strongest point—is the fact that you can query billions of documents in milliseconds with commodity hardware. And one of the reasons this is possible is its smart caching. You might have noticed that after indexing lots of data, the second query can be orders of magnitude faster than the first one. It's because of caching—for example, when you combine filters and queries—that the filter cache plays an important role in keeping your searches fast.

In this section we'll discuss the filter cache and two other types of caches: the shard query cache, useful when you run aggregations on static indices because it caches the overall result, and the operating system caches, which keep your I/O throughput high by caching indices in memory.

Finally, we'll show you how to keep all those caches warm by running queries at each refresh with index warmers. Let's start by looking at the main type of Elasticsearch-specific cache—the filter cache—and how you can run your searches to make the best use of it.

10.3.1 *Filters and filter caches*

In chapter 4 you saw that lots of queries have a filter equivalent. Let's say that you want to look for events on the get-together site that happened in the last month. To do that, you could use the range query or the equivalent range filter.

In chapter 4 we said that of the two, we recommend using the filter, because it's cacheable. The range filter is cached by default, but you can control whether a filter is cached or not through the `_cache` flag.

> **TIP** Elasticsearch 2.0 will cache, by default, only frequently used filters and only on bigger segments (that were merged at least once). This should prevent caching too aggressively but should also catch frequent filters and optimize them. More implementation details can be found in the Elasticsearch[5] and Lucene[6] issues about filter caching. This flag applies to all filters; for

---

[4] https://en.wikipedia.org/wiki/DEFLATE
[5] https://github.com/elastic/elasticsearch/pull/8573
[6] https://issues.apache.org/jira/browse/LUCENE-6077

example, the following snippet will filter events with `"elasticsearch"` in the
verbatim tag but won't cache the results:

```
% curl localhost:9200/get-together/group/_search?pretty -d '{
  "query": {
    "filtered": {
      "filter": {
        "term": {
          "tags.verbatim": "elasticsearch",
          "_cache": false
        }
      }
    }
  }
}'
```

NOTE Although all filters have the _cache flag, it doesn't apply in 100% of
cases. For the range filter, if you use `"now"` as one of the boundaries, the flag
is ignored. For the `has_child` or `has_parent` filters, the _cache flag doesn't
apply at all.

FILTER CACHE

The results of a filter that's cached are stored in the filter cache. This cache is allocated at the node level, like the index buffer size you saw earlier. It defaults to 10%,
but you can change it from elasticsearch.yml according to your needs. If you use filters
a lot and cache them, it might make sense to increase the size. For example:

```
indices.cache.filter.size: 30%
```

How do you know if you need more (or less) filter cache? By monitoring your actual
usage. As we'll explore in chapter 11 on administration, Elasticsearch exposes lots
of metrics, including the amount of filter cache that's actually used and the number of
cache evictions. An *eviction* happens when the cache gets full and Elasticsearch
drops the least recently used (LRU) entry in order to make room for the new one.

In some use cases, filter cache entries have a short lifespan. For example, users typically filter get-together events by a particular subject, refine their queries until they find
what they want, and then leave. If nobody else is searching for events on the same subject, that cache entry will stick around doing nothing until it eventually gets evicted. A
full cache with many evictions would make performance suffer because every search will
consume CPU cycles to squeeze new cache entries by evicting old ones.

In such use cases, to prevent evictions from happening exactly when queries are
run, it makes sense to set a time to live (TTL) on cache entries. You can do that on a
per-index basis by adjusting `index.cache.filter.expire`. For example, the following
snippet will expire filter caches after 30 minutes:

```
% curl -XPUT localhost:9200/get-together/_settings -d '{
  "index.cache.filter.expire": "30m"
}'
```

Besides making sure you have enough room in your filter caches, you need to run your filters in a way that takes advantage of these caches.

COMBINING FILTERS

You often need to combine filters—for example, when you're searching for events in a certain time range, but also with a certain number of attendees. For best performance, you'll need to make sure that caches are well used when filters are combined and that filters run in the right order.

To understand how to best combine filters, we need to revisit a concept discussed in chapter 4: bitsets. A *bitset* is a compact array of bits, and it's used by Elasticsearch to cache whether a document matches a filter or not. Most filters (such as the range and terms filter) use bitsets for caching. Other filters, such as the script filter, don't use bitsets because Elasticsearch has to iterate through all documents anyway. Table 10.1 shows which of the important filters use bitsets and which don't.

Table 10.1   Which filters use bitsets

Filter type	Uses bitset
term	Yes
terms	Yes, but you can configure it differently, as we'll explain in a bit
exists/missing	Yes
prefix	Yes
regexp	No
nested/has_parent/has_child	No
script	No
geo filters (see appendix A)	No

For filters that don't use bitsets, you can still set _cache to true in order to cache results of that exact filter. *Bitsets* are different than simply caching the results because they have the following characteristics:

- They're compact and easy to create, so the overhead of creating the cache when the filter is first run is insignificant.
- They're stored per individual filter; for example, if you use a term filter in two different queries or within two different bool filters, the bitset of that term can be reused.
- They're easy to combine with other bitsets. If you have two queries that use bitsets, it's easy for Elasticsearch to do a bitwise AND or OR in order to figure out which documents match the combination.

To take advantage of bitsets, you need to combine filters that use them in a bool filter that will do that bitwise AND or OR, which is easy for your CPU. For example, if you want to show only groups where either Lee is a member or that contain the tag elastic-search, it could look like this:

```
"filter": {
  "bool": {
    "should": [
      {
        "term": {
          "tags.verbatim": "elasticsearch"
        }
      },
      {
        "term": {
          "members": "lee"
        }
      }
    ]
  }
}
```

The alternative to combining filters is using the and, or, and not filters. These filters work differently because unlike the bool filter, they don't use bitwise AND or OR. They run the first filter, pass the matching documents to the next one, and so on. As a result, and, or, and not filters are better when it comes to combining filters that don't use bitsets. For example, if you want to show groups having at least three members, with events organized in July 2013, the filter might look like this:

```
"filter": {
  "and": [
    {
      "has_child": {
        "type": "event",
        "filter": {
          "range": {
            "date": {
              "from": "2013-07-01T00:00",
              "to": "2013-08-01T00:00"
            }
          }
        }
      }
    },
    {
      "script": {
        "script": "doc['members'].values.length > minMembers",
        "params": {
          "minMembers": 2
        }
      }
    }
  ]
}
```

If you're using both bitset and nonbitset filters, you can combine the bitset ones in a `bool` filter and put that `bool` filter in an `and/or/not` filter, along with the nonbitset filters. For example, in the next listing you'll look for groups with at least two members where either Lee is one of them or the group is about Elasticsearch.

Listing 10.6   Combine bitset filters in a `bool` filter inside an `and/or/not` filter

```
curl localhost:9200/get-together/group/_search?pretty -d'{
  "query": {
    "filtered": {
      "filter": {
        "and": [
          {
            "bool": {
              "should": [
                {
                  "term": {
                    "tags.verbatim": "elasticsearch"
                  }
                },
                {
                  "term": {
                    "members": "lee"
                  }
                }
              ]
            }
          },
          {
            "script": {
              "script": "doc[\"members\"].values.length > minMembers",
              "params": {
                "minMembers": 2
              }
            }
          }
        ]
      }
    }
  }
}'
```

The AND filter will run the bool filter first.

Filtered query means if you add a query here, it will run only on documents matching the filter.

bool is fast when cached because it makes use of the two bitsets of the term filters.

The script filter will work only on documents matching the bool filter.

Whether you combine filter with the `bool`, `and`, `or`, or `not` filters, the order in which those filters are executed is important. Cheaper filters, such as the `term` filter, should be placed before expensive filters, such as the `script` filter. This would make the expensive filter run on a smaller set of documents—those that already matched previous filters.

RUNNING FILTERS ON FIELD DATA

So far, we've discussed how bitsets and cached results make your filters faster. Some filters use bitsets; some can cache the overall results. Some filters can also run on field data. We first discussed field data in chapter 6 as an in-memory structure that keeps a mapping of documents to terms. This mapping is the opposite of the inverted index, which maps terms to documents. Field data is typically used when sorting and during aggregations, but some filters can use it, too: the `terms` and the `range` filters.

> **NOTE** An alternative to the in-memory field data is to use doc values, which are calculated at index time and stored on disk with the rest of your index. As we pointed out in chapter 6, doc values work for numeric and not-analyzed string fields. In Elasticsearch 2.0, doc values will be used by default for those fields because holding field data in the JVM heap is usually not worth the performance increase.

A `terms` filter can have lots of terms, and a `range` filter with a wide range will (under the hood) match lots of numbers (and numbers are also terms). Normal execution of those filters will try to match every term separately and return the set of unique documents, as illustrated in figure 10.6.

Filter: [apples, bananas]

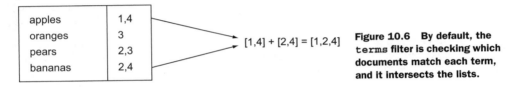

Figure 10.6 By default, the `terms` filter is checking which documents match each term, and it intersects the lists.

As you can imagine, filtering on many terms could get expensive because there would be many lists to intersect. When the number of terms is large, it can be faster to take the actual field values one by one and see if the terms match instead of looking in the index, as illustrated in figure 10.7.

Filter: [apples, bananas]

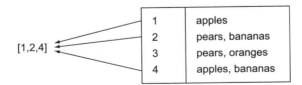

Figure 10.7 Field data execution means iterating through documents but no list intersections.

These field values would be loaded in the field data cache by setting `execution` to `fielddata` in the `terms` or `range` filters. For example, the following `range` filter will get events that happened in 2013 and will be executed on field data:

```
"filter": {
  "range": {
    "date": {
```

```
        "gte": "2013-01-01T00:00",
        "lt": "2014-01-01T00:00"
      },
      "execution": "fielddata"
    }
  }
}
```

Using field data execution is especially useful when the field data is already used by a sort operation or an aggregation. For example, running a `terms` aggregation on the `tags` field will make a subsequent `terms` filter for a set of tags faster because the field data is already loaded.

> **Other execution modes for the terms filter: bool and and/or**
>
> The `terms` filter has other execution modes, too. If the default execution mode (called `plain`) builds a bitset to cache the overall result, you can set it to `bool` in order to have a bitset for each term instead. This is useful when you have different `terms` filters, which have lots of terms in common.
>
> Also, there are `and`/`or` execution modes that perform a similar process, except the individual `term` filters are wrapped in an `and`/`or` filter instead of a `bool` filter.
>
> Usually, the `and`/`or` approach is slower than `bool` because it doesn't take advantage of bitsets. `and`/`or` might be faster if the first `term` filters match only a few documents, which makes subsequent filters extremely fast.

To sum up, you have three options for running your filters:

- Caching them in the filter cache, which is great when filters are reused
- Not caching them if they aren't reused
- Running `terms` and `range` filters on field data, which is good when you have many terms, especially if the field data for that field is already loaded

Next, we'll look at the shard query cache, which is good for when you reuse entire search requests over static data.

10.3.2   *Shard query cache*

The filter cache is purpose-built to make parts of a search—namely filters that are configured to be cached—run faster. It's also segment-specific: if some segments get removed by the merge process, other segments' caches remain intact. By contrast, the shard query cache maintains a mapping between the whole request and its results on the shard level, as illustrated in figure 10.8. If a shard has already answered an identical request, it can serve it from the cache.

As of version 1.4, results cached at the shard level are limited to the total number of hits (not the hits themselves), aggregations, and suggestions. That's why (in version 1.5, at least) shard query cache works only when your query has `search_type` set to `count`.

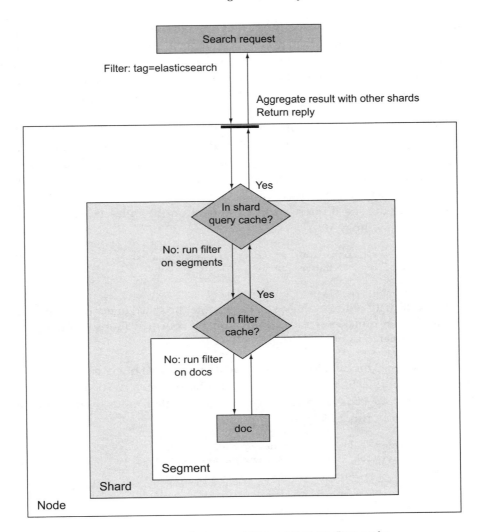

Figure 10.8   The shard query cache is more high-level than the filter cache.

NOTE   By setting `search_type` to `count` in the URI parameters, you tell Elasticsearch that you're not interested in the query results, only in their number. We'll look at `count` and other search types later in this section. In Elasticsearch 2.0, setting `size` to `0` will also work and `search_type=count` will be deprecated.[7]

---

[7]   https://github.com/elastic/elasticsearch/pull/9296

The shard query cache entries differ from one request to another, so they apply only to a narrow set of requests. If you're searching for a different term or running a slightly different aggregation, it will be a cache miss. Also, when a refresh occurs and the shard's contents change, all shard query cache entries are invalidated. Otherwise, new matching documents could have been added to the index, and you'd get out-dated results from the cache.

This narrowness of cache entries makes the shard query cache valuable only when shards rarely change and you have many identical requests. For example, if you're indexing logs and have time-based indices, you may often run aggregations on older indices that typically remain unchanged until they're deleted. These older indices are ideal candidates for a shard query cache.

To enable the shard query cache by default on the index level, you can use the indices update settings API:

```
% curl -XPUT localhost:9200/get-together/_settings -d '{
  "index.cache.query.enable": true
}'
```

> **TIP** As with all index settings, you can enable the shard query cache at index creation, but it makes sense to do that only if your new index gets queried a lot and updated rarely.

For every query, you can also enable or disable the shard query cache, overriding the index-level setting, by adding the `query_cache` parameter. For example, to cache the frequent `top_tags` aggregation on our get-together index, even if the default is disabled, you can run it like this:

```
% URL="localhost:9200/get-together/group/_search"
% curl "$URL?search_type=count&query_cache&pretty" -d '{
  "aggs": {
    "top_tags": {
      "terms": {
        "field": "tags.verbatim"
      }
    }
  }
}'
```

Like the filter cache, the shard query cache has a `size` configuration parameter. The limit can be changed at the node level by adjusting `indices.cache.query.size` from elasticsearch.yml, from the default of 1% of the JVM heap.

When sizing the JVM heap itself, you need to make sure you have enough room for both the filter and the shard query caches. If memory (especially the JVM heap) is limited, you should lower cache sizes to make more room for memory that's used anyway by index and search requests in order to avoid out-of-memory exceptions.

Also, you need to have enough free RAM besides the JVM heap to allow the operating system to cache indices stored on disk; otherwise you'll have a lot of disk seeks.

Next we'll look at how you can balance the JVM heap with the OS caches and why that matters.

10.3.3 *JVM heap and OS caches*

If Elasticsearch doesn't have enough heap to finish an operation, it throws an out-of-memory exception that effectively makes the node crash and fall out of the cluster. This puts an extra load on other nodes as they replicate and relocate shards in order to get back to the configured state. Because nodes are typically equal, this extra load is likely to make at least another node run out of memory. Such a domino effect can bring down your entire cluster.

When the JVM heap is tight, even if you don't see an out-of-memory error in the logs, the node may become just as unresponsive. This can happen because the lack of memory pressures the garbage collector (GC) to run longer and more often in order to free memory. As the GC takes more CPU time, there's less computing power on the node for serving requests or even answering pings from the master, causing the node to fall out of the cluster.

> ### Too much GC? Let's search the web for some GC tuning tips!
>
> When GC is taking a lot of CPU time, the engineer in us is tempted to find that magic JVM setting that will cure everything. More often than not, it's the wrong place to search for a solution because heavy GC is just a symptom of Elasticsearch needing more heap than it has.
>
> Although increasing the heap size is an obvious solution, it's not always possible. The same applies to adding more data nodes. Instead, you can look at a number of tricks to reduce your heap usage:
>
> - Reduce the index buffer size that we discussed in section 10.2.
> - Reduce the filter cache and/or shard query cache.
> - Reduce the `size` value of searches and aggregations (for aggregations, you also have to take care of `shard_size`).
> - If you have to make do with large sizes, you can add some non-data and non-master nodes to act as clients. They'll take the hit of aggregating per-shard results of searches and aggregations.
>
> Finally, Elasticsearch uses another cache type to work around the way Java does garbage collection. There's a young generation space where new objects are allocated. They're "promoted" to old generation if they're needed for long enough or if lots of new objects are allocated and the young space fills up. This last problem appears especially with aggregations, which have to iterate through large sets of documents and create lots of objects that might be reused with the next aggregation.
>
> Normally you want these potentially reusable objects used by aggregations to be promoted to the old generation instead of some random temporary objects that just happen to be there when the young generation fills up. To achieve this, Elasticsearch

(continued)

implements a PageCacheRecycler[8] where big arrays used by aggregations are kept from being garbage collected. This default page cache is 10% of the total heap, and in some cases it might be too much (for example, you have 30 GB of heap, making the cache a healthy 3 GB). You can control the size of this cache from elastic-search.yml via `cache.recycler.page.limit.heap`.

Still, there are times when you'd need to tune your JVM settings (although the defaults are very good), such as when you have almost enough memory but the cluster has trouble when some rare but long GC pauses kick in. You have some options to make GC kick in more often but stop the world less, effectively trading overall throughput for better latency:

- Increase the survivor space (lower -XX:SurvivorRatio) or the whole young generation (lower -XX:NewRatio) compared to the overall heap. You can check if this is needed by monitoring different generations.[9] More space should give more time for the young GC to clean up short-lived objects before they get promoted to the old generation, where a GC will stop the world for longer. But making these spaces too large will make the young GC work too hard and become inefficient, because longer-living objects have to be copied between the two survivor spaces
- Use the G1 GC (-XX:+UseG1GC), which will dynamically allocate space for different generations and is optimized for large-memory, low-latency use cases. It's not used as the default as of version 1.5 because there are still some bugs showing up[10] on 32-bit machines, so make sure you test it thoroughly before using G1 in production.

CAN YOU HAVE TOO LARGE OF A HEAP?

It might have been obvious that a heap that's too small is bad, but having a heap that's too large isn't great either. A heap size of more than 32 GB will automatically make pointers uncompressed and waste memory. How much wasted memory? It depends on the use case: it can vary from as little as 1 GB for 32 GB if you're doing mostly aggregations (which use big arrays that have few pointers) to something like 10 GB if you're using filter caches a lot (which have many small entries with many pointers). If you really need more than 32 GB of heap, you're sometimes better off running two or more nodes on the same machine, each with less than 32 GB of heap, and dividing the data between them through sharding.

> **NOTE** If you end up with multiple Elasticsearch nodes on the same physical machine, you need to make sure that two replicas of the same shard aren't allocated on the same physical machine under different Elasticsearch nodes. Otherwise, if a physical machine goes down, you'll lose two copies of that shard. To prevent this, you can use shard allocation, as described in chapter 11.

---

[8] https://github.com/elastic/elasticsearch/issues/4557
[9] Sematext's SPM can do that for you, as described in appendix D.
[10] https://wiki.apache.org/lucene-java/JavaBugs

Below 32 GB too much heap still isn't ideal (actually, at exactly 32 GB you already lose compressed pointers, so it's best to stick with 31 GB as a maximum). The RAM on your servers that isn't occupied by the JVM is typically used by the operating system to cache indices that are stored on the disk. This is especially important if you have magnetic or network storage because fetching data from the disk while running a query will delay its response. Even with fast SSDs, you'll get the best performance if the amount of data you need to store on a node can fit in its OS caches.

So far we've seen that a heap that's too small is bad because of GC and out-of-memory issues, and one that's too big is bad, too, because it diminishes OS caches. What's a good heap size, then?

IDEAL HEAP SIZE: FOLLOW THE HALF RULE
Without knowing anything about the actual heap usage for your use case, the rule of thumb is to allocate half of the node's RAM to Elasticsearch, but no more than 32 GB. This "half" rule often gives a good balance between heap size and OS caches.

If you can monitor the actual heap usage (and we'll show you how to do that in chapter 11), a good heap size is just large enough to accommodate the regular usage plus any spikes you might expect. Memory usage spikes could happen—for example, if someone decides to run a `terms` aggregation with size 0 on an analyzed field with many unique terms. This will force Elasticsearch to load all terms in memory in order to count them. If you don't know what spikes to expect, the rule of thumb is again half: set a heap size 50% higher than your regular usage.

For OS caches, you depend mostly on the RAM of your servers. That being said, you can design your indices in a way that works best with your operating system's caching. For example, if you're indexing application logs, you can expect that most indexing and searching will involve recent data. With time-based indices, the latest index is more likely to fit in the OS cache than the whole dataset, making most operations faster. Searches on older data will often have to hit the disk, but users are more likely to expect and tolerate slow response times on these rare searches that span longer periods of time. In general, if you can put "hot" data in the same set of indices or shards by using time-based indices, user-based indices, or routing, you'll make better use of OS caches.

All the caches we discussed so far—filter caches, shard query caches, and OS caches—are typically built when a query first runs. Loading up the caches makes that first query slower, and the slowdown increases with the amount of data and the complexity of the query. If that slowdown becomes a problem, you can warm up the caches in advance by using index warmers, as you'll see next.

10.3.4 Keeping caches up with warmers

A *warmer* allows you to define any kind of search request: it can contain queries, filters, sort criteria, and aggregations. Once it's defined, the warmer will make Elasticsearch run the query with every refresh operation. This will slow down the refresh, but the user queries will always run on "warm" caches.

Warmers are useful when first-time queries are too slow and it's preferable for the refresh operation to take that hit rather than the user. If our get-together site example had millions of events and consistent search performance was important, warmers would be useful. Slower refreshes shouldn't concern you too much, because you expect groups and events to be searched for more often than they're modified.

To define a warmer on an existing index, you'd issue a PUT request to the index's URI, with _warmer as the type and the chosen warmer name as an ID, as shown in listing 10.7. You can have as many warmers as you want, but keep in mind that the more warmers you have, the slower your refreshes will be. Typically, you'd use a few popular queries as your warmers. For example, in the following listing, you'll put two warmers: one for upcoming events and one for popular group tags.

Listing 10.7   Two warmers for upcoming events and popular group tags

```
curl -XPUT 'localhost:9200/get-together/event/_warmer/upcoming_events' -d '{
  "sort": [ {
    "date": { "order": "desc" }
  }]
}'
# {"acknowledged": true}
curl -XPUT 'localhost:9200/get-together/group/_warmer/top_tags' -d '{
  "aggs": {
    "top_tags": {
      "terms": {
        "field": "tags.verbatim"
      }
    }
  }
}'
# {"acknowledged": true}
```

Later on, you can get the list of warmers for an index by doing a GET request on the _warmer type:

```
curl localhost:9200/get-together/_warmer?pretty
```

You can also delete warmers by sending a DELETE request to the warmer's URI:

```
curl -XDELETE localhost:9200/get-together/_warmer/top_tags
```

If you're using multiple indices, it makes sense to register warmers at index creation. To do that, define them under the warmers key in the same way you do with mappings and settings, as shown in the following listing.

Listing 10.8   Register warmer at index creation time

```
curl -XPUT 'localhost:9200/hot_index' -d '{
"warmers": {
  "date_sorting": {
```

Name of this warmer. You can register multiple warmers, too.

```
            "types": [],
            "source": {
              "sort": [{
                "date": {
                  "order": "desc"
                }
              }]
            }
          }
        }
}}'
```

This warmer sorts by date. → (points to `"source": {`)

Under this key define the warmer itself.

Which types this warmer should run on. Empty means all types.

TIP If new indices are created automatically, which might occur if you're using time-based indices, you can define warmers in an index template that will be applied automatically to newly created indices. We'll talk more about index templates in chapter 11, which is all about how to administer your Elasticsearch cluster.

So far we've talked about general solutions: how to keep caches warm and efficient to make your searches fast, how to group requests to reduce network latency, and how to configure segment refreshing, flushing, and storing in order to make your indexing and searching fast. All of this also should reduce the load on your cluster.

Next we'll talk about narrower best practices that apply to specific use cases, such making your scripts fast or doing deep paging efficiently.

10.4 *Other performance tradeoffs*

In previous sections, you might have noticed that to make an operation fast, you need to pay with something. For example, if you make indexing faster by refreshing less often, you pay with searches that may not "see" recently indexed data. In this section we'll continue looking at such tradeoffs, especially those that occur in more specific use cases, by answering questions on the following topics:

- *Inexact matches*—Should you get faster searches by using ngrams and shingles at index time? Or is it better to use fuzzy and wildcard queries?
- *Scripts*—Should you trade some flexibility by calculating as much as possible at index time? If not, how can you squeeze more performance out of them?
- *Distributed search*—Should you trade some network round-trips for more accurate scoring?
- *Deep paging*—Is it worth trading memory to get page 100 faster?

By the time this chapter ends, we'll have answered all these questions and lots of others that will come up along the way. Let's start with inexact matches.

10.4.1 Big indices or expensive searches

Recall from chapter 4 that to get inexact matches—for example, to tolerate typos—you can use a number of queries:

- *Fuzzy query*—This query matches terms at a certain edit distance from the original. For example, omitting or adding an extra character would make a distance of 1.
- *Prefix query or filter*—These match terms starting with the sequence you provide.
- *Wildcards*—These allow you to use ? and * to substitute one or many characters. For example, `"e*search"` would match "elasticsearch."

These queries offer lots of flexibility, but they're also more expensive than simple queries, such as term queries. For an exact match, Elasticsearch has to find only one term in the term dictionary, whereas fuzzy, prefix, and wildcard queries have to find all terms matching the given pattern.

There's also another solution for tolerating typos and other inexact matches: ngrams. Recall from chapter 5 that ngrams generate tokens from each part of the word. If you use them at both index and query time, you'll get similar functionality to a fuzzy query, as you can see in figure 10.9.

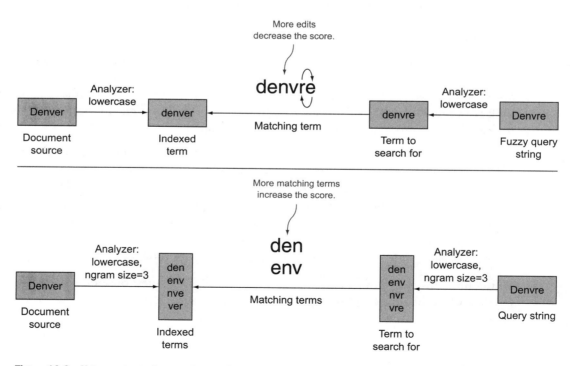

Figure 10.9 Ngrams generate more terms than you need with fuzzy queries, but they match exactly.

Which approach is best for performance? As with everything in this chapter, there's a tradeoff, and you need to choose where you want to pay the price:

- Fuzzy queries slow down your searches, but your index is the same as with exact matches.
- Ngrams, on the other hand, increase the size of your index. Depending on ngram and term sizes, the index size with ngrams can increase a few times. Also, if you want to change ngram settings, you have to re-index all data, so there's less flexibility, but searches are typically faster overall with ngrams.

The ngram method is typically better when query latency is important or when you have lots of concurrent queries to support, so you need each one to take less CPU. Ngrams cause indices to be bigger, but they need to still fit in OS caches or you need fast disks—otherwise performance will degrade because your index is too big.

The fuzzy approach, on the other hand, is better when you need indexing throughput, where index size is an issue, or you have slow disks. Fuzzy queries also help if you need to change them often, such as by adjusting the edit distance, because you can make those changes without re-indexing all data.

PREFIX QUERIES AND EDGE NGRAMS
For inexact matches, you often assume that the beginning is right. For example, a search for "elastic" might be looking for "elasticsearch." Like fuzzy queries, prefix queries are more expensive than regular term queries because there are more terms to look through.

The alternative could be to use edge ngrams, which were introduced in chapter 5. Figure 10.10 shows edge ngrams and prefix queries side by side.

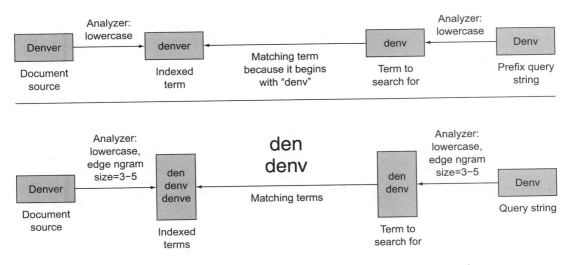

Figure 10.10   A prefix query has to match more terms but works with a smaller index than edge ngrams.

As with the fuzzy queries and ngrams, the tradeoff is between flexibility and index size, which are better in the prefix approach, and query latency and CPU usage, which are better for edge ngrams.

WILDCARDS

A wildcard query where you always put a wildcard at the end, such as `elastic*`, is equivalent in terms of functionality to a prefix query. In this case, you have the same alternative of using edge ngrams.

If the wildcard is in the middle, as with `e*search`, there's no real index-time equivalent. You can still use ngrams to match the provided letters *e* and *search*, but if you have no control over how wildcards are used, then the wildcard query is your only choice.

If the wildcard is always in the beginning, the wildcard query is typically more expensive than trailing wildcards because there's no prefix to hint in which part of the term dictionary to look for matching terms. In this case, the alternative can be to use the `reverse` token filter in combination with edge ngrams, as you saw in chapter 5. This alternative is illustrated in figure 10.11.

PHRASE QUERIES AND SHINGLES

When you need to account for words that are next to each other, you can use the `match` query with `type` set to `phrase`, as you saw in chapter 4. Phrase queries are slower because they have to account not only for the terms but also for their positions in the documents.

> **NOTE** Positions are enabled by default for all analyzed fields because `index_options` is set to `positions`. If you don't use phrase queries, only term queries, you can disable indexing positions by setting `index_options` to `freqs`. If you don't care about scoring at all—for example, when you index application logs and you always sort results by timestamp—you can also skip indexing frequencies by setting `index_options` to `docs`.

The index-time alternative to phrase queries is to use shingles. As you saw in chapter 5, shingles are like ngrams but for terms instead of characters. A text that was tokenized

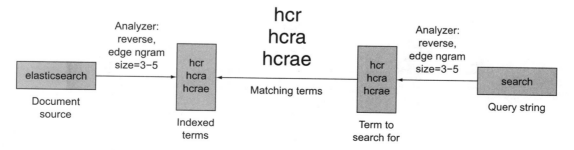

Figure 10.11   You can use the `reverse` and `edge ngram` token filters to match suffixes.

into `Introduction`, `to`, and `Elasticsearch` with a shingle size of 2 would produce the terms "Introduction to" and "to Elasticsearch."

The resulting functionality is similar to phrase queries, and the performance implications are similar to the ngram situations we discussed earlier: shingles will increase the index size and slow down indexing in exchange for faster queries.

The two approaches are not exactly equivalent, in the same way wildcards and ngrams aren't equivalent. With phrase queries, for example, you can specify a slop, which allows for other words to appear in your phrase. For example, a slop of 2 would allow a sequence like "buy the best phone" to match a query for "buy phone." That works because at search time, Elasticsearch is aware of the position of each term, whereas shingles are effectively single terms.

The fact that shingles are single terms allows you to use them for better matching of compound words. For example, many people still refer to Elasticsearch as "elastic search," which can be a tricky match. With shingles, you can solve this by using an empty string as a separator instead of the default white space, as shown in figure 10.12.

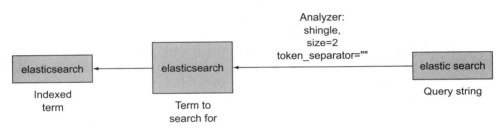

Figure 10.12   Using shingles to match compound words

As you've seen in our discussion of shingles, ngrams, and fuzzy and wildcard queries, there's often more than one way to search your documents, but that doesn't mean those ways are equivalent. Choosing the best one in terms of performance and flexibility depends a lot on your use case. Next we'll look more deeply at scripts, where you'll find more of the same: multiple ways to achieve the same result, but each method comes with its own advantages and disadvantages.

10.4.2   *Tuning scripts or not using them at all*

We first introduced scripts in chapter 3 because they can be used for updates. You saw them again in chapter 6, where you used them for sorting. In chapter 7 you used scripts again, this time to build virtual fields at search time using script fields.

You get a lot of flexibility through scripting, but this flexibility has an important impact on performance. Results of a script are never cached because Elasticsearch doesn't know what's in the script. There can be something external, like a random number, that will make a document match now but not match for the next run.

There's no choice for Elasticsearch other than running the same script for all documents involved.

When used, scripts are often the most time- and CPU-consuming part of your searches. If you want to speed up your queries, a good starting point is to try skipping scripts altogether. If that's not possible, the general rule is to get as close to native code as you can to improve their performance.

How can you get rid of scripts or optimize them? The answer depends heavily on the exact use case, but we'll try to cover the best practices here.

AVOIDING THE USE OF SCRIPTS

If you're using scripts to generate script fields, as you did in chapter 7, you can do this at index time. Instead of indexing documents directly and counting the number of group members in a script by looking at the array length, you can count the number of members in your indexing pipeline and add it to a new field. In figure 10.13, we compare the two approaches.

As with ngrams, this approach to doing the computation at index time works well if query latency is a higher priority than indexing throughput.

Besides precomputing, the general rule for performance optimization for scripting is to reuse as much of Elasticsearch's existing functionality as possible. Before using scripts, can you fulfill the requirements with the function score query that we discussed in chapter 6? The function score query offers lots of ways to manipulate the score. Let's say you want to run a query for "elasticsearch" events, but you'll boost the score in the following ways, based on these assumptions:

- *Events happening soon are more relevant.* You'll make events' scores drop exponentially the farther in the future they are, up to 60 days.
- *Events with more attendees are more popular and more relevant.* You'll increase the score linearly the more attendees an event has.

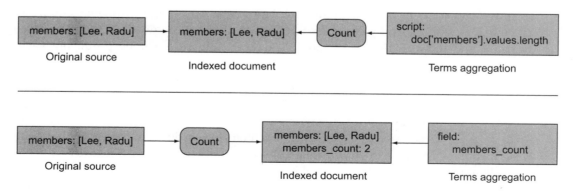

Figure 10.13 Counting members in a script or while indexing

If you calculate the number of event attendees at index time (name the field attendees_count), you can achieve both criteria without using any script:

```
"function_score": {
  "functions": [
    {
      "linear": {
        "date": {
          "origin": "2013-07-25T18:00",
          "scale": "60d"
        }
      }
    },
    {
      "field_value_factor": {
        "field": "attendees_count"
      }
    }
  ]
}
```

NATIVE SCRIPTS

If you want the best performance from a script, writing native scripts in Java is the best way to go. Such a native script would be an Elasticsearch plugin, and you can look in appendix B for a complete guide on how to write one.

The main disadvantage with native scripts is that they have to be stored on every node in Elasticsearch's classpath. Changing a script implies updating it on all the nodes of your cluster and restarting them. This won't be a problem if you don't have to change your queries often.

To run a native script in your query, set lang to native and the name of the script as the script content. For example, if you have a plugin with a script called number-OfAttendees that calculates the number of event attendees on the fly, you can use it in a stats aggregation like this:

```
"aggregations": {
  "attendees_stats": {
    "stats": {
      "script": "numberOfAttendees",
      "lang": "native"
    }
  }
}
```

LUCENE EXPRESSIONS

If you have to change scripts often or you want to be prepared to change them without restarting all your clusters, and your scripts work with numerical fields, Lucene expressions are likely to be the best choice.

With Lucene expressions, you provide a JavaScript expression in the script at query time, and Elasticsearch compiles it in native code, making it as quick as a native script.

The big limitation is that you have access only to indexed numeric fields. Also, if a document misses the field, the value of 0 is taken into account, which might skew results in some use cases.

To use Lucene expressions, you'd set `lang` to `expression` in your script. For example, you might have the number of attendees already, but you know that only half of them usually show up, so you want to calculate some stats based on that number:

```
"aggs": {
  "expected_attendees": {
    "stats": {
      "script": "doc['attendees_count'].value/2",
      "lang": "expression"
    }
  }
}
```

If you have to work with non-numeric or non-indexed fields and you want to be able to easily change scripts, you can use Groovy—the default language for scripting since Elasticsearch 1.4. Let's see how you can optimize Groovy scripts.

TERM STATISTICS

If you need to tune the score, you can access Lucene-level term statistics without having to calculate the score in the script itself—for example, if you only want to compute the score based on the number of times that term appears in the document. Unlike Elasticsearch's defaults, you don't care about the length of the field in that document or the number of times that term appears in other documents. To do that, you can have a script score that only specifies the term frequency (number of times the term appears in the document), as shown in the following listing.

Listing 10.9　Script score that only specifies term frequency

```
curl 'localhost:9200/get-together/event/_search?pretty' -d '{
  "query": {
    "function_score": {
      "filter": {
        "term": {
          "title": "elasticsearch"
        }
      },
      "functions": [
        {
          "script_score": {
            "script": "_index[\"title\"][\"elasticsearch\"].tf() +
            _index[\"description\"][\"elasticsearch\"].tf()",
            "lang": "groovy"
          }
        }
      ]
    }
  }
}'
```

Filter all documents with the term "elasticsearch" in the title field.

Compute relevancy by looking at the term's frequency in the title and description fields.

Access term frequency via the tf() function belonging to the term, which belongs to the field.

ACCESSING FIELD DATA

If you need to work with the actual content of a document's fields in a script, one option is to use the _source field. For example, you'd get the organizer field by using _source['organizer'].

In chapter 3, you saw how you can store individual fields instead of alongside _source. If an individual field is stored, you can access the stored content, too. For example, the same organizer field can be retrieved with _fields['organizer'].

The problem with _source and _fields is that going to the disk to fetch the field content of that particular field is expensive. Fortunately, this slowness is exactly what made field data necessary when Elasticsearch's built-in sorting and aggregations needed to access field content. Field data, as we discussed in chapter 6, is tuned for random access, so it's best to use it in your scripts, too. It's often orders of magnitude faster than the _source or _fields equivalent, even if field data isn't already loaded for that field when the script is first run (or if you use doc values, as explained in chapter 6).

To access the organizer field via field data, you'd refer to doc['organizer']. For example, you can return groups where the organizer isn't a member, so you can ask them why they don't participate to their own groups:

```
% curl 'localhost:9200/get-together/group/_search?pretty' -d '{
  "query": {
    "filtered": {
      "filter": {
        "script": {
          "script": "return
    doc.organizer.values.intersect(doc.members.values).isEmpty()",
        }
      }
    }
  }
}'
```

There's one caveat for using doc['organizer'] instead of _source['organizer'] or the _fields equivalent: you'll access the terms, not the original field of the document. If an organizer is 'Lee', and the field is analyzed with the default analyzer, you'll get 'Lee' from _source and 'lee' from doc. There are tradeoffs everywhere, but we assume you've gotten used to them at this point in the chapter.

Next, we'll take a deeper look at how distributed searches work and how you can use search types to find a good balance between having accurate scores and low-latency searches.

10.4.3 *Trading network trips for less data and better distributed scoring*

Back in chapter 2, you saw how when you hit an Elasticsearch node with a search request, that node distributes the request to all the shards that are involved and aggregates the individual shard replies into one final reply to return to the application.

Let's take a deeper look at how this works. The naïve approach would be to get *N* documents from all shards involved (where *N* is the value of size), sort them on the node that received the HTTP request (let's call it the coordinating node), pick the top *N* documents, and return them to the application. Let's say that you send a request with the default size of 10 to an index with the default number of 5 shards. This means that the coordinating node will fetch 10 whole documents from each shard, sort them, and return only the top 10 from those 50 documents. But what if there were 10 shards and 100 results? The network overhead of transferring the documents and the memory overhead of handling them on the coordinating node would explode, much like specifying large shard_size values for aggregations are bad for performance.

How about returning only the IDs of those 50 documents and the metadata needed for sorting to the coordinating node? After sorting, the coordinating node can fetch only the required top 10 documents from the shards. This would reduce the network overhead for most cases but will involve two round-trips.

With Elasticsearch, both options are available by setting the search_type parameter to the search. The naïve implementation of fetching all involved documents is query_and_fetch, whereas the two-trip method is called query_then_fetch, which is also the default. A comparison of the two is shown in figure 10.14.

The default query_then_fetch (shown on the right of the figure) gets better as you hit more shards, as you request more documents via the size parameter, and

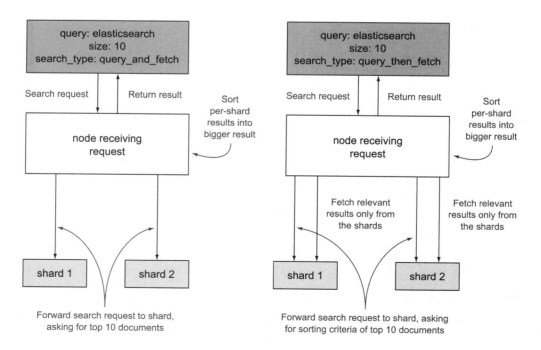

Figure 10.14 Comparison between query_and_fetch **and** query_then_fetch

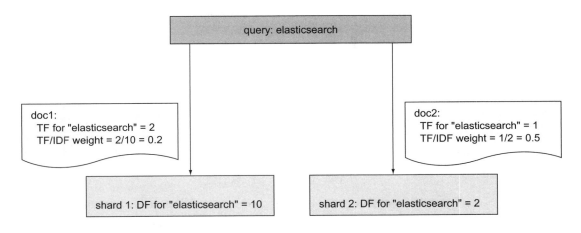

Figure 10.15 Uneven distribution of DF can lead to incorrect ranking.

as documents get bigger because it will transfer much less data over the network. `query_and_fetch` is only faster when you hit one shard—that's why it's used implicitly when you search a single shard, when you use routing, or when you only get the counts (we'll discuss this later). Right now you can specify `query_and_fetch` explicitly, but in version 2.0 it will only be used internally for these specific use cases.[11]

DISTRIBUTED SCORING

By default, scores are calculated per shard, which can lead to inaccuracies. For example, if you search for a term, one of the factors is the *document frequency* (DF), which shows how many times the term you search for appears in all documents. Those "all documents" are by default "all documents in this shard." If the DF of a term is significantly different between shards, scoring might not reflect reality. You can see this in figure 10.15, where doc 2 gets a higher score than doc 1, even though doc 1 has more occurrences of "elasticsearch," because there are fewer documents with that term in its shard.

You can imagine that with a high enough number of documents, DF values would naturally balance across shards, and the default behavior would work just fine. But if score accuracy is a priority or if DF is unbalanced for your use case (for example, if you're using custom routing), you'll need a different approach.

That approach could be to change the search type from `query_then_fetch` to `dfs_query_then_fetch`. The `dfs` part will tell the coordinating node to make an extra call to the shards in order to gather document frequencies of the searched terms. The aggregated frequencies will be used to calculate the score, as you can see in figure 10.16, ranking your doc 1 and doc 2 correctly.

---

[11] https://github.com/elastic/elasticsearch/issues/9606

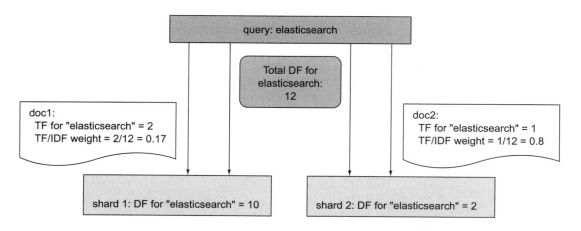

Figure 10.16   dfs search types use an extra network hop to compute global DFs, which are used for scoring.

You probably already figured out that DFS queries are slower because of the extra network call, so make sure that you actually get better scores before switching. If you have a low-latency network, this overhead can be negligible. If, on the other hand, your network isn't fast enough or you have high query concurrency, you may see a significant overhead.

RETURNING ONLY COUNTS

But what if you don't care about scoring at all and you don't need the document content, either? For example, you need only the document count or the aggregations. In such cases, the recommended search type is count. count asks the involved shards only for the number of documents that match and adds up those numbers.

> **TIP**   In version 2.0, adding size=0 to a query will automatically do the same logic that search_type=count currently does, and search_type=count will be deprecated. More details can be found here: https://github.com/elastic/elasticsearch/pull/9296.

10.4.4   *Trading memory for better deep paging*

In chapter 4, you learned that you'd use size and from to paginate the results of your query. For example, to search for "elasticsearch" in get-together events and get the fifth page of 100 results, you'd run a request like this:

```
% curl 'localhost:9200/get-together/event/_search?pretty' -d '{
  "query": {
    "match": {
      "title": "elasticsearch"
    }
  },
  "from": 400,
  "size": 100
}'
```

This will effectively fetch the top 500 results, sort them, and return only the last 100. You can imagine how inefficient this gets as you go deeper with pages. For example, if you change the mapping and want to re-index all existing data into a new index, you might not have enough memory to sort through all the results in order to return the last pages.

For this kind of scenario you can use the scan search type, as you'll do in listing 10.10, to go through all the get-together groups. The initial reply returns only the scroll ID, which uniquely identifies this request and will remember which pages were already returned. To start fetching results, send a request with that scroll ID. Repeat the same request to fetch the next page until you either have enough data or there are no more hits to return—in which case the hits array is empty.

Listing 10.10   Use scan search type

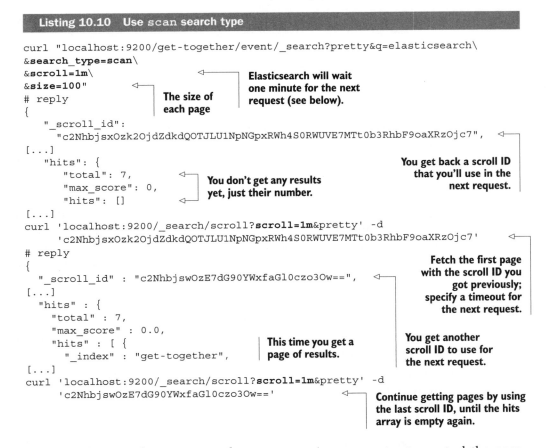

As with other searches, scan searches accept a size parameter to control the page size. But this time, the page size is calculated per shard, so the actual returned size would be size times the number of shards. The timeout given in the scroll parameter of each request is renewed each time you get a new page; that's why you can have a different timeout with every new request.

NOTE   It may be tempting to have big timeouts so that you're sure a scroll doesn't expire while you're processing it. The problem is that if a scroll is active and not used, it wastes resources, taking up some JVM heap to remember the current page and disk space taken by Lucene segments that can't be deleted by merges until the scroll is completed or expired.

The `scan` search type always returns results in the order in which it encounters them in the index, regardless of the sort criteria. If you need both deep paging and sorting, you can add a `scroll` parameter to a regular search request. Sending a GET request to the scroll ID will get the next page of results. This time, `size` works accurately, regardless of the number of shards. You also get the first page of results with the first request, just like you get with regular searches:

```
% curl 'localhost:9200/get-together/event/_search?pretty&scroll=1m' -d ' {
  "query": {
    "match": {
      "title": "elasticsearch"
    }
  }
}'
```

From a performance perspective, adding `scroll` to a regular search is more expensive than using the `scan` search type because there's more information to keep in memory when results are sorted. That being said, deep paging is much more efficient than the default because Elasticsearch doesn't have to sort all previous pages to return the current page.

Scrolling is useful only when you know in advance that you want to do deep paging; it's not recommended for when you need only a few pages of results. As with everything in this chapter, you pay a price for every performance improvement. In the case of scrolling, that price is to keep information about the current search in memory until the scroll expires or you have no more hits.

10.5 *Summary*

In this chapter we looked at a number of optimizations you can do to increase the capacity and responsiveness of your cluster:

- Use the bulk API to combine multiple `index`, `create`, `update`, or `delete` operations in the same request.
- To combine multiple `get` or `search` requests, you can use the multiget or multisearch API, respectively.
- A flush operation commits in-memory Lucene segments to disk when the index buffer size is full, the transaction log is too large, or too much time has passed since the last flush.
- A refresh makes new segments—flushed or not—available for searching. During heavy indexing, it's best to lower the refresh rate or disable refresh altogether.

- The merge policy can be tuned for more or less segments. Fewer segments make searches faster, but merges take more CPU time. More segments make indexing faster by spending less time on merging, but searches will be slower.

- An optimize operation forces a merge, which works well for static indices that get lots of searches.

- Store throttling may limit indexing performance by making merges fall behind. Increase or remove the limits if you have fast I/O.

- Combine filters that use bitsets in a `bool` filter and filters that don't in and/or/not filters.

- Cache counts and aggregations in the shard query cache if you have static indices.

- Monitor JVM heap and leave enough headroom so you don't experience heavy garbage collection or out-of-memory errors, but leave some RAM for OS caches, too.

- Use index warmers if the first query is too slow and you don't mind slower indexing.

- If you have room for bigger indices, using ngrams and shingles instead of fuzzy, wildcard, or phrase queries should make your searches faster.

- You can often avoid using scripts by creating new fields with needed data in your documents before indexing them.

- Try to use Lucene expressions, term statistics, and field data in your scripts whenever they fit.

- If your scripts don't need to change often, look at appendix B to learn how to write a native script in an Elasticsearch plugin.

- Use `dfs_query_then_fetch` if you don't have balanced document frequencies between shards.

- Use the `count` search type if you don't need any hits and the `scan` search type if you need many.

Administering your cluster

11

This chapter covers

- Improving default configuration settings
- Creating default index settings with templates
- Monitoring for performance
- Using backup and restore

We've covered a lot of material in this book, and we hope you now feel comfortable working with the Elasticsearch APIs. In this chapter you'll augment the APIs you've learned thus far and use them with the goal of monitoring and tuning your Elastic-search cluster for increasing performance and implementing disaster recovery.

Both developers and administrators will eventually be faced with the prospect of having to monitor and administer their Elasticsearch cluster. Whether your system is under high or moderate use, it will be important for you to understand and identify bottlenecks and be prepared in the event of a hardware or system failure.

This chapter covers Elasticsearch cluster administration operations using the REST API, which you should now feel comfortable with, given the exposure throughout this book. This will enable you to identify and address possible performance bottlenecks, using real-time monitoring and best practices.

To that end, we'll cover three overarching topics: improving defaults, monitoring for problems, and effectively using the backup system, with the simple premise that effective performance monitoring is necessary for system optimization and that understanding your system will aid in the planning of disaster scenarios.

11.1 *Improving defaults*

Although the out-of-the-box Elasticsearch configuration will satisfy the needs of most users, it's important to note that it's a highly flexible system that can be tuned beyond its default settings for increased performance.

Most uses of Elasticsearch in production environments may fall into the category of occasional full-text search, but a growing number of deployments are pushing formerly edge-case uses into more common installations, such as the growing trends of using Elasticsearch as a sole source of data, logging aggregators, and even using it in hybrid storage architectures where it's used in conjunction with other database types. These exciting new uses open the door for us to explore interesting ways in which to tune and optimize the Elasticsearch default settings.

11.1.1 *Index templates*

Creating new indices and associated mappings in Elasticsearch is normally a simple task once the initial design planning has been completed. But there are some scenarios in which future indices must be created with the same settings and mappings as the previous ones. These scenarios include the following:

- *Log aggregation*—In this situation a daily log index is needed for efficient querying and storage, much as rolling log file appenders work. A common example of this is found in cloud-based deployments, where distributed systems push their logs onto a central Elasticsearch cluster. Configuring the cluster to handle automatic templating of log data by day helps organize the data and eases searching for the proverbial needle in the haystack.
- *Regulatory compliance*—Here blocks of data must be either kept or removed after a certain time period to meet compliance standards, as in financial sector companies where Sarbanes-Oxley compliance is mandated. These sorts of mandates require organized record keeping where template systems shine.
- *Multi-tenancy*—Systems that create new tenants dynamically often have a need to compartmentalize tenant-specific data.

Templates have their uses when a proven and repeatable pattern is needed for homogenous data storage. The automated nature of how Elasticsearch applies templates is also an attractive feature.

CREATING A TEMPLATE
As the name suggests, an index template will be applied to any new index created. Indices that match a predefined naming pattern will have a template applied to them,

ensuring uniformity in index settings across all of the matching indices. The index-creation event will have to match the template pattern for the template to be applied. There are two ways to apply index templates to newly created indices in Elasticsearch:

- By way of the REST API
- By a configuration file

The former assumes a running cluster; the latter does not and is often used in pre-deployment scenarios that a dev ops engineer or system administrator would employ in a production environment.

In this section we'll illustrate a simple index template used for log aggregation, so your log aggregation tool will have a new index created per day. At the time of this writing, Logstash was the most popular log-aggregation tool used alongside Elasticsearch, and its integration was seamless, so focusing on Logstash-to-Elasticsearch index template creation makes the most sense.

By default, Logstash makes API calls using the daily timestamp appended to the index name; for example, logstash-11-09-2014. Assuming you're using the Elasticsearch default settings, which allow for automatic index creation, once Logstash makes a call to your cluster with a new event, the new index will be created with a name of logstash-11-09-2014, and the document type will be automapped. You'll use the REST API method first, as shown here:

```
curl -XPUT localhost:9200/_template/logging_index -d '{     ⟵   PUT command
    "template" : "logstash-*",                       ⟵
    "settings" : {                                         Applies this template
        "number_of_shards" : 2,                            to any index name that
        "number_of_replicas" : 1                           matches the pattern
    },
    "mappings" : { … },
    "aliases" : { "november" : {} }
}'
```

Using the PUT command, you instruct Elasticsearch to apply this template whenever an index call matching the logstash-* pattern is received. In this case, when Logstash posts a new event to Elasticsearch and an index doesn't exist by the name given, a new one will be created using this template.

This template also goes a bit further in applying an alias, so you can group all of these indices under a given month. You'll have to rename the index manually each month, but it affords a convenient way to group indices of log events by month.

TEMPLATES CONFIGURED ON THE FILE SYSTEM

If you want to have templates configured on the file system, which sometimes makes it easier to manage maintenance, the option exists. Configuration files must follow these simple rules:

- Template configurations must be in JSON format. For convenience, name them with a .json extension: <FILENAME>.json.

- Template definitions should be located in the Elasticsearch configuration location under a templates directory. This path is defined in the cluster's configuration file (elasticsearch.yml) as path.conf; for example, <ES_HOME>/config/templates/*.
- Template definitions should be placed in the directories of nodes that are eligible to be elected as master.

Using the previous template definition, your template.json file will look like this:

```
{
    "template" : "logstash-*",
    "settings" : {
        "number_of_shards" : 2,
        "number_of_replicas" : 1
    },
    "mappings" : { … },
    "aliases" : { "november" : {} }
}
```

Much like defining via the REST API, now every index matching the logstash-* pattern will have this template applied.

MULTIPLE TEMPLATE MERGING

Elasticsearch also enables you to configure multiple templates with different settings. You can then expand on the previous example and configure a template to handle log events by month and another that will store all log events in one index, as the following listing shows.

Listing 11.1 Configuring multiple templates

```
curl -XPUT localhost:9200/_template/logging_index_all -d '{
    "template" : "logstash-09-*",            ⟵
    "order" : 1,
    "settings" : {
        "number_of_shards" : 2,
        "number_of_replicas" : 1
    },
    "mappings" : {
        "date" : { "store": false }
    },
    "alias" : { "november" : {} }
}'
curl -XPUT http://localhost:9200/_template/logging_index -d '{
    "template" : "logstash-*",               ⟵
    "order" : 0,
    "settings" : {
        "number_of_shards" : 2,
        "number_of_replicas" : 1
    },
    "mappings" : {
      "date" : { "store": true }
    }
}'
```

Apply this template to any index beginning with "logstash-09-".

Apply this template to any index beginning with "logstash-*" and store the date field.

Highest order number will override the lowest order number setting

In the previous example, the topmost template will be responsible for November-specific logs because it matches on the pattern of index names beginning with `"logstash-09-"`. The second template acts as a catchall, aggregating all logstash indices and even containing a different setting for the `date` mapping.

One thing to note about this configuration is the `order` attribute. This attribute implies that the lowest order number will be applied first, with the higher order number then overriding it. Because of this, the two templates settings are merged, with the effect of all November log events *not* having the `date` field stored.

RETRIEVING INDEX TEMPLATES

To retrieve a list of all templates, a convenience API exists:

```
curl -XGET localhost:9200/_template/
```

Likewise, you're able to retrieve either one or many individual templates by name:

```
curl -XGET localhost:9200/_template/logging_index
```

```
curl -XGET localhost:9200/_template/logging_index_1,logging_index_2
```

Or you can retrieve all template names that match a pattern:

```
curl -XGET localhost:9200/_template/logging_*
```

DELETING INDEX TEMPLATES

Deleting a template index is achieved by using the template name. In the previous section, we defined a template as such:

```
curl -XPUT 'localhost:9200/_template/logging_index' -d '{ … }'
```

To delete this template, use the template name in the request:

```
curl -XDELETE 'localhost:9200/_template/logging_index'
```

11.1.2 Default mappings

As you learned in chapter 2, mappings enable you to define specific fields, their types, and even how Elasticsearch will interpret and store them. Furthermore, you learned how Elasticsearch supports dynamic mapping in chapter 3, removing the need to define your mappings at index-creation time; instead those mappings are dynamically generated based on the content of the initial document you index. This section, much like the previous one that covered default index templates, will introduce you to the concept of specifying default mappings, which act as a convenience utility for repetitive mapping creation.

We just showed you how index templates can be used to save time and add uniformity across similar datatypes. Default mappings have the same beneficial effects and can be thought of in the same vein as templates for mapping types. Default mappings are most often used when there are indices with similar fields. Specifying a default mapping in one place removes the need to repeatedly specify it across every index.

Mapping is not retroactive

Note that specifying a default mapping doesn't apply the mapping retroactively. Default mappings are applied only to newly created types.

Consider the following example, where you want to specify a default setting for how you store the _source for all of your mappings, except for a Person type:

```
curl -XPUT 'localhost:9200/streamglue/_mapping/events' -d ' {
    "Person" :
    {
        "_source" : {"enabled" : false}
    },
    "_default_" :
    {"_source" : {"enabled" : true }
    }
}'
```

In this case, all new mappings will by default store the document _source, but any mapping of type Person, by default, will not. Note that you can override this behavior in individual mapping specifications.

DYNAMIC MAPPINGS

By default, Elasticsearch employs *dynamic mapping:* the ability to determine the datatype for new fields within a document. You may have experienced this when you first indexed a document and noticed that Elasticsearch dynamically created a mapping for it as well as the datatype for each of the fields. You can alter this behavior by instructing Elasticsearch to ignore new fields or even throw exceptions on unknown fields. You'd normally want to restrict the new addition of fields to prevent data pollution and help maintain control over the schema definition.

DISABLING DYNAMIC MAPPING   Note also that you can disable the dynamic creation of new mappings for unmapped types by setting index.mapper.dynamic to false in your elasticsearch.yml configuration.

The next listing shows how to add a dynamic mapping.

Listing 11.2 Adding a dynamic mapping

```
curl -XPUT 'localhost:9200/first_index' -d
'{
    "mappings": {
        "person": {
            "dynamic":        "strict",      <-- Throw exception if an
            "properties": {                      unknown field is encountered
                "email":  { "type": "string"},   at index time.
                "created_date":  { "type": "date" }
            }
        }
    }
}'
```

```
curl -XPUT 'localhost:9200/second_index' -d
'{
    "mappings": {
        "person": {                              Allow the dynamic
            "dynamic":        "true",            creation of new
            "properties": {                   ◁┘ fields.
                "email":  { "type": "string"},
                "created_date":  { "type": "date" }
            }
        }
    }
}'
```

The first mapping restricts the creation of new fields in the person mapping. If you attempt to insert a document with an unmapped field, Elasticsearch will respond with an exception and not index the document. For instance, try to index a document with an additional first_name field added:

```
curl -XPOST 'localhost:9200/first_index/person' -d
'{
"email": "foo@bar.com",
"created_date" : "2014-09-01",
"first_name" : "Bob"
}'
```

Here's the response:

```
{
error: "StrictDynamicMappingException[mapping set to strict, dynamic
    introduction of [first_name] within [person] is not allowed]"
status: 400
}
```

DYNAMIC MAPPING AND TEMPLATING TOGETHER

This section wouldn't be complete if we didn't cover how dynamic mapping and dynamic templates work together, allowing you to apply different mappings depending on the field name or datatype.

Earlier we explored how index templates can be used to autodefine newly created indices for a uniform set of indices and mappings. We can expand on this idea now by incorporating what we've covered with dynamic mappings.

The following example solves a simple problem when dealing with data comprising UUIDs. These are unique alphanumeric strings that contain hyphen separators, such as "b20d5470-d7b4-11e3-9fa6-25476c6788ce". You don't want Elasticsearch analyzing them with a default analyzer because it would split the UUID by hyphen when building the index tokens. You want to be able to search by the complete string UUID, so you need Elasticsearch to store the entire string as a token. In this case, you need to instruct Elasticsearch to not analyze any string field whose name ends in "_guid":

```
curl -XPUT 'http://localhost:9200/myindex' -d '
{
    "mappings" : {
```

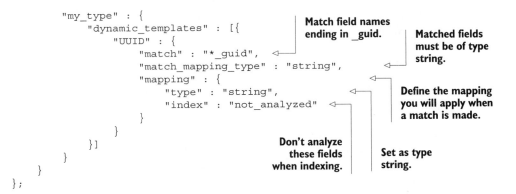

```
"my_type" : {
    "dynamic_templates" : [{
        "UUID" : {
            "match" : "*_guid",
            "match_mapping_type" : "string",
            "mapping" : {
                "type" : "string",
                "index" : "not_analyzed"
            }
        }
    }]
}
};
```

Match field names ending in _guid.

Matched fields must be of type string.

Define the mapping you will apply when a match is made.

Don't analyze these fields when indexing.

Set as type string.

In this example, the dynamic template is used to dynamically map fields that matched a certain name and type, giving you more control over how your data is stored and made searchable by Elasticsearch. As an additional note, you can use the path_match or path_unmatch keyword, which allows you to match or unmatch the dynamic template using dot notation—for instance, if you wanted to match something like person.*.email. Using this logic, you can see a match on a data structure such as this:

```
{
    "person" : {
        "user" : {
        "email": { "bob@domain.com" }
        }
    }
}
```

Dynamic templates are a convenient method of automating some of the more tedious aspects of Elasticsearch management. Next, we'll explore allocation awareness.

11.2 Allocation awareness

This section covers the concept of laying out cluster topology to reduce central points of failure and improve performance by using the concept of allocation awareness. *Allocation awareness* is defined as knowledge of where to place copies (replicas) of data. You can arm Elasticsearch with this knowledge so it intelligently distributes replica data across a cluster.

11.2.1 Shard-based allocation

Allocation awareness allows you to configure shard allocation using a self-defined parameter. This is a common best practice in Elasticsearch deployments because it reduces the chances of having a single point of failure by making sure data is evened out among the network topology. You can also experience faster read operations, as nodes deployed on the same physical rack will potentially have a proximity advantage of not having to go over the network.

Enabling allocation awareness is achieved by defining a grouping key and setting it in the appropriate nodes. For instance, you can edit elasticsearch.yml as follows:

```
cluster.routing.allocation.awareness.attributes: rack
```

> **NOTE** The awareness attribute can be assigned more than one value. `cluster`
> `.routing.allocation.awareness.attributes: rack, group, zone`

Using the previous definition, you'll segment your shards across the cluster using the awareness parameter `rack`. You alter the elasticsearch.yml for each of your nodes, setting the value the way you want your network configuration to be. Note that Elasticsearch allows you to set metadata on nodes. In this case, the metadata key will be your allocation awareness parameter:

```
node.rack: 1
```

A simple before-and-after illustration may help in this case. Figure 11.1 shows a cluster with the default allocation settings.

This cluster suffers from primary and replica shard data being on the same rack. With the allocation awareness setting, you can remove the risk, as shown in figure 11.2.

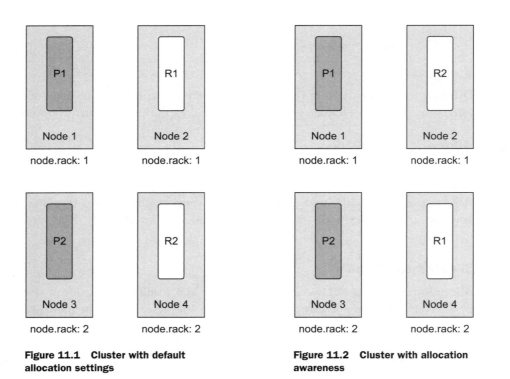

Figure 11.1 Cluster with default allocation settings

Figure 11.2 Cluster with allocation awareness

Wwith allocation awareness, the primary shards were not moved, but the replicas were moved to nodes with a different `node.rack` parameter value. Shard allocation is a convenient feature that insured against a central point of failure. A common use is separating cluster topology by location, racks, or even virtual machines.

Next, we'll take a look at forced allocation with a real-world AWS zone example.

11.2.2 Forced allocation awareness

Forced allocation awareness is useful when you know in advance the group of values and want to limit the number of replicas for any given group. A real-world example of where this is commonly used is in cross-zone allocation on Amazon Web Services or other cloud providers with multizone capabilities. The use case is simple: limit the number of replicas in one zone if another zone goes down or is unreachable. By doing this, you reduce the danger of overallocating replicas from another group.

For example, in this use case you want to enforce allocation at a zone level. First you specify your attribute, zone, as you did before. Next, you add dimensions to that group: us-east and us-west. In your elasticsearch.yml, you add the following:

```
cluster.routing.allocation.awareness.attributes: zone
cluster.routing.allocation.force.zone.values: us-east, us-west
```

Given these settings, let's play out this real-world scenario. Let's say you start a set of nodes in the East region with `node.zone: us-east`. You'll use the defaults here, leaving an index with five primary shards and one replica. Because there are no other zone values, only the primary shards for your indices will be allocated.

What you're doing here is limiting the replicas to balance only on nodes without your value. If you were to start up your West region cluster, with `node.zone: us-west`, replicas from us-east would be allocated to it. No replicas will ever exist for nodes defined as `node.zone: us-east`. Ideally, you'd do the same on `node.zone: us-west`, thereby ensuring that replicas never exist in the same location. Keep in mind that if you lose connectivity with us-west, no replicas will ever be created on us-east, or vice versa.

Allocation awareness does require some planning up front, but in the event that allocation isn't working as planned, these settings can all be modified at runtime using the Cluster Settings API. They can be persistent, where Elasticsearch applies the settings even after a restart, or temporary (transient):

```
curl -XPUT localhost:9200/_cluster/settings -d '{
      "persistent" : {
      "cluster.routing.allocation.awareness.attributes": zone
      "cluster.routing.allocation.force.zone.values": us-east, us-west
      }
}
```

Cluster allocation can make the difference between a cluster that scales and is resilient to failure and one that isn't.

Now that we've explored some of the finer adjustments that you can make to Elasticsearch default settings with shard allocation, let's look at how to monitor the general health of your cluster for performance issues.

11.3 *Monitoring for bottlenecks*

Elasticsearch provides a wealth of information via its APIs: memory consumption, node membership, shard distribution, and I/O performance. The cluster and node APIs help you gauge the health and overall performance metrics of your cluster. Understanding cluster diagnostic data and being able to assess the overall status of the cluster will alert you to performance bottlenecks, such as unassigned shards and missing nodes, so you can easily address them.

11.3.1 *Checking cluster health*

The cluster health API provides a convenient yet coarse-grained view of the overall health of your cluster, indices, and shards. This is normally the first step in being alerted to and diagnosing a problem that may be actively occurring in your cluster. The next listing shows how to use the cluster health API to check overall cluster state.

> **Listing 11.3   Cluster health API request**

```
curl -XGET 'localhost:9200/_cluster/health?pretty';
```

And the response:

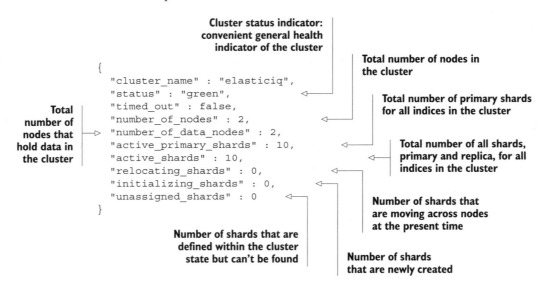

Taking the response shown here at face value, you can deduce a lot about the general health and state of the cluster, but there's much more to reading this simple output than what's obvious at first glance. Let's look a little deeper into the meaning of the last three indicators in the code: `relocating_shards`, `initializing_shards`, and `unassigned_shards`.

- `relocating_shards`—A number above zero means that Elasticsearch is moving shards of data across the cluster to improve balance and failover. This ordinarily occurs when adding a new node, restarting a failed node, or removing a node, thereby making this a temporary occurrence.
- `initializing_shards`—This number will be above zero when you've just created a new index or restarted a node.
- `unassigned_shards`—The most common reason for this value to be above zero is having unassigned replicas. The issue is common in development environments, where a single-node cluster has an index defined as having the default, five shards and one replica. In this case, there'll be five unassigned replicas.

As you saw from the first line of output, the cluster status is green. There are times when this may not be so, as in the case of nodes not being able to start or falling away from the cluster, and although the status value gives you only a general idea of the health of the cluster, it's useful to understand what those status values mean for cluster performance:

- *Green*—Both primary and replica shards are fully functional and distributed.
- *Yellow*—Normally this is a sign of a missing replica shard. The `unassigned_shards` value is likely above zero at this point, making the distributed nature of the cluster unstable. Further shard loss could lead to critical data loss. Look for any nodes that aren't initialized or functioning correctly.
- *Red*—This is a critical state, where a primary shard in the cluster can't be found, prohibiting indexing operations on that shard and leading to inconsistent query results. Again, likely a node or several nodes are missing from the cluster.

Armed with this knowledge, you can now take a look at a cluster with a yellow status and attempt to track down the source of the problem:

```
curl -XGET 'localhost:9200/_cluster/health?pretty';
{
  "cluster_name" : "elasticiq",
  "status" : "yellow",
  "timed_out" : false,
  "number_of_nodes" : 1,
  "number_of_data_nodes" : 1,
  "active_primary_shards" : 10,
  "active_shards" : 10,
  "relocating_shards" : 0,
  "initializing_shards" : 0,
  "unassigned_shards" : 5
}
```

Given this API call and response, you see that the cluster is now in yellow status, and as you've already learned, the likely culprit is the `unassigned_shards` value being above 0. The cluster health API provides a more fine-grained operation that will allow you to further diagnose the issue. In this case, you can look deeper at which indices are affected by the unassigned shards by adding the `level` parameter:

```
curl -XGET 'localhost:9200/_cluster/health?level=indices&pretty';
{
  "cluster_name" : "elasticiq",
  "status" : "yellow",
  "timed_out" : false,
  "number_of_nodes" : 1,
  "number_of_data_nodes" : 1,
  "active_primary_shards" : 10,
  "active_shards" : 10,
  "relocating_shards" : 0,
  "initializing_shards" : 0,
  "unassigned_shards" : 5,
  "indices" : {
    "bitbucket" : {
      "status" : "yellow",
      "number_of_shards" : 5,
      "number_of_replicas" : 1,
      "active_primary_shards" : 5,
      "active_shards" : 5,
      "relocating_shards" : 0,
      "initializing_shards" : 0,
      "unassigned_shards" : 5
    }...
```

Note that the cluster has only one node running.

The primary shards

Here you tell Elasticsearch to allocate one replica per primary shard.

Unassigned shards caused by a lack of available nodes to support the replica definition

The single-node cluster is experiencing some problems because Elasticsearch is trying to allocate replica shards across the cluster, but it can't do so because there's only one node running. This leads to the replica shards not being assigned anywhere and therefore a yellow status across the cluster, as figure 11.3 shows.

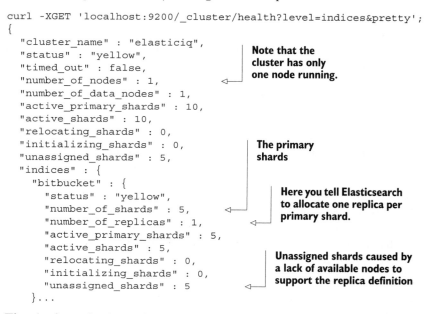

Yellow status: Single-node cluster with all shards confined to one node

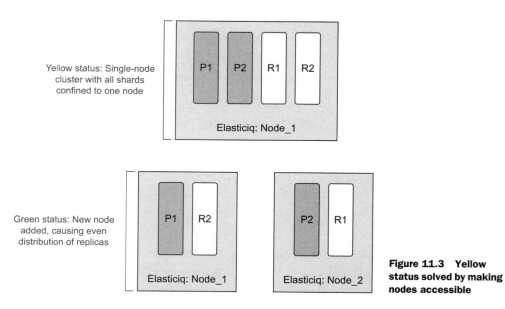

Green status: New node added, causing even distribution of replicas

Figure 11.3   Yellow status solved by making nodes accessible

As you can see, an easy remedy is to add a node to the cluster so Elasticsearch can then allocate the replica shards to that location. Making sure that all of your nodes are running and accessible is the easiest way to solve the yellow status issue.

11.3.2 *CPU: slow logs, hot threads, and thread pools*

Monitoring your Elasticsearch cluster may from time to time expose spikes in CPU usage or bottlenecks in performance caused by a constantly high CPU utilization or blocked/waiting threads. This section will help demystify some of these possible performance bottlenecks and provide you with the tools needed to identify and address these issues.

SLOW LOGS

Elasticsearch provides two logs for isolating slow operations that are easily configured within your cluster configuration file: slow query log and slow index log. By default, both logs are disabled. Log output is scoped at the shard level. That is, one operation can represent several lines in the corresponding log file. The advantage to shard-level logging is that you'll be better able to identify a problem shard and thereby a node with the log output, as shown here. It's important to note at this point that these settings can also be modified using the '{index_name}/_settings' endpoint:

```
index.search.slowlog.threshold.query.warn: 10s
index.search.slowlog.threshold.query.info: 1s
index.search.slowlog.threshold.query.debug: 2s
index.search.slowlog.threshold.query.trace: 500ms

index.search.slowlog.threshold.fetch.warn: 1s
index.search.slowlog.threshold.fetch.info: 1s
index.search.slowlog.threshold.fetch.debug: 500ms
index.search.slowlog.threshold.fetch.trace: 200ms
```

As you can see, you can set thresholds for both phases of a search: the query and the fetch. The log levels (warn, info, debug, trace) allow you finer control over which level will be logged, something that comes in handy when you simply want to grep your log file. The actual log file you'll be outputting to is configured in your logging.yml file, along with other logging functionality, as shown here:

```
index_search_slow_log_file:
  type: dailyRollingFile
  file: ${path.logs}/${cluster.name}_index_search_slowlog.log
  datePattern: "'.'yyyy-MM-dd"
  layout:
    type: pattern
    conversionPattern: "[%d{ISO8601}][%-5p][%-25c] %m%n"
```

The typical output on a slow log file will appear as this:

```
[2014-11-09 16:35:36,325][INFO ][index.search.slowlog.query] [ElasticIQ-
Master] [streamglue][4] took[10.5ms], took_millis[10], types[], stats[],
search_type[QUERY_THEN_FETCH], total_shards[10],
source[{"query":{"filtered":{"query":{"query_string":{"query":"test"}}}},...]
```

```
[2014-11-09 16:35:36,339][INFO ][index.search.slowlog.fetch] [ElasticIQ-
Master] [streamglue][3] took[9.1ms], took_millis[9], types[], stats[],
search_type[QUERY_THEN_FETCH], total_shards[10], ...
```

SLOW QUERY LOG

The important parts you're interested in for identifying performance issues are the
query times: took[##ms]. Additionally, it's helpful to know the shards and indices
involved, and those are identifiable by the [index][shard_number] notation; in this
case it's [streamglue][4].

SLOW INDEX LOG

Equally useful in discovering bottlenecks during index operations is the slow index
log. Its thresholds are defined in your cluster configuration file, or via the index update
settings API, much like the previous slow log:

```
index.indexing.slowlog.threshold.index.warn: 10s
index.indexing.slowlog.threshold.index.info: 5s
index.indexing.slowlog.threshold.index.debug: 2s
index.indexing.slowlog.threshold.index.trace: 500ms
```

As before, the output of any index operation meeting the threshold values will be written to your log file, and you'll see the [index][shard_number] ([bitbucket][2])
and duration (took[4.5ms]) of the index operation:

```
[2014-11-09 18:28:58,636][INFO ][index.indexing.slowlog.index] [ElasticIQ-
Master] [bitbucket][2] took[4.5ms], took_millis[4], type[test],
id[w0QyH_m6Sa2P-juppUy3Tw], routing[], source[] ...
```

Discovering where your slow queries and index calls are happening will go a long way
in helping remedy Elasticsearch performance problems. Allowing slow performance
to grow unbounded can cause a cascading failure across your entire cluster, leading to
it crashing entirely.

HOT_THREADS API

If you've ever experienced high CPU utilization across your cluster, you'll find the
hot_threads API helpful in identifying specific processes that may be blocked and
causing the problem. The hot_threads API provides a list of blocked threads for every
node in your cluster. Note that unlike other APIs, hot_threads doesn't return JSON but
instead returns formatted text:

```
curl -XGET 'http://127.0.0.1:9200/_nodes/hot_threads';
```

Here's the sample output:

```
::: [ElasticIQ-Master][AtPvr5Y3ReW-ua7ZPtPfuQ][loki.local][inet[/
127.0.0.1:9300]]{master=true}
   37.5% (187.6micros out of 500ms) cpu usage by thread
'elasticsearch[ElasticIQ-Master][search][T#191]
10/10 snapshots sharing following 3 elements
...
```

The output of the hot_threads API requires some parsing to understand correctly, so let's have a look at what information it provides on CPU performance:

```
::: [ElasticIQ-Master] [AtPvr5Y3ReW-ua7ZPtPfuQ] [loki.local] [inet[/
127.0.0.1:9300]]{master=true}
```

The top line of the response includes the node identification. Because the cluster presumably has more than one node, this is the first indication of which CPU the thread information belongs to:

```
   37.5% (187.6micros out of 500ms) cpu usage by thread
'elasticsearch[ElasticIQ-Master][search][T#191]
```

Here you can see that 37.5% of CPU processing is being spent on a search thread. This is key to your understanding, because you can then fine-tune your search queries that may be causing the CPU spike. Expect that the search value won't always be there. Elasticsearch may present other values here like `merge`, `index`, and the like that identify the operation being performed on that thread. You know this is CPU-related because of the `cpu usage` identifier. Other possible output identifiers here are `block usage`, which identifies threads that are blocked, and `wait usage` for threads in a WAITING state:

```
10/10 snapshots sharing following 3 elements
```

The final line before the stack trace tells you that Elasticsearch found that this thread with the same stack trace was present in 10 out of the 10 snapshots it took within a few milliseconds.

Of course, it's worth learning how Elasticsearch gathers the hot_threads API information for presentation. Every few milliseconds, Elasticsearch collects information about thread duration, its state (WAITING/BLOCKED), and the duration of the wait or block for each thread. After a set interval (500 ms by default), Elasticsearch does a second pass of the same information-gathering operation. During each of these passes, it takes snapshots of each stack trace. You can tune the information-gathering process by adding parameters to the hot_threads API call:

```
curl -XGET 'http://127.0.0.1:9200/_nodes/
hot_threads?type=wait&interval=1000ms&threads=3';
```

- `type`—One of `cpu`, `wait`, or `block`. Type of thread state to snapshot for.
- `interval`—Time to wait between the first and second checks. Defaults to 500 ms.
- `threads`—Number of top "hot" threads to display.

THREAD POOLS

Every node in a cluster manages thread pools for better management of CPU and memory usage. Elasticsearch will seek to manage thread pools to achieve the best performance on a given node. In some cases, you'll need to manually configure and override how thread pools are managed to avoid cascading failure scenarios. Under a heavy load, Elasticsearch may spawn thousands of threads to handle requests, causing your cluster to fail. Knowing how to tune thread pools requires intimate knowledge of how your application is using the Elasticsearch APIs. For instance, an application that uses mostly the bulk index API should be allotted a larger set of threads. Otherwise, `bulk index` requests can become overloaded, and new requests will be ignored.

You can tune the thread pool settings within your cluster configuration. Thread pools are divided by operation and configured with a default value depending on the operation type. For brevity, we're listing only a few of them:

- `bulk`—Defaults to a fixed size based on the number of available processors for all bulk operations.
- `index`—Defaults to a fixed size based on the number of available processors for index and delete operations.
- `search`—Defaults to a fixed size that's three times the number of available processors for count and search operations.

Looking at your elasticsearch.yml configuration, you can see that you can increase the size of the thread pool queue and number of thread pools for all bulk operations. It's also worth noting here that the Cluster Settings API allows you to update these settings on a running cluster as well:

```
# Bulk Thread Pool
threadpool.bulk.type: fixed
threadpool.bulk.size: 40
threadpool.bulk.queue_size: 200
```

Note that there are two thread pool types, `fixed` and `cache`. A `fixed` thread pool type holds a fixed number of threads to handle requests with a backing queue for pending requests. The `queue_size` parameter in this case controls the number of threads and defaults to the five times the number of cores. A cache thread pool type is unbounded, meaning that a new thread will be created if there are any pending requests.

Armed with the cluster health API, slow query and index logs, and thread information, you can diagnose CPU-intensive operations and bottlenecks more easily. The next section will cover memory-centric information, which can help in diagnosing and tuning Elasticsearch performance issues.

11.3.3   *Memory: heap size, field, and filter caches*

This section will explore efficient memory management and tuning for Elasticsearch clusters. Many aggregation and filtering operations are memory-bound within Elasticsearch, so knowing how to effectively improve the default memory-management settings in Elasticsearch and the underlying JVM will be a useful tool for scaling your cluster.

HEAP SIZE

Elasticsearch is a Java application that runs on the Java Virtual Machine (JVM), so it's subject to memory management by the *garbage collector*. The concept behind the garbage collector is a simple one: it's triggered when memory is running low, clearing out objects that have been dereferenced and thus freeing up memory for other JVM applications to use. These garbage-collection operations are time consuming and cause system pauses. Loading too much data in memory can also lead to `OutOfMemory` exceptions, causing failures and unpredictable results—a problem that even the garbage collector can't address.

For Elasticsearch to be fast, some operations are performed in memory because of improved access to field data. For instance, Elasticsearch doesn't just load field data for documents that match your query; it loads values for all the documents in your index. This makes your subsequent query much faster by virtue of having quick access to in-memory data.

The JVM heap represents the amount of memory allocated to applications running on the JVM. For that reason, it's important to understand how to tune its performance to avoid the ill effects of garbage collection pauses and `OutOfMemory` exceptions. You set the JVM heap size via the `HEAP_SIZE` environment variable. The two golden rules to keep in mind when setting your heap size are as follows:

- *Maximum of 50% of available system RAM*—Allocating too much system memory to the JVM means there's less memory allocated to the underlying file-system cache, which Lucene makes frequent use of.
- *Maximum of 32 GB RAM*—The JVM changes its behavior at over 32 GB allocated by not using compressed ordinary object pointers (OOP). This means that setting the heap size under 32 GB uses approximately half the memory space.

FILTER AND FIELD CACHE

Caches play an important role in Elasticsearch performance, allowing for the effective use of filters, facets, and index field sorting. This section will explore two of these caches: the filter cache and the field data cache.

The filter cache stores the results of filters and query operations in memory. This means that an initial query with a filter applied will have its results stored in the filter cache. Every subsequent query with that filter applied will use the data from the cache and not go to disk for the data. The filter cache effectively reduces the impact on CPU and I/O and leads to faster results of filtered queries.

Two types of filter caches are available in Elasticsearch:

- Index-level filter cache
- Node-level filter cache

The node-level filter cache is the default setting and the one we'll be covering. The index-level filter cache isn't recommended because you can't predict where the index will reside inside the cluster and therefore can't predict memory usage.

The node-level filter cache is an LRU (least recently used) cache type. That means that when the cache becomes full, cache entries that are used the least amount of times are destroyed first to make room for new entries. Choose this cache type by setting `index.cache.filter.type` to node, or don't set it at all; it's the default value. Now you can set the size with the `indices.cache.filter.size` property. It will take either a percentage value of memory (20%) to allocate or a static value (1024 MB) within your elasticsearch.yml configuration for the node. Note that a percentage property uses the maximum heap for the node as the total value to calculate from.

FIELD-DATA CACHE

The field-data cache is used to improve query execution times. Elasticsearch loads field values into memory when you run a query and keeps those values in the field-data cache for subsequent requests to use. Because building this structure in memory is an expensive operation, you don't want Elasticsearch performing this on every request, so the performance gains are noticeable. By default, this is an unbounded cache, meaning that it will grow until it trips the field-data circuit breaker (covered in the next section). By specifying a value for the field-data cache, you tell Elasticsearch to evict data from the structure once the upper bound is reached.

Your configuration should include an `indices.fielddata.cache.size` property that can be set to either a percentage value (20%) or a static value (16 GB). These values represent the percentage or static segment of node heap space to use for the cache.

To retrieve the current state of the field-data cache, there are some handy APIs available:

- Per-Node:

```
curl -XGET 'localhost:9200/_nodes/stats/indices/
fielddata?fields=*&pretty=1';
```

- Per-Index:

```
curl -XGET 'localhost:9200/_stats/fielddata?fields=*&pretty=1';
```

- Per-Node Per-Index:

```
curl -XGET 'localhost:9200/_nodes/stats/indices/
fielddata?level=indices&fields =*&pretty=1';
```

Specifying `fields=*` will return all field names and values. The output of these APIs looks similar to the following:

```
"indices" : {
  "bitbucket" : {
    "fielddata" : {
      "memory_size_in_bytes" : 1024mb,
      "evictions" : 200,
      "fields" : { … }
    }
  }, ...
```

These operations will break down the current state of the cache. Take special note of the number of `evictions`. Evictions are an expensive operation and a sign that the field-data cache may be set to too small of a value.

CIRCUIT BREAKER

As mentioned in the previous section, the field-data cache may grow to the point that it causes an `OutOfMemory` exception. This is because the field-data size is calculated after the data is loaded. To avoid such events, Elasticsearch provides circuit breakers.

Circuit breakers are artificial limits imposed to help reduce the chances of an `OutOf-Memory` exception. They work by introspecting data fields requested by a query to determine whether loading the data into the cache will push the total size over the cache size limit. Two circuit breakers are available in Elasticsearch, as well as a parent circuit breaker that sets a limit on the total amount of memory that all circuit breakers may use:

- `indices.breaker.total.limit`—Defaults to 70% of heap. Doesn't allow the field-data and request circuit breakers to surpass this limit.
- `indices.breaker.fielddata.limit`—Defaults to 60% of heap. Doesn't allow the field-data cache to surpass this limit.
- `indices.breaker.request.limit`—Defaults to 40% of heap. Controls the size fraction of heap allocated to operations like aggregation bucket creation.

The golden rule with circuit breaker settings is to be conservative in their values because the caches the circuit breakers control have to share memory space with memory buffers, the filter cache, and other Elasticsearch memory use.

AVOIDING SWAP

Operating systems use the swapping process as a method of writing memory pages to disk. This process occurs when the amount of memory isn't enough for the operating system. When the swapped pages are needed by the OS, they're loaded back in memory for use. Swapping is an expensive operation and should be avoided.

Elasticsearch keeps a lot of runtime-necessary data and caches in memory, as shown in figure 11.4, so expensive write and read disk operations will severely impact a running cluster. For this reason, we'll show how to disable swapping for faster performance.

The most thorough way to disable Elasticsearch swapping is to set `bootstrap.mlockall` to `true` in the elasticsearch.yml file. Next, you need to verify that the setting

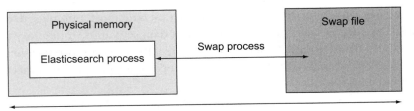

Figure 11.4   Elasticsearch keeps runtime data and caches in memory, so writes and reads can be expensive.

is working. Running Elasticsearch, you can either check the log for a warning or simply query for a live status:

- Sample error in the log:

```
[2014-11-21 19:22:00,612] [ERROR] [common.jna]
Unknown mlockall error 0
```

- API request:

```
curl -XGET 'localhost:9200/_nodes/process?pretty=1';
```

- Response:

```
...
  "process" : {
        "refresh_interval_in_millis" : 1000,
        "id" : 9809,
        "max_file_descriptors" : 10240,
        "mlockall" : false
    } ...
```

If either the warning is visible in the log or the status check results in `mlockall` being set to `false`, your settings didn't work. Insufficient access rights on the user running Elasticsearch are the most common reason for the new setting not taking affect. This is normally solved by running `ulimit -l unlimited` from the shell as the root user. It will be necessary to restart Elasticsearch for these new settings to be applied.

11.3.4 *OS caches*

Elasticsearch and Lucene leverage the OS file-system cache heavily due to Lucene's immutable segments. Lucene is designed to leverage the underlying OS file-system cache for in-memory data structures. Lucene segments are stored in individual immutable files. Immutable files are considered to be cache-friendly, and the underlying OS is designed to keep "hot" segments resident in memory for faster access. The end effect is that smaller indices tend to be cached entirely in memory by your OS and become diskless and *fast*.

Because of Lucene's heavy use of the OS file-system cache and the previous recommendation to set the JVM heap at half the physical memory, you can count on Lucene using much of the remaining half for caching. For this simple reason, it's considered best practice to keep the indices that are most often used on faster machines. The idea is that Lucene will keep hot data segments in memory for really fast access, and this is easiest to accomplish on machines with more non-heap memory allocated. But to make this happen, you'll need to assign specific indices to your faster nodes using routing.

First, you need to assign a specific attribute, `tag`, to all of your nodes. Every node has a unique value assigned to the attribute `tag`; for instance, `node.tag: mynode1` or `node.tag: mynode2`. Using the node's individual settings, you can create an index that will deploy only on nodes that have specific tag values. Remember, the point of this exercise is to make sure that your new, busy index is created only on nodes with more non-heap memory that Lucene can make good use of. To achieve this, your new index, `myindex`, will now be created only on nodes that have `tag` set to `mynode1` and `mynode2`, with the following command:

```
curl -XPUT localhost:9200/myindex/_settings -d '{
    "index.routing.allocation.include.tag" : "mynode1,mynode2"
}'
```

Assuming these specific nodes have a higher non-heap memory allocation, Lucene will cache segments in memory, resulting in a much faster response time for your index than the alternative of having to seek segments on disk.

11.3.5 *Store throttling*

Apache Lucene stores its data in immutable segment files on disk. Immutable files are by definition written only once by Lucene but read many times. Merge operations work on these segments because many segments are read at once when a new one is written. Although these merge operations normally don't task a system heavily, systems with low I/O can be impacted negatively when merges, indexing, and search operations are all occurring at the same time. Fortunately, Elasticsearch provides throttling features to help control how much I/O is used.

You can configure throttling at both the node level and the index level. At the node level, throttling configuration settings affect the entire node, but at the index level, throttling configuration takes effect only on the indices specified.

Node-level throttling is configured by use of the `indices.store.throre.throttle.type` property with possible values of `none`, `merge`, and `all`. The `merge` value instructs Elasticsearch to throttle I/O for merging operations across the entire node, meaning every shard on that node. The `all` value will apply the throttle limits to all operations for all of the shards on the node. Index-level throttling is configured much the same way but uses the `index.store.throttle.type` property instead. Additionally, it allows for a `node` value to be set, which means it will apply the throttling limits to the entire node.

Whether you're looking to implement node- or index-level throttling, Elasticsearch provides a property for setting the maximum bytes per second that I/O will use. For node-level throttling, use `indices.store.throttle.max_bytes_per_sec`, and for index-level throttling, use `index.store.throttle.max_bytes_per_sec`. Note that the values are expressed in megabytes per second:

```
indices.store.throttle.max_bytes_per_sec : "50mb"
```

or

```
index.store.throttle.max_bytes_per_sec : "10mb"
```

We leave as an exercise for you to configure the correct values for your particular system. If the frequency of I/O wait on a system is high or performance is degrading, lowering these values may help ease some of the pain.

Although we've explored ways to curtail a disaster, the next section will look at how to back up and restore data from/to your cluster in the event of one.

11.4   Backing up your data

Elasticsearch provides a full-featured and incremental data backup solution. The snapshot and restore APIs enable you to back up individual index data, all of your indices, and even cluster settings to either a remote repository or other pluggable backend systems and then easily restore these items to the existing cluster or a new one.

The typical use case for creating snapshots is, of course, to perform backups for disaster recovery, but you may also find it useful in replicating production data in development or testing environments and even as insurance before executing a large set of changes.

11.4.1 Snapshot API

Using the snapshot API to back up your data for the first time, Elasticsearch will take a copy of the state and data of your cluster. All subsequent snapshots will contain the changes from the previous one. The snapshot process is nonblocking, so executing it on a running system should have no visible effect on performance. Furthermore, because every subsequent snapshot is the delta from the previous one, it makes for smaller and faster snapshots over time.

It's important to note that snapshots are stored in repositories. A repository can be defined as either a file system or a URL.

- A file-system repository requires a shared file system, and that shared file system must be mounted on every node in the cluster.
- URL repositories are read-only and can be used as an alternative way to access snapshots.

In this section, we'll cover the more common and flexible file-system repository types, how to store snapshots in them, restoring from them, and leveraging common plugins for cloud vendor storage repositories.

11.4.2 Backing up data to a shared file system

Performing a cluster backup entails executing three steps that we'll cover in detail:

- *Define a repository*—Instruct Elasticsearch on how you want the repository structured.
- *Confirm the existence of the repository*—You want to trust but verify that the repository was created using your definition.
- *Execute the backup*—Your first snapshot is executed via a simple REST API command.

The first step in enabling snapshots requires you to define a shared file-system repository. The `curl` command in the following listing defines your new repository on a network mounted drive.

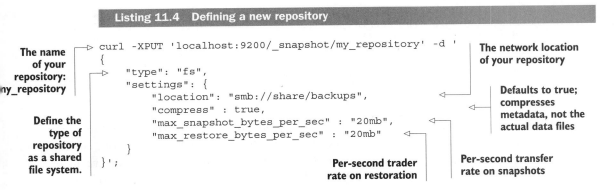

Listing 11.4   Defining a new repository

The name of your repository: my_repository

Define the type of repository as a shared file system.

The network location of your repository

Defaults to true; compresses metadata, not the actual data files

Per-second trader rate on restoration

Per-second transfer rate on snapshots

```
curl -XPUT 'localhost:9200/_snapshot/my_repository' -d '
{
    "type": "fs",
    "settings": {
        "location": "smb://share/backups",
        "compress" : true,
        "max_snapshot_bytes_per_sec" : "20mb",
        "max_restore_bytes_per_sec" : "20mb"
    }
}';
```

Once the repository has been defined across your cluster, you can confirm its existence with a simple GET command:

```
curl -XGET 'localhost:9200/_snapshot/my_repository?pretty=1';
{
  "my_repository" : {
    "type" : "fs",
    "settings" : {
      "compress" : "true",
      "max_restore_bytes_per_sec" : "20mb",
      "location" : "smb://share/backups",
      "max_snapshot_bytes_per_sec" : "20mb"
    }
  }
}
```

Note that as a default action, you don't have to specify the repository name, and Elasticsearch will respond with all registered repositories for the cluster:

```
curl -XGET 'localhost:9200/_snapshot?pretty=1';
```

Once you've established a repository for your cluster, you can go ahead and create your initial snapshot/backup:

```
curl -XPUT 'localhost:9200/_snapshot/my_repository/first_snapshot';
```

This command will trigger a snapshot operation and return immediately. If you want to wait until the snapshot is complete before the request responds, you can append the optional wait_for_completion flag:

```
curl -XPUT 'localhost:9200/_snapshot/my_repository/
first_snapshot?wait_for_completion=true';
```

Now take a look at your repository location and see what the snapshot command stored away:

```
./backups/index
./backups/indices/bitbucket/0/__0
./backups/indices/bitbucket/0/__1
```

```
./backups/indices/bitbucket/0/__10
./backups/indices/bitbucket/1/__c
./backups/indices/bitbucket/1/__d
./backups/indices/bitbucket/1/snapshot-first_snapshot
...
./backups/indices/bitbucket/snapshot-first_snapshot
./backups/metadata-first_snapshot
./backups/snapshot-first_snapshot
```

From this list, you can see a pattern emerging on what Elasticsearch backed up. The snapshot contains information for every index, shard, segment, and accompanying metadata for your cluster with the following file path structure: /<index_name>/<shard_number>/<segment_id>. A sample snapshot file may look similar to the following, which contains information about size, Lucene segment, and the files that each snapshot points to within the directory structure:

```
smb://share/backups/indices/bitbucket/0/snapshot-first_snapshot
{
  "name" : "first_snapshot",
  "index_version" : 18,
  "start_time" : 1416687343604,
  "time" : 11,
  "number_of_files" : 20,
  "total_size" : 161589,
  "files" : [ {
    "name" : "__0",
    "physical_name" : "_1.fnm",
    "length" : 2703,
    "checksum" : "1ot813j",
    "written_by" : "LUCENE_4_9"
  }, {
    "name" : "__1",
    "physical_name" : "_1_Lucene49_0.dvm",
    "length" : 90,
    "checksum" : "1h6yhga",
    "written_by" : "LUCENE_4_9"
  }, {
    "name" : "__2",
    "physical_name" : "_1.si",
    "length" : 444,
    "checksum" : "afusmz",
    "written_by" : "LUCENE_4_9"
  }
```

SECOND SNAPSHOT

Because snapshots are incremental, only storing the delta between them, a second snapshot command will create a few more data files but won't recreate the entire snapshot from scratch:

```
curl -XPUT 'localhost:9200/_snapshot/my_repository/second_snapshot';
```

Analyzing the new directory structure, you can see that only one file was modified: the existing /index file in the root directory. Its contents now hold a list of the snapshots taken:

```
{"snapshots":["first_snapshot","second_snapshot"]}
```

SNAPSHOTS ON A PER-INDEX BASIS

In the previous example, you saw how you can take snapshots of the entire cluster and all indices. It's important to note here that snapshots can be taken on a per-index basis, by specifying the index in the PUT command:

```
curl -XPUT 'localhost:9200/_snapshot/my_repository/third_snapshot' -d '
{
  "indices": "logs-2014,logs-2013"          ◁──── Comma-separated list of
};                                                 index names to snapshot
```

Retrieving basic information on the state of a given snapshot (or all snapshots) is achieved by using the same endpoint, with a GET request:

```
curl -XGET 'localhost:9200/_snapshot/my_repository/first_snapshot?pretty';
```

The response contains which indices were part of this snapshot and the total duration of the entire snapshot operation:

```
{
  "snapshots": [
    {
      "snapshot": "first_snapshot",
      "indices": [
        "bitbucket"
      ],
      "state": "SUCCESS",
      "start_time": "2014-11-02T22:38:14.078Z",
      "start_time_in_millis": 1414967894078,
      "end_time": "2014-11-02T22:38:14.129Z",
      "end_time_in_millis": 1414967894129,
      "duration_in_millis": 51,
      "failures": [],
      "shards": {
        "total": 10,
        "failed": 0,
        "successful": 10
      }
    }
  ]
}
```

Substituting the snapshot name for _all will supply you with information regarding all snapshots in the repository:

```
curl -XGET 'localhost:9200/_snapshot/my_repository/_all';
```

Because snapshots are incremental, you must take special care when removing old snapshots that you no longer need. It's always advised that you use the snapshot API in removing old snapshots because the API will delete only currently unused segments of data:

```
curl -XDELETE 'localhost:9200/_snapshot/my_repository/first_snapshot';
```

Now that you have a solid understanding of the options available when backing up your cluster, let's have a look at restoring your cluster data and state from these snapshots, which you'll need to understand in the event of a disaster.

11.4.3 *Restoring from backups*

Snapshots are easily restored to any running cluster, even a cluster the snapshot didn't originate from. Using the snapshot API with an added _restore command, you can restore the entire cluster state:

```
curl -XPOST 'localhost:9200/_snapshot/my_repository/first_snapshot/_restore';
```

This command will restore the data and state of the cluster captured in the given snapshots: first_snapshot. With this operation, you can easily restore the cluster to any point in time you choose.

Similar to what you saw before with the snapshot operation, the restore operation allows for a wait_for_completion flag, which will block the HTTP call you make until the restore operation is fully complete. By default, the restore HTTP request returns immediately, and the operation executes in the background:

```
curl -XPOST 'localhost:9200/_snapshot/my_repository/first_snapshot/
_restore?wait_for_completion=true';
```

Restore operations also have additional options available that allow you to restore an index to a newly named index space. This is useful if you want to duplicate an index or verify the contents of a restored index from backup:

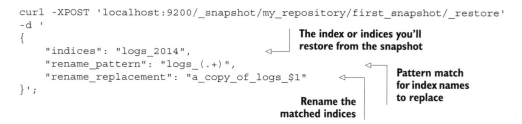

```
curl -XPOST 'localhost:9200/_snapshot/my_repository/first_snapshot/_restore'
-d '
{
    "indices": "logs_2014",
    "rename_pattern": "logs_(.+)",
    "rename_replacement": "a_copy_of_logs_$1"
}';
```

The index or indices you'll restore from the snapshot

Pattern match for index names to replace

Rename the matched indices

Given this command, you'll restore only the index named logs_2014 from the snapshot and ignore restoring any other indices found in the snapshot. Because the index name matches the pattern you defined as the rename_pattern, the snapshot data will reside in a new index named a_copy_of_logs_2014.

NOTE When restoring an existing index, the running instance of the index must be closed. Upon completion, the restore operation will open the closed indices.

Now that you understand how the snapshot API works to enable backups in a network-attached-storage environment, let's explore some of the many plugins available for performing backups in a cloud-based vendor environment.

11.4.4 Using repository plugins

Although snapshotting and restoring from a shared file system is a common use case, Elasticsearch and the community also provide repository plugins for several of the major cloud vendors. These plugins allow you to define repositories that use a specific vendor's infrastructure requirements and internal APIs.

AMAZON S3

For those deploying on an Amazon Web Services infrastructure, there's a freely available S3 repository plugin available on GitHub and maintained by the Elasticsearch team: https://github.com/elasticsearch/elasticsearch-cloud-aws#s3-repository.

The Amazon S3 repository plugin has a few configuration variables that differ from the norm, so it's important to understand what functionality each of them controls. An S3 repository can be created as such:

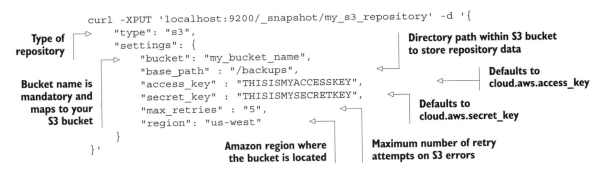

```
curl -XPUT 'localhost:9200/_snapshot/my_s3_repository' -d '{
    "type": "s3",
    "settings": {
        "bucket": "my_bucket_name",
        "base_path" : "/backups",
        "access_key" : "THISISMYACCESSKEY",
        "secret_key" : "THISISMYSECRETKEY",
        "max_retries" : "5",
        "region": "us-west"
    }
}'
```

Type of repository

Bucket name is mandatory and maps to your S3 bucket

Directory path within S3 bucket to store repository data

Defaults to cloud.aws.access_key

Defaults to cloud.aws.secret_key

Amazon region where the bucket is located

Maximum number of retry attempts on S3 errors

Once enabled, the S3 plugin will store your snapshots in the defined bucket path. Because HDFS is compatible with Amazon S3, you may be interested in reading the next section, which covers the Hadoop HDFS repository plugin, as well.

HADOOP HDFS

The HDFS file system can be used as a snapshot/restore repository with this simple plugin, built and maintained by the Elasticsearch team that's part of the more general Hadoop plugin project: https://github.com/elasticsearch/elasticsearch-hadoop/tree/master/repository-hdfs.

You must install the latest stable release of this plugin on your Elasticsearch cluster. From the plugin directory, use the following command to install the desired version of the plugin directly from GitHub:

```
bin/plugin -i elasticsearch/elasticsearch-repository-hdfs/2.x.y
```

Once it's installed, it's time to configure the plugin. The HDFS repository plugin configuration values should be placed within your elasticsearch.yml configuration file. Here are some of the important values:

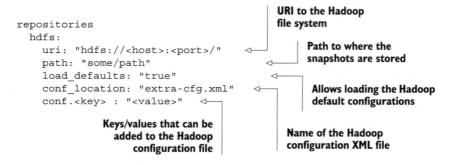

```
repositories
  hdfs:
    uri: "hdfs://<host>:<port>/"
    path: "some/path"
    load_defaults: "true"
    conf_location: "extra-cfg.xml"
    conf.<key> : "<value>"
```

URI to the Hadoop file system

Path to where the snapshots are stored

Allows loading the Hadoop default configurations

Keys/values that can be added to the Hadoop configuration file

Name of the Hadoop configuration XML file

Now, with your HDFS repository plugin configured, your snapshot and restore operations will execute using the same snapshot API as covered earlier. The only difference is that the method of snapshotting and restoring will be from your Hadoop file system.

In this section we explored various ways to back up and restore cluster data and state using the snapshot API. Repository plugins provide a convenience for those deploying Elasticsearch with public cloud vendors. The snapshot API provides a simple and automated way to store backups in a networked environment for disaster recovery.

11.5   *Summary*

We've covered a lot of information in this chapter, with the main focus being administration and optimization of your Elasticsearch cluster. Now that you have a firm understanding of these concepts, let's recap:

- Index templates enable autocreation of indices that share common settings.
- Default mappings are convenient for the repetitive tasks of creating similar mappings across indices.
- Aliases allow you to query across many indices with a single name, thereby allowing you to keep your data segmented if needed.
- The cluster health API provides a simple way to gauge the general health of your cluster, nodes, and shards.
- Use the slow index and slow query logs to help diagnose index and query operations that can be affecting the performance of the cluster.
- Armed with a solid understanding of how the JVM, Lucene, and Elasticsearch allocate and use memory, you can prevent the operating system from swapping processes to disk.
- The snapshot API provides a convenient way to back up and restore your cluster with network-attached storage. Repository plugins expand this functionality to public cloud vendors.

appendix A
Working with
geospatial data

Geospatial data makes your search application location-aware. For example, to search for events that are close to you, to find restaurants in a certain area, or to see which park's area intersects with the area of the city center, you'd work with geospatial data.

We'll call events and restaurants in this context *points* because they're essentially points on the map. We'll put areas, such as a country or a rectangle that you draw on a map, under the generic umbrella of *shapes*. Geospatial search works with points, shapes, and various relations between them:

- *Distance between a point and another point*—If where you are is a point and swimming pools are other points, you can search for the closest swimming pools. Or you can filter only pools that are reasonably close to you, or use aggregations to see how many of them are within 10 km, how many are between 10 and 20 km, and so on.

- *A shape containing a point*—If you select an area on the map, like the area where you work, you can filter only restaurants that are in that area, or you can use the geo_bounds aggregation to find out which area a set of points belongs in.

- *A shape overlapping with another shape*—For example, you can search for parks in the city center.

This appendix will show you how to search, sort, and aggregate documents in Elasticsearch, based on their distance from a reference point on the map. You'll also learn how to search for points that fall into a rectangle and how to search shapes that intersect with a certain area you define on the map.

A.1   *Points and distances between them*

To search for points, you first have to index them. Elasticsearch has a *geo point* type especially for that. You can see an example of how to use it in the code samples by looking at mapping.json.

> **NOTE** The code samples for this book, along with instructions on how to use them, can be found at https://github.com/dakrone/elasticsearch-in-action.

Each event has a `location` field, which is an object that includes the `geolocation` field as a `geo_point` type:

```
"geolocation" : { "type" : "geo_point"}
```

With the geo point type defined in your mapping, you can index points by giving the latitude and longitude, as you can see in populate.sh:

```
"geolocation": "39.748477,-104.998852"
```

> **TIP** You can also provide the latitude and longitude as properties, an array, or a geohash. This doesn't change the way points are indexed; it's just for your convenience, in case you have a preferred way. You can find more details at www.elastic.co/guide/en/elasticsearch/reference/current/mapping-geo-point-type.html.

Having geo points indexed as part of your event documents (from the dataset used throughout the book) enables you to add distance criteria to your searches in the following ways:

- *Sort results by the distance from a given point*—This makes the event closest to you appear first.
- *Filter results by distance*—This lets you display only events that are within a certain range—for example, 100 kilometers from you.
- *Aggregate results by distance*—This allows you to create buckets of ranges. For example, you can get the number of events within 100 km from you, the number of events from 100 km to 200 km, and so on.

A.2   *Adding distance to your sort criteria*

Using the get-together example from the main chapters of the book, let's say your coordinates are 40,–105 and you need to find the event about Elasticsearch closest to you. To do that, you need to add a sort criteria called `_geo_distance`, where you specify your current location, as shown in the following listing.

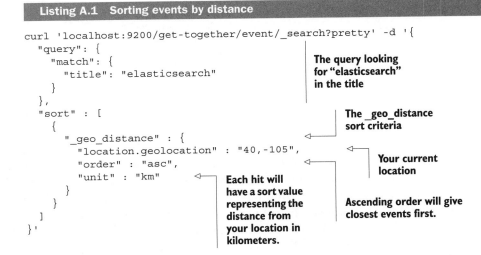

Listing A.1 Sorting events by distance

```
curl 'localhost:9200/get-together/event/_search?pretty' -d '{
  "query": {
    "match": {                           The query looking
      "title": "elasticsearch"           for "elasticsearch"
    }                                     in the title
  },
  "sort" : [                             The _geo_distance
    {                                    sort criteria
      "_geo_distance" : {
        "location.geolocation" : "40,-105",
        "order" : "asc",                       Your current
        "unit" : "km"                          location
      }
    }                     Each hit will
  ]                       have a sort value    Ascending order will give
}'                        representing the     closest events first.
                          distance from
                          your location in
                          kilometers.
```

You can also specify an array of multiple reference points and use `mode` to decide whether the sort value will be the `mim`/`max`/`avg` distance between the reference points and the point stored in the document:

```
"_geo_distance" : {
  "location.geolocation" : ["40,-105", "42,-107"],
  "order" : "asc",
  "unit" : "km",
  "mode" : "avg"
```

This is useful, for example, when you have multiple points of interest and you want to find a hotel that's close to all of them.

A.2.1 Sorting by distance and other criteria at the same time

A search like the previous one is useful when distance is your only criteria. If you want to include other criteria in the equation, such as the document's score, you can use the `function_score` query that we introduced in chapter 6. This way, you can generate a final score based on the initial score from your query plus the distance from your point of interest.

The following listing shows such a query: an event will score linearly lower the farther it is from you. At 100 km, the original score would be cut by half (`decay=0.5`).

Listing A.2 Taking distance into account when calculating the score

```
curl 'localhost:9200/get-together/event/_search?pretty' -d '{
  "query": {
    "function_score": {
      "query": {                        Query looking for
        "match": {                      "elasticsearch"
          "title": "elasticsearch"      returns a score
        }
```

```
    },
    "linear": {
      "location.geolocation": {
        "origin": "40, -105",
        "scale": "100km",
        "decay": 0.5
      }
    }
  }
 }
}'
```

> linear decay function reduces an event's score the farther it is from origin

You might be tempted to think that such scripts bring the best of both worlds: relevance from your query and the geospatial dimension. Although the function_score query is very powerful indeed, running it as shown in listing A.2 is expensive in terms of speed, especially when you have lots of documents, because it has to calculate the distance from origin of all matching documents. A faster way could be to search your events as usual and filter only those that are within a certain distance.

A.3 Filter and aggregate based on distance

Let's say you're looking for events within a certain range from where you are, as in figure A.1.

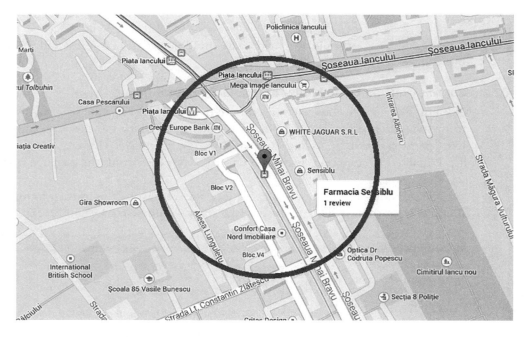

Figure A.1 You can filter only points that fall in a certain range from a specified location.

To filter such events, you'd use the geo distance filter. The parameters it needs are your reference location and the limiting distance, as shown here:

```
% curl 'localhost:9200/get-together/event/_search?pretty' -d '{
  "query": {
    "filtered": {
      "filter": {
        "geo_distance": {
          "distance": "50km",
          "location.geolocation": "40.0,-105.0"
        }
      }
    }
  }
}'
```

In this default mode, Elasticsearch will calculate the distance from 40.0,–105.0 to each event's geolocation and return only those that are under 50 km. You can set the way the distance is calculated via the distance_type parameter, which will go next to the distance parameter. You have three options:

- sloppy_arc (default)—It calculates the distance between the two points by doing a faster approximation of an arc of a circle. This is a good option for most situations.
- arc—It actually calculates the arc of a circle, making it slower but more precise than sloppy_arc. Note that you don't get 100% precision here, either, because the Earth isn't perfectly round. Still, if you need precision, this is the best option.
- plane—This is the fastest but least precise implementation because it assumes the surface between the two points is a plane. This option works well when you have many documents and the distance limit is fairly small.

Performance optimization doesn't end with distance algorithms. There's another parameter to the geo distance filter called optimize_bbox. bbox stands for *bounding box*, which is a rectangle that you define on a map that contains all the points and areas of interest.

Using optimize_bbox will first check if events match a square that contains the circle describing the distance range. If they match, Elasticsearch filters further by calculating the distance.

If you're asking yourself whether the bounding box optimization is actually worth it, you'll be happy to know that for most cases, it is. Verifying whether a point belongs to a bounding box is much faster than calculating the distance and comparing it to your limit.

It's also configurable. You can set optimize_bbox to none and check whether your query times are faster or slower. The default value is memory and you can set it to indexed.

Are you curious about what the difference between memory and indexed is? We'll discuss this difference in the beginning of the next section. If you're not curious and you don't want to obsess about performance improvements, sticking with the default should be good enough for most cases.

374 APPENDIX A *Working with geospatial data*

DISTANCE RANGE FILTER

The geo distance range filter allows you, for example, to search for events between 50 and 100 kilometers from where you are. Besides its from and to distance options, it accepts the same parameters as the geo distance filter:

```
"filter": {
  "geo_distance_range": {
    "from": "50km",
    "to": "100km",
    "location.geolocation": "40.0,-105.0"
  }
}
```

DISTANCE RANGE AGGREGATION

Users will probably search for events farther from their point of reference because the ones they found close by weren't satisfying—for example, if the events' dates are too far in the future. In such situations, it might be handy for the user to see in advance how many events are, say, within 50 km, between 50 and 100, between 100 and 200, and so on.

For this use case, the geo distance range aggregation will come in handy. It looks similar to the range and date range aggregations you saw in chapter 7. In this case, you'll specify a reference point (origin) and the distance ranges you need:

```
"aggs" : {
  "events_ranges" : {
    "geo_distance" : {
      "field" : "location.geolocation",
      "origin" : "40.0, -105.0",
      "unit": "km",
      "ranges" : [
        { "to" : 100 },
        { "from" : 100, "to" : 5000 },
        { "from" : 5000 }
      ]
    }
  }
}
```

Elasticsearch will return how many events it finds for each distance range:

```
"aggregations" : {
  "events_ranges" : {
    "buckets" : [ {
      "key" : "*-100.0",
      "from" : 0.0,
      "to" : 100.0,
      "doc_count" : 8
    }, {
      "key" : "100.0-5000.0",
      "from" : 100.0,
      "to" : 5000.0,
      "doc_count" : 3
    }, {
```

```
        "key" : "5000.0-*",
        "from" : 5000.0,
        "doc_count" : 3
      } ]
    }
  }
```

So far we've covered how to search and aggregate points based on distances. Next, we'll look at searching and aggregating them based on shapes.

A.4   Does a point belong to a shape?

Shapes, especially rectangles, are easy to draw interactively on a map, as you can see in figure A.2. It's also faster to search for points in a shape than to calculate distances because searching in a shape only requires comparing the coordinates of the point with the coordinates of the shape's corners.

There are three types of shapes on the map that you can match points to, or you can match points to events if you're thinking of the get-together example we used throughout the chapters:

- *Bounding boxes (rectangles)*—These are fast and give you the flexibility to draw any rectangle.
- *Polygons*—These allow you to draw a more precise shape, but it's difficult to ask a user to draw a polygon, and the more complex the polygon is, the slower the search.
- *Geohashes (squares defined by a hash)*—These are the least flexible because hashes are fixed. But, as you'll see later, they're typically the fastest implementation of the three.

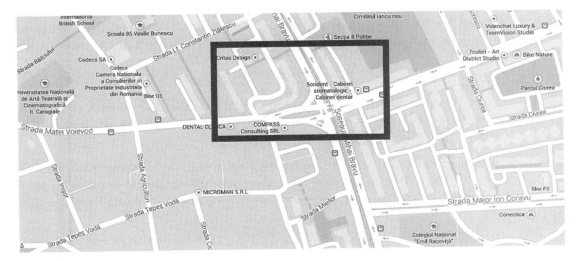

Figure A.2   You can filter points based on whether they fall within a rectangle on the map.

A.4.1   *Bounding boxes*

To search whether a point falls within a rectangle, you'd use the bounding box filter. This is useful if your application allows users to click a point on the map to define a corner of the rectangle and then click again to define the opposite corner. The result could be a rectangle like the one from figure A.2.

To run the bounding box filter, specify the coordinates for the top-left and bottom-right points that describe the rectangle:

```
% curl 'localhost:9200/get-together/event/_search?pretty' -d '{
  "query": {
    "filtered": {
      "filter": {
        "geo_bounding_box": {
          "location.geolocation": {
            "top_left": "40, -106",
            "bottom_right": "38, -103"
          }
        }
      }
    }
  }
}'
```

The default implementation of the bounding box filter is to load the points' coordinates in memory and compare them with those provided for the bounding box. This is the equivalent of setting the type option under geo_bounding_box to memory.

Alternatively, you can set type to indexed and Elasticsearch will do the same comparison using range filters, like the ones you learned about in chapter 4. For this implementation to work, you need to index the point's latitude and longitude in their own fields, which aren't enabled by default.

To enable indexing latitude and longitude separately, you have to set lat_lon to true in your mapping, making your geolocation field definition look like this:

```
"geolocation" : { "type" : "geo_point", "lat_lon": true }
```

> **NOTE**   If you make this change to mapping.json from the code samples, you'll need to run populate.sh again to re-index the sample dataset and have your changes take effect.

The indexed implementation is faster, but indexing latitude and longitude will make your index bigger. Also, if you have more geo points per document—such as an array of points for a restaurant franchise—the indexed implementation won't work.

> **Polygon filter**
>
> If you want to search for points matching a more complex shape than a rectangle, you can use the geo polygon filter. It allows you to enter the array of points that describe the polygon. More details about the geo polygon filter can be found here: www.elastic.co/guide/en/elasticsearch/reference/current/query-dsl-geo-polygon-filter.html.

If you use the geo bounding box filter to search for documents that fall in an area, you can use the geo bounds aggregation to do the opposite—get the bounding box that includes all points resulting from your search:

```
"aggs" : {
  "events_box": {
    "geo_bounds": {
      "field": "location.geolocation"
    }
  }
}
# returns
"aggregations" : {
  "events_box" : {
    "bounds" : {
      "top_left" : {
        "lat" : 51.524806,
        "lon" : -122.399801
      },
      "bottom_right" : {
        "lat" : 37.787742,
        "lon" : -0.099095
      }
    }
  }
}
```

A.4.2 Geohashes

The last point-matches-shape method you can use is matching geohash cells. Geohash, which is a system invented by Gustavo Niemeyer when building geohash.org,[1] works as suggested in figure A.3, which is a screenshot from http://geohash.gofreerange.com. The Earth is divided into 32 rectangles/cells. Each cell is identified by an alphanumeric character, its hash. Then each rectangle—for example, d—can be further divided into 32 rectangles of its own, generating d0, d1, and so on. You can repeat the process virtually forever, generating smaller and smaller rectangles with longer and longer hash values.

---

[1] https://en.wikipedia.org/wiki/Geohash

Figure A.3   The world divided in 32 letter-coded cells. Each cell is divided into 32 cells and so on, making longer hashes.

GEOHASH CELL FILTER

Because of the way geohash cells are defined, each point on the map belongs to an infinite number of such geohash cells, like d, d0, d0b, and so on. Given such a cell, Elasticsearch can tell you which points match with the geohash cell filter:

```
% curl 'localhost:9200/get-together/event/_search?pretty' -d '{
  "query": {
    "filtered": {
      "filter": {
        "geohash_cell": {
          "location.geolocation": "9xj"
        }
      }
    }
  }
}'
```

Even though a geohash cell is a rectangle, this filter works differently than the bounding box filter. First, geo points have to get indexed with a geohash that describes them—for example, 9xj6. Then, you also have to index all the ngrams of that hash, like 9, 9x, 9xj, and 9xj6, which describe all the parent cells. When you run the filter, the hash from the query is matched against the hashes indexed for that point, making a geohash cell filter similar in implementation to the term filter you saw in chapter 4, which is very fast.

To enable indexing the geohash in your geo point, you have to set geohash to true in the mapping. To index that hash's parents (edge ngrams), set geohash_prefix to true, as well. Indexing prefixes will help make filters faster because they'll do an exact match on the prefixes already indexed instead of a more expensive wildcard search.

> **TIP** Because a cell will never be able to perfectly describe a point, you have to choose how precise (or big) that rectangle needs to be. The default setting for precision is 12, which creates hashes like 9xj64sswpkdq with an accuracy of a few centimeters. Because you'll also index all the parents, you may want to trade some precision for index size and search performance. You can also specify the precision as length (like 10m), and Elasticsearch will set the corresponding numeric value.

GEOHASH GRID AGGREGATION

Just as you can do aggregations with distances, you can cluster documents that match your search by the geohash cells they belong to. The size of these geohash cells is configured through the precision option:

```
"aggs" : {
  "events_clusters": {
    "geohash_grid": {
      "field": "location.geolocation",
      "precision": 5
    }
  }
}
```

This would return buckets like these:

```
"events_clusters" : {
  "buckets" : [ {
    "key" : "9xj64",
    "doc_count" : 6
  }, {
    "key" : "gcpvj",
    "doc_count" : 3
```
...

Understanding geohash cells is important even if you're not going to use the geohash filters and aggregations because in Elasticsearch, geohashes are the default way of representing shapes. We'll explain how shapes use geohashes in the next section.

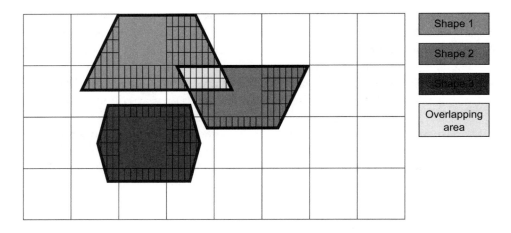

Figure A.4 Shapes represented in geohashes. Searching for shapes matching shape 1 will return shape 2.

A.5   *Shape intersections*

Elasticsearch can index documents with shapes, such as polygons showing the area of a park, and filter documents based on whether parks overlap other shapes, such as the city center. It does this by default through the geohashes discussed in the previous section. The process is described in figure A.4: each shape is approximated (we'll discuss precision later) to a group of rectangles defined by geohashes. When you search, Elasticsearch will easily find out if at least one geohash of a certain shape overlaps a geohash of another shape.

A.5.1   *Indexing shapes*

Let's say you have a shape of a park that's a polygon with four corners. To index it, you'd first have to define a mapping of that shape field—let's call it area—of type geo_shape. With the mapping in place, you can start indexing documents: the area field of each document would have to mention that the shape's type is polygon and show the array of coordinates for that polygon, as shown in the next listing.

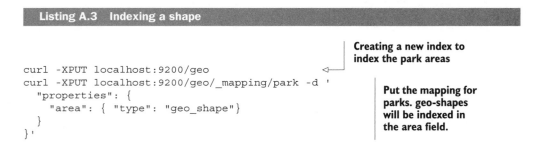

Listing A.3 Indexing a shape

```
curl -XPUT localhost:9200/geo                          ◁── Creating a new index to
curl -XPUT localhost:9200/geo/_mapping/park -d '            index the park areas
  "properties": {
    "area": { "type": "geo_shape"}                     Put the mapping for
  }                                                     parks. geo-shapes
}'                                                      will be indexed in
                                                        the area field.
```

```
curl -XPUT localhost:9200/geo/park/1 -d '{
  "area": {                                    A polygon is indexed
    "type": "polygon",                         in the area field.
    "coordinates": [
      [[45, 30], [46, 30], [45, 31], [46, 32]]        Coordinates for
    ]                                                  the polygon
  }
}'            This first array describes the outer
              boundary. Optionally, other arrays can be
              added to define holes in the polygon.
```

NOTE Polygons aren't the only shape type Elasticsearch supports. You can have multiple polygons in a single shape (type: multipolygon). There are also the point and multipoint types, one or more chained lines (linestring, multilinestring), rectangles (envelope), and more. You can find the complete list here: www.elastic.co/guide/en/elasticsearch/reference/current/mapping-geo-shape-type.html.

The amount of space a shape occupies in your index depends heavily on how you index it. Because geohashes can only approximate most shapes, it's up to you to define how small those geohash rectangles can be. The smaller they are, the better the resolution/approximation, but your index size increases because smaller geohash cells have longer strings and—more importantly—more parent ngrams to index as well. Depending on where you are in this tradeoff, you'll specify a precision parameter in your mapping, which defaults to 50m. This means the worst-case scenario is to get an error of 50m.

A.5.2 *Filtering overlapping shapes*

With your park documents indexed, let's say you have another four-cornered shape that represents your city center. To see which parks are at least partly in the city center, you'd use the geo shape filter. You can provide the shape definition of your city center in the filter, as shown in the following listing.

Listing A.4   geo shape filter example

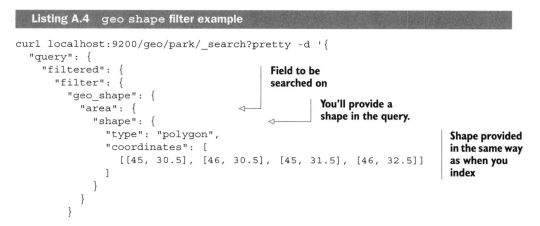

```
curl localhost:9200/geo/park/_search?pretty -d '{
  "query": {
    "filtered": {                          Field to be
      "filter": {                          searched on
        "geo_shape": {
          "area": {                             You'll provide a
            "shape": {                          shape in the query.
              "type": "polygon",
              "coordinates": [                        Shape provided
                [[45, 30.5], [46, 30.5], [45, 31.5], [46, 32.5]]   in the same way
              ]                                        as when you
            }                                          index
          }
        }
      }
    }
```

```
            }
          }
        }
      }
    }'
```

If you followed listing A.3, you should see that the indexed shape matches. Change the query to something like `[[95, 30.5], [96, 30.5], [95, 31.5], [96, 32.5]]`, and the query won't return any hits because there's no common geohash to trigger an overlap.

Geohashes are powerful because they provide a way to do geospatial search using the same underlying mechanisms as the `term` queries we discussed throughout the book. Although geohashes are only an approximation of a point or a shape, using them is typically faster than doing calculations or range filtering on raw latitude and longitude numbers, as you saw in the first part of the appendix.

appendix B
Plugins

Plugins are a powerful way to extend or enhance the functionality that Elasticsearch provides out of the box. A default installation of Elasticsearch comes with no plugins installed, but many are available on GitHub for you to download and play around with.

This appendix shows you how to install, access, and manage plugins in Elasticsearch.

B.1   Working with plugins

Plugins are split into two categories: site plugins and code plugins. A *site plugin* is one that provides no additional functionality; it simply provides a web page served by Elasticsearch. Some examples of site plugins are the elasticsearch-head plugin, elasticsearch-kopf, bigdesk, elasticsearch-hq, and whatson. For example, you may remember the screenshot from chapter 2 shown in figure B.1, showing shards allocated on two different nodes on the kopf plugin.

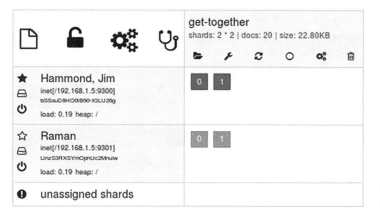

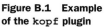

Figure B.1   Example of the kopf plugin

You can see in the figure that the `kopf` plugin shows information about the Elasticsearch cluster; Elasticsearch isn't running any different code and hasn't had any behavior on the server changed at all. The alternative to this is a code plugin.

A *code plugin* is any plugin that includes JVM code that Elasticsearch executes; this can include plugins that add features to Elasticsearch such as the AWS plugin, used to add the ability to snapshot indices to Amazon S3, as well as plugins like the ICU analysis plugin, which is used to better handle language-specific characteristics of text during analysis. There are even plugins that replace internal parts of Elasticsearch such as the shard distributor and discovery mechanisms.

Some examples of code plugins are the `elasticsearch-aws` and `elasticsearch-azure` plugins and the multiple `elasticsearch-lang-*` plugins such as `elasticsearch-lang-python` and `elasticsearch-lang-ruby` that add support for additional scripting languages. There are also plugins that add query capabilities such as additional highlighters and new types of aggregations. Because a code plugin is just a .jar file, it can add any kind of functionality that a developer can think of to Elasticsearch.

Although we said that plugins were split into two categories, that isn't entirely true. It's possible for a code plugin to also include basic HTML, image, and JavaScript files that Elasticsearch can serve to provide an interface as well. An example of a plugin like this is the `elasticsearch-marvel` plugin (www.elastic.co/products/marvel/), which includes Java code that collects and stores metrics, as well as the site portion, which includes an interface to display analytic information about data in Elasticsearch.

Now that we've covered the two different types of Elasticsearch plugins, let's talk about how to install and start using them.

B.2   *Installing plugins*

In order to use a plugin, you first need to install it. Plugins come in many forms, but they're most frequently .zip files. You can choose to manually extract a .zip file to the plugins directory, or you can use the bin/plugin tool to install it by downloading it either from the internet or from a local zip file.

You'll start by installing the `elasticsearch-head` plugin, as shown in the following listing. You can find the plugin here: https://mobz.github.io/elasticsearch-head/. You'll install it using the built-in plugin shell script that comes with Elasticsearch. On Windows, you can use the plugin.bat script to install plugins.

Listing B.1   Installing the `elasticsearch-head` plugin

```
$ cd /path/to/elasticsearch
$ ls
LICENSE.txt  NOTICE.txt  README.textile  bin  config  lib  logs
$ bin/plugin -install mobz/elasticsearch-head            ◁──┐  Installing the
-> Installing mobz/elasticsearch-head...                    │  plugin with the
Trying https://github.com/mobz/elasticsearch-head/archive/master.zip...   bin/plugin script
```

```
Downloading ........................................................DONE
Installed mobz/elasticsearch-head into /data/elasticsearch-1.5.1/plugins/head
Identified as a _site plugin, moving to _site structure ...                    ⟵┐
```
**Elasticsearch detected the
plugin was a site plugin.**

Here you can see that the plugin script has downloaded the plugin from github.com and installed the `elasticsearch-head` plugin into the plugins/head directory. It also has detected that the plugin is a site plugin.

You can list plugins that have been installed by using the `-l` or `--list` parameters to the plugin script, as shown in the next listing.

Listing B.2 Listing installed plugins

```
$ bin/plugin --list
Installed plugins:
    - head
```

In this case, you install a site plugin that was automatically downloaded from GitHub, but there are also other ways to install plugins. Running the bin/plugin script without any parameters shows you all of the options available. See the next listing.

Listing B.3 Available options of the plugin script

```
$ bin/plugin
Usage:
    -u, --url       [plugin location]   : Set exact URL to download the plugin
       from
    -i, --install [plugin name]         : Downloads and installs listed
       plugins [*]
    -t, --timeout [duration]            : Timeout setting: 30s, 1m, 1h...
       (infinite by default)
    -r, --remove   [plugin name]        : Removes listed plugins
    -l, --list                          : List installed plugins
    -v, --verbose                       : Prints verbose messages
    -s, --silent                        : Run in silent mode
    -h, --help                          : Prints this help message

  [*] Plugin name could be:
      elasticsearch/plugin/version for official elasticsearch plugins
      (download from download.elasticsearch.org)
      groupId/artifactId/version   for community plugins (download from maven
      central or oss sonatype)
      username/repository          for site plugins (download from github
      master)
```

Here you can see at the bottom of the output the three different kinds of plugins that can be automatically downloaded—from Elasticsearch, from Maven Central, or directly from GitHub. You can also specify the URL manually, as shown in listing B.4, using the `--url` parameter, which allows you to install from a local file as well.

For example, if you had a plugin downloaded locally that you wanted to install, you could install it by prepending file:/// to the full path of the ZIP file. But if you do this, you'll need to manually specify the name of the plugin you're installing.

Listing B.4 Manually installing a plugin from a local ZIP file

```
$ bin/plugin --url file:///downloads/elasticsearch-head.zip --install head
-> Installing head...
Trying file:/downloads/elasticsearch-head.zip...
Downloading ........DONE
Installed head into /Users/hinmanm/ies/elasticsearch-1.5.1/plugins/head
Identified as a _site plugin, moving to _site structure ...
```

Now that you've installed the plugin by either having the plugin tool download the plugin or installing from a local file, you'll want to be able to access the plugin from Elasticsearch.

B.3   *Accessing plugins*

If you start Elasticsearch now that you've installed the elasticsearch-head plugin, you'll see the log lines shown in the next listing.

Listing B.5 Example output starting Elasticsearch with the head plugin installed

```
[INFO ][node                 ] [Black Widow] version[1.5.1], pid[33030],
    build[5e38401/2015-04-09T13:41:35Z]
[INFO ][node                 ] [Black Widow] initializing ...
[INFO ][plugins              ] [Black Widow] loaded [], sites [head]
[INFO ][node                 ] [Black Widow] initialized
[INFO ][node                 ] [Black Widow] starting ...
[INFO ][transport            ] [Black Widow] bound_address {inet[/
    0:0:0:0:0:0:0:9300]}, publish_address {inet[/192.168.0.4:9300]}
[INFO ][discovery            ] [Black Widow] elasticsearch/evzmesg5QlmRjffe-
    HnGIw
[INFO ][cluster.service      ] [Black Widow] new_master [Black
    Widow][evzmesg5QlmRjffe-HnGIw][Xanadu-2.domain][inet[/
    192.168.0.4:9300]], reason: zen-disco-join (elected_as_master)
[INFO ][http                 ] [Black Widow] bound_address {inet[/
    0:0:0:0:0:0:0:9200]}, publish_address {inet[/192.168.0.4:9200]}
[INFO ][node                 ] [Black Widow] started
```

Pay close attention to the loaded [], sites [head] text. This text indicates which plugins Elasticsearch has loaded; in this case, the empty [] means that there are no code plugins installed. The [head] text shows that the head plugin has been installed and detected correctly by Elasticsearch. If the plugin doesn't show up in these log messages, it most likely hasn't been installed correctly.

Once Elasticsearch has been started with a site plugin installed, you can navigate to the HTML for the plugin by going to http://localhost:9200/_plugin/head in any web browser.

Figure B.2 is an example screenshot of the elasticsearch-head plugin running.

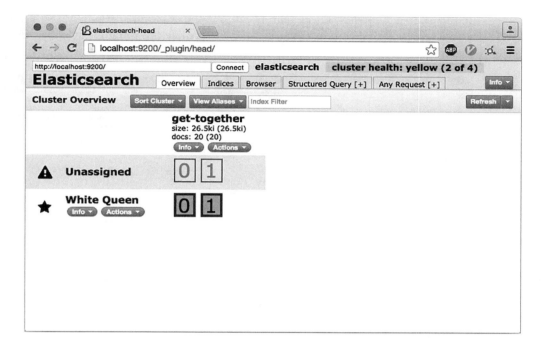

Figure B.2   Screenshot of the `elasticsearch-head` plugin

To access a site plugin, visit http://localhost:9200/_plugin/<name>, where <name> is the name of the plugin that you've installed. This works for all site plugins, but what about code plugins? Other than seeing the name of the plugin in the `loaded [myplugin]` log message when starting Elasticsearch, how you access a code plugin will differ depending on what the plugin is doing. A plugin that adds different analyzers for Elasticsearch will be used by specifying the new analyzer name in the mapping; a plugin that adds a new type of query will be accessed through the regular query DSL. These plugins may also require configuration via values added to the elasticsearch.yml file. Check the documentation for the plugin you're installing to see how it should be correctly configured.

B.4   Telling Elasticsearch to require certain plugins

When deploying Elasticsearch, it can be helpful to require certain plugins to be installed. This means that Elasticsearch will refuse to start until these plugins are installed and detected. This is accomplished by using the `plugin.mandatory` setting. For example, to require that the `elasticsearch-head` and ICU analysis plugins are both installed, you'd add this line to elasticsearch.yml:

```
plugin.mandatory: analysis-icu,head
```

If you then try to start Elasticsearch without these plugins installed, you'll see that Elasticsearch at first refuses to start. But it starts once the plugins have been installed, as shown in the next listing.

Listing B.6   Making plugins mandatory for the Elasticsearch service

> **Elasticsearch refuses to start because the plugins aren't installed.**

```
$ bin/elasticsearch                                          ◁─┐
[INFO ][node                  ] [Carrion] version[1.5.1], pid[46463],
    build[5e38401/2015-04-09T13:41:35Z]
[INFO ][node                  ] [Carrion] initializing ...
{1.5.1}: Initialization Failed ...
- ElasticsearchException[Missing mandatory plugins [analysis-icu, head]]
```

Installing the required plugins

```
$ bin/plugin --install mobz/elasticsearch-head
-> Installing mobz/elasticsearch-head...
Trying https://github.com/mobz/elasticsearch-head/archive/master.zip...
Downloading ........................DONE
Installed mobz/elasticsearch-head into /Users/hinmanm/ies/elasticsearch-
    1.5.1/plugins/head
Identified as a _site plugin, moving to _site structure ...

$ bin/plugin --install elasticsearch/elasticsearch-analysis-icu/2.5.0
-> Installing elasticsearch/elasticsearch-analysis-icu/2.5.0...
Trying http://download.elasticsearch.org/elasticsearch/elasticsearch-
    analysis-icu/elasticsearch-analysis-icu-2.5.0.zip...
Downloading ......................................DONE
Installed elasticsearch/elasticsearch-analysis-icu/2.5.0 into /Users/hinmanm/
    ies/elasticsearch-1.5.1/plugins/analysis-icu
```

Elasticsearch now starts.

```
$ bin/elasticsearch
[INFO ][node                  ] [ISAAC] version[1.5.1], pid[46698],
    build[5e38401/2015-04-09T13:41:35Z]
[INFO ][node                  ] [ISAAC] initializing ...
[INFO ][plugins               ] [ISAAC] loaded [analysis-icu], sites [head]   ◁─┐
[INFO ][node                  ] [ISAAC] initialized
[INFO ][node                  ] [ISAAC] starting ...
[INFO ][node                  ] [ISAAC] started
```

> **The analysis-icu and head plugins are loaded.**

B.5   *Removing or updating plugins*

If you decide you no longer want to have a plugin installed, you can remove the plugin using bin/plugin -r or bin/plugin --remove followed by the name of the plugin. For example, to remove the elasticsearch-analysis-icu plugin you installed in the earlier section, you'd use the code shown in the following listing.

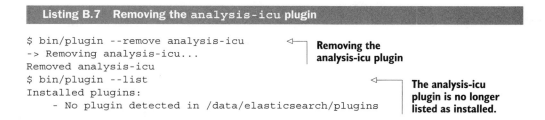

Listing B.7   Removing the `analysis-icu` plugin

```
$ bin/plugin --remove analysis-icu
-> Removing analysis-icu...
Removed analysis-icu
$ bin/plugin --list
Installed plugins:
    - No plugin detected in /data/elasticsearch/plugins
```

◁— **Removing the analysis-icu plugin**

◁— **The analysis-icu plugin is no longer listed as installed.**

Updating plugins uses this same functionality, but there's no upgrade option on the plugin tool. Instead, to update a plugin you must remove the old version and then install the version you want. To upgrade the `elasticsearch-head` plugin, you'd run `bin/plugin --remove head` followed by `bin/plugin --install mobz/elasticsearch-head`.

As you can see, managing plugins is easy with Elasticsearch's included plugin script. For a list of helpful plugins managed by both Elastic and the community, check out the following URL: www.elastic.co/guide/en/elasticsearch/reference/current/modules-plugins.html#known-plugins.

appendix C
Highlighting

Highlighting indicates why a document results from a query by emphasizing matching terms, giving the user an idea of what the document is about, and also showing its relationship to the query, as shown in figure C.1.

Although figure C.1 is taken from DuckDuckGo, Elasticsearch offers highlighting functionality, too. For example, you can search for "elasticsearch" in get-together event titles and make that word stand out like this:

```
"title" : [ "Introduction to <em>Elasticsearch</em>" ],
```

To get such highlighting, you'll need three things, and we'll discuss them in detail in this appendix:

- A `highlight` part of your search request, which will go on the same level as `query` and `aggregations`
- A list of fields you want to be highlighted, like the event name or its description
- Highlighted fields included in `_source` or stored individually

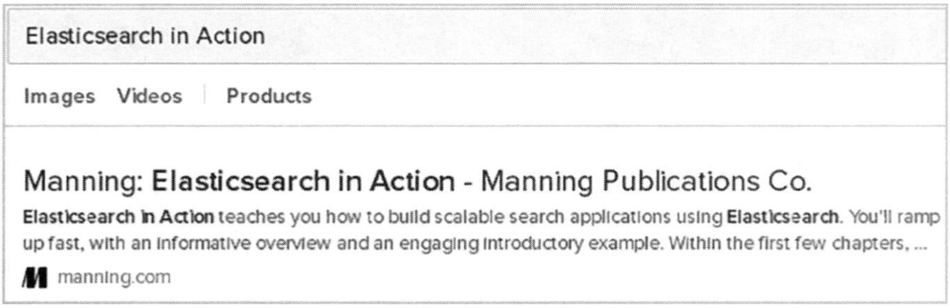

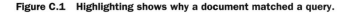

Elasticsearch in Action

Images Videos | Products

Manning: Elasticsearch in Action - Manning Publications Co.

Elasticsearch In Action teaches you how to build scalable search applications using **Elasticsearch**. You'll ramp up fast, with an informative overview and an engaging introductory example. Within the first few chapters, ...

M manning.com

Figure C.1 Highlighting shows why a document matched a query.

> **NOTE**   All fields are included in _source by default but aren't stored individually. You can find more information about _source and stored fields in chapter 3, section 3.4.1.

After you do the basic highlighting, you might want to turn some knobs. In this appendix, we'll also discuss the most important highlighting options:

- *What to match*—You can decide, for example, to show a snippet of a field, even if there are no terms to highlight in there, to show the same fields for all documents. Or you might want to use a different query for highlighting than the one you use for searching.
- *How fragments should look*—With large fields, you typically don't get back all their contents with highlighted terms; you just get one or more fragments of text around those terms. You can configure how many fragments to allow, which order they should be shown, and how big they should be in.
- *How to highlight*—You can change the default <em> and </em> tags to something else. If you stick to HTML tags, you can have Elasticsearch encode the whole fragments in HTML (for example, by escaping ampersand (&) characters) so you can render those fragments correctly in your application.

We'll also discuss different highlighting implementations. The default implementation is called plain and relies on re-analyzing the text from stored fields in order to highlight relevant terms. This process might become too expensive for big fields, like the contents of a blog post. Alternatively, you can use the Postings Highlighter or the Fast Vector Highlighter. Both require you to change the mapping to make Elasticsearch store additional data: term offsets for the Postings Highlighter and term vectors for the Fast Vector Highlighter. Both changes will increase your index size and use more computing power while indexing.

Each highlighting implementation comes with its own set of features, and we'll talk about them later in this appendix. But first, let's deal with the basics of highlighting.

C.1   *Highlighting basics*

To start, you'll recreate the highlighting snippet from the introduction. In listing C.1, you'll run a search on the get-together events for the term "elasticsearch" in the name and will highlight this term in the title and the description fields.

> **NOTE**   For the listing to work, you need to download the code samples for this book by cloning the Git repository from https://github.com/dakrone/elasticsearch-in-action and running populate.sh to index the sample data.

Listing C.1   Highlighting terms in two fields

```
curl localhost:9200/get-together/event/_search?pretty -d '{
  "query": {
    "match": {
      "title": "elasticsearch"                    Typical match query
    }                                              for Elasticsearch;
  }                                                nothing new here
```

```
      },
      "highlight": {
        "fields": {
          "title": {},
          "description": {}
        }
      }
    }
  }'
# reply
    "hits" : [ {
      "_index" : "get-together",
      "_type" : "event",
      "_id" : "103",
      "_score" : 0.9581454,
      "_source":{
    "host": "Lee",
    "title": "Introduction to Elasticsearch",
    "description": "An introduction to ES and each other. We can meet and
    greet and I will present on some Elasticsearch basics and how we use it.",
    [...]
        "highlight" : {
          "title" : [ "Introduction to <em>Elasticsearch</em>" ],
          "description" : [ "can meet and greet and I will present on some
    <em>Elasticsearch</em> basics and how we use it." ]
        }
    [...]
    "title": "Elasticsearch and Logstash",
    "description": "We can get together and talk about Logstash -
    http://logstash.net with a sneak peek at Kibana",
    [...]
        "highlight" : {
          "title" : [ "<em>Elasticsearch</em> and Logstash" ]
        }
```

Include which fields you want to highlight.

The reply will contain _source as before...

...but also the highlighted fields, if they match the term "elastic-search".

Highlighting works here because, by default, the `title` and `description` fields are included in _source. If they had been stored individually (by setting `store` to `true` in the mapping of that field), Elasticsearch would have extracted the contents from the stored field instead of retrieving it from _source.

> **TIP** Storing a field and not going through _source can be faster if you're highlighting a single field. If you're highlighting multiple fields, using _source is typically faster because all fields are fetched in the same trip to the disk. You can force using _source even for stored fields by setting `force_source` to `true` in your highlighting request. For most use cases, it's best to stick with the default of using _source alone—both in the mapping and for highlighting.

Depending on your use case, the results from listing C.1 might not be what you need. Let's look at two of the most common problems and how you can fix them.

C.1.1 What should be passed on to the user

Results from listing C.1 contain the _source field, plus the `title` and/or `description` fields if there's something to highlight in them. Assuming you want to return the title and description fields to the user, you'll have to implement something like this in your application:

- Check if the field (title or description, in this case) is highlighted.
- If it is, show the highlighted fragment. If it's not, take the original field content from _source.

A more elegant solution is to have the highlighter return fragments of both the title and the description fields, regardless of whether there's something to highlight in there or not. You'll do that in listing C.2 by setting no_match_size to the number of characters you want the fragment to have, if the field doesn't match. The default is 0, which is why fields that don't match don't appear at all.

> **NOTE** Configuring the fragment size is useful when you can't control how large fields are. If you take an event description from _source and it fills one page, for example, it will ruin the UI. We'll discuss more about fragment sizes and other fragment options in section C.2.1.

With the highlighter returning all fields you need, the _source field from the results becomes redundant, so you can skip returning it by setting _source to false in your search request, as shown in the next listing.

Listing C.2 Forcing the highlighter to return the needed fields with no_match_size

```
curl localhost:9200/get-together/event/_search?pretty -d '{
  "query": {
    "match": {
      "title": "elasticsearch"
    }
  },
  "highlight": {
    "no_match_size": 100,          Show up to 100
    "fields": {                    characters of a field
      "title": {},                 that doesn't match.
      "description": {}
    }                              You have all the needed
  },                               information in the highlighted
  "_source": false                 fields, so you disable _source.
}'
# reply
    "hits" : [ {
      "_index" : "get-together",
      "_type" : "event",
      "_id" : "103",
      "_score" : 0.9581454,                              No _source
      "highlight" : {                                    in the results
        "title" : [ "Introduction to <em>Elasticsearch</em>" ],
        "description" : [ "can meet and greet and I will present on some
      em>Elasticsearch</em> basics and how we use it." ]
      }
  [...]
```

```
"highlight" : {
  "title" : [ "<em>Elasticsearch</em> and Logstash" ],
  "description" : [ "We can get together and talk about Logstash -
➥ http://logstash.net with a sneak peek at Kibana" ]                    ◄──┐
```

This description doesn't match, but the field is shown anyway for completeness.

Highlighting the same fields regardless of whether they match or not is a common use case. Next we'll look at a different (though still common) use case.

C.1.2 *Too many fields contain highlighted terms*

If you pass on the highlighted results of listing C.2 to users, they might get confused by getting elasticsearch descriptions highlighted anyway because they searched only in the title field. To highlight only fields matching the query, you can set require_field_match to true, as in the following listing. Now if the query matches the title field, only the title field gets its terms highlighted.

Listing C.3   Highlighting only fields matching the query

```
curl localhost:9200/get-together/event/_search?pretty -d '{
  "query": {
    "match": {
      "title": "elasticsearch"
    }
  },
  "highlight": {
    "require_field_match": true,
    "fields": {
      "title": {},
      "description": {}
    }
  }
}'
# reply
      "highlight" : {
        "title" : [ "Introduction to <em>Elasticsearch</em>" ]
      }
[...]
      "highlight" : {
        "title" : [ "<em>Elasticsearch</em> and Logstash" ]
      }
```

Only the title field is highlighted now.

Another method to get to the same result is to figure out that the search goes to the title field and add only title in the list of highlighted fields. This might work, but sometimes you don't have control over which fields are searched on. For example, if you're using the query_string query that we discussed in chapter 4, someone could introduce description:elasticsearch, even if the default searched field is something else.

`require_field_match` and `no_match_size` are just two of the available highlighting options. There are many more you may find useful, and we'll discuss them in the next sections.

C.2   *Highlighting options*

Besides choosing which fields to work with, you can configure highlighting with other options, like these:

- Adjusting the size of highlighted fragments and their number
- Changing highlighting tags and encoding
- Specifying a different query for highlighting, instead of the main query

We'll discuss all of these next.

C.2.1   *Size, order, and number of fragments*

Highlighting `elasticsearch` in an event's `description` field will show only a fragment of about 100 characters around the highlighted terms. As you might have noticed from listings C.1 and C.2, this doesn't always contain the whole field, so the context could be too large or too small:

```
        "description" : [ "can meet and greet and I will present on some
➥ <em>Elasticsearch</em> basics and how we use it." ]
```

We say *about* 100 characters because Elasticsearch tries to make sure that words aren't truncated.

FRAGMENT SIZE

Naturally, there's a `fragment_size` option to change the default fragment size. Setting it to `0` will show the entire field content, which works nicely for short fields like names.

 You can set fragment size globally for all fields and individually for each field. Individual settings override global settings, as shown in the next listing, where you'll search for "Elasticsearch," "Logstash," and "Kibana" in the `description` field.

> **Listing C.4   Field-specific `fragment_size` setting overrides the global setting**

```
curl localhost:9200/get-together/event/_search?pretty -d '{
  "query": {
    "match": {
      "description": "elasticsearch logstash kibana"
    }
  },
  "highlight": {
    "fragment_size": 20,            Global fragment size
    "fields": {                     applies to all fields
      "title": {},
      "description": {
        "fragment_size": "40"       Field-specific fragment
      }                             size overrides the
    }                               global setting
  }
```

```
    }
  }'
  # reply
        "highlight" : {
          "title" : [ "Logging and <em>Elasticsearch</em>" ],
          "description" : [ "dive for what <em>Elasticsearch</em> is and how
⟶  it", "logging with <em>Logstash</em> as well as <em>Kibana</em>!" ]
        }
     [...]
        "highlight" : {
          "title" : [ "<em>Elasticsearch</em> and <em>Logstash</em>" ],
          "description" : [ "together and talk about <em>Logstash</em> -
⟶  http://logstash", "with a sneak peek at <em>Kibana</em>" ]
        }
     [...]
        "highlight" : {
          "title" : [ "<em>Elasticsearch</em> at" ],
          "description" : [ "how they use <em>Elasticsearch</em>" ]
        }
```

Fragments showing only part of the field

You can see from this listing that if the fragment size is small enough and there are enough occurrences of the term, multiple fragments are generated.

ORDER OF FRAGMENTS

By default, fragments are returned in the order in which they appear in the text, as you saw in listing C.4. This works well for short texts, where the natural order of fragments gives a better overview of the whole content. For example, the description fragments you got back in listing C.4 do a good job of showing the description.

For large documents, such as books, the natural order doesn't work so well because fragments can be far apart, so the user won't see any link. For example, if you searched for "elasticsearch parent child" in this book, the top two fragments might look like this:

```
"we will discuss how Elasticsearch works and"
"the child aggregation works on buckets generated by"
```

Not terribly relevant, assuming you were looking for parent-child relationships in Elasticsearch. Even though the book itself is relevant because it discusses the topic, it would have been nicer to show a fragment that appears later in the book:

```
"parent-child relationships work with different Elasticsearch documents"
```

When you're highlighting large fields, it makes sense to arrange fragments in the order of their relevance to the query because users are likely to be interested in seeing those relevant parts in order, so they can decide if the result is what they expected.

The highlighter calculates a TF-IDF score for each fragment, much as it calculates scores for documents within the index. To order fragments by this score, you have to set order to score in the highlight part of the request. As is done with fragment sizes, you can set the order individually and/or globally. For example, the following highlight section will change the order of fragments for the "elasticsearch logstash kibana" query you ran in listing C.4:

```
"highlight": {
  "fields": {
    "description": {
      "fragment_size": 40,
      "order": "score"
    }
  }
}
```

You can see that the fragment matching more terms appears first because it has a higher score:

```
"description" : [ "logging with <em>Logstash</em> as well as
    <em>Kibana</em>!", "dive for what <em>Elasticsearch</em> is and how it" ]
```

NUMBER OF FRAGMENTS

With big documents such as books, it makes sense to show only one large, relevant fragment. Multiple small fragments work better for describing smaller fields, like the event descriptions you've worked with so far. You can adjust the number of fragments by setting number_of_fragments (shocker!), which defaults to 5:

```
"highlight": {
  "fields": {
    "description": {
      "number_of_fragments": 1
    }
  }
}
```

For really small fields, such as names or short descriptions, you can set number_ of_fragments to 0. This will skip using fragments altogether and return the whole field as a single fragment, ignoring the value of fragment_size.

With the size, order, and number of fragments figured out, let's move on to configuring how those fragments are returned.

C.2.2   *Highlighting tags and fragment encoding*

You can change the <em> and </em> tags that are used by default through the pre_tags and post_tags options. In the following listing, you'll use <b> and </b> instead.

> **Listing C.5   Custom highlighting tags**

```
curl localhost:9200/get-together/event/_search?pretty -d '{
  "query": {
    "match": {
      "title": "elasticsearch"
    }
  },
```

```
    "highlight": {
      "pre_tags" : ["<b>"],
      "post_tags" : ["</b>"],          Global tags; you can
      "fields": {                      also define different
        "title": {}                    tags for each field.
      }
    }
}'                                                New tags are used
# reply                                           in the highlighted
        "highlight" : {                                  fragments.
          "title" : [ "<b>Elasticsearch</b> at Rangespan and Exonar" ]   ◁────
        }
```

If your custom tags are HTML like the default ones, you probably want to render the fragments in HTML to show them in some user interface. Here you might encounter a problem: by default, Elasticsearch returns fragments without any encoding, so they won't render properly if there are special characters, such as the ampersand (&). For example, a fragment that's highlighted as select&copy would appear as shown in figure C.2, because the &copy sequence is interpreted as the copyright character.

Figure C.2   The lack of fragment encoding can make the browser interpret HTML incorrectly.

The ampersand needs to be escaped as &. You can do that by setting encoder to html:

```
    "highlight": {
      "encoder": "html",
      "fields": {
        "title": {}
      }
    }
```

The HTML encoder will make the text render properly, as shown in figure C.3.

Figure C.3   Using the HTML encoder avoids parsing mistakes.

Now that we've gone through customizing the contents of fragments, let's take a step back and look at the query that generated the highlighted fragments in the first place. By default, terms from the main query are used, but you can define a custom query.

C.2.3 Highlight query

Using the main query for highlighting works for most use cases, but there are some that require special care—for example, if you use rescore queries.

You first met rescoring in chapter 6 when we discussed relevancy, because rescoring allows you to improve the ranking of results by running alternative—often expensive—queries only on the top *N* of the overall result set. Elasticsearch then combines the original score with the score from the rescore queries to get the final ranking. The problem: rescore queries don't apply to highlighting.

This is where custom highlight queries become useful—for example, if the main query is looking for groups with elasticsearch or simply search in their name, and you also want to boost the presence of tags that end with search, like enterprise search. A wildcard query for *search is expensive, as you saw in chapter 10, section 10.4.1, so you can put this criterion in a rescore query that runs on only the top 200 documents.

In the listing that follows, you'll see how you can put elasticsearch and search names plus *search tags in the highlight query to highlight all the terms involved in the search. You can see that wildcards are expanded and highlight matching tags like enterprise search.

Listing C.6 Highlight query contains terms from the main and the rescore query

```
curl localhost:9200/get-together/group/_search?pretty -d '{
    "query" : {
      "match" : {
        "name" : "elasticsearch search"          Main query matches
      }                                           elasticsearch and search
    },                                            in the name field
    "rescore" : {
      "window_size": 200,
      "query" : {
        "rescore_query" : {
          "wildcard" : {
            "tags.verbatim" : "*search"           Rescore query
          }                                       matches tags
        }                                         ending in search
      }
    },
    "highlight": {
      "highlight_query": {
        "query_string": {
          "query": "name:elasticsearch name:search tags.verbatim:*search"
        }
      },                                          Highlight query
      "fields": {                                 matches all main and
        "name": {},                               rescore query criteria
        "tags.verbatim": {}
      }
    }
  }'
```

```
# reply
    "highlight" : {
        "name" : [ "<em>Elasticsearch</em> Denver" ],
        "tags.verbatim" : [ "<em>elasticsearch</em>" ]
    [...]

    "highlight" : {
        "name" : [ "Enterprise <em>search</em> London get-together" ],
        "tags.verbatim" : [ "<em>enterprise search</em>" ]
```

elastic-
search and
search are
highlighted
in the name
field.

**All tags
ending in
search are
highlighted,
too.**

Now let's take a deeper look at how highlighting works under the hood. This will allow you to choose the implementation that works best for your use case.

C.3   *Highlighter implementations*

So far we've assumed that you're using the default highlighter implementation called Plain. The Plain Highlighter works by re-analyzing the text from each field to identify terms to highlight and where those terms are located in the text. This is good for most use cases and only requires highlighted fields to be stored, either independently or in the _source field. Because it has to analyze the text again, the Plain Highlighter can be slow for large fields; for example, when you index books or blog post contents.

For such use cases, two other implementations come in handy:

- Postings Highlighter
- Fast Vector Highlighter

Both are faster than the Plain Highlighter on large fields, but both require additional data to be stored in the index—data on which their speed is based. Both also come up with their unique features, which will be discussed next.

If it's not obvious which one is best for you, we suggest starting with the Plain Highlighter and moving on to the Postings Highlighter for fields where the Plain Highlighter proves to be too slow, because the Postings Highlighter adds little overhead in terms of index size and also works well if fields are smaller. If the Postings Highlighter doesn't give you the needed functionality, try the Fast Vector Highlighter.

C.3.1   *Postings Highlighter*

The Postings Highlighter requires you to set index_options to offsets for high-lighted fields, which will store each term's location (position and offset) in the index. As you can see in listing C.7, offsets indicate the exact position of a certain term in the text, and with this information, the Postings Highlighter is able to identify which terms to highlight without having to re-analyze the text.

In this listing you'll use the Analyze API, which you first encountered in chapter 5 on analysis.

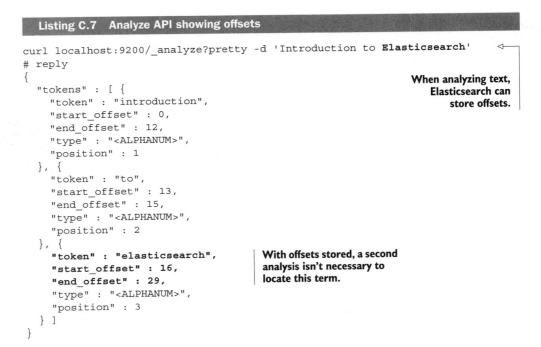

```
curl localhost:9200/_analyze?pretty -d 'Introduction to Elasticsearch'
# reply
{
  "tokens" : [ {
    "token" : "introduction",
    "start_offset" : 0,
    "end_offset" : 12,
    "type" : "<ALPHANUM>",
    "position" : 1
  }, {
    "token" : "to",
    "start_offset" : 13,
    "end_offset" : 15,
    "type" : "<ALPHANUM>",
    "position" : 2
  }, {
    "token" : "elasticsearch",
    "start_offset" : 16,
    "end_offset" : 29,
    "type" : "<ALPHANUM>",
    "position" : 3
  } ]
}
```

Listing C.7 Analyze API showing offsets

When analyzing text, Elasticsearch can store offsets.

With offsets stored, a second analysis isn't necessary to locate this term.

When analyzing the text, Elasticsearch is able to extract each term's offsets in order to store its exact location. With offsets stored, Elasticsearch doesn't have to analyze the text again during highlighting in order to locate each term. Adding term offsets to the index is a typical tradeoff where you allow slower indexing and a bigger index in order to get better query latency. You saw many such performance tradeoffs in chapter 10.

When you set `index_options` to `offsets`, the Postings Highlighter is used automatically. For example, in the next listing you'll enable offsets for the `content` field of a new index, add two documents, and highlight them.

Listing C.8 Using the Postings Highlighter

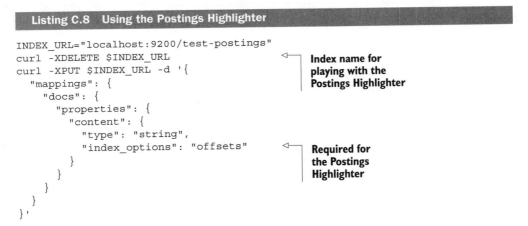

```
INDEX_URL="localhost:9200/test-postings"
curl -XDELETE $INDEX_URL
curl -XPUT $INDEX_URL -d '{
  "mappings": {
    "docs": {
      "properties": {
        "content": {
          "type": "string",
          "index_options": "offsets"
        }
      }
    }
  }
}'
```

Index name for playing with the Postings Highlighter

Required for the Postings Highlighter

**Indexing
two sample
documents**

```
curl -XPUT $INDEX_URL/docs/1 -d '{
    "content": "Postings Highlighter rocks. It stores offsets in postings."
}'
curl -XPUT $INDEX_URL/docs/2 -d '{
    "content": "Postings are a generic name for the inverted part of the
       ➥ index: term dictionary, term frequencies, term positions."
}'
curl -XPOST $INDEX_URL/_refresh
curl "$INDEX_URL/_search?q=content:postings&pretty" -d '{       ⟵
    "highlight": {
        "fields": {
            "content": {}
        }
    }                                                           ⟵
}'
# reply
        "highlight" : {
            "content" : [ "<em>Postings</em> Highlighter rocks.", "It stores
  ➥ offsets in <em>postings</em>." ]
        }
[...]
        "highlight" : {
            "content" : [ "<em>Postings</em> are a generic name for the inverted
  ➥ part of the index: term dictionary, term frequencies, term positions." ]
        }
```

> **Query for postings
> in the content
> field; Postings
> Highlighter is used
> automatically.**

You can see from this listing that the highlighted samples are sentences, whether large
or small. The Postings Highlighter will ignore the `fragment_size` option if you set it;
fragments will always be sentences unless you set `number_of_fragments` to 0, in which
case the whole field is treated as one fragment.

> **TIP** If you want to set the highlighter implementation manually, you can do
> so by setting `type` to `plain` (for the Plain Highlighter), `postings` (for the
> Postings Highlighter), or `fvh` (for the Fast Vector Highlighter). This can be
> done globally or per field and is useful if you change your mind about the
> implementation and you don't want to re-index. For example, you index off-
> sets but don't like the sentence-as-fragment approach of the Postings High-
> lighter, so you need a way to get back to using the Plain Highlighter.

Internally, the Postings Highlighter breaks the field into sentences (which then
become fragments) and treats those sentences as separate documents, scoring them
by using BM25 similarity. As we discussed in chapter 6, BM25 is a TF-IDF–based similarity that works well for short fields, like your sentences are supposed to be.

Because of the way it creates and scores fragments, the Postings Highlighter works
well when you're indexing natural language, such as books or blogs. It might not work
so well when you're indexing code, for example, because the concept of a sentence
often doesn't work, and you can end up with the entire field as a single fragment and
no options to reduce the fragment size.

Another downside of the Postings Highlighter is that, at least in version 1.4, it
doesn't work well with phrase queries because it only accounts for individual terms.

For example, in the next listing you'll look for the phrase "Elasticsearch intro" by using a match_phrase query.

Listing C.9 Postings Highlighter matches all the terms and discounts phrases

```
curl -XPUT localhost:9200/test-postings/docs/2 -d '{
  "content": "Elasticsearch intro - first you get an intro of the core
➡ concepts, then we move on to the advanced stuff"
}'
curl localhost:9200/test-postings/_search?pretty -d '{
  "query": {
    "match_phrase": {
      "content": "Elasticsearch intro"
    }
  },
  "highlight": {
    "encoder": "html",
    "fields": {
      "content": {}
    }
  }
}'
# reply
"highlight": {
  "content": ["<em>Elasticsearch</em> <em>intro</em> - first you get an
➡ <em>intro</em> of the core concepts, then we move on to the advanced
    stuff"]
}
curl localhost:9200/test-postings/_search?pretty -d '{
  "query": {
    "match_phrase": {
      "content": "Elasticsearch intro"
    }
  },
  "highlight": {
    "encoder": "html",
    "fields": {
      "content": {
        "type": "plain"
      }
    }
  }
}'
#reply
"highlight" : {
  "content" : [ "<em>Elasticsearch</em> <em>intro</em> - first you get an
➡ intro of the core concepts, then we move on to the advanced stuff" ]
}
```

Second occurrence of intro is highlighted, even though it's not part of the phrase

With the Plain Highlighter, only the phrase is highlighted.

You get individual terms highlighted even if they don't belong to the phrase, which doesn't happen with the Plain Highlighter. On the upside, although indexing offsets increase your index size and slow down indexing a bit, the overhead is lower than what you get when adding term vectors, which are needed by the Fast Vector Highlighter.

C.3.2 *Fast Vector Highlighter*

To enable the Fast Vector Highlighter for a field, you have to set `term_vector` to `with_positions_offsets` in the mapping. This will allow Elasticsearch to identify terms as well as their location in the text without re-analyzing the field content. For large fields—for example, those over 1 MB—the Fast Vector Highlighter is faster than the Plain Highlighter.

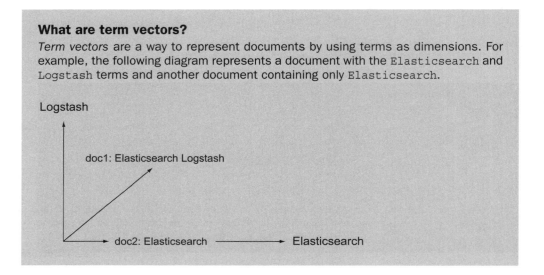

What are term vectors?

Term vectors are a way to represent documents by using terms as dimensions. For example, the following diagram represents a document with the `Elasticsearch` and `Logstash` terms and another document containing only `Elasticsearch`.

Logstash

doc1: Elasticsearch Logstash

doc2: Elasticsearch ⟶ Elasticsearch

Metadata, vectors, and rankings

You can also represent a query as another vector and rank documents based on the distance between the query vector and each document's vector. Another application is to add other metadata to each document—for example, the field's total size—that will influence ranking. For more information about term vectors and their use, go to https://en.wikipedia.org/wiki/Vector_space_model.

For highlighting, this metadata has to be the list of positions and offsets for each term. This is why the Fast Vector Highlighter needs the `with_positions_offsets` setting. Alternative settings are `no` (default), `yes`, `with_positions`, and `with_offsets`.

Compared to the Postings Highlighter, the Fast Vector Highlighter takes up more space and requires more computation during indexing, because both need positions and offsets, but only the Fast Vector Highlighter has to compute the term vectors themselves, which are disabled by default.

When `term_vector` is set to `with_positions_offsets` for a field, Elasticsearch automatically uses the Fast Vector Highlighter for that field. For example, the get-together event and group descriptions from the code samples use this highlighter by default. Here's a relevant snippet from the mapping:

```
"group" : {
  "properties" : {
    "description" : {
      "type" : "string",
      "term_vector": "with_positions_offsets"
```

Compared to the Postings Highlighter, this offers better phrase highlighting. Instead of highlighting every matching term, the Fast Vector Highlighter highlights only terms belonging to the phrase—as the Plain Highlighter did in listing C.9.

The Fast Vector Highlighter also comes with unique functionality:

- It works nicely with multi-fields, because it's able to combine matches from multi-fields into the same set of fragments,
- If there are multiple words to highlight, you can highlight them with different tags.
- You can configure how the boundaries of a fragment are selected.

Let's take a deeper look at each of these features.

HIGHLIGHTING MULTI-FIELDS

You met multi-fields in chapter 3, section 3.3.2, as a way to index the same text in multiple ways. Multi-fields are a great way to refine your searches, but highlighting them properly may be tricky if variations of the same field produce different matches. Take the following listing, for example, where the `description` field is analyzed in two ways: the default is the `english` analyzer, which uses stemming to match `search` with `searching`. The `suffix` subfield uses a custom analyzer that makes use of Edge ngrams to match words with common suffixes, such as `elasticsearch` and `search`. When you do a `multi_match` query on both of them, the Plain Highlighter can match only one field at a time.

Listing C.10 Plain Highlighter doesn't work well with multi-fields

```
curl -XPUT localhost:9200/multi -d '{
  "settings": {
    "analysis": {
      "analyzer": {
        "my-suffix": {
          "tokenizer": "standard",
          "filter": ["lowercase","suffix"]
        }
      },
      "filter": {
        "suffix": {
          "type": "edgeNGram",
          "min_gram": 5,
          "max_gram": 5,
```

Custom analyzer that accounts for only the last five letters of each term

```
                        "side": "back"
                    }
                }
            }
        },
        "mappings": {
            "event": {
                "properties": {
                    "description": {
                        "type": "string",
                        "analyzer": "english",
                        "term_vector": "with_positions_offsets",
                        "fields": {
                            "suffix": {
                                "type": "string",
                                "analyzer": "my-suffix",
                                "term_vector": "with_positions_offsets"
                            }
                        }
                    }
                }
            }
        }
    }'
curl -XPUT localhost:9200/multi/event/1 -d '{
    "description": "elasticsearch is about searching"
}'
curl localhost:9200/multi/_refresh
curl -XGET localhost:9200/multi/event/_search -d'
{
    "query": {
        "multi_match": {
            "query": "search",
            "fields": ["description", "description.suffix"]
        }
    },
    "highlight": {
        "type": "plain",
        "fields": {
            "description": {},
            "description.suffix": {}
        }
    }
}'
# reply
"highlight": {
    "description": ["elasticsearch is about <em>searching</em>"],
    "description.suffix": ["<em>elasticsearch</em> is about searching"]
```

English analyzer does stemming on the default field, matching search with searching

Custom analyzer takes suffixes only, matching elasticsearch with search

Plain Highlighter can highlight only one match or the other.

Here's where the Fast Vector Highlighter comes to the rescue because it can combine both multi-fields into one and highlight all the matches. It only requires term_vector to be set to with_positions_offsets on all the fields you need to highlight (which is the requirement for the Fast Vector Highlighter to work in the first place). You already added this in this listing. To combine multiple subfields into one, you have to indicate which subfields you want to highlight with the `matched_fields` option:

```
"highlight": {
  "fields": {
    "description": {
      "matched_fields": ["description","description.suffix"]
    }
  }
}
```

With the document and the query from listing C.10, you'll have the highlighting that you'd expect:

```
"highlight": {
  "description": ["<em>elasticsearch</em> is about <em>searching</em>"]
```

USING DIFFERENT TAGS FOR DIFFERENT FRAGMENTS

To **bold** the first highlighted word and *italicize* the second, you can specify an array of tags:

```
"highlight": {
  "fields": {
    "description": {
      "pre_tags": ["<b>", "<em>"],
      "post_tags": ["</b>", "</em>"]
```

If there are more than two words to highlight, the Fast Vector Highlighter starts over: bold the third, italicize the fourth, and so on. If you have many words to highlight, you might want to keep track of their number. You can do that by setting `tags_schema` to styled, like in this query:

```
"query": {
  "match": {
    "description": "elasticsearch logstash kibana"
  }
},
"highlight": {
  "tags_schema": "styled",
  "fields": {
    "description": {}
```

If you run it on the documents from the code samples, you'll get the first hit highlighted like this:

```
"highlight": {
    "description": [
        "for what <em class=\"hlt1\">Elasticsearch</em> is and how
  it can be used for logging with <em class=\"hlt2\">Logstash</em> as well
  as <em class=\"hlt3\">Kibana</em>!"
```

This allows you to take the class name (`hltX`) and figure out which words matched first, second, and so on.

CONFIGURING BOUNDARY CHARACTERS

Recall from section C.2.1 that we said `fragment_size` is approximate because Elasticsearch tries to make sure words aren't truncated. If you thought then that the explanation is a bit vague, it's because the behavior depends on the highlighter implementation.

With the Postings Highlighter, fragment size is irrelevant because it breaks the text down into sentences. The Plain Highlighter adds terms around the highlighted term until it gets close to the fragment size, which means the boundary is always a term. As you've seen in the listings of this chapter, this works well for natural language, but it might become problematic in other use cases where the word and term concepts don't overlap. For example, if you're indexing code, you may have variable definitions like this:

```
variable_with_a_very_very_very_very_long_name = 1
```

To search this kind of text effectively, you'll need an analyzer that can break this long variable and allow you to search for terms within it.

> **TIP**   You can do this with the Pattern Tokenizer, where you specify a pattern that includes underscores—for example, (\\ |_)—which will tokenize on spaces and underscores. In chapter 5 you'll find more information about analyzers and tokenizers.

If the analyzer will break the variable into tokens, the Plain Highlighter will break it, too, even if you don't want it to. For example, a search for `long` with a fragment size of 20 would give you this:

```
_very_very_very_very_<em>long</em>_name = 1
```

The Fast Vector Highlighter works differently because words aren't the same as terms. Words are strings delimited by the following characters: . , ! ? \t\n. You can change the list through the `boundary_chars` option. When it builds fragments, it seeks those characters for `boundary_max_scan` characters (defaults to 20) from the limits that are normally set by `fragment_size`. If it doesn't find such boundary characters while scanning, the fragment is truncated. By default, the Fast Vector Highlighter will truncate the code sample while highlighting `long`:

```
ry_very_<em>long</em>_name = 1
```

You can fix this by changing the defaults in two ways. One is to add the underscore to the list of boundary characters. This will still truncate the variable but in a more predictable way:

```
"highlight": {
  "fields": {
    "description": {
```

```
      "fragment_size": 20,
      "boundary_chars": ".,!? \t\n_"
# will yield
very_very_<em>long</em>_name = 1
```

The other option is to leave `boundary_chars` set to the default and extend `boundary_max_scan` instead, which will increase the chances of having the whole variable included in the fragment, even if it implies a higher fragment size for this particular fragment:

```
variable_with_a_very_very_very_very_<em>long</em>_name = 1
```

Issues with fragment boundaries are typically visible when you need small fragments. For bigger chunks, inaccurate boundaries are less likely to be visible to users because their attention tends to focus on the highlighted bits and the words around them, not on the fragment as a whole. Another parameter to configure for the Fast Vector Highlighter is the `fragment_offset`. With this parameter you can control the margin to start the highlighting from.

LIMITING THE NUMBER OF MATCHES FOR THE FAST VECTOR HIGHLIGHTER

The final configuration option we discuss is the `phrase_limit` parameter. If the Fast Vector Highlighter matches many phrases, it could consume a lot of memory. By default, only the 256 first matches are used. You can change this amount using the `phrase_limit` parameter.

appendix D
Elasticsearch
monitoring plugins

The Elasticsearch community offers a wide array of monitoring plugins that make it easier to manage cluster state and indices and to perform queries via attractive user interfaces. Many of these plugins are available freely and are in active development thanks to well-documented plugin and REST APIs and the ever-vibrant Elasticsearch community.

In this section, we'll cover a few of the most popular plugins available:

- Bigdesk
- ElasticHQ
- Head
- Kopf
- Elasticsearch Marvel

Each of these plugins is well documented and actively supported by either the open-source community or, in the case of Elasticsearch Marvel or Sematext SPM, Elastic, Inc. and Sematext, Inc., respectively. Often the question of which monitoring or management interface to choose is a personal one. If it's commercial support you're looking for, the decision is a binary one. Both Marvel and Sematext, in this regard, are affordable and actively maintained/backed by proven companies. Sematext has the additional benefit of offering more than Elasticsearch monitoring, but unless you're looking for sitewide monitoring of your infrastructure, the choice becomes clearer. Bigdesk, ElasticHQ, Head, and Kopf share many similarities in functionality, making your decision a bit trickier. Because this batch of solutions is

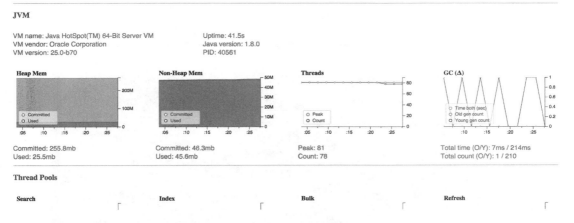

Figure D.1   Website: http://bigdesk.org/ License: Apache License v2.0

either hosted or installable within minutes, it has been our experience that most users simply try each until they find the one that's best for them. Sometimes it all comes down to the ease of use of the user interface.

D.1   *Bigdesk: visualize your cluster*

Bigdesk, shown in figure D.1, is the creation of Lukáš Vlček and has provided a solid monitoring plugin user interface since version 0.17.0 of Elasticsearch. Bigdesk offers live charts and statistics, allowing you to visualize changes occurring across your cluster in real time.

One of the most desirable features of Bigdesk, and a rarity among most of the available plugins, is the ability to visualize your cluster topography. The cluster you built using the get-together application in the book is shown in figure D.2.

This feature is rather fine-grained in that it allows you to see nodes, shards, and indices deployed across your cluster in great detail.

Because Bigdesk communicates via the Elasticsearch REST API, you can use it in three ways:

- As a server-side installed plugin
- From the Bigdesk.org website: http://bigdesk.org
- Downloaded and installed locally

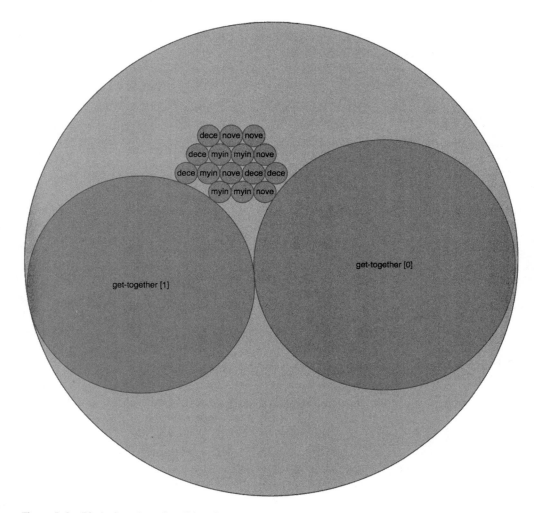

Figure D.2   Bigdesk makes visualizing the get-together cluster easy.

D.2   *ElasticHQ: monitoring with management*

ElasticHQ offers a real-time analytics display for monitoring; the ability to create, edit, and delete aliases, mappings, and indices for management; and a query interface for easy searching on Elasticsearch clusters. This is a recent trend, in that many of the monitoring plugins are now branching out into management and query interfaces for testing and maintenance. Figure D.3 shows the main index-management screen

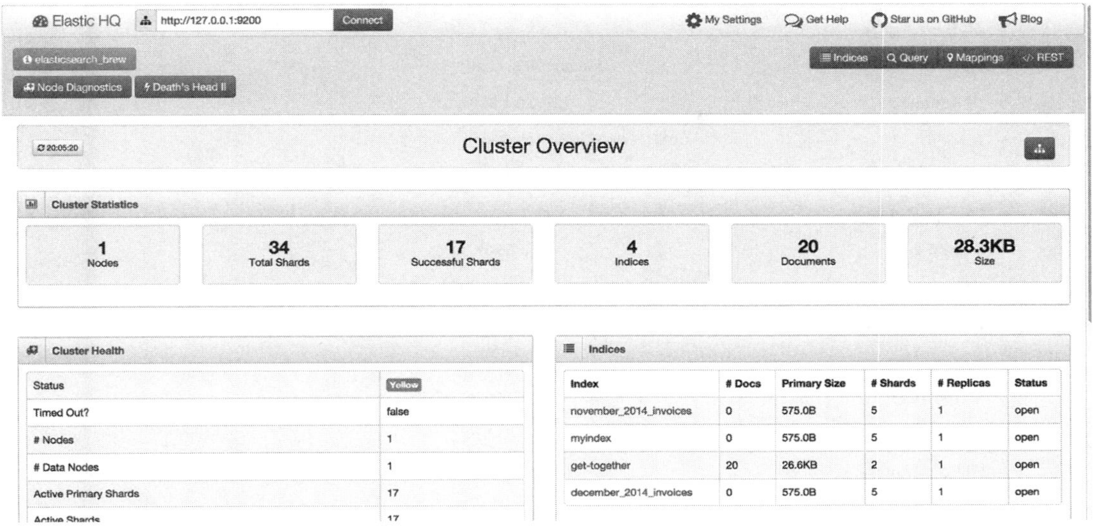

Figure D.3   Website: www.elastichq.org/ License: Apache License v2.0

for ElasticHQ, which allows users to modify their indices in real time via an easy-to-use interface.

More than just a real-time monitoring plugin, it allows the creation of indices and mappings, and it includes a query interface and a REST UI that allows you to tinker with the Elasticsearch endpoint requests.

By far, the most useful feature of this plugin is its ability to diagnose your cluster, applying rules that can alert you to the source of problems within your cluster. These diagnostic rules measure the values of process, operating-system, and UI variables in Elasticsearch and trigger warnings and alerts if they exceed a certain threshold, as shown in figure D.4.

Because ElasticHQ communicates via the Elasticsearch REST API, it can be used in three ways:

- As a server-side installed plugin
- From the ElasticHQ.org website: www.elastichq.org
- Downloaded and installed locally

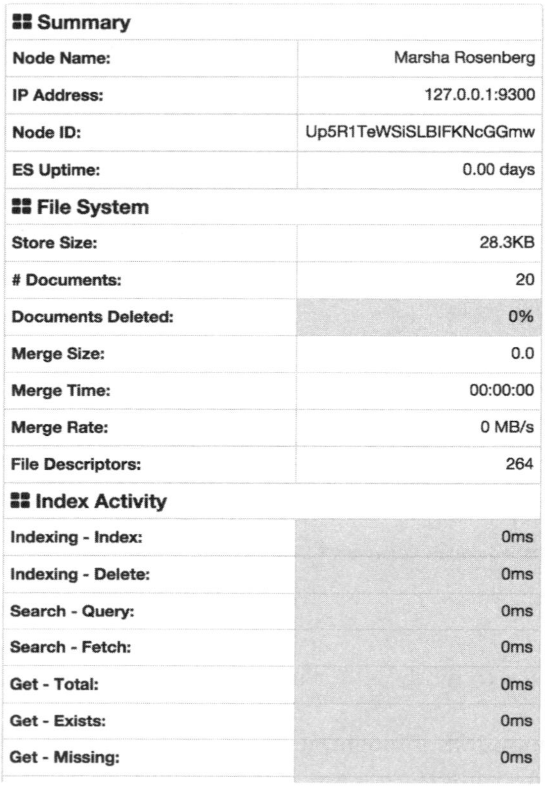

⠿ Summary	
Node Name:	Marsha Rosenberg
IP Address:	127.0.0.1:9300
Node ID:	Up5R1TeWSiSLBIFKNcGGmw
ES Uptime:	0.00 days
⠿ File System	
Store Size:	28.3KB
# Documents:	20
Documents Deleted:	0%
Merge Size:	0.0
Merge Time:	00:00:00
Merge Rate:	0 MB/s
File Descriptors:	264
⠿ Index Activity	
Indexing - Index:	0ms
Indexing - Delete:	0ms
Search - Query:	0ms
Search - Fetch:	0ms
Get - Total:	0ms
Get - Exists:	0ms
Get - Missing:	0ms

Figure D.4   Node diagnostics screen

D.3   *Head: advanced query building*

The Head plugin was one of the first on the scene. Even though it's been around the longest and its user interface hasn't changed much, it's still in active development, adding new features and supporting newer versions of Elasticsearch.

Head has an easy-to-use interface (shown in figure D.5) and features a powerful query-builder tool that allows you to create complex queries without the need for cURL or manually crafting them in a command-line REST tool.

Head can be run in two ways:

- As a server-side installed plugin
- Downloaded and installed locally: https://github.com/mobz/elasticsearch-head

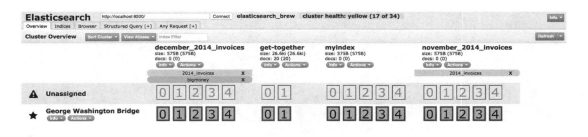

Figure D.5   Website: https://github.com/mobz/elasticsearch-head License: Apache License v2.0

D.4   *Kopf: snapshots, warmers, and percolators*

Kopf, a German word that translates to "head" in English, is a relative newcomer on the scene, offering a complete administrative interface to Elasticsearch via an easy-to-use and attractive UI, shown in figure D.6.

Kopf contains many features that some of the other plugins listed here do not, such as access to the snapshots, percolator, and warmer APIs. Both the percolator and warmer user interfaces come in handy for users wanting to use these features without having to learn all of the API commands. Kopf even includes a REST user interface for those who want tighter control over their administrative interactions with their Elasticsearch instance, allowing users to execute formatter JSON requests to a running cluster.

Kopf can be run in the following ways:

- As a server-side plugin
- Online at http://lmenezes.com/elasticsearch-kopf/
- Downloaded and installed locally

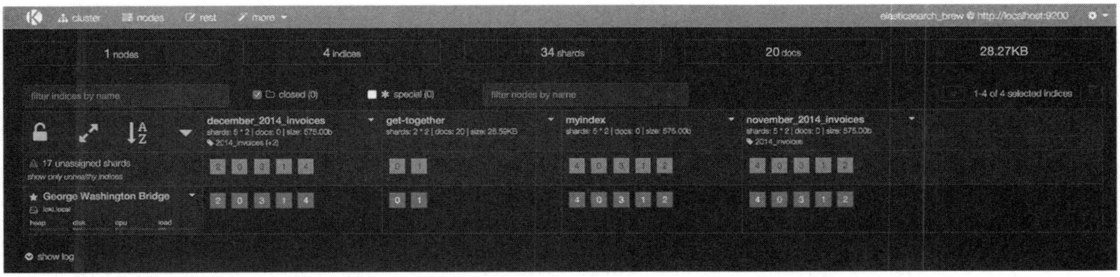

Figure D.6   Website: https://github.com/lmenezes/elasticsearch-kopf License: MIT

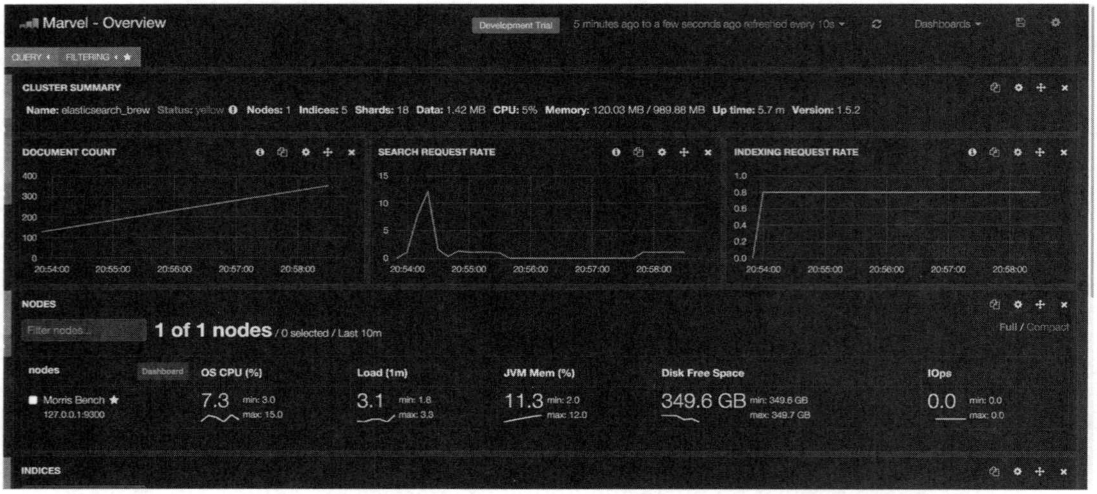

Figure D.7   Website: www.elastics.co/overview/marvel/ License: Commercial

D.5   *Marvel: fine-grained analysis*

Elasticsearch Marvel is a commercial monitoring solution offered by Elasticsearch. It's a visually appealing user interface (shown in figure D.7), allowing for deep insight into your running cluster, such as drill-down views of OS, JVM, search, and index request performance.

As a server-side installed plugin, Marvel has the advantage of providing historical data analysis, as well as real-time performance information on cache sizes, memory details, and thread pools.

As far as REST API interfaces go, Marvel contains the most powerful set of features with advanced functionality, such as context-sensitive suggestions and autocompletion of terms and endpoints (figure D.8).

At the time of this writing, Marvel is available free for development use. A production install of Marvel begins at $1000/year for the first five nodes. Elasticsearch Marvel is available only as a server-side installation because of its ability to store and analyze historic data. The manner of installation differs from the previously mentioned plugins; Marvel must be installed directly on the server and accessed via a web browser.

D.6   *Sematext SPM: the Swiss Army knife*

Sematext has long been known as a provider of cloud-hosted centralized log management. In recent years, its product portfolio has expanded into the world of real-time performance monitoring for distributed systems, including Elasticsearch. Sematext SPM,

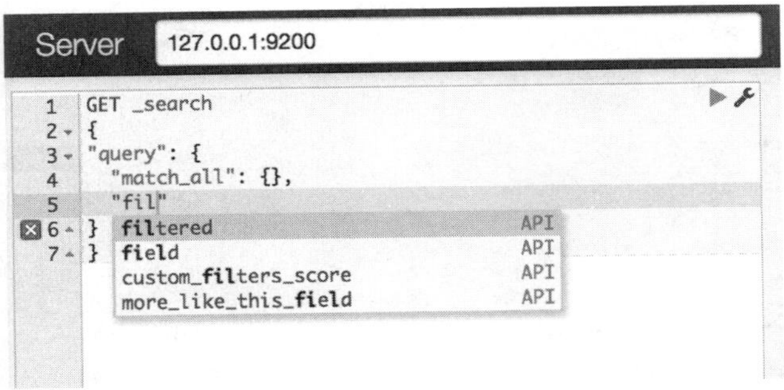

Figure D.8 Autocompletion of REST calls

shown in figure D.9, offers performance monitoring, querying capabilities, alerting, and anomaly detection in a cloud or on-premise offering.

SPM goes a step beyond the solutions mentioned previously by offering a rich set of alerts and notification settings for Elasticsearch and across other infrastructure you may have deployed, such as Apache Kafka, NGINX, Hadoop, MySQL, and others. Alerts can be email-based, and they can post the alert data to another web service or even integrate with other monitoring or collaboration applications, such as Atlassian HipChat or Nagios.

Still, what appeals to us most about SPM is the all-in-one performance monitoring dashboard idea, allowing users to see the big picture across every piece of their deployed architecture or simply drill down into the real-time metrics being gathered

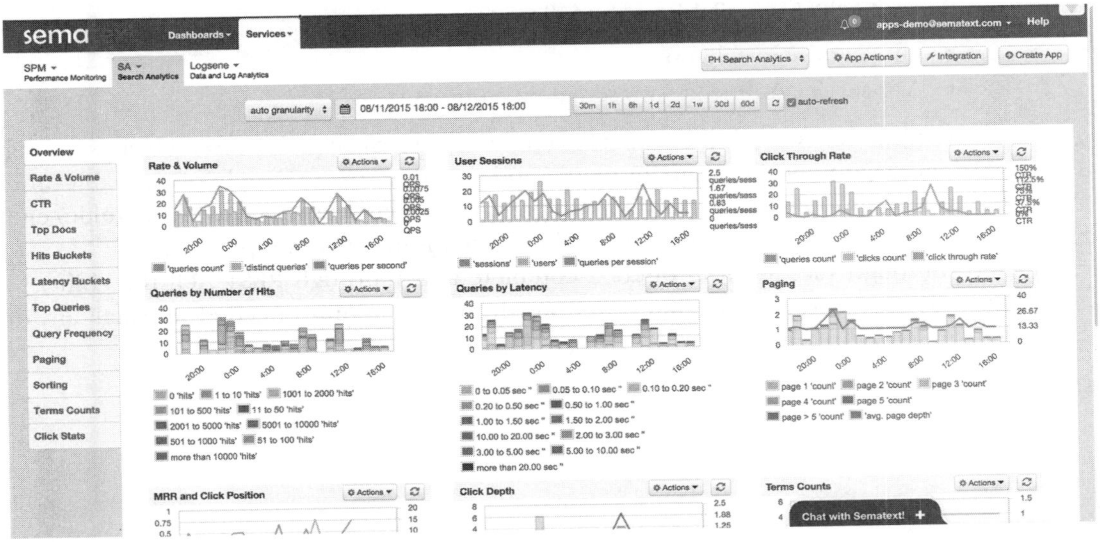

Figure D.9 Website: www.sematext.com License: Commercial

Application Alerts

Alerts   Alert Rules   Notification Transports   PagerDuty   Nagios   WebHooks   HipChat

Alerts

Integrate with PagerDuty »

Show 10 ⇕

Search by message:

Message ⇕	When ▾	Sent ⇕	Back to normal ⇕
The avg(nodes) < 2.0 for 300 seconds for application Event.Prod.Elasticsearch . Current value is 1.91. Triggered at 07-14-2015 06:42:00 UTC.	1 month ago	No	No
The avg(nodes) < 2.0 for 300 seconds for application Event.Prod.Elasticsearch . Current value is 1.73. Triggered at 07-14-2015 06:41:00 UTC.	1 month ago	No	No
The avg(nodes) < 2.0 for 300 seconds for application Event.Prod.Elasticsearch . Current value is 1.60. Triggered at 07-14-2015 06:40:00 UTC.	1 month ago	No	No
The avg(nodes) < 2.0 for 300 seconds for application Event.Prod.Elasticsearch . Current value is 1.40. Triggered at 07-14-2015 06:39:00 UTC.	1 month ago	No	No
The avg(nodes) < 2.0 for 300 seconds for application Event.Prod.Elasticsearch . Current value is 1.18. Triggered at 07-14-2015 06:38:00 UTC.	1 month ago	No	No
The avg(nodes) < 2.0 for 300 seconds for application Event.Prod.Elasticsearch . Current value is 1.00. Triggered at 07-14-2015 06:37:00 UTC.	1 month ago	No	No
The avg(nodes) < 2.0 for 300 seconds for application Event.Prod.Elasticsearch . Current value is 1.00. Triggered at 07-14-2015 06:36:00 UTC.	1 month ago	No	No
The avg(nodes) < 2.0 for 300 seconds for application Event.Prod.Elasticsearch . Current value is 1.00. Triggered at 07-14-2015 06:35:00 UTC.	1 month ago	No	No
The avg(nodes) < 2.0 for 300 seconds for application Event.Prod.Elasticsearch . Current value is 1.00. Triggered at 07-14-2015 06:34:00 UTC.	1 month ago	No	No
The avg(nodes) < 2.0 for 300 seconds for application Event.Prod.Elasticsearch . Current value is 1.00. Triggered at 07-14-2015 06:33:00 UTC.	1 month ago	No	No

Showing 1 to 10 of 24 entries

First   Previous   1   2   3   Next   Last

Figure D.10   Alerts and notifications configuration

on their Elasticsearch cluster (see figure D.10). That being said, SPM isn't free like some of the other options we discussed, but the pricing is variable depending on usage (cpu/hour) and can be found here: http://sematext.com/spm/index.html.

Sematext SPM is available in the following ways:

- On-premise installation
- As-a-service online at www.sematext.com

This appendix covered just a small sample of the existing Elasticsearch monitoring and management solutions available today. The current batch of available and community-supported monitoring plugins can be found at www.elastic.co/guide/en/elasticsearch/reference/current/modules-plugins.html#known-plugins.

Although Elasticsearch offers a complete and thorough REST API, the ability to visualize live and historic data is well worth the few minutes needed to install any of the plugins discussed here.

appendix E
Turning search upside down with the percolator

The Elasticsearch percolator is typically defined as "search upside down" for the following reasons:

- You index queries instead of documents. This registers the query in memory, so it can be quickly run later.
- You send a document to Elasticsearch instead of a query. This is called percolating a document, basically indexing it into a small, in-memory index. Registered queries are run against the small index, so Elasticsearch finds out which queries match.
- You get back a list of queries matching the document, instead of the other way around like a regular search.

The typical use case for percolation is alerting. As shown in figure E.1, you can notify users when new documents (matching their interests) appear.

As the figure shows, using the get-together site example we've used throughout the book, you could let members define their interests, and you'd save them as percolator queries. When a new event is added, you can percolate it against those queries. Whenever there are matches, you can send emails to the respective users to notify them of new events relevant to their interests.

Next, we'll describe how to implement those alerts using the percolator. After that, we'll explain how it works under the hood, and then we'll move on to performance and functionality tricks.

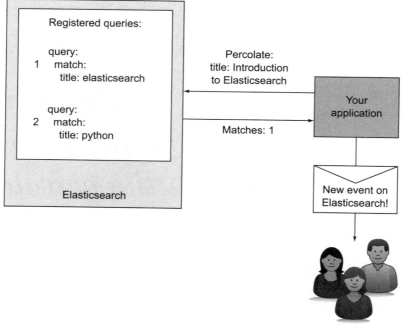

Figure E.1   Typical use case: percolating a document enables the application to send alerts to users if their stored queries match the document.

E.1   *Percolator basics*

There are three steps needed for percolation:

1 Make sure there's a mapping in place for all the fields referenced by the registered queries.
2 Register the queries themselves.
3 Percolate documents.

Figure E.2 shows these steps.

We'll take a closer look at these three steps next, and then we'll move on to how the percolator works and what its limitations are.

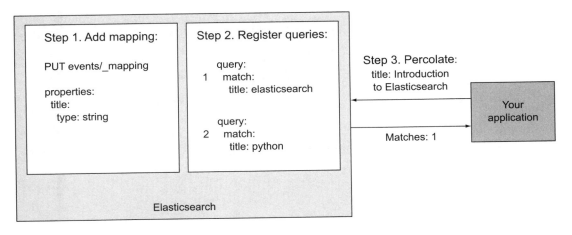

Figure E.2 You need a mapping and some registered queries in order to percolate documents.

E.1.1 *Define a mapping, register queries, then percolate documents*

Assume you want to send alerts for any new events about the Elasticsearch percolator. Before registering queries, you need a mapping for all the fields you run queries on. In the case of our get-together example, you might already have mappings for groups and events if you ran populate.sh from the code samples. If you didn't do that already, you can download the code samples from https://github.com/dakrone/elasticsearch-in-action so you can run populate.sh.

With the data from the code samples in place, you can register a query looking for `Elasticsearch Percolator` in the `title` field. You already have the mapping for `title` in place because you ran populate.sh:

```
% curl -XPUT 'localhost:9200/get-together/.percolator/1' -d '{
  "query": {
    "match": {
      "title": "elasticsearch percolator"
    }
  }
}'
```

Note that the body of your request is the `match` query, but to register it, you have to send it through a `PUT` request as you would while adding a document. To let Elasticsearch know this isn't your average document but a percolator query, you have to specify the `.percolator` type.

> **NOTE** As you might expect, you can add as many queries as you want, at any point in time. The percolator is real time, so a new query will account for percolation right after it's added.

With your mapping and queries in place, you can start percolating documents. To do that, you'll hit the _percolate endpoint of the type where the document would go and put the contents of the document under the doc field:

```
% curl 'localhost:9200/get-together/event/_percolate?pretty' -d '{
  "doc": {
    "title": "Discussion on Elasticsearch Percolator"
  }
}'
```

You'll get back a list of matching queries, identified by the index name and ID:

```
"total" : 1,
"matches" : [ {
  "_index" : "get-together",
  "_id" : "1"
} ]
```

> **TIP** If you have lots of queries registered in the same index, you might want only the IDs to shorten the reply. To do that, add the percolate_format=ids parameter to the request URI.

Next, let's look at how the percolator works and what kind of limitations you can expect.

E.1.2   *Percolator under the hood*

In the percolation you just did, Elasticsearch loaded the registered query and ran it against a tiny, in-memory index containing the document you percolated. If you had registered more queries, all of them would have been run on that tiny index.

REGISTERING QUERIES

It's convenient that in Elasticsearch, queries are normally expressed in JSON, just as documents are; when you register a query, it's stored in the .percolator type of the index you point it to. This is good for durability because those queries would be stored like any other documents. In addition to storing the query, Elasticsearch loads it in memory so it can be executed quickly.

> **WARNING** Because registered queries are parsed and kept in memory, you need to make sure you have enough heap on each node to hold those queries. As we'll see in section E.2.2 of this appendix, one way to deal with large amounts of queries would be to use a separate index (or more indices) for percolation. This way you can scale out with percolation independent of the actual data.

UNREGISTERING QUERIES

To unregister a query, you have to delete it from the index using the .percolator type and the ID of the query:

```
% curl -XDELETE 'localhost:9200/get-together/.percolator/1'
```

Because queries are also loaded in memory, deleting a query doesn't always unregister the query. A delete-by-ID does remove the percolation query from the memory, but as of version 1.4, a delete-by-query request doesn't unregister matching queries from memory. For that to happen, you'd need to reopen the index; for example:

```
% curl -XDELETE 'localhost:9200/get-together/.percolator/_query?q=*:*'
# right now, any deleted queries are still in memory
% curl -XPOST 'localhost:9200/get-together/_close'
% curl -XPOST 'localhost:9200/get-together/_open'
# now they're unregistered from memory, too
```

PERCOLATING DOCUMENTS

When you percolate a document, that document is first indexed in an in-memory index; then all registered queries are run against that index to see which ones match.

Because you can only percolate one Elasticsearch document at a time, as of version 1.4 the parent-child queries you saw in chapter 8 don't work with percolator because they imply multiple documents. Plus, you can always add new children to the same parent, so it's difficult to keep all relevant data in the in-memory index.

By contrast, nested queries work because nested documents are always indexed together in the same Elasticsearch document. You can see such an example in the following listing, where you'll percolate events with attendee names as nested documents.

Listing E.1   Using percolator with nested attendee names

```
curl -XPUT 'localhost:9200/get-together/_mapping/nested-events' -d '{
  "properties": {
    "title": { "type": "string" },
    "attendee-name": {                          Defining attendee-name
      "type": "nested",                         as nested
      "properties": {
        "first": { "type": "string" },
        "last": { "type": "string" }
      }
    }
  }
}'
curl -XPUT 'localhost:9200/get-together/.percolator/1' -d '{
  "query": {
    "nested": { "path": "attendee-name",        Registering a
      "query": {                                nested query
        "bool": {
          "must": [
            { "match": {
                "attendee-name.first": "Lee"
            }},
            { "match": {
                "attendee-name.last": "Hinman"
            }}
          ]
        }
      }
    }
```

```
        }
      }
    }
  }'
curl 'localhost:9200/get-together/nested-events/_percolate?pretty' -d '{
  "doc": {
    "title": "Percolator works with nested documents",
    "attendee-name": [
      { "first": "Lee", "last": "Hinman" },        ◁───┐ This nested document
      { "first": "Radu", "last": "Gheorghe" },           will match the
      { "first": "Roy", "last": "Russo" }                registered query.
    ]
  }
}'
```

As the number of queries grows, percolating a single document requires more CPU. That's why it's important to register cheap queries wherever possible; for example, by using ngrams instead of wildcards or regular expressions. You can look back at chapter 10 for performance tips, and section 10.4.1 describes the tradeoff between ngrams and wildcards.

Percolation performance may be a concern for you, and in the next section we'll show you percolator-specific tips depending on your use case.

E.2   Performance tips

For different percolator use cases, there are different things you can do to improve performance. In this section, we'll look at the most important techniques and divide them into two categories:

- *Optimizations to the format of the request or the reply*—You can percolate existing documents, percolate multiple documents in one request, and ask for only the number of matching queries, instead of the whole list of IDs.
- *Optimizations to the way you organize queries*—As we mentioned earlier, you can use one or more separate indices to store registered queries. Here, you'll apply this advice, and we'll also look at how you can use routing and filtering to reduce the number of queries being run for each percolation.

E.2.1   Options for requests and replies

In some use cases, you can get away with fewer requests or less data going through the network. Here, we'll look at three ways to achieve this:

- Percolating existing documents
- Using multi percolate, which is the bulk API of percolation
- Counting the number of matching queries instead of getting the full list

PERCOLATING EXISTING DOCUMENTS

This works well if what you percolate is what you index, especially if documents are big. For example, if you index blogs, it might be slow to send every post twice over HTTP: once for indexing and once for alerting subscribers of posts matching their interests. In such cases, indexing a document and then percolating it by ID, instead of submitting it again, makes sense.

> **NOTE** Percolating existing documents doesn't work well for all use cases. For example, if social media posts have a geo point field, you can register geo queries matching each country's area. This way, you can percolate each post to determine its country of origin and add this information to the post before indexing it. In such use cases, you need to percolate and then index; it doesn't make sense to do it the other way around. The use case to determine the country of origin is described in the following blog post by Elastic: www.elastic.co/blog/using-percolator-geo-tagging/.

In the next listing, you'll register a query for groups matching `elasticsearch`. Then you'll percolate the group with ID 2 (Elasticsearch Denver), which is already indexed, instead of sending its content all over again.

Listing E.2 Percolating an existing group document

```
curl -XPUT 'localhost:9200/get-together/.percolator/2' -d '{
  "query": {
    "match": {                              Query matching groups about
      "name": "elasticsearch"               Elasticsearch; the .percolator ID 2
    }                                       is not related to group ID 2.
  }
}'
curl 'localhost:9200/get-together/group/2/_percolate?pretty'   ◁─┤ Percolating the
                                                                   existing Elasticsearch
                                                                   Denver group (ID 2)
```

MULTI PERCOLATE API

Whether you percolate existing documents or not, you can do multiple percolations at once. This works well if you also index in bulks. For example, you can use the percolator for some automated tagging of blog posts by having one query for each tag. When a batch of posts arrives, you can do as shown in figure E.3:

1. Percolate them all at once through the multi percolate API. Then, in your application, append matching tags. Be aware that the percolate API returns only the IDs of the matching queries. Your application has to map the IDs of the percolation queries to the tags, so it has to map 1 to `elasticsearch`, 2 to `release`, and 3 to `book`. Another approach would be to give the percolation queries the ID equal to the tag.
2. Finally, index all posts at once through the bulk API we introduced in chapter 10.

Be aware that sending the document twice, once for percolation and once for indexing, does imply more network traffic. The advantage would be that you wouldn't have to re-index the document if you added the tag using an update. That would be the alternative if you indexed the document first, did the percolation by ID, and used the multi update API to update the indexed documents.

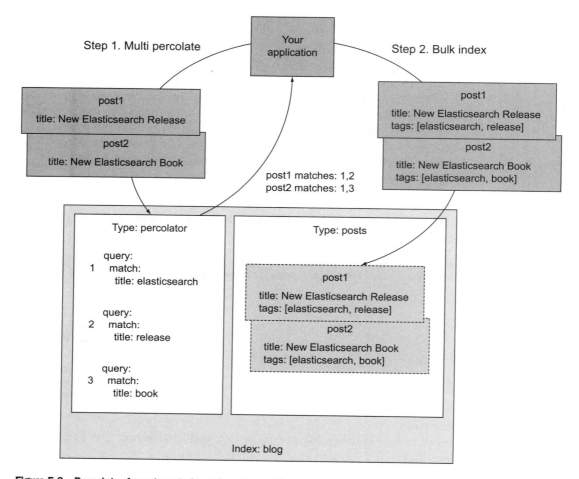

Figure E.3   Percolator for automated tagging. The multi percolate and bulk APIs reduce the number of requests. Before step 1, the percolation queries have been indexed. In step 1 you use the multi percolate API to find matching percolation queries. The application maps the IDs to the tags and adds them to the documents to index. In step 2 you use the bulk index API to index the documents.

In the following listing you'll apply what's described in figure E.3.

Listing E.3   Using the multi percolate and bulk APIs for automated tagging

```
curl -XPUT localhost:9200/blog -d '{
  "mappings": {
    "posts": {
      "properties": {
        "title": {
          "type": "string"
        }
```
| Create the index first, with the
| mapping for the title field.

```
            }
          }
        }
      }
    }'
    echo '{"index" : {"_index" : "blog", "_type" : ".percolator", "_id": "1"}}
    {"query": {"match": {"title": "elasticsearch"}}}
    {"index" : {"_index" : "blog", "_type" : ".percolator", "_id": "2"}}
    {"query": {"match": {"title": "release"}}}
    {"index" : {"_index" : "blog", "_type" : ".percolator", "_id": "3"}}
    {"query": {"match": {"title": "book"}}}
    ' > bulk_requests_queries
    curl 'localhost:9200/_bulk?pretty' --data-binary @bulk_requests_queries
    echo '{"percolate" : {"index" : "blog", "type" : "posts"}}
    {"doc": {"title": "New Elasticsearch Release"}}
    {"percolate" : {"index" : "blog", "type" : "posts"}}
    {"doc": {"title": "New Elasticsearch Book"}}
    ' > perc_requests
    curl 'localhost:9200/_mpercolate?pretty' --data-binary @perc_requests
    echo '{"index" : {"_index" : "blog", "_type" : "posts"}}
    {"title": "New Elasticsearch Release", "tags": ["elasticsearch", "release"]}
    {"index" : {"_index" : "blog", "_type" : "posts"}}
    {"title": "New Elasticsearch Book", "tags": ["elasticsearch", "book"]}
    ' > bulk_requests
    curl 'localhost:9200/_bulk?pretty' --data-binary @bulk_requests
```

can use the bulk API to ster queries, ust as you've ed the index API so far.

lti percolate will return matches for each percolated document.

Knowing which tag corresponds to which post, you can index posts with tags, too.

Note how similar the multi percolate API is to the bulk API:

- Every request takes two lines in the request body.
- The first line shows the operation (percolate) and identification information (index, type, and for existing documents, the ID). Note that the bulk API uses underscores like _index and _type, but multi percolate doesn't (index and type).
- The second line contains metadata. You'd put the document in there under the doc field. When you're percolating existing documents, the metadata JSON would be empty.
- Finally, the body of the request is sent to the _mpercolate endpoint. As with the bulk API, this endpoint can contain the index and the type name, which can later be omitted from the body.

GETTING ONLY THE NUMBER OF MATCHING QUERIES

Besides the percolate action, the multi percolate API supports a count action, which will return the same reply as before with the total number of matching queries for each document, but you won't get the matches array:

```
echo '{"count" : {"index" : "blog", "type" : "posts"}}
{"doc": {"title": "New Elasticsearch Release"}}
{"count" : {"index" : "blog", "type" : "posts"}}
{"doc": {"title": "New Elasticsearch Book"}}
' > percolate_requests
curl 'localhost:9200/_mpercolate?pretty' --data-binary @percolate_requests
```

Using count doesn't make sense for the tagging use case, because you need to know which queries match, but this might not be the case everywhere. Let's say you have an online shop and you want to add a new item. If you collect user queries and register them for percolation, you can percolate new items against those queries to predict how many users will find them while searching.

In the get-together site example, you could get an idea of how many attendees to expect for an event before submitting it—assuming you can get each user's availability and register time ranges as queries.

You can, of course, get counts for individual percolations, not just multi percolations. Add /count to the _percolate endpoint:

```
% curl 'localhost:9200/get-together/event/_percolate/count?pretty' -d '{
  "doc": {
    "title": "Discussion on Elasticsearch Percolator"
  }
}'
```

Counting will help with performance the more queries match because Elasticsearch won't have to load all their IDs in memory and send them over the network. But if you have many queries to begin with, you might want to look into keeping them in separate indices and make sure you run only the relevant ones. We'll look at how you can do that next.

E.2.2 *Separating and filtering percolator queries*

If you're registering lots of queries and/or percolating lots of documents, you're probably looking for scaling and performance tips. Here we'll discuss the most important ones:

- *Keep percolations in a separate index.* This lets you scale them separately from the rest of your data, especially if you store these indices in a separate Elasticsearch cluster.
- *Reduce the number of queries run for each percolation.* Strategies include routing and filtering.

USING SEPARATE INDICES FOR PERCOLATOR

When you register queries in a separate index, the thing to keep in mind is to define a mapping for all the fields you want to query. In the get-together example, if you want percolator queries to run on the title field, you need to define it in the mapping. You can do this while creating the index, at which time you can also specify other index-specific settings, such as the number of shards:

```
% curl -XPUT 'localhost:9200/attendance-percolate' -d '{
  "settings": {
    "number_of_shards": 4
  },
  "mappings": {
    "event": {
```

```
      "properties": {
        "title": {
          "type": "string"
        }
      }
    }
  }
}'
```

Your new attendance-percolate index has four shards, compared to the existing get-together index with two. This means you can potentially run a single percolation on up to four nodes. Such an index can also be stored in a separate Elasticsearch cluster so that percolations don't take CPU away from the queries you'd run on the get-together index.

Once your separate index is set up with the mapping, you'd register queries and run percolations in the same way you did in section E.1.1:

```
% curl -XPUT 'localhost:9200/attendance-percolate/.percolator/1' -d '{
  "query": {
    "match": {
      "title": "elasticsearch percolator"
    }
  }
}'
% curl 'localhost:9200/attendance-percolate/event/_percolate?pretty' -d '{
  "doc": {
    "title": "Discussion on Elasticsearch Percolator"
  }
}'
```

Most of the scaling strategies you saw in chapter 9 apply to percolator as well. You can use multiple indices—for example, one per customer—to make sure you run only the queries that are relevant for each percolation. You can also use aliases to limit the customer in your query; that way you overcome the too-many-indices problem if each customer gets their own index.

USING PERCOLATOR WITH ROUTING

Percolator also supports routing, another scaling strategy discussed in chapter 9. Routing works well when you have many nodes as well as many users running many percolations. Routing lets you keep each user's queries in a single shard, avoiding the excessive chatter between nodes shown in figure E.4.

> **NOTE** The main downside of routing is that shards might become imbalanced because queries won't be distributed randomly as they are by default. If you have some users with more queries than others, their shards might become bigger and thus more difficult to scale. See chapter 9 for more information.

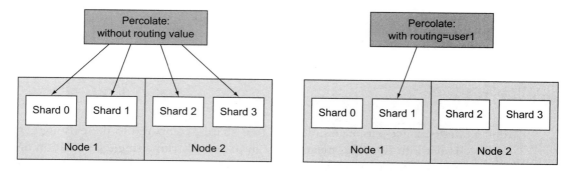

Figure E.4   A percolate request with routing reduces the number of queries and also hits fewer shards.

To use routing, you'd register queries with a `routing` value:

```
% curl -XPUT 'localhost:9200/\
attendance-percolate/.percolator/1?routing=radu' -d '{
  "query": {
    "match": {
      "title": "Elasticsearch Aggregations"
    }
  }
}'
```

Then you'd percolate with routing by specifying the same value:

```
% curl 'localhost:9200/\
attendance-percolate/event/_percolate?routing=radu&pretty' -d '{
  "doc": {
    "title": "Introduction to Aggregations"
  }
}'
```

Or you'd percolate against all registered queries by omitting the `routing` value. Beware that you'll lose the advantage of sending the queries to appropriate shards only:

```
% curl 'localhost:9200/attendance-percolate/event/_percolate?pretty' -d '{
  "doc": {
    "title": "Introduction to Aggregations"
  }
}'
```

FILTERING REGISTERED QUERIES

Percolator performance depends directly on the number of queries being run, and filtering can help keeping this number at bay.

Typically, you'd add some metadata next to the query and filter on it. The names for these fields can be chosen freely. Because these fields are metadata fields and not part of the documents to match, these fields aren't added to the mapping. For example, you can tag queries for events:

```
% curl -XPUT 'localhost:9200/\
attendance-percolate/.percolator/1' -d '{
  "query": {
    "match": {
      "title": "introduction to aggregations"
    }
  },
  "tags": ["elasticsearch"]
}
```

Then, when percolating documents, add a filter for that tag to make sure only the relevant queries are being run:

```
% curl 'localhost:9200/attendance-percolate/event/_percolate?pretty' -d '{
  "doc": {
    "title": "nesting aggregations"
  },
  "filter": {
    "term": {
      "tags": "elasticsearch"
    }
  }
}'
```

Alternatively, you can filter on the query itself. This requires a mapping change because the query object isn't indexed by default, as if the mapping for the .percolator type looked like this:

```
".percolator": {
  "properties": {
    "query": {
      "type": "object",
      "enabled": false
    }
  }
}
```

TIP You can find more information about objects and their options in chapter 7, section 7.1.

In the next listing, you'll change the mapping to enable the query object and then use the filter on the query string itself.

> **Listing E.4 Filtering queries by their content**

```
curl -XPUT 'localhost:9200/smart-percolate' -d '{
  "mappings": {
    "event": {
```

```
        "properties": {
      "title": { "type": "string" }
        }
      },
      ".percolator": {
        "properties": {
      "query": { "type": "object", "enabled": true }
        }
      }
    }
  }
}'
curl -XPUT 'localhost:9200/smart-percolate/.percolator/1' -d '{
   "query": {
      "match": {
         "title": "Elasticsearch Aggregations"
      }
   }
}'
curl 'localhost:9200/smart-percolate/event/_percolate?pretty' -d '{
   "doc": {
      "title": "Nesting Elasticsearch Aggregations"
   },
   "filter": {
      "query": {
         "match": {
            "query.match.title": "Elasticsearch"
         }
      }
   }
}'
```

> **Create a new index with the title field in the event mapping and the query object enabled.**

> **Add a query about Elasticsearch aggregations.**

> **Percolate an event about aggregations, but filter only queries about Elasticsearch.**

There are advantages and disadvantages to both methods. Metadata filtering works well when you have clear categories to filter on. On the other hand, filtering on the query text might work like a heuristic mechanism when metadata isn't available or reliable.

You may be wondering why you wrapped a query in a filter in listing F.4. It's because you didn't need the score when filtering registered queries for this use case. As you saw in chapter 4, filters are faster because they don't calculate scores and are cacheable. But there are use cases where the score—or other features, such as highlighting or aggregations—turns out to be useful during percolation. We'll discuss such use cases next.

E.3   *Functionality tricks*

Just as you can filter registered queries based on their metadata, you can query on this metadata and use the score to decide which query is more relevant. In this section, we'll look at how this works and also at using aggregations to get better insights on matching queries.

> **NOTE** Remember that for queries and aggregations, you'll run them on the registered queries, not on the percolated documents. This means you'll get ranking and statistics on the queries, not on the documents.

If the logic of querying queries sounds a bit twisted, let's start with another functionality trick: highlighting. This one is more straightforward because the highlighted text comes from the percolated document.

E.3.1 Highlighting percolated documents

Highlighting will let you know which words from the document you're percolating matched the query. In appendix C we discussed the features of highlighting in the context of regular queries, but all of them work with the percolator, too.

If you ran listing F.4, you can try a highlighted percolation by adding a `highlight` section to your percolate request. You should also specify a `size` value in order to place a limit on how many queries to highlight:

```
% curl 'localhost:9200/smart-percolate/event/_percolate?pretty' -d '{
  "doc": {
    "title": "Nesting Elasticsearch Aggregations"
  },
  "highlight": {
    "fields": {
      "title": {}
    }
  },
  "size": 2
}'
```

For each query, you'll see the matching terms from the percolated document:

```
    "_index" : "smart-percolate",
    "_id" : "1",
    "highlight" : {
      "title" : [ "Nesting <em>Elasticsearch</em> <em>Aggregations</em>" ]
    }
```

Scoring, on the other hand, works "upside down," just like the percolator itself: queries are scored, not the percolated documents.

E.3.2 Ranking matching queries

Let's take the use case of contextual advertising. A user is looking at blog posts on your website, and you have some ads registered as queries. During page load, you can percolate the post against those queries to see which ads are appropriate for the displayed content. This allows you to show tech ads for tech posts, holiday ads for holiday posts, and so on. But you have limited ad space, so which ads are you going to show?

How about sorting ads by some criterion, like the revenue you get for each ad? Then you can use a `size` value to get back only as many ads as you can display.

To sort registered queries by the value of a field, you can use the `function score` query, which was introduced in chapter 6. In the following listing, you'll use it to sort ads by the value of `ad_price`.

Listing E.5 Sorting registered queries by a metadata value

```
curl -XPUT 'localhost:9200/blog-ad/' -d '{
  "mappings": {
    "posts": {
      "properties": {
        "text": {
          "type": "string"
        }
      }
    }
  }
}'
curl -XPUT 'localhost:9200/blog-ad/.percolator/1' -d '{
  "query": {
    "match": {
      "text": "new cars"
    }
  },
  "ad_price": 5.4
}'
curl -XPUT 'localhost:9200/blog-ad/.percolator/2' -d '{
  "query": {
    "match": {
      "text": "used cars"
    }
  },
  "ad_price": 2.1
}'

curl 'localhost:9200/blog-ad/posts/_percolate?pretty' -d '{
  "doc": {
    "text": "This post is about cars"
  },
  "query": {
    "function_score": {
      "field_value_factor": {
        "field": "ad_price"
      }
    }
  },
  "size": 5,
  "sort": "_score"
}'
```

> Obligatory mapping for the text field in the posts, on which queries will run

> Add a price metadata field to the stored query.

> Function score query makes the score equal to the ad price

> How many ads you want to show

> Specify that you sort on score, which is now the ad price.

Note that the function score query doesn't do any filtering—although that's possible, too—it simply defines the _score value, which is used for sorting.

At this point, you might be wondering why you sort on _score and not on the ad_price field directly. There are two reasons:

- Percolator supports sorting only on _score (as of version 1.4).
- In practice, you probably want to combine multiple sort criteria.

In the case of ads, you might want to throw a random value into the mix to make sure you show all ads eventually; just increase the odds for the expensive ones. The function score query allows you to define different weights for different criteria and combine them.

Finally, you might want to get more insight about how matching queries are distributed. You can get this through aggregations.

E.3.3 Aggregations on matching query metadata

Let's say you're responsible for an online shop's search feature. When a new product is added, you want to make sure the description matches searches of users normally looking for this type of product.

If you register user searches as percolator queries, you can percolate a product document before submitting it to predict how often that product would show up in searches. If the product shows in too few or too many searches, it could be a problem. In these situations, you can get more information about the distribution of these matching queries by running an aggregation on a metadata field or even the actual query text.

In the listing that follows, you'll prepare and then run a percolation on user searches, aggregating on the query terms. In this example, the term cheap will appear in the top terms for matching queries, suggesting that price is important for users looking at this type of product.

Listing E.6 Using aggregations to get matching query metadata and term statistics

```
curl -XPUT 'localhost:9200/shop' -d '{
  "mappings": {
    "items": {
      "properties": {
        "name": { "type": "string" }       <─┐ Queries will run on the
      }                                         name field, so you define
    },                                          it in the mapping.
    ".percolator": {
      "properties": {
        "query": { "type": "object", "enabled": true }   <─┐ Enabling the query
      }                                                       object will let you
    }                                                         aggregate on
  }                                                           query terms.
}'
curl -XPUT 'localhost:9200/shop/.percolator/1' -d '{
  "query": {
    "match": {
      "name": "cheap PC Linux"       <─┐
    }                                    Registering some
  }                                      queries that look
}'                                       like user searches
curl -XPUT 'localhost:9200/shop/.percolator/2' -d '{
  "query": {
    "match": {
      "name": "cheap PC"       <─┘
```

```
      }
    }
}'
curl -XPUT 'localhost:9200/shop/.percolator/3' -d '{
  "query": {
    "match": {
      "name": "Mac Pro latest"                    ◁──┐  Registering some
    }                                                 │  queries that look like
  }                                                   │  user searches
}'
curl 'localhost:9200/shop/items/_percolate/count?pretty' -d '{
  "doc": {
    "name": "PC with preinstalled Linux"        ◁──┐  Percolating this new
  },                                               │  product will match the
  "aggs": {                                        │  first two queries.
    "top_query_terms": {
      "terms": { "field": "query.match.name" }   ◁──┐  Aggregation running on query
    }                                              │  text shows that cheap and pc
  }                                                │  appear twice and linux once.
}'
```

The aggregation part of the response for the query would be like this:

```
"aggregations" : {
  "top_query_terms" : {
    "doc_count_error_upper_bound" : 0,
    "sum_other_doc_count" : 0,
    "buckets" : [ {
      "key" : "cheap",
      "doc_count" : 2
    }, {
      "key" : "pc",
      "doc_count" : 2
    }, {
      "key" : "linux",
      "doc_count" : 1
    } ]
  }
}
```

If cheap is the top term here, and the computer you're adding is indeed cheap, it would be good to add it to the description so that people searching for this type of product will find it.

The key thing to remember here is that as with most of this appendix, features like aggregations work on registered queries and not on the percolated documents. We don't call percolation "search upside down" for nothing!

appendix F
Using suggesters
for autocomplete and
did-you-mean functionality

You now expect search engines not only to return good results but also to improve your queries. Take Google, for instance: if you make a typo, Google tells you about it and recommends a correction or even runs it directly, as shown in figure F.1.

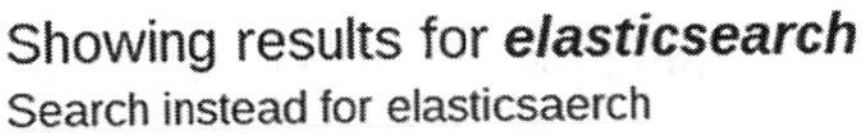

Showing results for *elasticsearch*
Search instead for elasticsaerch

Figure F.1   Spell checking by Google

Google also tries to prevent typos by offering autocomplete, which also makes queries faster and shows you topics that you might find interesting, as shown in figure F.2.

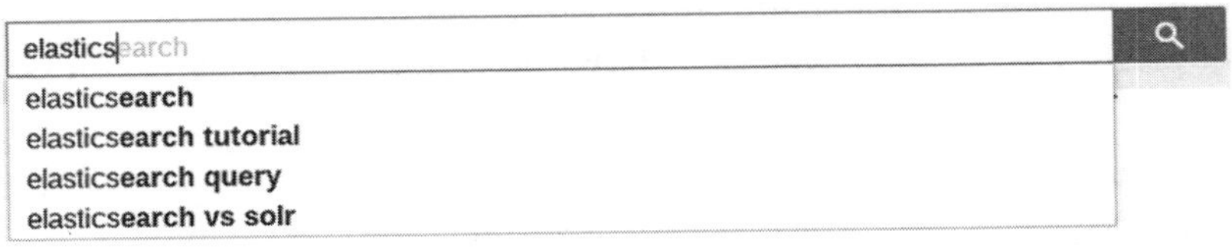

elastics**earch**	🔍
elastics**earch**	
elastics**earch tutorial**	
elastics**earch query**	
elastics**earch vs solr**	

Figure F.2   Autocomplete on Google

Elasticsearch offers both did-you-mean (DYM) and autocomplete functionality through the Suggesters module. The point of a suggester is to take a given text and return better keywords.

In this appendix we'll cover four types of suggesters:

- *Term suggester*—For each term in the provided text, it suggests keywords from the index. It works well for DYM on short fields, such as tags.
- *Phrase suggester*—You can think of it as an extension of the term suggester that provides DYM alternatives for the whole text instead of individual terms. It accounts for how often terms appear next to each other, making it especially better for longer fields, such as product descriptions.
- *Completion Suggester*—This provides autocomplete functionality based on term prefixes. It works with in-memory structures, making it faster than the prefix queries you saw in chapter 4.
- *Context Suggester*—This is an extension of the Completion Suggester that allows you to filter alternatives based on terms (categories) or geo-point locations.

NOTE Work is being done on a new suggester based on the NRT suggester. More options will be included like geo distance and filters. This new suggester is planned for version 2.0; the current suggesters will keep working as described here. More information on the new suggester can be found here: https://github.com/elastic/elasticsearch/issues/8909.

F.1   Did-you-mean suggesters

Term and phrase suggesters can help you avoid those nasty "0 results found" pages by eliminating typos and/or showing more popular variations of the original keywords. For example, you may suggest *Lucene/Solr* for *Lucene/Solar*.

You can leave it up to the user to run the suggester query:

(Did you mean *Lucene/Solr?*)

Or you can run it automatically:

(Showing results for *Lucene/Solr*. Click here for *Lucene/Solar*).

Typically, you'd run the suggested query automatically if the original query produces no results or just a few results with tiny scores.

Before we dive into the details of how you'd use the term and phrase suggesters, let's look at how they compare:

- The term suggester is basic and fast, working well when you care only about the occurrence of each word, like when you search code or short texts.
- The phrase suggester, on the other hand, takes the input text as a whole. This is slower and more complicated, as we'll see in a bit, but also works much better for natural languages or other places where you need to consider the sequence of words, like product names. For example, *apple iphone* is probably

a better suggestion than *apple phone*, even if the word *phone* appears more often in the index.

Both the term and the phrase suggester use Lucene's SpellChecker module at their core. They look at terms from the index to come up with suggestions, so you can easily add DYM functionality on top of existing data if your data can be trusted. Otherwise, if your data would often contain typos—for example, if you're indexing social media content—you might be better off maintaining a separate index with suggestions as a "dictionary." That separate index could contain queries that are run often and return results that are typically clicked on.

F.1.1 Term suggester

The term suggester takes the input text, analyzes it into terms, and then provides a list of suggestions for each term. This process is best illustrated in listing F.1, where you provide suggestions for group members of the get-together site example you've been running throughout the book.

The term suggester's structure applies to other types of suggesters as well:

- Suggest options go under a `suggest` element at the root of the JSON—at the same level as `query` or `aggregations`, for example.
- You can have one or more suggestions, each having a name, as you can with the aggregations we discussed in chapter 7. In listing F.1 you have `dym-members`.
- Under each suggestion, you provide the `text` and the suggestion type; in this case, `term`. Under it, you'd put type-specific options. In the term suggester's case, the only mandatory option is the field to use for getting suggestions. In this case, you'll use the `members` field.

NOTE For listing F.1 to work properly, you must download the code samples from https://github.com/dakrone/elasticsearch-in-action and run populate.sh to index some sample data.

Listing F.1 Using the term suggester to correct member typos

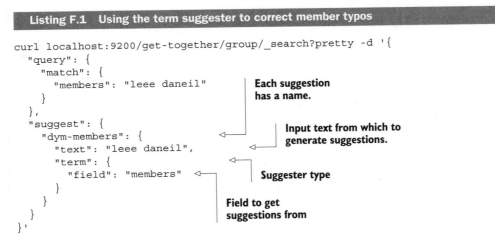

```
curl localhost:9200/get-together/group/_search?pretty -d '{
  "query": {
    "match": {
      "members": "leee daneil"          Each suggestion
    }                                    has a name.
  },
  "suggest": {
    "dym-members": {                     Input text from which to
      "text": "leee daneil",             generate suggestions.
      "term": {
        "field": "members"               Suggester type
      }
    }                          Field to get
  }                            suggestions from
}'
```

```
# reply snippet
  "hits" : {                          Search doesn't return any
    "total" : 0,                      hits because of the typos.
    "max_score" : null,
    "hits" : [ ]
  },
  "suggest" : {
    "dym-members" : [ {
      "text" : "leee",
      "offset" : 0,
      "length" : 4,
      "options" : [ {
        "text" : "lee",
        "score" : 0.6666666,
        "freq" : 3
      } ]
    }, {                              For each term in
      "text" : "daneil",             the input text,
      "offset" : 5,                   you get an array
      "length" : 6,                   of suggestions.
      "options" : [ {
        "text" : "daniel",
        "score" : 0.8333333,
        "freq" : 1
      } ]
    } ]
  } ]
```

If you need only suggestions and not the query results, you can use the _suggest end-point, skip the query object, and only pass the suggest object as a payload without the surrounding suggest keyword:

```
% curl localhost:9200/get-together/_suggest?pretty -d '{
  "dym-members": {
    "text": "leee daneil",
    "term": {
      "field": "members"
    }
  }
}'
```

This is useful when you want to check for missing terms before running the query, allowing you to correct the keywords instead of returning a potential "no results found" page.

RANKING SUGGESTIONS

By default, the term suggester offers a number of suggestions (up to the value of size) for each provided term. Suggestions are sorted by how close they are to the provided text. For example, if you provide Willian you'll get back William and then Williams. Of course, you can only get back these two values if they are available terms in the index. Also, Elasticsearch will provide suggestions only if the initial term Willian doesn't exist in the index.

This won't be ideal if you're searching though documents about Formula 1, where Williams is more likely to be searched for than either William or Willian. And you probably want to show Williams even if Willian actually exists in the index.

As you might expect, you can change all these. You can rank popular words higher by changing sort to frequency instead of the default score. Finally, you can change suggest_mode to decide when to show suggestions. Compared to the default value of missing, popular will come up with terms with higher frequencies than the one provided, and always will come up with suggestions anyway.

In the next listing, you'll get only the most popular suggestion for the event attendee mick.

Listing F.2 Getting the most popular suggestion for a term

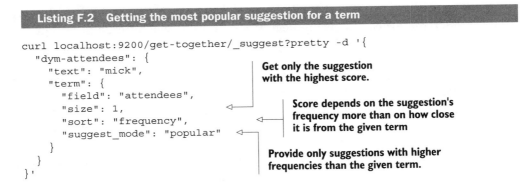

```
curl localhost:9200/get-together/_suggest?pretty -d '{
  "dym-attendees": {
    "text": "mick",                        Get only the suggestion
    "term": {                              with the highest score.
      "field": "attendees",
      "size": 1,                            Score depends on the suggestion's
      "sort": "frequency",                  frequency more than on how close
      "suggest_mode": "popular"            it is from the given term
    }
  }                                         Provide only suggestions with higher
}'                                          frequencies than the given term.
```

CHOOSING WHICH TERMS TO BE CONSIDERED

In listing F.2 you got the winning suggestion, but who competed for that one spot? Let's see how the term suggester works in order to understand which suggestions were considered in the first place.

As we mentioned before, the term suggester uses Lucene's SpellChecker module. This returns terms from the index at a maximum edit distance from the provided term. You saw an example of how edit distance works in the fuzzy query in chapter 4; for example, to get from mik to mick you need to add a letter, so the edit distance between them is 1.

Like the fuzzy query, the term suggester has a number of options that let you balance flexibility and performance:

- max_edits—This limits the edit distance from the provided term to the terms that might be suggested. For performance reasons, this is limited to values of 1 and 2, with 2 being the default value.
- prefix_length—How much of the beginning of the word to assume is correct. The bigger the prefix, the faster Elasticsearch will find suggestions, but you also have a higher risk of typos in that prefix. The default for prefix_length is 1.

If you're concerned about performance, you might also want to tweak these options:

- `min_doc_freq`, which limits candidate suggestions to popular enough terms
- `max_term_freq`, which excludes popular terms in the input text from being corrected in the first place

You can find more details about them in the documentation at www.elastic.co/guide/en/elasticsearch/reference/current/search-suggesters-term.html.

If you're more concerned about accuracy, take a look at the phrase suggester as well. It should provide better suggestions, especially on larger fields.

F.1.2   *Phrase suggester*

The phrase suggester also provides did-you-mean functionality, like the terms suggester, but instead of giving suggestions for individual terms, it gives suggestions for the overall text. This has a couple of advantages when you have multiple words in your search.

First, there's less client-side logic to apply. For example, if you're using the terms suggester for the input text `abut using elasticsarch`, you'll probably get `about` as a suggestion for `abut` and `elasticsearch` for `elasticsarch`. Your application has to figure out that `using` has no suggestion and build up a message like "did you mean: about using elasticsearch."

As you'll see in the following listing, the phrase suggester gives you `about using elasticsearch` out of the box. Plus, you can use highlighting to show the user which of the original terms have been corrected.

Listing F.3   Phrase suggester working with highlighting

```
curl localhost:9200/get-together/_suggest?pretty -d '{
  "dym-attendees": {
    "text": "abut using elasticsarch",
    "phrase": {                              ⟵   Suggester type
      "field": "description",                    changes to phrase
      "highlight": {
        "pre_tag": "<em>",           Highlighting needs tags, like the
        "post_tag": "</em>"          ones you saw in appendix C.
      }
    }
  }
}'
# reply snippet
  "dym-attendees" : [ {
    "text" : "abut using elasticsarch",                    Suggestions for
    "offset" : 0,                                          the overall text,
    "length" : 23,                                         ranked and
    "options" : [ {                                        highlighted
      "text" : "about using elasticsearch",
      "highlighted" : "<em>about</em> using <em>elasticsearch</em>",   ⟵
      "score" : 0.004515128
    }, {
```

```
    "text" : "about using elasticsarch",
    "highlighted" : "<em>about</em> using elasticsarch",      ◁─┐  Suggestions for
    "score" : 0.002511514                                         │  the overall text,
  }, {                                                            │  ranked and
    "text" : "abut using elasticsearch",                         │  highlighted
    "highlighted" : "abut using <em>elasticsearch</em>",      ◁─┘
    "score" : 0.0022977828
  } ]
} ]
```

Then you can expect suggestions to be better ranked, especially if you're searching natural language, such as book content. The phrase suggester does that by adding new logic on top of the terms suggester to weigh candidate phrases based on how terms occur together in the index. This ranking technique is called *ngram-language model*, and it works if you have a shingle field with the same content as the field you're searching on. You can get shingles by using the shingle token filter that we discussed in chapter 5; remember, this means you have to configure shingles in the mapping to create the index appropriately.

More on n-grams, shingles, and n-gram models

An *n-gram* is defined as a contiguous sequence of *n* items from a given sequence of text or speech.[1] These items could be letters or words, and in Elasticsearch we say *n-grams* for letter n-grams and *shingles* for word n-grams.

An *n-gram model* uses frequencies of existing word n-grams (shingles, in Elasticsearch money) to determine the likelihood of different words existing next to each other. For example, a speech recognition device is more likely to encounter `yellow fever` than `hello fever`, assuming it finds more `yellow fever` than `hello fever` shingles in the training data.

The phrase suggester uses n-gram models to score candidate phrases based on the occurrence of consecutive words in a shingle field. You can expect a phrase suggestion like `John has yellow fever` to be scored higher than `John has hello fever`.

The `shingles` field is used for ranking suggestions by checking how often suggested words occur next to each other, as shown in figure F.3.

As you might expect, there are many options that allow you to configure much of this process, and we'll discuss the most important ones here:

- How candidate generators come up with candidate terms
- How overall phrases get scored based on the `shingles` field
- How shingles of different sizes influence a suggestion's score
- How to include and exclude suggestions based various criteria, such as score or whether they'll actually return results

---

[1] https://en.wikipedia.org/wiki/N-gram

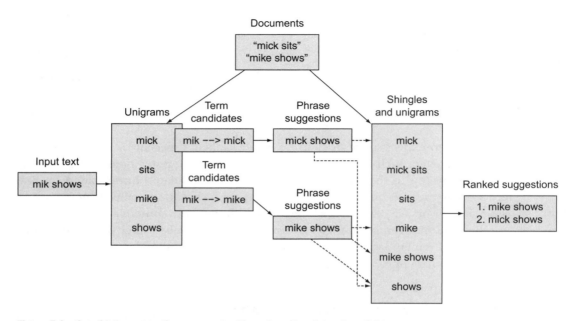

Figure F.3   Candidate suggestions are ranked based on the `shingles` field.

CANDIDATE GENERATORS

The responsibility of the candidate generators is to come up with a list of possible terms based on the terms in the provided text. As of version 1.4, there's only one type of candidate generator, called `direct_generator`. It works in a similar way to the terms suggester in that it finds suggestions for every term of the input text.

The direct generator has similar options to the term suggester, like `max_edits` or `prefix_length`. But the phrase suggester supports more than one generator, and it also allows you to specify an analyzer that is applied to input terms before they get spell checked (pre-filter), and one that is applied to suggested terms before they are returned.

Having multiple generators and filters lets you do some neat tricks. For instance, if typos are likely to happen both at the beginning and end of words, you can use multiple generators to avoid expensive suggestions with low prefix lengths by using the `reverse` token filter, as shown in figure F.4.

You'll implement what's shown in figure F.4 in listing F.4:

- First, you'll need an analyzer that includes the reverse token filter.
- Then you'll index the correct product description in two fields: one analyzed with the standard analyzer and one with the reverse analyzer.

When you run the suggester, you can specify two candidate generators: one running on the standard field and one on the reversed field, which will make use of the reverse pre- and post-filters.

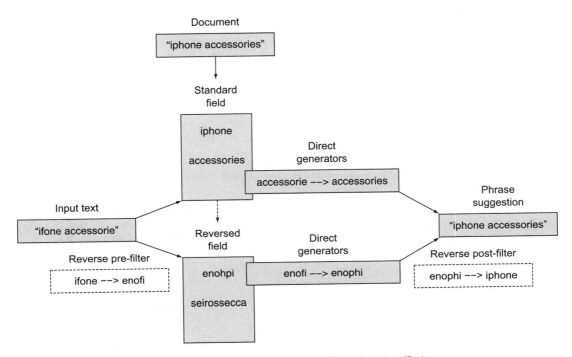

Figure F.4 Using filters and two direct generators to correct both prefix and suffix typos

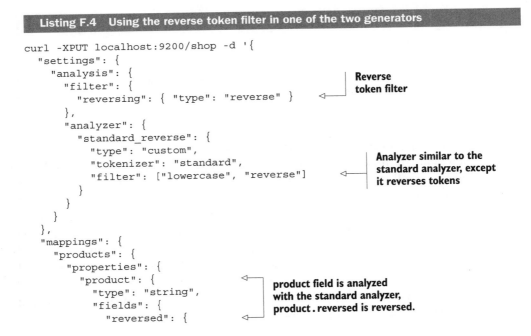

Listing F.4 Using the reverse token filter in one of the two generators

```
curl -XPUT localhost:9200/shop -d '{
  "settings": {
    "analysis": {
      "filter": {
        "reversing": { "type": "reverse" }          ⟵  Reverse
      },                                                 token filter
      "analyzer": {
        "standard_reverse": {
          "type": "custom",
          "tokenizer": "standard",
          "filter": ["lowercase", "reverse"]        ⟵  Analyzer similar to the
        }                                                standard analyzer, except
      }                                                  it reverses tokens
    }
  },
  "mappings": {
    "products": {
      "properties": {
        "product": {                         ⟵
          "type": "string",                        product field is analyzed
          "fields": {                              with the standard analyzer,
            "reversed": {                    ⟵     product.reversed is reversed.
```

```
                        "type": "string",
                        "analyzer": "standard_reverse"
                      }
                    }
                  }
                }
              }
            }
          }
        }'
curl -XPUT localhost:9200/shop/products/1 -d '{
  "product": "iphone accessories"
}'
curl -XPOST localhost:9200/shop/_suggest?pretty -d '{
    "dym": {
      "text": "ifone accesorie",
      "phrase": {
        "field": "product",
        "max_errors": 2,
        "direct_generator": [
          {
            "field": "product",
            "prefix_length": 3
          },
          {
            "field": "product.reversed",
            "prefix_length": 3,
            "pre_filter": "standard_reverse",
            "post_filter": "standard_reverse"
          }
        ]
      }
    }
}'
# reply snippets
    "text" : "iphone accessories",
        "score" : 0.48023444
    "text" : "iphone accesorie",
        "score" : 0.38765374
    "text" : "ifone accessories",
        "score" : 0.35540017
```

max_errors dictates how many corrections are allowed in a suggestion.

Regular generator corrects suffixes, reversed generator corrects prefixes

Both terms are corrected in suggestions.

USING A SHINGLES FIELD FOR SCORING CANDIDATES

Now that you have good candidates, you'll use a shingles field for ranking. In listing F.5, you'll use the shingle token filter to define another multi-field for the shop product descriptions.

You'll have to decide how many consecutive words to allow in a shingle, or the shingle size. This is usually a tradeoff between performance and accuracy: lower-level shingles are needed in order to get partial matches, like boosting a suggestion for United States based on an indexed text saying United States of America. Higher-level shingles are good for boosting exact matches of longer texts such as United States of America above United States of Americas. The problem is, the more shingle sizes you add, the bigger your index gets, and suggestions will take longer.

A good balance for most use cases is to index sizes from 1 to 3. You can do it by setting `min_shingle_size` to 2 and `max_shingle_size` to 3, because the shingle filter outputs unigrams by default.

With the `shingles` field in place, you need to specify it as the `field` of your phrase suggester, whereas the regular `description` field will go under each candidate generator.

Listing F.5   Using a `shingles` field to get better ranking for suggestions

```
curl -XPUT localhost:9200/shop2 -d '{
"settings": {
  "analysis": {
    "filter": {
      "shingle": {
        "type": "shingle",
        "min_shingle_size": 2,
        "max_shingle_size": 3
      }
    },
    "analyzer": {
      "shingler": {
        "type": "custom",
        "tokenizer": "standard",
        "filter": ["lowercase", "shingle"]
      }
    }
  }
},
"mappings": {
  "products": {
    "properties": {
      "product": {
        "type": "string",
        "fields": {
          "shingled": {
            "type": "string",
            "analyzer": "shingler"
          }
        }
      }
    }
  }
}
}}'
curl -XPUT localhost:9200/shop2/products/1 -d '{
  "product": "iphone accessories"
}'
curl localhost:9200/shop2/_suggest?pretty -d '{
  "dym": {
    "text": "ifone accesorie",
    "phrase": {
      "field": "product.shingled",
      "max_errors": 2,
      "direct_generator": [{
        "field": "product"
```

Shingle analyzer that outputs unigrams, bigrams, and trigrams

Field using the shingle analyzer

Shingle field is used for scoring, unigram field for candidates

```
        }]
      }
    }
  }'
# reply snippet
    "text" : "iphone accessories",
        "score" : 0.44569767
    "text" : "ifone accessories",
        "score" : 0.16785859
    "text" : "iphone accesorie",
        "score" : 0.16785859
```

Score gap increases compared to listing F.4, because the first suggestion matches a bigram

USING SMOOTHING MODELS TO SCORE SHINGLES OF DIFFERENT SIZES

Take two possible suggestions: Elasticsearch in Action and Elasticsearch is Auction. If the index contains the trigram Elasticsearch in Action, you'd expect this suggestion to rank higher. But if term frequencies are the only criterion, and the unigram auction appears many times in the index, Elasticsearch is Auction might win.

In most use cases, you want the score to be given not only by the frequency of a shingle but also by the shingle's size. Luckily, there are *smoothing models* that do just that. By default, Elasticsearch uses an algorithm called *Stupid Backoff* in the phrase suggester. The name implies that it's simple, but it works well:[2] it takes the highest order shingles as the reference—trigrams in the case of listing F.5. If no trigrams are found, it looks for bigrams but multiplies the score by 0.4. If no bigrams are found, it goes to unigrams but lowers the score once again by 0.4. The whole process is shown in figure F.5.

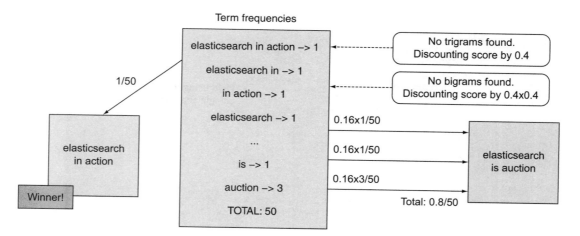

Figure F.5 Stupid Backoff discounts the score of lower-order shingles.

---

[2] Stupid Backoff was the original name, because authors assumed such a simple algorithm couldn't possibly work. It turns out it works, but the name stuck. More details here: www.aclweb.org/anthology/D07-1090.

That 0.4 multiplier can be configured through the `discount` parameter:

```
% curl localhost:9200/shop2/_suggest?pretty -d '{
  "dym": {
    "text": "ifone accesories",
    "phrase": {
      "field": "product.shingled",
      "smoothing": {
        "stupid_backoff": {
          "discount": 0.5
        }
      },
      "direct_generator": [{
          "field": "product"
      }]
    }
  }
}'
```

> **NOTE** Usually, Stupid Backoff works well, but there are other smoothing models available, such as Laplace smoothing or linear interpolation. For more information about them, go to www.elastic.co/guide/en/elasticsearch/reference/current/search-suggesters-phrase.html#_smoothing_models.

EXCLUDING SUGGESTIONS BASED ON DIFFERENT CRITERIA

Besides ranking suggestions based on ngram-language models, you can include or exclude them based on certain criteria. Back in listing F.4, you saw `max_errors`, which allows only suggestions that correct a maximum number of terms. It's usually recommended to set `max_errors` to a low value (it defaults to 1); otherwise, the suggest request will take a long time because it has to score too many suggestions.

You can also include or exclude possible suggestions based on their score or whether they would actually produce results, should you run a query with the suggested text.

For filtering by score, the main option is `confidence`—the higher the value, the more confident you are that the input text doesn't need suggestions. It works like this: the phrase suggester scores the input text as well as possible suggestions. Suggestions with a score less than the input text's score multiplied by `confidence` (which defaults to 1) are eliminated. Increasing the value improves performance and helps you get rid of embarrassing suggestions like "Did you mean lucene/*solar*?" On the other hand, a value that's too high might miss providing suggestions for "solr panels."

`confidence` works hand in hand with `real_word_error_likelihood`, which should describe the proportion of misspelled words in the index itself (defaults to 0.95). Possible suggestions have their score multiplied by this value, so lowering it reduces chances of returning a misspelled word as a suggestion, because the score of that suggestion is more likely to be lower than that of the input text (multiplied by `confidence`). If you set it too low though, good suggestions might be missed as well, so it's usually best to set `real_word_error_likelihood` to a value that describes the real likelihood of a misspelling in the index.

Finally, what happens if the query you suggest won't return any results? That would be pretty bad, but luckily you can have Elasticsearch verify that for each suggestion. In the following listing, you'll use the `collate` option to have Elasticsearch return only suggestions that return results. You need to specify a query, and in that query you'll refer to the suggestion itself as the `{{suggestion}}` variable. Note how suggestions such as `ifone accessories` are removed from the list.

Listing F.6 Using `collate` to see which suggestions would return results

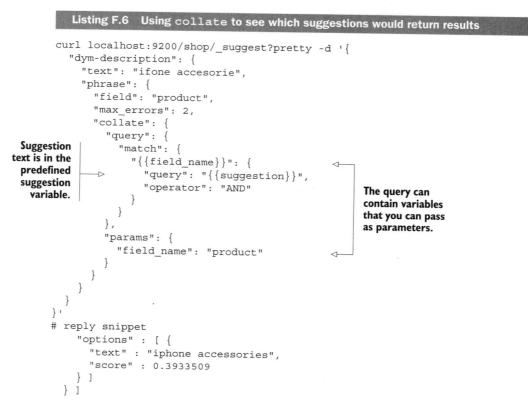

```
curl localhost:9200/shop/_suggest?pretty -d '{
  "dym-description": {
    "text": "ifone accesorie",
    "phrase": {
      "field": "product",
      "max_errors": 2,
      "collate": {
        "query": {
          "match": {
            "{{field_name}}": {
              "query": "{{suggestion}}",
              "operator": "AND"
            }
          }
        },
        "params": {
          "field_name": "product"
        }
      }
    }
  }
}'
# reply snippet
    "options" : [ {
      "text" : "iphone accessories",
      "score" : 0.3933509
    } ]
  } ]
```

Suggestion text is in the predefined suggestion variable.

The query can contain variables that you can pass as parameters.

> **NOTE** These are Mustache templates (more details at https://mustache .github.io) and can also be used for predefining regular queries. You can find more details on query templates here: www.elastic.co/guide/en/elasticsearch/ reference/current/query-dsl-template-query.html.

Collating works well for ironing out a few bad suggestions. If you have a high rate of bad suggestions, consider running the phrase suggester against a separate index with successful queries. This requires a lot of maintenance, but you should get much more relevant suggestions. And because that index will probably be much smaller, you'll get better performance, too.

Next, we'll move on to autocomplete suggesters. You're very likely to run them on separate indices, because they typically have to be very fast and relevant.

F.2 Autocomplete suggesters

If autocomplete was cool in 2005, now it's a must—any search without it looks ancient. You expect a good autocomplete to help you search faster (especially on mobile devices) and better (you type in *e*, so it should know you're looking for *Elasticsearch*) but also to allow you to explore popular options ("elasticsearch tutorial"—that's actually a good idea!). Finally, a good autocomplete will reduce the load on your main search system, especially if you have some sort of instant search available—when you jump directly to a popular result without executing the full-blown search.

A good autocomplete has to be fast and relevant: fast because it has to generate suggestions as the user is typing, and relevant because you don't want to suggest a query with no results or one that isn't likely to be useful.

You can help with the quality of suggestions by keeping what would be good candidates, such as successful products or queries, in a separate index. You could then run the prefix queries we introduced in chapter 4 to generate suggestions. But those queries might not be fast enough because ideally you need to come up with a suggestion before the user types the next character.

The completion and context suggesters help you build a faster autocomplete. They're built on Lucene's Suggest module, keeping data in memory in finite state transducers (FSTs). FSTs are essentially graphs that are able to store terms in a way that's compressed and easy to retrieve. Figure F.6 illustrates how the terms *index*, *search*, and *suggest* would be stored.

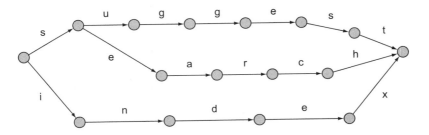

Figure F.6 In-memory FSTs help you get fast suggestions based on a prefix.

The actual implementation is a bit more complex—because it allows you to add weights, for instance—but you can imagine why in-memory FSTs are fast: you just have to follow the paths and see that prefix *s* would lead to *search* and *suggest*.

Next, we'll look at how the Completion Suggester works, then move on to the Context Suggester, which is an extension of it, much like the phrase suggester we discussed earlier is an extension of the simpler term suggester.

NOTE For versions 2.0 and later, a new Completion Suggester is planned. It should have all the features of the current Completion and Context suggesters, plus a few more (like flexible scoring based on geo distance or edit distance). The basic principles remain the same, though. For more information on Completion Suggester Version 2, take a look at the main issue here: https://github.com/elastic/elasticsearch/issues/8909. When this suggester is released, you should see updated documentation in the Suggesters page: www.elastic.co/guide/en/elasticsearch/reference/current/search-suggesters .html.

F.2.1 Completion Suggester

To tell Elasticsearch that you meant to store suggestions in FSTs for autocomplete, you need to define a field in the mapping with `type` set to `completion`. The easiest way to store suggestions is by adding such a field as a multi-field to a field that you're already indexing, like in the following listing. There, you'll index places like restaurants, and you'll add a `suggest` subfield to each place's name field.

Listing F.7 Simple autocomplete based on existing data

```
curl -XPUT 'localhost:9200/places' -d '{
"mappings": {
  "food": {
    "properties": {
      "name": {
          "type": "string",
        "fields": {
          "suggest": {                          Suggestions would
            "type": "completion"      <───      be stored in the
          }                                      completion field.
        }
      }
    }
  }
}
}}'
curl -XPUT 'localhost:9200/places/food/1' -d '{ "name": "Pizza Hut" }'
curl 'localhost:9200/places/_suggest?pretty' -d '{
  "name-autocomplete": {
    "text": "p",
    "completion": {                    Completion suggest requests
      "field": "name.suggest"          run on the completion field.
    }
  }
}'
#reply
  "name-autocomplete" : [ {
    "text" : "p",
    "offset" : 0,
    "length" : 1,                       The indexed name
    "options" : [ {                     is returned as a
      "text" : "Pizza Hut",   <───      suggestion.
      "score" : 1.0
    } ]
```

If such a simple autocomplete implementation isn't enough—for example, because results aren't ranked—there are quite a few options that can help you improve relevancy. Some of them have to be done at index time (for example, you can add a weight to each suggestion), whereas others work at search time (you can enable fuzziness). On top of all this, suggestions can have payloads, where you can store document IDs that you can use for instant search.

IMPROVING RELEVANCY AT INDEX TIME

As with regular searches on string fields, the input text is analyzed at both index time and search time. That's why `Pizza Hut` matched p. You can control analysis through the `index_analyzer` and `search_analyzer` options. For example, if you wanted case-sensitive suggesting (so that only P matches, not p), you can use the keyword analyzer:

```
"suggest": {
  "type": "completion",
  "index_analyzer": "keyword",
  "search_analyzer": "keyword"
```

If you need more information about analysis, you'll find it in chapter 6.

In most cases, you'll keep suggestions in a separate field, index, or even a separate Elasticsearch cluster. This helps when you want to control suggestions based on how they perform and also to be able to scale suggesters separately from the main search system.

When suggestions are in a different field, you can separate the inputs you match from the suggestion you provide (output). For example, a document like this

```
{
  "name": {
    "input": "phone",
    "output": "iphone"
  }
}
```

would let you suggest `iphone` for the input text ph. Also, you can provide multiple inputs:

```
{
  "name": {
    "input": ["iphone", "phone"],
    "output": "iphone"
  }
}
```

Finally, you can rank suggestions based on weights you provide at index time. In the next listing, you'll combine inputs, outputs, and weights to implement autocomplete on top of group tags for the get-together use case you've been running for most of this book.

Listing F.8   Using weights, inputs, and outputs

```
curl -XPUT 'localhost:9200/autocomplete' -d '{
"mappings": {
  "group": {
    "properties": {
      "tags": { "type": "completion" }
    }
  }
}}'
curl -XPUT 'localhost:9200/autocomplete/group/1' -d '{
"tags": {
  "input": ["big data", "data"],
  "output": "big data",
  "weight": 8
}}'
curl -XPUT 'localhost:9200/autocomplete/group/2' -d '{
"tags": {
  "input": ["data visualization", "visualization"],
  "output": "data visualization",
  "weight": 5
}}'
curl 'localhost:9200/autocomplete/_suggest?pretty' -d '{
"tags-autocomplete": {
  "text": "d",
  "completion": {
    "field": "tags"
  }
}}'
# reply
  "tags-autocomplete" : [ {
    "text" : "d",
    "offset" : 0,
    "length" : 1,
    "options" : [ {
      "text" : "big data",
      "score" : 8.0
    }, {
      "text" : "data visualization",
      "score" : 5.0
    } ]
  } ]
```

When using separate fields, you can separate inputs, outputs, and weights.

Suggestions are the outputs ranked by weight.

IMPROVING RELEVANCY AT SEARCH TIME

When you run the suggest request, you can decide which suggestions will appear. Like with other suggesters, size lets you control how many suggestions to return. Then, if you want to tolerate typos, you need a fuzzy object under the completion object of your suggest request. With fuzzy search enabled this way, you can configure additional options, like the following:

- fuzziness, which allows you to specify the maximum allowed edit distance
- min_length, where you specify at which length of the input text to enable fuzzy search

- `prefix_length`, which improves performance at the cost of flexibility by considering these first characters correct

All those options go under the `completion` object of your suggest request:

```
% curl 'localhost:9200/autocomplete/_suggest?pretty' -d '{
"tags-autocomplete": {
  "text": "daata",
  "completion": {
    "field": "tags",
    "size": 3,
    "fuzzy": {
      "fuzziness": 2,
      "min_length": 4,
      "prefix_length": 2
    }
  }
}}'
```

IMPLEMENTING INSTANT SEARCH WITH PAYLOADS

Many search solutions let you go directly to a specific result when clicking on a suggestion instead of running that search. Figure F.7 shows an example from SoundCloud.

Figure F.7 Instant search lets you jump to the result without running an actual search.

To implement this in Elasticsearch, you'd put a payload in your `completion` field, and that payload would be the ID of the document you're suggesting. You can then use the ID to get the document, as you'll do in the next listing.

Listing F.9 Payload lets you get documents instead of searching for the suggested text

```
curl -XPUT 'localhost:9200/autocomplete/_mapping/group' -d '{
"properties": {
  "name": {
    "type": "completion",        ◁— Enabling payloads in
    "payloads": true                 the mapping of the
  }                                   completion field
}}'
```

```
curl -XPUT 'localhost:9200/autocomplete/group/3' -d '{
"name": {
  "input": "Elasticsearch San Francisco",          ◄─┤ If input is the same as
  "payload": {                                          output, you can omit it.
    "groupId": 3
  }                                                  ◄─┐ Adding payload to
}}'                                                    │ the document
curl 'localhost:9200/autocomplete/_suggest?pretty' -d '{
"name-autocomplete": {
  "text": "elastic",
  "completion": {
    "field": "name"
  }
}}'
# reply
    "options" : [ {
      "text" : "Elasticsearch San Francisco",
      "score" : 1.0,                                 ◄─┤ Payload comes back with the
      "payload":{"groupId":3}                            suggestion. Now you can GET
    } ]                                                  the document with ID 3.
```

The Completion Suggester returns all results matching the input text, which might work well with something like SoundCloud. But some use cases require filtering, like your get-together site: you only want to suggest events reasonably close to the user and ignore the others. To do this, you'll need the Context Suggester, which is built to add filtering functionality on top of the Completion Suggester.

F.2.2   Context Suggester

The Context Suggester allows you to filter on a context, which can be a category (term) or a geo location. To enable these contexts, you need to specify them in the mapping and then provide contexts in documents and in your suggest requests.

DEFINING CONTEXTS IN THE MAPPING

You can add one or more context values to your completion field in the mapping. Each context has a type, which can be either category or geo. For geo contexts, you need to specify a precision value:

```
"name": {
  "type": "completion",
  "context": {
    "location": {
      "type": "geo",
      "precision": "100km"
    },
    "category": {
      "type": "category"
    }
  }
}
```

Contexts under the hood

Contexts work on top of the same FST structure that the Completion Suggester uses. To enable filtering, the context would be used as a prefix to the actual suggestion, like `search_lucene` if `search` is the category and `lucene` is the text you want to match.

For `geo` contexts, the prefix is a geohash, like `abcde`. As you saw in appendix A about geo search, a geohash indicates a rectangular area on the map, and the longer the string, the higher the precision. For example, *gc* is a rectangle taking up most of Britain and Ireland, whereas *gcp* only goes from London to Southampton.[3]

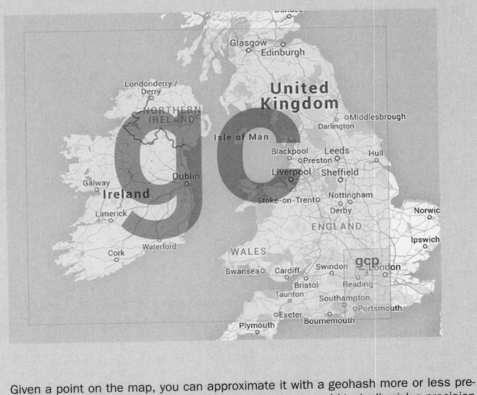

Given a point on the map, you can approximate it with a geohash more or less precisely, depending on the hash length. For suggestions, you'd typically pick a precision that would reflect how near a point of interest should be to the current location. For example, restaurants would work with more precise hashes (like 10 km wide) than get-together events (which may be 100 km wide), assuming that users are more likely to drive farther for a monthly event than for a burger.

---

[3] Snapshot taken from GeohashExplorer: http://geohash.gofreerange.com/.

ADDING CONTEXTS TO DOCUMENTS AND SUGGEST REQUESTS

With the mapping in place, you'd put contexts in documents under the context field of your completion:

```
{
  "name": {
    "input": "Elasticsearch Denver",
    "context": {
      "location": {
        "lat": 39.752337,
        "lon": -105.00083
      },
      "category": ["big data"]
    }
  }
}
```

When fetching suggestions, you should add a context value to your completion request as well:

```
% curl 'localhost:9200/autocomplete/_suggest?pretty -d '{
  "name-autocomplete": {
    "text": "denv",
    "completion": {
      "field": "name",
      "context": {
        "category": "big data",
        "location": {
          "lat": 39,
          "lon": -105
        }
      }
    }
  }
}'
```

TROUBLESHOOTING CONTEXT (AND COMPLETION) SUGGESTER ERRORS

Normally, if you define contexts and run the Context Suggester with no context in the request, you'll get an error for every shard:

```
"reason": "BroadcastShardOperationFailedException[[autocomplete][0] ];
nested: ElasticsearchException[failed to execute suggest]; nested:
ElasticsearchIllegalArgumentException[suggester [completion] requires context
to be setup]; "
```

But if you really need to specify contexts to only some of your requests and documents, you can specify a default value in the mapping:

```
"name": {
  "type": "completion",
  "context": {
    "category": {
      "type": "category",
      "default": "default_category"
    }
```

```
    }
  }
```

Then you can index documents without categories:

```
{
  "name": {
    "input": "test meeting"
  }
}
```

Finally, if the user doesn't enter any filtering context, you can fill in the default value on your application; this is also possible with a geo context:

```
"name-autocomplete": {
  "text": "te",
  "completion": {
    "field": "name",
    "context": {
      "category": "default_category"
    }
  }
}
```

From a functionality standpoint, this works as if you have the Context Suggester when you need it and the Completion Suggester when you don't. But in both cases you might get suggestions from deleted documents. This happens because the FSTs used under the hood are built for each Lucene segment in the index, and they never get changed until the segment is deleted during merging (when the FST gets deleted as well). As you may recall from chapter 3, when a document is deleted, it's not really gone from the segment; it's just marked as deleted.

Although searches are smart enough to filter out deleted documents, suggesters are not, at least in version 1.4. Until this is addressed in the new Completion Suggester (see https://github.com/elastic/elasticsearch/issues/8909), you can work around this issue by changing your merge policy or optimizing so you have as few deleted documents in the index as possible. For more information on merges, go to chapter 10, section 10.2.2.

index

plugins *(continued)*
  Marvel 416–417
  Sematext SPM 416
  overview 383–384
  removing 388–389
  requiring installation of 387–388
  updating 388–389
porter_stem filter 145
post filter 185
Postings Highlighter 400–403
post_tags option 397
precision parameter 381
precision_threshold parameter 191–192
predefined fields
  _all 67–68
  fields parameter and 67
  overview 65–66
  _source 66
  _uid 68–69
prefix filter 111–112, 314
prefix queries 111–112, 117, 327–328
prefix_length option 441
pre_tags option 397

Q

queries
  boosting at query time 156
  checking for field existence with filters
    exists filter 114
    missing filter 114–115
    overview 113–114
    transforming any query into filter 115–116
  choosing best for situation 116–117
  compound
    bool filter 107–109
    bool query 105–106
  deleting by 80
  for denormalized data 253–255
  match query and term filter
    boolean query behavior 102
    overview 92–95, 102
    phrase query behavior 102–103
  match_all query 96
  multi_match query 104
  for objects 223–225

parent-child relationships
  children aggregation 245–247
  getting child documents in results 243
  has_child query and filter 241–243
  has_parent query and filter 244–245
  overview 240–241
phrase_prefix query 103–104
prefix query 111–112
query_string query 96–98
range query 109–111
term query and term filter 98–100
terms query 100–102
wildcard query 112–113
query rescoring 160–162
query_and_fetch vs. query_then_fetch methods 333–335
query_cache parameter 320
query_string query 96–98
query_weight parameter 161
queue_size parameter 356

R

random_score function 166–167
range aggregation
  date_range aggregation 201–202
  overview 200–201
  uses for 204
range filter 109–111
range query 109–111, 117
real_word_error_likelihood option 449
Red Hat Linux 16
refresh thresholds 302–303
regexp filter 314
registering queries 422
regulatory compliance 341
relationships
  application-side joins 255
  denormalizing data
    defined 220
    deleting members 253
    indexing 252
    overview 247–248
    querying 253–255
    representation of one-to-many relationship 251

    side to be denormalized 251
    updating documents 252
    use cases for 248–250
nested type
  aggregating scores of nested objects 231–232
  defined 218–219
  getting which inner document matched 232–233
  mapping and indexing 226–229
  nested and reverse nested aggregations 234–235
  nested query and filter 230
  nested sorting 233–234
  overview 225–226
  performance considerations 235–236
  searching in multiple levels of nesting 231
object type
  defined 217–218
  mapping and indexing 222–223
  overview 221–222
  searching in objects 223–225
  overview 215–217
parent-child relationships
  defined 219–220
  deleting documents 240
  indexing and retrieving 239–240
  mapping 239
  overview 236–238
  searching in parent and child documents 240–247
  updating child documents 240
relevancy
  boosting
    at index time 155–156
    overview 154–155
    at query time 156
    specifying boost for multi_match 157–158
  custom scoring
    combining scores 164
    configuration options 169–170
    decay functions 167–169
    example of 170–171
    field_value_factor function 164–165